MW00526773

This volume is a brilliant capstone to David VanDrunen's project on Reformed political and legal teachings. It again features probing exegesis of biblical teachings and their reception history; creative retrieval and reconstruction of natural law theories, Two Kingdoms ontologies, and covenantal theology; and a bracing engagement with enduring questions of authority and liberty, justice and mercy, custom and community, rights and resistance. This volume and its prequels have earned VanDrunen a place high on the honor roll of law and religion scholarship and of Reformed political theology.

—JOHN WITTE JR., director of the Center for the
Study of Law and Religion, Emory University

Idolatry leaves us empty, and politics is no exception. Christians have good reason to be discouraged: we've placed too much hope in the powers of this world, and we have neglected love of neighbor and maintenance of peace as two of the primary goals of politics. Into this muddled context, David VanDrunen presents a timely and compelling theological vision for political community. Appealing to Scripture and acknowledging a crucial role for prudence and good judgment, VanDrunen outlines a much-needed path forward for Christian conviction and integrity in political life.

—BEN SASSE, United States senator from Nebraska

In *Politics after Christendom*, David VanDrunen develops a political theology worthy of his most august predecessors in the Two Kingdoms tradition in Reformed theology. VanDrunen's great innovation is to place the insights of this tradition into the context of God's covenant with Noah. After making his case for a Noahic perspective, VanDrunen applies it to a wide range of political concerns, including justice and rights, religious freedom, the role of the family, and authority and resistance. Beautifully and clearly written, *Politics after Christendom* will be a touchstone even for those of us who are not fully persuaded by the Two Kingdoms perspective.

—DAVID SKEEL, S. Samuel Arsht Professor of Corporate
Law, University of Pennsylvania Carey Law School

In this pioneering and provocative work, David VanDrunen brings to impressive completion his longstanding project of retrieving neglected themes in classic Reformed political theology—"natural law," "Two Kingdoms," and the "Noahic covenant"—and deploying them for our pluralistic "post-Christendom" context. It is the most substantial biblical and theological case for what the author calls a "conservative liberalism" to have appeared in many years, and future debates about Reformed political theology will not be able to bypass it. Even those unpersuaded by some of the book's core theological and political judgments will be enriched by the author's erudition and argumentative vigour and in turn challenged to come up better arguments for their own positions.

—JONATHAN CHAPLIN, independent researcher and writer, member of Cambridge University Divinity Faculty

Two problems bedevil nearly every Christian political theology, whether you encounter it in an academic's tome or a nonacademic's water-cooler opinions. First, Christians too often begin with ideological or partisan foundations. Second, they build on those foundations with a favorite biblical prooftext, often one meant for ancient Israel or the church but wrongly applied to nation-states and their governments. Therefore, it's difficult to overstate the importance of building our political theology on the whole Bible's covenantal structure, with specific attention given to the Noahic covenant. Whether you count yourself a Two Kingdoms theologian or not (I don't), every political theologian needs to follow VanDrunen precisely here. To put it simply, I believe that VanDrunen's emphasis on the Noahic covenant is the way forward for Christian political theology. Other books offer helpful emphases or counterpoints, but *Politics after Christendom* offers the starting point for anyone who wants to lay a foundation on the Bible. It just moved into pole position for my top recommendation in the field.

—JONATHAN LEEMAN, author of *Political Church* and *How the Nations Rage*

At last, a biblically grounded, credible alternative to the eschatology-driven messianisms that have dominated political theology for a very long time. Taking his cue from the Noahic covenant, VanDrunen builds a political vision that is universal and pluralist, legitimating a common, provisional polity in which families can be a blessing and commerce can thrive.

VanDrunen engages the significant thinkers from Augustine to Yoder, but his treatment is far more than theoretical; it is concrete, practical, and contemporary—a political theology for the fallen world as it really is rather than for the world the philosophers wish it to be. This clear and thoughtful work is a game changer.

—JOHN BOLT, Jean and Kenneth Baker Professor of Systematic Theology emeritus, Calvin Theological Seminary

Few people are experts on Scripture, Augustine, Aquinas, Luther, or Calvin. David VanDrunen is an expert on all five. His wisdom is on full display in *Politics after Christendom: Political Theology in a Fractured World*. In the current challenging cultural moment for Christians, he gives a thoughtful argument for a Two Kingdoms/Two Covenants approach. It deserves careful consideration alongside the Benedict/separatist and conversionist options of recent years. VanDrunen's treatment of the Noahic covenant as the key to understanding a Christian's (and everyone's) relationship with the state is unique, thoughtful, and challenging.

—ROBERT F. COCHRAN JR., Louis D. Brandeis Professor of Law at Pepperdine University, coeditor, *Agape, Justice, and Law*

Politics after Christendom is an extraordinary achievement, one that will be a defining work of political theology for a generation. David VanDrunen's analysis of the Noahic covenant, its application to contemporary society, and its perennial dilemmas concerning rights, justice, pluralism, and religious liberty demonstrates that Protestant Christians understand that these issues are not unique to liberal democracy but pertain to the order of creation. Advocating for a broad framework rather than rigid prescriptions for society, VanDrunen argues lucidly that society is constrained by a politics of creation that every political community, regardless of geography or culture, finds itself living within. *Politics after Christendom* helps explain and resolve the intractable disputes of human societies. The exhausted trope that Protestants lack a clear, coherent, compelling, and translatable political theology can be put to rest with the publication of this volume.

—ANDREW T. WALKER, associate professor of Christian ethics, Southern Baptist Theological Seminary, executive director, Carl F. H. Henry Institute for Evangelical Engagement

POLITICS
after
CHRISTENDOM

POLITICAL THEOLOGY IN A
FRACTURED WORLD

DAVID VANDRUNEN

ZONDERVAN
ACADEMIC

ZONDERVAN ACADEMIC

Politics after Christendom
Copyright © 2020 by David VanDrunen

Requests for information should be addressed to:
Zondervan, *3900 Sparks Dr. SE, Grand Rapids, Michigan 49546*

ISBN 978-0-310-10884-9 (softcover)

ISBN 978-0-310-10885-6 (ebook)

Cover design: Tammy Johnson
Cover photo: © Sahas2015;Christina Romero Palma; Oleg7799; DaGa5/Shutterstock
Interior design: Kait Lamphere

Printed in the United States of America

20 21 22 23 24 25 26 27 28 29 30 /LSC/ 20 19 18 17 16 15 14 13 12 11 10 9 8 7 6 5 4 3 2 1

CONTENTS

FOREWORD

It is clear that the church in the West is facing a political situation in which it has lost most, if not all, of its traditional power and influence. If this happened in Europe over an extended period of time in the nineteenth and twentieth centuries, it is occurring with startling speed in the Americas in the twenty-first. Many Christians feel a mix of creeping fear and vertiginous confusion as things such as marriage and gender—upon which everyone, Christian and non-Christian, seemed to agree in the recent past—are now points of conflict. Ordinary believers find themselves decried as idiots at best and bigots at worst simply for holding to traditional moral norms. Once unquestioned social virtues, such as freedom of speech and religion, are now coming under pressure as popular opinion moves against them. And many Christians have no idea how to respond.

What we are witnessing is the undoing of the project that began in the fourth century. First, Constantine granted Christianity legal toleration within the Roman empire. Then the Empire adopted Christianity as its official religion. Thus began a close and fruitful connection between what we now call the secular state and the church. It is the last vestiges of the cultural fruits of this—the close correlation between Christian virtues and civic values—that is rapidly dissolving before our eyes. Many Christians are concerned that we now face the unknown without the resources to begin to address the situation.

In fact, as David VanDrunen makes clear in this book, there is no need to panic or despair. The situation that has been the historical norm, a close connection between Christianity and the values of the wider culture, is actually the theological exception. Nothing in the Bible should lead us to think that the church would ever have enjoyed the political power and cultural cachet it did for some 1,500 years. The New Testament presents the church as community of sojourners, of pilgrims, whose home is not in this world.

9

There is an obvious danger with this (obvious) New Testament teaching: it might tempt Christians to abandon civic life entirely and become sectarians or cultists, huddling together in some isolated compound waiting for the end of time. But that is not necessary and is arguably as unbiblical as the theocratic pretensions of its opposite—the theonomists of the political right and left. As VanDrunen demonstrates, the Bible points to resources that allow a thoughtful Christian to respond to the current changes in society without becoming either isolationists or those who engage in futile efforts to reinstate some putative Christian commonwealth (which was always more real in the imagination of those who confuse church and nation than in reality). It is possible to be a Christian citizen without the state being Christianized.

Yet VanDrunen offers Protestants more than simply a model for understanding how the church and the secular state should relate. He also opens up possibilities for social and ethical thinking that are needed at a time when technology, especially in the sphere of medicine, raises challenges so complex and so constantly changing that few of us know where to start thinking about such things, let alone come to clear conclusions.

Roman Catholics have in recent years far outstripped Protestants in thoughtful engagement with our current cultural moment. This is because Rome has a long and deep tradition of social thought built upon careful reflection upon natural law. What VanDrunen does is point Protestants back to our heritage in this matter and supplement it with a distinctively Reformed approach to the present. Building on his early scholarly work, VanDrunen points the reader to a number of biblically grounded concepts—natural law, Augustine's two cities, the two kingdoms, and the variegated covenant structure of God's relationship to his creatures. In so doing, he begins the important work of developing the kind of framework for social thought that is going to be of inestimable importance and utility in the coming years.

This is therefore an important book. It is clear and accessible, though built upon a wealth of learning, reading, and careful thought. It should be read—and inwardly digested—by pastors, by teachers, and indeed by any Christian who wishes to understand how the old polarities of "Christendom or cult compound" are not the biblical way and who wish to develop their political, civic, and ethical thinking in the light of biblical principles. VanDrunen has done the church a great service in his previous scholarly work and an even greater service in now presenting the fruits of that work in this learned and lucid synthesis of his earlier work now applied to our present cultural climate.

Carl R. Trueman, Grove City College

ACKNOWLEDGMENTS

In many respects, this book is the culmination of twenty-five years of serious reflection on political theology. This has brought me into contact with so many interesting people and institutions around the world that I cannot even begin to recognize all those who have contributed to my work in one way or another. But I am pleased to be able to thank a number of individuals who have been especially helpful to me as I created this volume.

I wish first to recognize the board and staff at my employer, Westminster Seminary California, and especially my students and faculty colleagues. I can hardly imagine producing this volume without the opportunities for teaching, research, student interaction, and faculty collaboration that WSC has given me. It is a privilege to work for an institution that values the sort of inquiry this book represents.

I also offer profound thanks to John Witte and his colleagues at the Center for the Study of Law and Religion at Emory University, especially Amy Wheeler. Prof. Witte has been a great encouragement to me for many years as I have pondered the natural law tradition, the two kingdoms doctrine, and challenges of political theology. He is a model of scholarly grace, and I thank him for all the help he has offered me, in this project and beyond. I'm especially grateful for his organizing a virtual symposium on a draft manuscript of the present volume, which was of great assistance in refining my work. Thank you to the symposium participants: Nick Aroney, Jonathan Burnside, Jonathan Chaplin, Sam Gregg, Michael Welker, and Nicholas Wolterstorff. I wish I could have presented to them the final version of this book and heard their comments on that instead of on an inferior draft. But I recognize that their critical interaction with that draft was an important step in producing a better version.

I also extend my thanks to the Henry Luce Foundation and the Association of Theological Schools for awarding me a Henry Luce III Fellowship in Theology for 2016–17. This was a great honor and an amazing opportunity for me as a scholar. The timing of the fellowship was absolutely perfect and allowed me to write a complete draft of this book during a period of peaceful focus that would have been impossible otherwise. Thanks especially to Stephen Graham for his skillful administration of this program, and for others who supported it, including Margaret Fitzgerald, Michael Gilligan, Jonathan VanAntwerpen, and Leah Wright.

I express my gratitude also to the Kern Family Foundation, and especially to Greg Forster, for awarding me a grant some years earlier. This grant funded several research trips that allowed me to develop some of the earliest material that would find its way into this book.

Thank you to several friends and colleagues who took the time to read the whole of my draft manuscript and offered extensive comments on the whole (no small task, I well recognize): Allison and Greg Church, Mike Horton, Lance Kinzer, Manfred Svensson, and Matt Tuininga. I especially appreciate Manfred's willingness to fly all the way from Chile to Pittsburgh to present a few of his comments publicly.

Many others sacrificed their time to give me valuable feedback on smaller pieces of this project or to give me opportunities to present my ideas-in-progress. I do not take this generosity for granted. With apologies to those I have surely failed to mention, let me express gratitude to Raju Abraham, Neil Arner, Steve Baugh, Tom Bell, Hays Bierman, John Bolt, Bill Brewbaker, Ad de Bruijne, Elizabeth Agnew Cochran, Bob Cochran, Doug Coyle, Jon Crowe, Perry Dane, Mike De Boer, Eric Descheemaeker, Bryan Estelle, John Fesko, Mark Graham, Jennifer Herdt, Dennis Johnson, Simon Jooste, Constance Youngwon Lee, Brad Littlejohn, Josh Maloney, Bill Reddinger, Rebecca Rine, Donald Roth, Josh Van Ee, Koos Vorster, Nico Vorster, Pieter Vos, and Kevin Walton.

Many thanks to Zondervan for taking up this project. I thank Ryan Pazdur, in particular, for his enthusiasm for my book and for his many helpful ideas for bringing it to its final form.

Most of all, my thanks to Katherine and Jack for all sorts of support and encouragement along the way. They would deserve the highest appreciation even if the former wasn't an inter-library-loaner extraordinaire and the latter didn't want to have long conversations about polycentrism and conservative liberalism.

Several parts of this book originated in articles I have written over the past decade exploring issues addressed here. I am grateful to the respective editors and publishers for permission to adapt material from these pieces: "Legal Polycentrism: A Christian Theological and Jurisprudential Evaluation," *Journal of Law and Religion* 32, no. 3 (November 2017): 383–405; "Justice Tempered by Forbearance: Why Christian Love Is an Improper Category to Apply to Civil Law," in *Agape, Justice, and Law: How Might Christian Love Shape Law?*, ed. Robert F. Cochran Jr. and Zachary R. Calo (Cambridge: Cambridge University Press, 2017), 125–47; "Learning the Natural Law as Maturation in Wisdom," *In die Skriflig/In Luce Verbi* 50, no. 1 (2016): 1–9; "Power to the People: Revisiting Civil Resistance in Romans 13:1–7 in Light of the Noahic Covenant," *Journal of Law and Religion* 31, no. 1 (March 2016): 4–18; "The Protectionist Purpose of Law: A Moral Case from the Biblical Covenant with Noah," *Journal of the Society of Christian Ethics* 35, no. 2 (Fall/ Winter 2015): 101–17; "Natural Law for Reformed Theology: A Proposal for Contemporary Reappropriation," *Journal of Reformed Theology* 9 (2015): 117–30; "Natural Rights in Noahic Perspective," *Faulkner Law Review* 6, no. 1 (Fall 2014): 103–34; "The Natural Law and Liberal Traditions: Heritage (and Hope?) of Western Civilization," in *The Law of God: Exploring God and Civilization*, ed. Pieter Vos and Onno Zijlstra (Leiden: Brill, 2014), 64–83; "The Market Economy and Christian Ethics: Refocusing Debate Through the Two-Kingdoms Doctrine," *Journal of Markets and Morality* 17 (Spring 2014): 11–45; and "A Natural Law Right to Religious Freedom: A Reformed Perspective," *International Journal for Religious Freedom* 5, no. 2 (2012): 135–46.

Perhaps this book reflects the spirit of my great-great-great-grandfather, Bastiaan van Drunen, who defied the state and (the state) church by hosting Reformed worship in his home in the mid to late 1830s in Sleeuwijk, North Brabant, Netherlands.

Matthew 8:20.

INTRODUCTION

To say that there are deep divisions within Western political communities is to state the obvious. As sharp as the disagreements are about identity politics, nationalism, or democratic socialism, at least everyone seems to agree that Western societies are plagued by profound disagreements and mutual suspicion. The historical events that have brought us to our current state of affairs are complex. But one way to describe our contemporary situation is that we are wrestling with life after Christendom.

By *Christendom* I mean the vision of Christian civilization that emerged in the very early medieval period and stretched well into the modern era, primarily in the West. Under Christendom, Christianity sought to be a civil power as well as a spiritual power. Most Western Christians lived within institutionally unified Christian societies in which political officials supported and protected the (true) church while suppressing heresies and non-Christian religions. While church, state, and other social institutions were technically distinct, they were linked in devotion to a common Christian culture. Few people would have found it controversial to say that their community was a "Christian society." While the sixteenth-century Protestant Reformation changed the character of Christendom in profound ways, it did not end Christendom itself.

That began to change as Western history moved into the so-called modern era. Various Enlightenment philosophies challenged orthodox theological beliefs, and political liberalism challenged the civil influence of churches and other traditional bodies. Communities began to grant new liberties to religious dissenters, and churches began to reexamine their long-standing objections to such liberties. Of course, Christendom did not die all at once or in the same way in every place. Yet slowly but surely, the habits, assumptions, and structures of Christendom withered away. Western societies became openly pluralistic in ways previous generations could not have imagined. New ways of thinking and acting came to prominence that no one could mistake for Christianity. Christian faith and Christian churches did not disappear, but Christendom gradually did.

Was the fall of Christendom a positive development? That has been a controversial question, even among Christians themselves. For the many Christians who held minority convictions in their societies, a post-Christendom world has brought new opportunities to express and promote their faith without persecution. The demise of Christendom has also corresponded with a period of unprecedented technological development and economic growth, which has produced a meteoric increase of health, wealth, and longevity for billions of people around the globe. Yet even many Christians with affection for religious liberty and capitalism find weighty reasons for unease. Amid the expanding opportunities and material prosperity, the post-Christendom world has witnessed the rise of violent ideologies, worldwide wars, upheavals in moral standards, and a decline in church attendance throughout the West. Life after Christendom has been a mixed experience. Christians have been trying to figure out how to navigate faithfully in such a world for quite a while now but seem to be as puzzled and divided about it as ever.

This is a book about politics after Christendom, but only in part. It does indeed attempt to set out a political theology appropriate for the pluralistic world that post-Christendom societies have become. But I also make a bigger claim: Christians do not need a new and special kind of political theology for life after Christendom. Rather, Scripture itself provides a political-theological vision perfectly suited for a post-Christendom world. The New Testament envisions Christians living in a world such as this and prepares them for it. Scripture equips Christians to understand and function within societies that will remain foreign and often hostile to them. And it never hints that Christians ought to seek the kind of integrated Christian society that Christendom represented, even were that possible. A politics after Christendom is a perennial political theology.

A POLITICAL-THEOLOGICAL VISION

What does this look like? Part 1 presents a biblical vision for *political theology*. That is to say, part 1 reflects theologically upon public life and political community in these last days following Christ's resurrection and ascension.[1] By "political community," I refer to the social life of the *polis*, that is, the "city": not smaller and often voluntary communities such as families, clubs, or businesses, but the larger community in a geographical region in which individuals and smaller communities interrelate.[2] Political communities ordinarily have governments, but government is not the same thing as political community. *Political* is a broader term than *governmental*.[3] From a Christian theological perspective, civil government is only one of many distinct but related institutions that God has ordained to promote a degree of justice, peace, and prosperity in common human life.

The theological vision of part 1 identifies four key characteristics of political institutions. First, political institutions are *legitimate*. God himself has ordained the existence and authority of our civil laws, governments, and officials. Second, political institutions are *provisional*. God has ordained them not as enduring bodies that will govern us in the new creation but as temporary bodies meant to promote a measure of peace and justice in this present, fallen world. Third, political institutions are *common*. God did not establish these institutions simply for the benefit of Christians, or simply for the benefit of people from a certain location or ethnicity, but for the benefit of all humans alike. Finally, political institutions are *accountable*. These institutions are under God's law and God's authority. He established them to promote peace and justice, and thus political institutions must ultimately answer to God himself.

---

1. My nontechnical use of *political theology* may bear resemblance to Mark Lilla's broad conception of political theology as the mode of thinking of people who "have appealed to God" when reflecting on "political questions," or as "discourse about political authority based on a revealed divine nexus." See *The Stillborn God: Religion, Politics, and the Modern West* (New York: Knopf, 2007), 3, 23.

2. This conception resembles Aristotle's basic idea of the *polis* as the association that is highest and inclusive of all other associations, such as the household. See his *Politics* 1.A.1.1 (1252a). But my understanding of political communities as instituted and sustained by God's temporal, common grace, in distinction from God's redemptive grace that brings new creation—as I will explain and defend at some length—makes me hesitant to use Aristotle's language of the *polis* as the "final and perfect association" that exists "for the sake of a good life"; see *Politics* 1.A.2.8 (1252b). For English translation, see *The Politics of Aristotle*, ed. and trans. Ernest Barker (New York: Oxford University Press, 1962). From my theological perspective, I might have opted for a broader definition of "political." For example, Jonathan Leeman defines "politics" as the "*mediating of God's covenantal rule*" (italics his) and thus argues that the church is a political institution; see *Political Church: The Local Assembly as Embassy of Christ's Rule* (Downers Grove, IL: IVP Academic, 2016), 237. The church is indeed "political" under such a definition. But this is not my working definition here.

3. James K. A. Smith takes a similar view of political theology and thus chooses to call it "public theology." See *Awaiting the King: Reforming Public Theology* (Grand Rapids: Baker Academic, 2017), 11–13. Another term I perhaps could have used is *civil society*, although that too has had a variety of nuances. "Civil society" is basically just the Latin version of the Greek *koinonia politike*. See Stephen B. Smith, *Modernity and Its Discontents: Making and Unmaking the Bourgeois from Machiavelli to Bellow* (New Haven: Yale University Press, 2016), 156.

In accord with these four characteristics, the political theology of part 1 rejects the notion that Christians should identify their political communities with the kingdom of God proclaimed in the New Testament. Many of the most popular contemporary political theologies contend that Christians should seek to redeem or transform their political communities so that these communities might somehow manifest and anticipate Christ's coming kingdom. This book promotes a different view. God has instituted and rules political communities, and Christians should be active within them and promote their welfare. But Christians ought not to seek the kingdom within such communities. The kingdom of God proclaimed in the New Testament is ultimately the coming new creation, and *the church of Jesus Christ* is the one present community God has appointed to manifest and anticipate that kingdom here and now. The fact that Christians are already citizens of Christ's kingdom means that they are always homeless in this world to some degree. To use Scripture's own language, Christians are *sojourners* and *exiles* within their political communities.

This perspective encourages contemporary Christians to be circumspect and thus to avoid the temptations of cultural pessimism and optimism. This book does not embrace the pessimistic outlook of some recent writers who portray the West as moving unstoppably into a dark age in which Christians will be mostly shut out of ordinary political life. But neither does it embrace a narrative of inevitable cultural progress. The short-term future is uncertain, and the long-term future all the more so. God's providence is mysterious, and one thing we know about the future is that it will defy our confident predictions. But if, theologically speaking, Christians are *always* sojourners and exiles in this present world, they should always strive for a healthy balance of vigilance in the face of opposition and confidence in God's preserving mercies. Some periods of time are relatively peaceful and prosperous for Christians and other periods more dire. But in all circumstances, Christians need healthy churches, a critical posture toward the deceits of the world, an appreciation for the goods and blessings around them, and an eagerness to participate with excellence in their political communities.

Part 2 moves from political theology to political ethics.[4] It seeks to answer some more specific questions: How should this biblical vision shape the way Christians think about pressing issues of political and legal theory? What are

---

4. I borrow this terminology from Oliver O'Donovan, who acknowledges the imprecision of distinguishing these disciplines in this manner; see *The Ways of Judgment* (Grand Rapids: Eerdmans, 2005), ix–x.

the implications of a biblical political theology for controversies about religious liberty, justice, rights, authority, resistance, and related matters? Part 2 does *not* argue that there is a single, detailed public policy agenda that all Christians are obligated to embrace. Rather, it explores what sort of *framework* the political theology of part 1 provides for Christians confronting ongoing debates in the public square. In summary, I propose a framework that suggests a strong measure of political tolerance and religious liberty, the foundational importance of marriage and family for the health of human communities, the benefits (and risks) of a market or enterprise economy, the necessity of pursuing justice (a justice that is retributive, compensatory, forbearing, and restorative), the good of the rule of law rather than human will, the legitimate authority of civil government under certain conditions, and the lawfulness of resistance to unjust authorities.

The final chapter reflects on the highly controversial ideas of *liberalism*, *conservatism*, *progressivism*, and *nationalism*, and traditions that lie behind them. How people evaluate such ideas depends in part on how they define them, which is always up for debate. But as a way of bringing my broader argument to conclusion, I will suggest that a Christian political theology points in the direction of a *conservative liberalism*. Such an outlook is liberal because it recognizes the inevitability of pluralism in our political communities and seeks just and peaceful ways for different kinds of people to live together. And it is conservative because it honors the wisdom accumulated in previous generations and values (critically) the traditions that embody it.

Throughout the book, I will interact with writers coming from many different perspectives and drawing on various fields of expertise. Among my interlocutors are Christian theologians of various eras (including Augustine, Aquinas, and Calvin), prominent political theologians of recent years (including Hauerwas, O'Donovan, and Wolterstorff), contemporary Christian cultural commentators (including MacIntyre, Hunter, and Dreher), and secular legal and political theorists (including Rawls, Hayek, and Dworkin).

THE THEOLOGICAL IDEAS AT WORK

To develop and defend the political theology summarized above, I make use of several classical theological doctrines. Although I present a political-theological vision different from the long-standing vision of Christendom, I am not inventing new categories or vocabulary. Some readers may be sympathetic to this book's political theology yet prefer not to speak of one or more of the classical doctrines I utilize. That could simply be a healthy disagreement among friends. Yet I believe these doctrines are of enduring value for understanding the issues before us. I mention four of them here.

The first is *natural law*. Natural law, in short, refers to God's basic moral will for the human race, revealed in the created order itself, such that all people have the capacity to understand and respond to it (although they also sinfully distort it). Natural law was a staple of medieval and Reformation theology, and of many Christian thinkers since. Although many twentieth-century Protestants came to regard natural law as foreign to Reformation Christianity, there has been a renaissance of interest in Protestant natural-law theory in the early twenty-first century. This present book, in part, seeks to contribute to that renaissance. It makes a new argument for the traditional Christian idea that natural law is foundational for human law.

This book makes use of another classical idea: Augustine's *two cities*. For Augustine, Christians are citizens of the city of God, the heavenly new creation, while unbelievers are citizens of another city, doomed to destruction. Through his two-cities imagery, Augustine described Christians as pilgrims in this world, on the way to their everlasting home. Christians intermingle with unbelievers during their pilgrimage and share many earthly things in common with them. Nevertheless, a strong spiritual antithesis distinguishes one from the other. The present book portrays the Christian life as one of pilgrimage and thereby stands in the two-cities tradition.

But this book also makes use of the idea of *two kingdoms*, particularly as developed in early Reformed theology. This idea is different from Augustine's two cities, though it is compatible with it. It teaches that God rules all things but does so in a twofold way. God exercises a *common* rule by which he preserves the world and ordains political government and other social institutions. God also exercises a *redemptive* rule by which he builds his church and brings the new creation. By analyzing political communities in terms of God's common rule, this book works within the two-kingdoms tradition.

A fourth traditional idea this book utilizes is familiar to everyone who reads Scripture: the *biblical covenants*. At key junctures in biblical history, God entered into covenants with his creatures. In my own Reformed tradition, theologians have often used these biblical covenants as a way to organize and interpret the broader message of Scripture. While this book gives attention to many of the biblical covenants, it makes special use of the covenant with Noah (Gen 8:21–9:17). The Noahic covenant, I argue, is foundational for understanding the revelation of God's will in the natural law, the character of Christians' pilgrimage in the present age, and the nature of God's common rule. Although a multitude of Christian writers have utilized doctrines of natural law, the two cities, and the two kingdoms to try to understand Christians' place in their political communities, the present book is unique in trying to explain all of these ideas in the context of the biblical covenants.

Christians have been arguing about the issues before us for a very long time and undoubtedly will continue to do so until Christ returns. That should put this present contribution to political theology in perspective. Yet Christians can surely agree that living just and fruitful lives that bless our neighbors is an important part of Christian responsibility in this age as we "serve the living and true God" and "wait for his Son from heaven" (1 Thess 1:9–10). I hope this volume can promote that goal in some way.

PART 1

POLITICAL
THEOLOGY

CHAPTER 1

LEGITIMATE, BUT PROVISIONAL, COMMON, BUT ACCOUNTABLE

The Contours of a Christian Political Theology

Political theology is complex and controversial, and it is not at all obvious where to start. I believe it will be helpful to begin by identifying and defending a few basic ideas that provide an overview of a biblically grounded political theology. This should lay an excellent foundation for our study in the chapters that follow. After this, I will step back and consider where these foundational ideas fit in the long history of Christian political-theological reflection. This discussion will help readers understand how my project resembles and differs from other important political theologies of past and present.

The foundational political-theological ideas of this book are simple to state and crucial to understand but, as Christian theological history suggests, not easy to work out in detail. The ideas are these: God has ordained civil government—as the ruling authority of political communities—to be *legitimate*, but *provisional*, and to be *common*, but *accountable*. Let us consider each of these in turn.

LEGITIMATE

First, civil government is legitimate. By this I mean that civil government has a right and even an obligation to carry out its proper work. As argued later, civil government's proper work is to promote justice. Thus when civil governments and political officials promote justice within a particular society, they are not engaging in an act of usurpation but exercising legitimate authority. Although they may come to power by different routes, furthermore, God is the ultimate source of their legitimacy.

Several New Testament texts speak explicitly of civil government and have been foundational for Christian thinking about legitimate political authority. According to Paul, there is no governing authority "except from God, and those that exist have been instituted by God" (Rom 13:1). God establishes these authorities for beneficial purposes, namely, to approve of those who do good and to "bear the sword" as "an avenger who carries out God's wrath on the wrongdoer" (Rom 13:3–4). Along similar lines, Peter writes of governors "as sent by him [God] to punish those who do evil and to praise those who do good" (1 Pet 2:14). As such, these magistrates are God's "servants" and "ministers" (Rom 13:4, 6). Doing their work well enables Christians to "lead a peaceful and quiet life" (1 Tim 2:2). Since God has ordained civil magistrates for such propitious ends, Christians ought to submit to them, honor them, pay taxes (Matt 22:16–21; Rom 13:1–2, 5–7; Tit 3:1; 1 Pet 2:13–17), and pray for them (1 Tim 2:1–2).

While these texts directly affirm political legitimacy, Acts does so indirectly through its account of the early church. Here the apostles implicitly acknowledge the legitimate authority of civil officials and the legal structures in which they operate. Paul had frequent confrontations with the powers of his day, and though they sometimes treated him roughly, he never challenged their offices or the governing laws. On several memorable occasions, he asserted his rights under Roman law, both to have a trial before punishment (Acts 16:37; 22:25) and to appeal to Caesar (25:11). In Corinth Paul was ready to defend himself in court, until the judge dismissed the charges (18:14–15), and in Caesarea he defended himself repeatedly (24:10–21; 26:2–23). In one of his court appearances, he addressed the governor with the sort of respect he commends in Romans 13: "Knowing that for many years you have been a judge over this nation, I cheerfully make my defense" (Acts 24:10). In fact, the various civil magistrates readers meet in the course of Paul's ministry often act rather sensibly, recognizing what is just and acknowledging the limits of their jurisdiction (Acts 16:38–39; 18:14–16; 19:35–41; 22:25–29; 23:16–35; 27:42–43).

In the New Testament, Christians are not only obligated to recognize legitimate political authority but also free to hold civil office. Zacchaeus was a chief tax collector (Luke 19:2), a position the people despised. After seeing Jesus from a sycamore tree and hosting him at his house, Zacchaeus promised restitution for those he defrauded but did not demit his office—and Jesus approved (19:8–10). Cornelius, a centurion of the Italian Cohort, was a God-fearing gentile who sought Peter's preaching and was subsequently baptized (Acts 10). Some Jewish Christians initially objected to granting him full fellowship with the church because he was an uncircumcised gentile (11:1–3), but no one objected to admitting him because of his military office. Shortly thereafter, Sergius Paulus, a proconsul in Cyprus and "man of intelligence," believed in Christ through Paul's teaching (Acts 13:6–12). In these and other instances (cf. Luke 3:13–14; Rom 16:23), holding civil office created no obstacle to Christian faith. Although the New Testament never comments normatively on government work as a vocation for Christians, the fact that civil office was a nonissue in the conversion of political officials is consistent with the New Testament's general affirmation of the state's legitimacy.

This evidence for the legitimacy of state authority is not unique to the New Testament, for the Old Testament provided ample witness of it long before Christ's coming. One of the important claims of the present book is that the transition from Old to New through Christ's ministry effects no essential change in the nature, purpose, or legitimate authority of civil government, and we can begin to see evidence for this claim already here. In what follows, I comment only on what the Old Testament says about civil governments among the gentile nations. Legitimate political authority also existed among the Israelites as they lived in their promised land under the law of Moses, but their experience was unique in important respects. Chapters 2 and 3 address this issue. For now, I simply consider some of the extensive evidence for polit-ical legitimacy among the gentile nations, among which the Roman Empire later emerged.

The Old Testament often recounts how God used civil magistrates to accomplish his good purposes, particularly with respect to his covenant people. Pharaoh, ruler of Egypt, offered provision and protection for Jacob's family during famine (Gen 47), the king of Moab sheltered David and his family from the tyranny of Saul (1 Sam 22:3–4), and Israel in Babylonian exile enjoyed a degree of prosperity under Nebuchadnezzar (Jer 29:5–7). Subsequently, Cyrus the Persian restored the Israelites to their land (2 Chr 36:22–23; Ezra 1; Isa 45:1–13), and his successors supported them at several points of crisis (Ezra 6:1–5; Neh 2:1–8).

Although these incidents display how God used civil authority in his providential government of the world, they do not necessarily prove its legiti-macy, since God sometimes uses evil things for his own ends. But legitimacy is clearly evident in several other texts, in which God's people, with implicit or explicit divine blessing, actively acknowledge the work of gentile governments and participate in it. Three interesting things deserve mention. First, God's servants occasionally made covenants with rulers of gentile nations. It is striking that the same Hebrew word describes both God's covenants with human partners and intrahuman political treaties. These political covenants are solemn oaths that establish mutual recognition and responsibilities. Abraham entered such a covenant with King Abimelech of Gerar (Gen 21:22–32), and his son Isaac followed suit (Gen 26:26–31). Kings David and Solomon had friendly relationships with several foreign rulers (e.g., 2 Sam 10:1–2; 1 Kgs 10:1–13), but the most important seems to be the partnership with Hiram king of Tyre, with whom Solomon did extensive business (1 Kgs 5) and entered a covenant (5:12; 5:26). The Mosaic law prohibited Israel from making covenants with nations within the bounds of their promised land (Deut 7:1–2). Yet Solomon's covenant with Hiram, a manifestation of his wisdom (1 Kgs 5:12), indicates that legitimate civil authority continued to exist among gentile nations elsewhere, even during the golden age of the Israelite theocracy.

Second, a number of Old Testament saints held high political office under gentile governments. Joseph, a God-fearing man who maintained hope in the promises to Abraham (e.g., 39:4–12; 42:18; 50:24–25), was second only to Pharaoh in the land of Egypt (41:38–44). During the exile, the godly Daniel, Shadrach, Meshach, and Abednego entered the Babylonian civil service with distinction (Dan 1) and later assumed positions of power (Dan 2:48–49). After the Medes and Persians overthrew Babylon, Daniel assumed another high position under Darius (Dan 6:1–3). He was such a faithful Persian civil servant that his enemies could find no ground to accuse him "with regard to the [Persian] kingdom" (6:4). The zealously pious Nehemiah (e.g., Neh 13) was cupbearer to a later Persian king, Artaxerxes (Neh 1–2). Another Persian king, Ahasuerus, took a Jew for his queen (Esther 2) and elevated her uncle Mordechai to second in command (10:3). It would be remarkable enough to know that members of God's covenant people held even lowly civil office under three of the most powerful kingdoms of the ancient world; it is a wonder to learn that they assumed positions of the greatest authority short of being head of state.

Third, Jeremiah 27 and 29 provide perhaps the closest Old Testament counterpart to the explicit descriptions of government legitimacy and its corresponding obligations found in Romans 13 and 1 Peter 2. As God prepared

Judah for exile, he declared to the rulers of Edom, Moab, Ammon, Tyre, and Sidon, as well as to Judah, that he gives the earth to whomever he pleases and that he had given their lands to his servant Nebuchadnezzar (Jer 27:2–6). Therefore, they were all to submit to Nebuchadnezzar for their own good (27:7–22). Accordingly, Jeremiah's letter to the first wave of Jewish exiles exhorted them not only to live normal lives in Babylon (29:5–6) but also to seek its welfare and to pray for it (29:7). Thus a great many pieces of New Testament teaching about the legitimacy of civil authority find precedent here: God's appointment, the magistrate as divine servant, and the peoples' obligation to submit to their magistrates and pray for them.

LEGITIMATE, BUT PROVISIONAL

The legitimacy of civil government needs to be complemented by another crucial biblical idea: civil government is provisional. "Provisional" refers to something set in place for a limited time and purpose until something greater arrives. Civil government is an important institution but will not endure forever. It is a valuable institution but not of highest value. It is penultimate rather than ultimate. Only the kingdom of the Lord Jesus Christ, inchoately manifest now in the church and climactically revealed in the New Jerusalem, is of ultimate value and importance.

Civil government is legitimate but provisional. A Christian political theology ought to affirm both simultaneously.

Daniel 2 captures this point vividly. Nebuchadnezzar dreamed of an imposing image with head of gold, chest and arms of silver, midsection and thighs of bronze, legs of iron, and feet of iron and clay. A stone of nonhuman origin struck the image and broke it into pieces, which the wind carried away without leaving a trace (2:31–35). God revealed the interpretation to Daniel. God had granted Nebuchadnezzar a great kingdom and made him the head of gold. After his kingdom, God would raise up other, weaker kingdoms, represented by the lower parts of the image. But in the days of the latter kings "the God of heaven will set up a kingdom that shall never be destroyed, nor shall the kingdom be left to another people. It shall break in pieces all these kingdoms and bring them to an end, and it shall stand forever" (2:36–45). Earthly kings and kingdoms are provisional. They come and go. But the eschatological kingdom of God will endure.

The New Testament texts considered in the previous section also communicate the provisionality of civil government. God commissions civil magistrates to promote justice by praising the good and punishing evildoers (Rom 13:3–4; 1 Pet 2:14), and in so doing they enable people to live peaceful and quiet lives (1 Tim 2:2). These are genuine goods, objects of thanksgiving for those who enjoy them. But the New Testament nowhere ascribes any greater task to civil government. Magistrates do not forgive sins, reconcile people with God, or usher in the new creation. Civil officials may bear the sword (Rom 13:4), but they do not wield the "keys of the kingdom," which Christ entrusted to his church (Matt 16:18–19).

Thus it is no surprise that the New Testament steers Christians away from staking very much upon government institutions. Christians may avail themselves of civil justice, pray for their civil authorities, and even exercise political office, but they should always keep affairs of state in proper perspective. No affection Christians may feel toward their political communities can compare to their allegiance toward Christ's heavenly kingdom. The Philippian Christians lived in a Roman colony, yet Paul declared that their "citizenship is in heaven" (Phil 3:20). Christians, already raised up with Christ, should "seek the things that are above," not "things that are on earth"; their lives are "hidden with Christ in God" (Col 3:1–3). Long ago, Abraham, living by faith, "was looking forward to the city that has foundations, whose designer and builder is God" (Heb 11:10). Abraham sought a "homeland," "a better country, that is, a heavenly one" (Heb 11:14, 16). Thus believers today say, "Here we have no lasting city, but we seek the city that is to come" (Heb 13:12). Paul warns Christians about becoming absorbed in the affairs of the world, such as marriage or commerce, "for the present form of this world is passing away" (1 Cor 7:29–31). Christians do not avoid such affairs but retain a modest detachment and refuse to grant them all-consuming importance. They may have citizen status in their cities of residence, but they are sojourners and exiles on earth, as the saints of old (1 Pet 2:11; Heb 11:13).

Scripture also communicates the provisional character of legitimate civil institutions by highlighting the precarious and fleeting nature of political power. God repeatedly exposes the weakness of those who appear to be strong. The mighty Pharaoh helplessly watched the divine plagues destroy his country and, like the lowliest pauper, lost his firstborn son (Exod 7–12). The indomitable Sennacherib, king of Assyria, lost 185,000 soldiers in a single night by the angel of the Lord and then returned home to be killed by his sons (2 Kgs 18–19). Nebuchadnezzar, while admiring Babylon and basking in his own majesty, was driven into the fields and grew claws, ate grass, and lived with the beasts (Dan 4). The last king of the Babylonian empire,

Belshazzar, gave a feast for a thousand of his lords and then lost control of his bowels before them when a mysterious hand wrote on the wall. Later that night he lost his kingdom (Dan 5). Shortly after King Herod executed the apostle James, he was struck down by the angel of the Lord and eaten by worms while wearing his finest apparel (Acts 12). As Isaiah declares, "Behold, the nations are like a drop from a bucket, and are accounted as the dust on the scales" (40:15). God

> brings princes to nothing,
>> and makes the rulers of the earth as emptiness.
> Scarcely are they planted, scarcely sown,
>> scarcely has their stem taken root in the earth,
> when he blows on them, and they wither,
>> and the tempest carries them off like stubble. (40:23–24)

Scripture displays the provisionality of legitimate civil authority in at least one other striking way: though God commissions magistrates to promote justice, they are among the grandest perpetrators of evil. Authority itself is a good. But civil governments in a fallen world are intractably sinful institutions. The power of the sword that enables them to keep some evil at bay also enables them to do evil on a more vicious scale than private parties. Civil governments and civil offices are part of this present age that is passing away.

Biblical examples are legion. The first civil officials to appear in the biblical canon are polygamist kings who take whatever women they choose (Gen 6:1–4) and mighty warriors who wreak violence on the earth (Gen 6:11). The last civil officials to appear in the canon lament the fall of the mysterious "Babylon," that great enemy of God, and gather to make war against God on the last day (Rev 18:9–10; 19:17–19). In between, we find Pharaoh enslaving Israel and ordering the mass murder of its baby boys (Exod 1:8–22), Nebuchadnezzar requiring worship of an idol under threat of death by fiery furnace (Dan 3), Darius requiring exclusive prayer to himself under threat of death by lions' den (Dan 6), Haman planning genocide (Esther 3), Herod beheading James and imprisoning Peter (Acts 12:1–5), and anonymous magistrates beating Paul and Silas and imprisoning them without trial (Acts 16:19–24). Satan claimed power over the kingdoms of the world (Luke 4:6), and a certain sway he surely enjoys (e.g., Eph 2:2). Christians may seek and pray for justice from civil officials, but they should not be surprised to be persecuted instead.

Civil government is thus legitimate but provisional. Neither its legitimacy nor its provisionality cancels out the other. The political theology unfolded in this book strives to uphold both legitimacy and provisionality simultaneously.

COMMON

The other pair of truths is that civil governments are common but accountable. God has ordained civil government to wield authority in political communities for the benefit of the human race in common. Government is not for some sorts of people rather than other sorts. One type of government is not to serve those of one ethnic or religious identity and an essentially different type of government to serve those of a different identity. Yet civil governments are also morally accountable. They should not be, and in fact cannot be, neutral. The way to achieve and maintain commonality is not by seeking a legal framework that makes no moral judgments and is hence independent of any philosophical or theological perspective. Instead, civil governments are accountable to God and his standards of justice. Therefore, a Christian political theology ought to teach and defend simultaneously that God designed civil governments to be common but accountable. This is a fiendishly difficult subject in need of much reflection in later chapters. For now, I simply outline some of the basic biblical evidence pointing in this direction.

Turning first to the theme of commonality, we find help again in Romans 13. Several features of the text point to the common nature of civil government. Paul begins by exhorting "every person" to be subject to the governing authorities and then adds that "there is no authority except from God, and those that exist have been instituted by God" (13:1). This means, at least generally, that everywhere civil government exists it is divinely ordained and thus legitimate and that everyone who lives in a community with a government should submit to its authority. Paul also identifies the basic purpose for which government exists: to be a "servant of God, an avenger who carries out God's wrath on the wrongdoer" (13:4).

If we put these pieces together, we do not get a complete theory of political commonality, but we begin to see a basic outline. Where government exists, it is obligated to promote justice on God's behalf, approving those doing good and punishing wrongdoers. Paul does not specify that this is for gentiles rather than Jews (or vice versa) or for Romans rather than Scythians (or vice versa). Neither does Paul specify that this is for Christians rather than for pagans (or vice versa). The apostle implies that civil government is obligated to administer justice toward the entire human community within its jurisdiction without discriminating by ethnic or religious identity. To be sure, in order to carry out its responsibilities civil government must make judgments that discriminate between good acts deserving praise and evil acts deserving punishment, and such moral judgments are inseparable from one's cultural background and religious convictions (to anticipate the "accountable" discussion below). Yet Paul's use of generic terms for "good" and "evil" in Romans 13:1–7 is striking in context and carries important implications. While Paul unpacks an explicitly Christ-shaped and Christ-directed ethic for the Christian community in the texts immediately preceding and immediately following, in 13:1–7 he makes no mention of Christ or redemption but merely speaks of good and evil in general for the entire human community before God. By implication, government's discernment of good and evil for purposes of civil judgment is not meant to discriminate between Christian and non-Christian. From the other direction, every person within the jurisdiction of a civil government is obligated to honor and submit to it as it carries out its obligation to administer justice. According to Paul, Jews and gentiles, Romans and Scythians, and Christians and pagans have identical responsibilities toward their civil officials. In light of all this, to attempt to establish a designer government or boutique state aiming to serve one particular ethnic or religious constituency would run afoul of Paul's teaching.

It is helpful again to consider the Old Testament roots of these New Testament ideas. The Old Testament speaks of many ancient governments and political rulers and, as considered above, confirms their legitimacy. Excluding again the unique case of Israel under the Mosaic law, we recognize that every one of these governments ruled communities that were predominantly if not exclusively gentile, and their magistrates, with possible exceptions, did not worship the God of Abraham. These ancient governments, we begin to see, were common to the human race, ruling all sorts of people.

This commonality becomes all the more evident when we remember that some members of Abraham's household and of the holy nation of Israel had occasion to live under such governments, participate in the communities they ruled, and even assume civil office within them. Despite their ethnic and religious differences, when Israelite worshipers of Yahweh interacted with gentile idolaters in communities ruled by these governments, there were "things that ought not to be done" that both sides expected the other to avoid (see Gen 20:9; 34:7). This points to a common standard of justice akin to Paul's appeal to "good" and "evil" in Romans 13. Old Testament saints did not believe their different religious or ethnic status disqualified them from seeking the welfare of these political communities, either as ordinary citizens (e.g., Jer 29:7) or as civil officials (e.g., Daniel). Furthermore, the saints who attained high political office showed no interest in using their power to turn their communities into holy theocracies. Joseph did not try to expunge Egyptian religion and permit only the worship of the God of Abraham; Daniel did not try to turn Babylon into a new Jerusalem.

Thus both Old and New Testaments indicate that God has ordained civil governments to be common, that is, to administer justice on behalf of all people within their jurisdiction. They are not meant to discriminate against people on the basis of their ethnic or religious identities.

COMMON, BUT ACCOUNTABLE

While affirming this notion of commonality, Christian political theology also ought to affirm that civil governments are morally accountable. Just as political legitimacy may tempt a person to deny political provisionality, so also political commonality may tempt a person to portray politics as morally neutral. After all, how can a political or legal system be structured so that it maintains an even hand when dealing with people of different ethnic origin or religious conviction? One attractive answer, popular in the contemporary West, is that laws and governmental institutions should be based upon notions of human reason that do not favor one group of people over another, providing a level playing field in which individuals and groups can freely live according to their own beliefs and values. This, it would seem, provides a setting that perfectly protects commonality.

Defining the precise nature of commonality and determining how to attain it are very difficult issues, but this quest for neutrality is not the solution. On the one hand, even were it desirable, such neutrality is simply impossible to attain. Many Christian and non-Christian writers have exposed the idea of neutral reason as a myth. Universal faculties of human reason exist, but how people understand and use them are inseparably intertwined with their fundamental religious and moral assumptions, whether they are consciously aware of them or not. Such notions also inevitably shape convictions about justice that underlie human laws and government institutions. The critiques of the quest for a religiously and morally neutral public life are so numerous and compelling that I say no more about it here.

But it is important to add, as a matter of Christian political theology, that this quest for neutrality, even were it possible to attain, is theologically problematic. Romans 13 is helpful again. As we have seen, Paul does not simply assert that God has ordained civil magistrates but that God has ordained them for a specific task, the administration of justice through approving good and punishing evil (13:3–4; cf. 1 Pet 2:14). Civil officials are not their own bosses (even in an autocracy), and the people they govern are also not their bosses (even in a democracy). Magistrates are "servants" and "ministers" of God (Rom 13:4, 6), who is the only ultimate authority. In this text, Paul does not delegate authority to magistrates to *define* what is good and evil but to *recognize* what is good and evil so that they might administer justice accordingly. The judgments of civil magistrates are always morally freighted because they either advance or resist a divine commission.

Once again, none of this is new to the New Testament. The Old Testament contains many accounts of judgment God brought, or promised to bring, upon wicked gentile nations and their rulers. In one of the most famous, God rained fire and brimstone from heaven upon Sodom and Gomorrah (Gen 19:24–25) in response to the great "outcry" against these cities and their "very grave" sin (18:20; cf. 19:1–22). The Old Testament prophets also provide numerous examples through their oracles against non-Israelite communities. Such oracles appear in all of the major prophets (Isa 13–23; Jer 46–51; Ezek 25–32) and some of the minor prophets (e.g., Amos 1:2–2:3). The oracles serve different purposes in different contexts, but many of them announce coming divine judgment against these nations' sins, and some of them address rulers specifically. They often target nations that have oppressed or mocked God's covenant people Israel (e.g., Ezek 25)—surely a source of encouragement for the church and of warning for hostile governments today. God held all of these nations accountable and permitted them no space for neutrality. It is remarkable that in the texts cited above God never judges these nations or their rulers for idolatry as he did with Israel. This indicates that he did not condemn them for failure to establish true religious worship and exclude the noncompliant. God condemned them instead for egregious acts of injustice or crimes against humanity. In Amos 1–2, for example, he brings charges for acts such as slave trading, violating treaties, and ripping open pregnant women. This makes sense. God holds governments and their officials accountable for promoting justice but does not wish them to exclude people on the basis of religious identity. God ordains commonality and accountability simultaneously.

Christian political theology necessarily rejects any government's claim to be morally neutral, but this prompts questions about how civil officials know the standard of justice to which God holds them accountable. Affirming commonality makes these questions even more acute, since it takes away easy answers that merely point to the Bible as the source for knowing God's will. If the legitimacy of government does not depend upon what religion its officials profess, and if God does not presently judge communities for idolatrous worship, then there is something at least initially suspicious about any claim that governments depend upon knowledge of Scripture and its moral claims. In any case, many nations and their rulers have not had and do not have knowledge of the Christian Scriptures, and God holds them accountable for administering justice nonetheless.

Consistent with these observations, Scripture testifies to the reality of an objective moral order that all human beings know through their ordinary faculties whether or not they have read the Old or New Testaments. The gentile Abimelech knew that there were "things that ought not to be done" (Gen 20:9). A certain "fear of God" served as a check upon injustice in several gentile contexts (Gen 20:11; 42:18; Exod 1:17) or served as a source of accusation when it was missing (Deut 25:17–19). The wisdom necessary to perceive what is just was present among gentile peoples, at least to some meaningful degree (1 Kgs 4:30; Jer 49:7; Obad 8; Ezek 14:14, 20; 28:3), such that Proverbs could incorporate foreign wisdom material into its corpus (in Prov 22–24, 30, 31). "By me kings reign," says personified Wisdom, "and rulers decree what is just; by me princes rule, and nobles, *all* who govern justly" (Prov 8:15–16, emphasis added). Paul confirms the presence of universally known moral truth. God "has made plain" his "eternal power and divine nature" in "the things that have been made," such that all human beings are "without excuse" for failing to honor God (Rom 1:19–21). All people "know" that their wicked deeds deserve death (Rom 1:32). In other words, Paul claims that God, somehow or other, reveals himself and his moral will in the natural order and that he holds the entire human race accountable for their response to it (cf. Rom 2:14–15). This points to the reality of a natural law, to be considered further below.

Thus God has ordained civil government to be common but accountable. A sound Christian political theology must recognize both and seek to explain their harmony.

THE CONTEXT OF THIS POLITICAL THEOLOGY

The preceding discussions identified some basic contours of a Christian political theology that, in my judgment, meet several fundamental tenets of biblical teaching concerning civil community and public life. Affirming "legitimate but provisional" and "common but accountable" is hardly all that political theology needs to do, and even affirming them in general terms leaves many important questions unanswered. But failing to embrace these basic contours is almost sure to guarantee missteps in a more detailed political-theological inquiry.

Thus it is worth asking where those who affirm these basic contours will land if they attempt to situate themselves in the broader landscape of Christian political theology. In the remainder of this chapter, I suggest a way to answer this question. I first identify an approach to political-theological issues in the broader Christian tradition that I believe provides the best resources and categories for explaining how political institutions are legitimate but provisional, common but accountable. The present volume embraces this approach while also seeking to refine and improve it. Second, I briefly consider several other popular paradigms for Christian political theology and explain why I conclude that each, despite genuine strengths, is less than satisfactory, in large part because each paradigm fails to reckon sufficiently with either legitimacy or provisionality.

Affirming Two

There are many ways to try to make sense of the complex development of Christian thinking about government and civil society over two millennia. One helpful way is tracing the varied expositions of "the Two." In many different social and theological contexts, Christian thinkers have spoken of Two Cities, Two Swords, Two Powers, Two Kingdoms, and Two Governments. These do not mean the same things, although some are (at least potentially) compatible with each other, and it seems fair to say that their advocates proposed them in order to address a set of interrelated issues. These advocates recognized that Christians need to make certain distinctions in order to understand the social realities of this present world properly. Earthly communities must be distinguished from the heavenly community, the church must be distinguished from the state, and so on. Theologians have long recognized that good distinctions make for good theology. Theologians distinguish person and nature, body and soul, and justification and sanctification, for example, striving to explain what differentiates one from the other as well as how they relate. Christian thinkers rightly sensed the need for good distinctions regarding the institutions and activities of the present life as well.

In the present study, I join this inquiry about "the Two." As I understand it, my political theology affirms and refines the idea of the Two Kingdoms as developed within the Reformed theological tradition, situated within a broader framework of the Two Cities as pioneered by Augustine.[1] I do not claim that Christian thinkers who choose not to embrace these categories of the Two are necessarily in error, although they too must find ways to make appropriate distinctions. But I myself gladly identify with this line of analysis despite the unfortunate connotations that taint the idea of the Two Kingdoms in the minds of many. An important reason why I identify with this line of analysis is because it is my own tradition. I am a Reformed minister and theologian, and I wish to work within the confessional and theological heritage of my churches. But I am also convinced that this line of analysis offers a uniquely helpful way to encapsulate a sound biblical-theological understanding of political institutions and public life. I believe that older Reformed expositions of the Two Kingdoms should be refined and enriched, but its basic ideas provide a solid foundation and strong structure in which to keep living while doing the work of refurbishment.

I have not written this book as merely a contribution to parochial Reformed debates, however. While continuing, and I hope contributing to, the Reformed tradition, this study attempts to focus upon biblical, theological, moral, legal, and political argumentation that those from other Christian traditions can understand and appreciate. After all, interpretation of Scripture should be of great interest to all professing Christians, and my line of inquiry is rooted in patristic and medieval Christianity, which the Reformation sought to reform, not reject.

Augustine's *The City of God* was obviously not the first Christian foray into political theology, but it was a monumental work that remains impossible to ignore. Augustine proposed that there are two cities, the earthly city and the heavenly city of God. These two cities are not church and state or church and civil society. They transcend any institutional distinction of this present world. Instead, Augustine's two cites correspond to two peoples: one the people of God, redeemed through Christ, on pilgrimage here and now on their way to the eschatological new creation, and the other the rest of fallen

---

1. In *Awaiting the King: Reforming Public Theology* (Grand Rapids: Baker Academic, 2017), 45–47, James K. A. Smith represents my interpretation of Augustine's Two Cities and the Reformation Two Kingdoms as if I think the latter was a helpful morphing of the former into something more complex, as if the Two Cities gets spatialized into a civil realm, the realm of nature rather than grace. But as I explain in *Natural Law and the Two Kingdoms: A Study in the Development of Reformed Social Thought* (Grand Rapids: Eerdmans 2010), the Two Cities and Two Kingdoms are different categories that address different issues. Augustine's "earthly city" is *not* the "common kingdom" (or whatever one calls it).

humanity, also living presently in this world but destined for eschatological death. A key trait distinguishing the people of these two cities is their two loves. Citizens of the city of God love their Creator above all while loving created things only in relation to God and for his sake. Citizens of the earthly city, on the other hand, set their chief affection on themselves. In terms of both destiny and love, therefore, a stubborn antithesis separates the two sets of citizens. Yet in this world they intermingle. Church and political community are not identical to the heavenly and earthly cities, respectively, because both church and political community are mixed societies. Some citizens of the earthly city are members of the church, while citizens of the heavenly city participate in civil communities. And as Christians participate in their civil communities, they have no objection to sharing many things in common with citizens of the other city, whether manners, laws, clothing, or other necessities of life, provided they do not hinder faith or worship of the true God. Christians thus seek the welfare of their civil communities and make use of whatever peace it enjoys, even while recognizing that only the heavenly city provides true peace and justice.[2]

Augustine's meditations on the movement of history and God's work of redemption surely get many things correct, and profoundly so. In terms of earlier discussion—legitimate but provisional, common but accountable—Augustine seems to point us largely in the right direction. He expressed a genuine, if appropriately measured, appreciation for earthly political communities as common, for he encouraged Christians to share many things with unbelievers without scruple and to support the attainment of temporal peace (although he also advocated the state's use of coercion to compel recalcitrant people into the church). Yet this commonality did not deny moral accountability. *The City of God* critiqued earthly societies and their alleged virtues and insisted that Christians cannot share in common those things that divert them from God. Augustine was also clear about the provisional character of political communities, which endure only for a time and fall far short of the heavenly. But this great work may be somewhat insufficient with respect to legitimacy. While Augustine did not oppose the state or its pursuit of justice, he seems to have fallen short of a full-fledged theological account of its divine institution. The basic Two Cities category itself, in any case, does not imply such an account.

---

2. See especially *The City of God*, book 19. Cf. VanDrunen, *Natural Law and the Two Kingdoms*, 26–32.

Augustine's notion of the Two Cities, therefore, offers a very helpful paradigm for building a Christian political theology, although one might question its sufficiency in some respects. There was room, it would seem, for further political-theological development. Thus, in hindsight, it is no surprise that Christian thinkers continued inquiry into the Two.

In the late fifth century, Pope Gelasius I propounded a doctrine of Two Powers, the civil and the ecclesiastical, or that of emperor and priest. While Augustine had proposed a distinction between two peoples with different loves and destinies, who nevertheless commingle in this world, Gelasius asserted a distinction between two powers, both from God, that exercise authority in this world. These two powers rule over the same people but have different jurisdictions. The emperor has authority over "mundane" and "temporal affairs" for the goal of "public order"; the priest is concerned with the sacraments and "spiritual activities" toward the goal of "eternal life." Priest and emperor should submit to one another in their proper spheres.[3]

Several features of Gelasius's doctrine of the Two fit within the framework of legitimate but provisional, common but accountable. His doctrine affirms the legitimacy of civil authority as divinely established, which was not clearly present in Augustine. By associating civil authority with mundane and temporal affairs, Gelasius also suggests the provisional character of civil government. His paradigm, furthermore, embraces no myth about the state's moral neutrality. More doubtful is whether Gelasius's Two Powers could sufficiently account for commonality. His paradigm presumed the joint rule of pope and emperor over a unified Christian society and the emperor's humble submission to the pope in all spiritual things. In this respect, it seems to suffer tension with the idea that God has ordained political institutions and public life for all human beings. And if the vision of a unified Christian society constituted an attempt to realize the new Jerusalem ahead of God's own schedule—which I fear it did—then this paradigm may also have compromised the provisional character of civil government.

The Two Powers category, for obvious reasons, would prove to be an attractive way to think about civil authority and its relation to the church in the context of Western Christendom. It achieved something valuable by affirming that government is legitimate even while distinguishing government's work from that of the church (although some of its versions compromised

---

3. For English translation of Gelasius's letter to Emperor Anastasius (494) and his treatise *On the Bond of Anathema* (496), see Brian Tierney, *The Crisis of Church and State: 1050–1300* (Englewood Cliffs, NJ: Prentice-Hall, 1964), 13–15. Cf. VanDrunen, *Natural Law and the Two Kingdoms*, 32–34.

this achievement—I think especially of Pope Boniface VIII's notion of Two Swords, which reduced the civil power to a vassal serving at the church's good pleasure).[4] But insofar as Christendom imposed legal sanctions upon those who did not profess Christianity or professed it in unapproved ways, it had a serious flaw, at least if political authority ought to be *common* to the human race.

In the Reformation and beyond, many Protestant theologians developed another category of the Two: the Two Kingdoms. Different versions (and caricatures) of the Two Kingdoms have existed within the Protestant traditions. The category is usually associated with Lutheran theology, in which it has indeed played an important role. But I focus upon its Reformed version, since this is my own tradition and, I believe, the most theologically compelling. To introduce this paradigm briefly, I utilize the work of seventeenth-century theologian Francis Turretin, an eminent representative of the period of "Reformed orthodoxy," and then consider a more recent traveler in this tradition.[5]

The (Reformed) Two Kingdoms category generally resembles the Two Powers in its interest in how God rules the present world by means of human institutions and authorities, but its scope extends considerably further than this. Turretin's understanding of the two kingdoms is rooted in Christology and specifically in the nature of Christ's kingship. When beginning his treatment of this topic, he comments, "But before all things we must distinguish the twofold kingdom, belonging to Christ: the one natural or essential; the other mediatorial and economical." Christ rules the former as true God and Logos, the second specifically as the incarnate God-Man. He rules the first through his work of providence, the second by redemptive grace. The natural

---

4. For English translation of Boniface's *Unam Sanctam* (1302), see Tierney, *The Crisis of Church and State*, 188–89. Cf. VanDrunen, *Natural Law and the Two Kingdoms*, 34–36.

5. The basic paradigm I present here, via Turretin, was not the unanimous view among classical Reformed theologians, although it seems to have become the predominant view among both Presbyterians and the continental Reformed. For an example of another two-kingdoms paradigm, see the recent exposition and defense of Reformed (Anglican) theologian Richard Hooker's view by W. Bradford Littlejohn in *The Peril and Promise of Christian Liberty: Richard Hooker, the Puritans, and Protestant Political Theology* (Grand Rapids: Eerdmans, 2017). Hooker, following a more Lutheran line of two-kingdoms thought, identified the spiritual kingdom with Christ's direct rule over the believer in the inner forum of conscience and the civil kingdom with God's outer and indirect rule through human authorities, in both church and state. To my mind, this paradigm is neither biblically persuasive nor practically attractive. Since Scripture presents God's rule over creation in its various aspects in terms of *covenant*, I believe the two kingdoms are best seen as grounded in two covenants, as I will defend in subsequent chapters. This paradigm supports the basic Reformed version of the two kingdoms as represented by Turretin, or so I will argue.

kingdom extends over all creatures equally, and the mediatorial kingdom over the church uniquely. Accordingly, Christ administers the mediatorial kingdom through the calling, government, and protection of the church, and its perfection in the age to come.[6] In terms relevant for political theology, first, the mediatorial kingdom consists fundamentally of Christ's rule over his redeemed and perfected people in the age to come, and the church is the one institutional expression of this kingdom in the present world. Second, Turretin and other Reformed orthodox theologians saw the "natural kingdom" idea as especially relevant for understanding the nature and authority of civil government. Nevertheless, since Christ's natural kingdom extends equally over all creatures, presumably all other legitimate institutions of this world also reflect and express this universal providential rule of Christ in some way.

Turretin proposed a sevenfold distinction between ecclesiastical and political authority. (1) Political authority originates in God the Creator, while ecclesiastical authority originates in Christ, the head of the church; only the church's ministers, not civil magistrates, promote the mediatorial kingdom of Christ "properly and formally." (2) Non-Christians can hold political office, but ecclesiastical office belongs only to believers. (3) Political authorities can make, improve, and change laws, which they enforce through physical coercion, while ministers of the gospel have power only to promulgate the laws of Christ, and they do not bear the sword. (4) The supreme end of civil magistrates is the glory of God the Creator, who preserves the human race and rules the world, and their subordinate end is public peace and the temporal good of the community. The supreme end of the Christian ministry, however, extends to the glory of Christ the mediator, the king of his church, and its subordinate end is the welfare of the church and the advance of Christ's mediatorial kingdom. (5) Political authority concerns the external things of the present life, while ecclesiastical authority concerns sacred things that pertain to salvation. (6) Civil magistrates attend to external concerns in a political way and for a political end, while the church's ministers attend to spiritual concerns in a spiritual way and for a spiritual end. (7) Finally, political authority is regulated by natural reason and human laws, but ecclesiastical authority is governed by the word of God alone.[7]

---

6. Francis Turretin, *Institutes of Elenctic Theology*, 3 vols., trans. George Musgrave Giger, ed. James T. Dennison Jr. (Phillipsburg, NJ: P&R, 1992–1997), 2:486–87. Cf. VanDrunen, *Natural Law and the Two Kingdoms*, 173–82.

7. Turretin, *Institutes*, 3:278–79. Cf. VanDrunen, *Natural Law and the Two Kingdoms*, 182–89.

Dutch theologian and statesman Abraham Kuyper (1837–1920) was the most influential Reformed social theorist of the past several centuries. Kuyper's social thought developed the earlier Two Kingdoms paradigm, although scholars often overlook this. Three features of the way he adapted this paradigm are noteworthy for the present study. First, Kuyper developed a detailed doctrine of common grace and special grace. The former refers to God's preservation of the present world and the latter to God's redemptive achievement of new creation. Kuyper attributed common grace and special grace to Christ as mediator of creation and mediator of redemption, respectively, mirroring appeals to the twofold kingship of Christ in earlier centuries. Second, Kuyper grounded common grace especially in God's covenant with Noah after the great flood. Finally, through his notion of sphere sovereignty, Kuyper identified many independent activities and institutions of human life, which develop organically as common grace sustains the various capacities of human beings created in God's image and permits these capacities to blossom as civilization expands.[8]

How should one evaluate the Reformed idea of the Two Kingdoms? Although I would wish to nuance or qualify Turretin's statements at several points, I believe his paradigm reckons well with the basic contours of a sound Christian political theology suggested above: legitimate but provisional, common but accountable.

Turretin roots political authority in the ordination of God the creator and sustainer of all things, and specifically in the exercise of Christ's natural or universal kingship. Civil office is thus legitimate. At the same time, political magistrates do not exercise a spiritual authority that directly promotes Christ's mediatorial kingdom, but they bear the sword to advance temporal ends concerning the peace and order of the civil community. Thus Turretin's paradigm affirms political provisionality alongside legitimacy. Turretin also

---

8. See especially Abraham Kuyper, *Lectures on Calvinism* (Grand Rapids: Eerdmans, 1931); and Abraham Kuyper, *Common Grace*, vol. 1, parts 1–3, trans. Nelson D. Kloosterman and Ed M. van der Maas, ed. Jordan J. Ballor and Stephen J. Grabill (Grand Rapids: Christian's Library Press, 2013–14). Cf. VanDrunen, *Natural Law and the Two Kingdoms*, 276–315. Among other scholars interpreting Kuyper as member of a broader two-kingdoms tradition, see, e.g., Cornelis van der Kooi, "A Theology of Culture. A Critical Appraisal of Kuyper's Doctrine of Common Grace," in *Kuyper Reconsidered: Aspects of His Life and Work*, ed. Cornelis van der Kooi and Jan de Bruijn (Amsterdam: VU Uitgeverij, 1999), 98–100; Jacob Klapwijk, "Antithesis and Common Grace," in *Bringing into Captivity Every Thought: Capita Selecta in the History of Christian Evaluations of Non-Christian Philosophy*, ed. Jacob Klapwijk, Sander Griffioen, and Gerben Groenewoud (Lanham, MD: University Press of America, 1991), 170–79; and John Halsey Wood Jr., "Theologian of the Revolution: Abraham Kuyper's Radical Proposal for Church and State," in *Kingdoms Apart: Engaging the Two Kingdoms Perspective*, ed. Ryan C. McIlhenny (Phillipsburg, NJ: P&R, 2012), 155–71.

touches upon commonality. He affirms that Christ's natural kingdom extends to all creatures equally and that non-Christians as well as Christians may hold civil office. Yet the common character of political authority is obviously morally accountable: Turretin places political authority under the ultimate authority of Christ the king so that it will promote the divinely instituted ends of temporal life.

This Two Kingdoms paradigm, however, does raise questions similar to those I mentioned regarding the Two Powers. Turretin maintained a vision of a unified Christian society in which political magistrates, despite having no spiritual authority over the church or individual conscience, ought to wield their physical sword in support of the true church and keep threats of heresy and blasphemy at bay.[9] This at least raises questions whether Turretin's exposition sufficiently accounts for the commonality and provisionality of political life.

In the end, I judge that the basic idea of the Two Kingdoms that Turretin represents is a theologically sound structure, a home in which Reformed Christians do well to keep living—and a home to which they may gladly invite guests from other traditions. Two things might enhance the attractiveness of this home. First, understanding the Two Kingdoms against the background of the Two Cities may help the Two Kingdoms tradition to account adequately for notions of commonality and provisionality that popular visions of Christendom underappreciated. Second, supplementing the Two Kingdoms distinction with aspects of Kuyper's ideas about common grace, the Noahic covenant, and sphere sovereignty may enrich and deepen older paradigms such as Turretin's. Old homes frequently need update and refurbishment, especially when many wish to condemn the house altogether. The present study, in part, undertakes such an updating and refurbishing effort.

Paths Not Taken

I now mention a few other popular approaches to political theology. I consider approaches within both the Reformed and other Christian traditions, for Christian political-theological debates seldom merely involve one

---

9. Turretin, *Institutes*, 3:316–36. Cf. VanDrunen, *Natural Law and the Two Kingdoms*, 192–206. I believe it is a cause for gratitude that most Reformed believers and church communities moved away from this view between the eighteenth and twentieth centuries. American Presbyterians, for example, modified the *Westminster Confession of Faith* and Catechisms at several points in 1788 to reflect this change of conviction, and many Reformed churches throughout the world with roots in continental Europe have modified Belgic Confession Article 31 in similar fashion. These issues are a major concern of chapter 7 below.

confessional tradition battling another. As the following pages indicate, debates within Roman Catholic and Eastern Orthodox circles often bear remarkable similarity to those within Reformed circles. I focus now upon the idea that political authority is legitimate but provisional. These other approaches I discuss fall short in one aspect or the other, either failing sufficiently to affirm legitimacy or failing sufficiently to affirm provisionality. Needless to say, their proponents did not volunteer to have their work evaluated by means of these categories. But reflecting on their work in this way maintains the coherence of this chapter and indicates why I do not walk their paths in the chapters that follow.

LEGITIMACY DENIED

Most churches and theologians have not denied the legitimacy of civil government. The Reformed, Lutheran, Roman Catholic, and Eastern Orthodox traditions generally affirm that civil magistrates have some God-ordained authority to promote justice, backed by coercion. Advocates of nonviolence identified with the so-called Radical Reformation of the sixteenth century and their spiritual heirs are a prominent exception. While nonviolence has ordinarily lurked outside the mainstream of the Christian world, it gained new intellectual respectability in recent decades through the work of theologians such as John Howard Yoder, Stanley Hauerwas, and Richard Hays. Thus their nonviolent vision serves as an appropriate example of a popular path I am not taking.

Crucial to this nonviolent vision is a principled rejection of the long experiment with Christendom. One theologian within this circle of thought describes Christendom as "the concept of Western civilization as having a religious arm (the church) and a secular arm (civil government), both of which are united in their adherence to Christian faith. . . . Within this Christian civilization, the state and the church have different roles to play, but, since membership in both is coterminous, both can be seen as aspects of one unified reality."[10] Advocates of the nonviolent vision do not simply claim that Christendom had abuses and excesses—which few Christians of any sort would deny—but assert that Christendom itself was a fundamental error that perverted the gospel and betrayed Christ's teaching.[11] From the perspective of my earlier discussion, one might conclude that this polemic

---

10. Craig A. Carter, *Rethinking Christ and Culture: A Post-Christendom Perspective* (Grand Rapids: Brazos, 2006), 14.

11. E.g., see Carter, *Rethinking*, 22, 78, 92–93.

against Christendom insightfully upholds the provisional character of civil government (although "provisional" may not be the word advocates of nonviolence would choose). Indeed, I believe this perspective is correct to reject the idea that coercion-backed civil government should join the church to form two aspects of a unified Christian civilization.

But their robust affirmation of provisionality entails rejection of legitimacy. Yoder's position is unambiguous. Two features of his interpretation of Romans 13:1–7 stand out. First, Yoder states, "God is not said to *create* or *institute* or *ordain* the powers that be, but only to *order* them, to put them in their place." God does not mandate any given government or make it a channel of his will, but simply uses it in his ordering of the cosmos.[12] Second, Yoder observes, in the broader context of Romans 12 and 13, that Paul tells Christians never to exercise vengeance (12:19), even while recognizing that civil authorities do precisely this (13:4). Jesus's teaching in the Sermon on the Mount and Paul's exhortations in Romans 12–13 are not in any tension but command the same thing.[13] Hence, "the function exercised by government is not the function to be exercised by Christians."[14] In short, Yoder does not believe that the coercion-backed state is divinely ordained or that Christians should participate in its punishment of wrongdoers.

Other proponents of the nonviolent vision agree that the New Testament forbids Christian participation in the state's coercive activity but seem to leave open some God-ordained role for civil government. Hays, for example, states that "though the governing authority bears the sword to execute God's wrath (13:4), that is not the role of believers. Those who are members of the one body in Christ (12:5) are never to take vengeance (12:19)."[15] In his view, the New Testament evidence against violence is overwhelming, and Christians therefore ought to "relinquish positions of power and influence insofar as the exercise of such positions becomes incompatible with the teaching and example of Jesus."[16] Arguably, this conclusion keeps Christians only from government jobs that directly involve the infliction of violence—say, from military and police service. Nevertheless, *everything* civil government does is

---

12. John Howard Yoder, *The Politics of Jesus: Vicit Agnus Noster* (Grand Rapids: Eerdmans, 1972), 203–4.

13. Yoder, *The Politics of Jesus*, 213–14.

14. Yoder, *The Politics of Jesus*, 199.

15. Richard B. Hays, *The Moral Vision of the New Testament: Community, Cross, New Creation: A Contemporary Introduction to New Testament Ethics* (San Francisco: HarperSanFrancisco, 1996), 331; cf. 340–42; also see Carter, *Rethinking*, 104–5.

16. Hays, *The Moral Vision*, 340–42.

grounded in at least the threat of coercion. To adhere consistently to Hays's conclusion seems to require abstention from working on government-funded infrastructure projects and for government-funded social services, for example, since such funding comes from taxes, which governments collect with whatever violence they deem necessary.

Hauerwas considers similar matters in his reconception of Christian social ethics. He famously claims that "the first social ethical task of the church is to be the church."[17] But he insists that this does not express disinterest in the broader world. Rather, when the church is the church, it shows the world what the world was meant to be. Christians do not join the world in practicing politics or seeking justice with the aid of coercion, but they do look for people who manifest God's peace better than they themselves do, and they seek to cooperate with them. This cooperation in promoting true peace and justice results from the wideness of God's kingdom, not from any universal natural law morality.[18] The church's "task is not to *make* the world the kingdom, but to be faithful to the kingdom by showing to the world what it means to be a community of peace."[19] For Hauerwas, therefore, Christians cannot participate in the state's activity as described in Romans 13, but the church does attempt to show the broader world what the peace of Christ's kingdom is. Where that peace is manifest, there the kingdom is present, even beyond the church's bounds.

For these advocates of nonviolence, therefore, civil government is less than fully legitimate. Some of these theologians believe government altogether lacks divinely ordained authority to pursue justice backed by coercion. Others at least deny that Christians should participate in this work. In my judgment, these nonviolent visions correctly grasp that the sword-wielding state cannot be identified with the kingdom Jesus proclaimed, but they improperly refuse to recognize the state's legitimacy.[20]

PROVISIONALITY COMPROMISED

Most churches and theologians do not deny the legitimacy of civil government, despite widespread interest in the work of Yoder, Hauerwas, and Hays. The more common shortcoming in Christian political theology, it seems to me,

---

17. Stanley Hauerwas, *The Peaceable Kingdom: A Primer in Christian Ethics* (Notre Dame: University of Notre Dame Press 1983), 99.

18. Hauerwas, *The Peaceable Kingdom*, 100–104.

19. Hauerwas, *The Peaceable Kingdom*, 103.

20. For another recent critical interaction with these theologians, see Nigel Biggar, *In Defence of War* (Oxford: Oxford University Press, 2013), ch. 1.

is to affirm legitimacy without a corresponding provisionality, or at least without a provisionality that is sufficiently robust. The core problem is that these political theologians place an eschatological burden upon political activity and institutions. Many political-theological visions see the work of civil government as (at least potentially) part of the realization of the kingdom Jesus proclaimed. That is to say, these visions believe that legitimate political institutions, in some way or another, participate in the redemptive work of Christ. Such a perspective compromises the provisional character of political institutions.

In the broader history of Christian theology, it is difficult to think of a more poignant (and hardly subtle) compromise of provisionality than the concluding narratives of Eusebius of Caesarea's *Ecclesiastical History*. Eusebius did not intend these narratives to be a systematic theological analysis of Constantine and the Roman Empire, but he describes them in a way that associates a *particular* state, and even a particular political ruler, with the fulfillment of Old Testament prophecy and thus with the realization of Christ's kingdom on earth. He portrays Constantine as a man of profound piety who, with God's help, rescued Rome from tyranny as Moses overthrew Pharaoh. Thus in their own day, Eusebius writes, they had seen the fulfillment of Psalms 46:9–10 and 37:35–36, which prophesied that war would cease and the wicked be cut off. Constantine cleansed the world of its hatred for God.[21]

Our present focus, however, is on prominent contemporary approaches to political theology. Although these approaches do not exalt particular states and rulers, a number of recent political theologies hold that Christian redemption extends to political life generally and that well-executed civil authority is a realization of Christ's kingdom here and now.

So-called liberation theologies present an important and rather radical example of this perspective. I recognize the danger in subjecting liberation theologies to critical examination. These theologies typically arise from those who have suffered genuine injustice and have legitimate grievances. People who evaluate a liberation theology invite critique that they do not understand or sympathize with the suffering behind it. I will not defend myself against such charges except to say that I hope subsequent reflections on pluralism, economics, justice, and resistance will offer constructive treatment of some of the grievances that have inspired liberationists. In any case, theology written for the broader public subjects itself to critical examination, and the claims of liberation theology are pertinent to the present discussion.

---

21. See Eusebius of Caesarea, *Ecclesiastical History*, 9.9; 10.1, 9.

James Cone's "black theology" offers a good example. As Cone has attempted to rethink theology for the African American community in a series of books over the past half-century, he frequently polemicizes against an otherworldly spirituality that whites foisted upon black churches and that the latter largely accepted. This entailed belief in salvation as a forgiveness of sins that prepared people for heaven, where they would one day escape present suffering. Although Cone does not altogether deny a future aspect to the kingdom or the expectation of life after death, he views emphasis upon such things as a Platonic distortion of Christianity that keeps the oppressed from fighting for justice in this life, which was exactly what their white oppressors wanted.[22] Over against this, Cone asserts, "Jesus' work is essentially one of liberation."[23] The *kingdom of God* releases people from all human evils in the present and is being realized in "the black revolution" and "the liberation struggle in the black community."[24] Likewise, *salvation* is an earthly "liberation from bondage," manifest when the helpless and poor rise up against their oppressors and demand justice now.[25] In short, the overturning of unjust political and other social structures is of the essence of the kingdom Jesus proclaimed and the salvation he offered.[26] Liberation from present injustice realizes the kingdom.

Rosemary Radford Ruether's feminist theology advances many of the same themes. She rejects "the classical theology of the cross."[27] This rests in traditional Christian ideas about God as omnipotent and compassionate, human beings as fallen and guilty, and the atonement as God's gracious intervention to pay for sins.[28] For Ruether, redemption does not come through someone's unjust torture and death, and Jesus did not come in order to suffer and die. Instead, Jesus came to share "experiences of liberation and abundance

---

22. E.g., James H. Cone, *Black Theology and Black Power* (New York: Seabury, 1969), 37, 122–25; and James H. Cone, *A Black Theology of Liberation*, 2nd ed. (Maryknoll, NY: Orbis, 1986), 126, 137, 140–42.

23. Cone, *Black Theology and Black Power*, 35

24. Cone, *Black Theology and Black Power*, 37; *A Black Theology of Liberation*, 124–25.

25. Cone, *A Black Theology of Liberation*, 127–28.

26. Cf. Jürgen Moltmann, *On Human Dignity: Political Theology and Ethics*, trans. M. Douglas Meeks (Minneapolis: Fortress, 2007), 110: "There can be no economic justice without political freedom, no improvement of socioeconomic conditions without overcoming cultural alienation and without personal conversion from apathy to hope. Whoever does not understand salvation in the most comprehensive literal sense and does not strive for a network of saving anticipations over the various fields of devastation does not understand salvation holistically."

27. Rosemary R. Ruether, *Introducing Redemption in Christian Feminism* (Sheffield: Sheffield Academic Press, 1998), 104.

28. Ruether, *Introducing Redemption*, 97–98.

of life" with the powerless. Redemption is "transformation that brings abundant life in loving mutuality." It comes about "through processes or practices that actually create and promote mutual flourishing" and "through resistance to the sway of evil, and in the experiences of conversion and healing by which communities of well-being are created."[29] Ruether denies altogether the hope of an eschatological new creation. We should accept our mortality and transience, she says, rather than try to solve it as Greek spirituality did.[30] For Ruether, therefore, redemption is wholly imminent. Present liberation from injustice and flourishing earthly communities are the only visions Jesus inspired.

These liberation theologians advocate a stark rejection of the kind of provisionality I described above, as they themselves would surely agree. I wish to shift focus now to subtler challenges to such provisionality. For examples, I call upon writers from three different traditions: Reformed, Roman Catholic, and Eastern Orthodox. I do not mean to conflate their broader political-theological views. But in their own ways they are united in seeing the redemptive work of Christ extend to the transformation of government and other social institutions. They do not deny or downplay the hope of an eschatological new creation, as do liberation theologians, but they do link present political activity with the kingdom Jesus proclaimed.[31] I do not describe their views comprehensively or critique them here but only highlight this particular point.

Political theorist James Skillen provides a Reformed example. Skillen works in the "neo-Calvinist" line of thought popular in many Reformed circles over the past century. Skillen's general theological outlook follows the typical neo-Calvinist scheme, emphasizing God's good creation of all things, the disordering of creation through the fall into sin, and God's redemption of the whole creation through Christ.[32] He also relies particularly on Anglican

29. Ruether, *Introducing Redemption*, 101, 104–5.

30. Ruether, *Introducing Redemption*, 106, 119–20.

31. The work of influential Anglican theologian John Milbank, I believe, also insufficiently accounts for provisionality. Milbank subjects all social institutions to a withering critique on the basis of a Christian ontology of peace, and his positive prescriptions—of "Christian socialism," for example—seek to realize something of this eternal peace in present human communities. See especially *Theology and Social Theory: Beyond Secular Reason* (Malden, MA: Blackwell, 1990); also see "Socialism of the Gift, Socialism by Grace," *New Blackfriars* 77 (1996): 532–48.

32. E.g., see Albert M. Wolters, *Creation Regained: Biblical Basics for a Reformational Worldview* (Grand Rapids: Eerdmans, 1985). Someone has suggested to me that there may be significant agreement between the second of my two sets of criteria (common but accountable) and the neo-Calvinist distinction between a creaturely thing's "structure" and its "direction." From neo-Calvinist perspective, a thing's structure (or essence) reflects God's created law for it and thus remains sound in a fallen world, while its

New Testament scholar N. T. Wright for his conception of how the broader biblical story unfolds.[33] Following a theme popular for both Wright and neo-Calvinists, as well as for Cone and Ruether, Skillen emphasizes that Scripture is not about the "salvation of souls" and warns against an undue (or even Neoplatonic) focus on the life to come.[34] Skillen does battle on many fronts, but he finds the idea of Two Kingdoms an especially useful foil when presenting his own vision, although he recognizes that other Reformed writers—including John Calvin and the present author—have held versions of this idea.[35] For Skillen, God has only ever had one kingdom—from the first creation to its consummation. This kingdom "embraces all human governing experiences in this age," and thus "good government in this age does not belong to a kingdom separate from God's kingdom but is part of the building material God is using to construct the kingdom of our Lord Jesus Christ." Present political life "find[s] its fulfillment in the kingdom Jesus is establishing."[36] Skillen connects political activity not only to Christ's kingdom but also to his work of redemption. "Every dimension of life in this world is being renewed by the Spirit of Christ," he writes, for "the mission of Jesus in announcing the fulfillment of God's purposes with creation was to reconcile and redeem all that is human—all shepherding, schooling, family relationships, economic institutions, and political practices."[37] Thus the vision of Christ's kingdom should guide Christians' political engagement as they seek "a better and more integrated view of the relation of earthly life to the fulfillment of creation in the age to come."[38]

Roman Catholic theologian David L. Schindler has defended analogous ideas that, in my judgment, compromise political provisionality. Schindler unfolds his ideas in the context of the *communio* ecclesiology advanced at

---

direction has been sinfully distorted and needs to be restored. E.g., see Wolters, *Creation Regained*, 72–73. Likewise, so the suggestion goes, political institutions are common insofar as appointed by God for all human beings but accountable insofar as their moral direction has become distorted and falls under God's judgment. I agree that there is similarity of concern, although the neo-Calvinist view of the restoration of proper direction reflects a redemptive-transformationist perspective that I reject, and which I believe entails (among other things) an insufficient appreciation for provisionality, as discussed here.

33. Evident especially in James W. Skillen, *The Good of Politics: A Biblical, Historical, and Contemporary Introduction* (Grand Rapids: Baker Academic, 2014), ch. 1.

34. E.g., Skillen, *The Good of Politics*, xx, 3, 24, 55. This theme is pervasive in N. T. Wright, *Surprised by Hope: Rethinking Heaven, the Resurrection, and the Mission of the Church* (San Francisco: HarperOne, 2008).

35. See Skillen, *The Good of Politics*, ch. 3. On Calvin and VanDrunen, see *The Good of Politics*, 94–95, 121, 200n2.

36. Skillen, *The Good of Politics*, 8, 34, 39.

37. Skillen, *The Good of Politics*, xix, 10.

38. Skillen, *The Good of Politics*, 122–23.

the Second Vatican Council. He contrasts his work with a different stream of Roman Catholic thought, which has been influential during the past half century. John Courtney Murray, Richard John Neuhaus, and Michael Novak, for example, have proposed a benign, conservative interpretation of the Anglo-American liberal tradition that makes it harmonious with Roman Catholicism. Over against this, Schindler seeks to unmask liberalism as an insidious worldview or ideology whose views on freedom, neutrality, and the like are opposed to fundamental Roman Catholic convictions.[39] According to Schindler, who works from a conception of the nature-grace relationship different from Murray's,[40] "the Christian's mission in the world . . . is to be present *as Church*, and thereby to assist in drawing into *communio* all of nature and all of the anthropological (political, economic, cultural) orders that extend nature into culture." The world, he explains, "with all of its political, economic, and cultural orders," is only fully the *world* as it attains this *communio*. Thus the mission of the church, which represents the entire cosmos, "lies in bodying forth the *communio*-Church into all areas of worldly existence," although complete *communio* is achieved only in the age to come.[41] While maintaining the juridical distinctness of church and state and forswearing any use of coercion to attain these goals,[42] Schindler argues that the church must be "penetrating the world—and hence the world's social-economic-cultural orders—*with* itself," and only by participating in *communio* can any aspect of reality "be liberated to give glory to God."[43] Every Christian must ask "how I, concretely, day by day, can penetrate with the love of Jesus Christ the social, economic, political, and educational institutions with which I am most directly involved."[44]

Vigen Guroian adds an Eastern Orthodox voice to these Reformed and Roman Catholic voices. Whereas Skillen and Schindler address the Western political tradition as Westerners, Guroian writes as part of the post-Ottoman, post-Communist Orthodox dispersion to the West and sees his own theological

---

39. As summarized in David L. Schindler, *Heart of the World, Center of the Church:* Communio *Ecclesiology, Liberalism, and Liberation* (Grand Rapids: Eerdmans, 1996), xiv–xv, 31–34. Cf. John Courtney Murray, *We Hold These Truths: Catholic Reflections on the American Proposition* (Kansas City: Sheed and Ward, 1960); Michael Novak, *The Spirit of Democratic Capitalism* (New York: Simon & Schuster, 1982); and Richard John Neuhaus, *The Naked Public Square* (Grand Rapids: Eerdmans, 1984).

40. See Schindler, *Heart of the World*, 75–80. Schindler largely embraces the work of Henri de Lubac.

41. Schindler, *Heart of the World*, xi, xiii.

42. Schindler, *Heart of the World*, 84–85.

43. Schindler, *Heart of the World*, 10–11 (emphasis original).

44. Schindler, *Heart of the World*, 136.

tradition as a stranger to Western ways of discussing political-theological top-ics.[45] Guroian examines his tradition critically. He confesses that the Eastern church often erred in refusing to resist imperial claims that Byzantium was the kingdom of God already on earth, and he declines association with "Orthodoxy's Constantinian legacy."[46] Nevertheless, he also rejects popular Western options, claiming that Orthodox ecclesiology is incompatible with the "metaphysical dualisms" underlying the "Gelasian theory of the two swords, Luther's notion of the two realms, and the American principle of separation of church and state," although there may be pragmatic reasons to live with the American order. In this light, he too, like Schindler, dissents from John Courtney Murray's approach.[47] The church's proper mission is "to sanctify all things, making it known that there is no final polarity of nature and grace, state and church, world and Kingdom of God," or in other words "to make the Kingdom of God present by redeeming and transfiguring the world." Hence, appealing to H. Richard Niebuhr's famous fifth paradigm for the relationship of Christ and culture, Guroian claims that Orthodox social ethics is "consistently transformationist or conversionist."[48] While denying that politics "belong[s] to the Kingdom" or that the imperfect achievements of political life" can be "equate[d] . . . with the values of the Kingdom of God," he asserts that "political life is part of that material of the Kingdom which the Church must take within its own life, sanctify, and return to God. Politics reforms; the Church transfigures."[49] The church is a "Eucharistic public which is sent out into the society to transform it into the image of God's Kingdom of light, liberty, and love."[50]

CONCLUDING SUMMARY

We have considered two popular political-theological paths that the present study does not follow. On the one hand, proponents of a nonviolent vision, contemporary heirs of the Radical Reformation, correctly recognize that sword-bearing civil government cannot be an expression or manifestation

---

45. See Vigen Guroian, *Incarnate Love: Essays in Orthodox Ethics* (Notre Dame: University of Notre Dame Press, 1987), 4, 156–57.

46. Guroian, *Incarnate Love*, 123, 143–44.

47. Guroian, *Incarnate Love*, 154–57. For an Eastern Orthodox political theology much more favorable to Murray and to the liberal tradition generally, see Aristotle Papanikolaou, *The Mystical as Political: Democracy and Non-Radical Orthodoxy* (Notre Dame: University of Notre Dame Press, 2012).

48. Guroian, *Incarnate Love*, 24. Cf. H. Richard Niebuhr, *Christ and Culture* (New York: Harper, 1951), ch. 6.

49. Guroian, *Incarnate Love*, 25.

50. Guroian, *Incarnate Love*, 67.

of the kingdom Jesus proclaimed but fail to affirm its God-ordained legiti-macy. On the other hand, representatives of certain streams of the Reformed, Roman Catholic, and Eastern Orthodox traditions correctly acknowledge the God-ordained legitimacy of civil government but fail to account for its provisionality by portraying it as (at least potentially) a manifestation of Christ's kingdom, which his redemptive grace penetrates. These two prom-inent streams of thought place Christians in an uncomfortable dilemma: either affirm the peaceful character of the kingdom Jesus proclaimed at the expense of political legitimacy or affirm political legitimacy at the cost of expecting that kingdom to advance and be manifest, in part, by the edge of a human sword.

To understand this dilemma better, with the hope of extricating ourselves from it, we might observe several similarities between these two paths, despite their apparently vast differences. First and most important, both paths link the concept of legitimacy to the manifestation of Christ's eschatological king-dom. That is, both paths hold that Christians may approve of and participate in human institutions other than the church, but only insofar as Christ's king-dom and redemptive grace extend to them. To put it another way, Christians may promote the work of various human institutions, but only if they seek to saturate these institutions with the grace and ethic of the coming new creation. Both camps thus embrace a redemptive-transformationist vision of Christian public life. For advocates of nonviolence, this means opposing the coercion-backed state as inimical to the kingdom and thus seeking alternative ways to promote justice. For the likes of Skillen, Schindler, and Guroian, this means conceiving the coercion-backed state itself as a manifestation of the kingdom and thus promoting justice through it.

A second similarity between these paths, following from the first, is that both tend to adopt a skeptical posture toward the tradition of political lib-eralism as exemplified by the American constitutional order (not to be con-fused with "liberalism" as left-wing politics, as in contemporary American jargon). Proponents of a nonviolent vision are naturally critical of the liberal tradition as another attempt to legitimize what should not be legitimized, namely, coercive governmental institutions. The evaluation of liberalism is less straightforward for those on the second path considered above. They do not oppose the state's existence in principle and can appreciate political, legal, and economic achievements of the liberal tradition, especially in comparison to other systems. But while others in their own ecclesiastical traditions take a more grateful posture toward the liberal tradition as perhaps the best kind of arrangement Christians can hope for in the present age,[51] travelers on the second path above seem more intent to unmask the ideological dangers of liberalism in opposition to Christian faith. This difference of perspective within Reformed, Roman Catholic, and Eastern Orthodox traditions is not that one side advocates theocracy and religious persecution while the other does not. The difference seems to revolve around issues of political provisionality. Those on one side have a more robust view of it and hence appreciate the fact that the traditionally liberal state does not claim to be a manifestation of Christ's eschatological kingdom. Those on the other side, with a less robust view of provisionality, interpret the liberal state as an attempt to declare autonomy and neutrality in the face of the all-penetrating claims of the coming new creation.

This present study is hardly a wholesale rejection of either of these two paths not taken. But it does seek to address the uncomfortable dilemma these two paths have created and to offer Christian political theology an alternative. To do so, I reject the fundamental idea these two paths hold in common: that legitimate political institutions should be redemptively transformed and can thereby manifest the new-creation kingdom. Civil government and other human institutions can be legitimate without having to bear such an eschatological burden. In other words, Christians can and should embrace both legitimacy and provisionality.

Thus in the following chapters I must offer a theological account of how and why civil government is legitimate, but in a way that maintains its distinction from Christ's eschatological kingdom. This account must also explain how and why civil government is common to all human beings while remaining morally accountable. I begin by discussing the biblical covenants and the relationship of nature and grace.

---

51. This is the case for Roman Catholics Murray, Novak, and Neuhaus, and for Eastern Orthodox Papanikolaou, all cited above. This is also the case for the present study; see chapter 12. Of course, it is possible to be *both* grateful for *and* critical of political liberalism, and that is probably an accurate way to describe all of the people mentioned in this discussion. But I suspect it is generally accurate to say that gratitude predominates more in those who recognize greater provisionality and critique predominates more in those who recognize less.

CHAPTER 2

NATURE, GRACE, AND THE BIBLICAL COVENANTS

Political-theological debates are perennially complicated. In part, this is because our political communities themselves are complex and confront us with constantly changing circumstances. But these debates are complicated also because political theology is never independent of a myriad of other biblical and theological convictions. That is, a person's political theology is intertwined with that person's broader theology and interpretation of the biblical story. To communicate my own political theology as clearly as possible, and for readers to be able to evaluate it intelligently, it will be helpful for me to explain some of the broader biblical and theological convictions that undergird the political theology developed in the rest of part 1. That is the goal of this chapter.

To accomplish this, I address two main issues. The first is the *biblical covenants*. These covenants, we will see, are a kind of scaffold that organizes and structures the biblical story. Consideration of the covenants will thus identify the primary themes of Scripture and describe how it fits together as a whole. This discussion will summarize the plot of the biblical narrative that underlies the political theology of following chapters. Second, I turn to the famous question about the relationship of *nature and grace*, which asks, What does the grace of Christ do to nature, which was created by God but then corrupted by evil? Answers to this question inevitably draw upon convictions about human nature, sin, Christology, salvation, the church, and eschatology. Describing and defending my view of the relationship of nature and grace is thus a good way to summarize the broader theology that informs the political theology of the pages ahead.

Although this chapter is not directly political-theological, therefore, it provides important background for much that follows. Discussion of the biblical covenants should be illuminating because I stake much of my political theology on the distinctive nature and purposes of the Noahic covenant (Gen 8:21–9:17). And discussion of nature and grace should be illuminating because my political theology builds on the idea that the Noahic covenant is a covenant of *common grace* that *preserves nature*. In short, subsequent chapters will argue that political community and civil government are rooted in God's preservative grace administered through the Noahic covenant.

THE BIBLICAL COVENANTS

This first main section of the chapter presents the basic understanding of the biblical story that undergirds the political theology of this book. Summarizing the biblical narrative by means of the *covenants* makes the most sense to me. In part, this is because approaching Scripture through the lens of covenant is a common and distinctive mark of Reformed theology.[1] Hence, this covenantal focus reflects my desire, expressed in chapter 1, to honor and refine my own Reformed tradition as I develop a political theology in these pages.

But there are also good theological reasons for this focus. For one thing, the divine covenants are a systemic theme in Scripture. God established covenants at crucial points of biblical history—the beginning of the new world under Noah, the call of Abraham, the exodus from Egypt, the appointment of King David, and the crucifixion of Christ—and thus studying these covenants provides a promising way to chart the progress of the biblical story, with respect to both its underlying unity and the distinctiveness of its parts. In addition, by making the theme of covenant so prominent, Scripture communicates that people do not deal with God in the abstract or at a distance but in relationship. Through covenants, God enters intimate bonds with his creation and promises to deal with human beings according to established terms. Accordingly, if the Noahic covenant is the source of our political

---

1. E.g., see R. Scott Clark, "Christ and Covenant: Federal Theology in Orthodoxy," in *Companion to Reformed Orthodoxy*, ed. Herman Selderhuis (Leiden: Brill, 2013), 403–28; Richard A. Muller, "Divine Covenants, Absolute and Conditional: John Cameron and the Early Orthodox Development of Reformed Covenant Theology," *Mid-America Journal of Theology* 17 (2006): 11–56; and Geerhardus Vos, "The Doctrine of the Covenant in Reformed Theology," in *Redemptive History and Biblical Interpretation: The Shorter Writings of Geerhardus Vos*, ed. Richard B. Gaffin Jr. (Phillipsburg, NJ: P&R, 1980), 234–67.

communities (as I will argue), then legal and political institutions are gifts flowing out of a relationship with God, and thus we are responsible before God for how we develop and respond to these institutions. A covenantal perspective presents our political activity as an aspect of our moral vocation before the Almighty rather than as merely a horizontal, intrahuman affair.

Created in the Image: The Covenant of Creation

A survey of the biblical plot begins fittingly with the creation narratives. Although Genesis 1–2 does not use the term *covenant*, Reformed theology has usually understood the original relationship between God and the human race (represented by Adam) as covenantal in character—often referred to as the "covenant of works." I have defended the covenantal nature of this primordial divine-human relationship in a previous book and will not repeat the argument here.[2] Whether it is proper to see a covenant in Genesis 1–2 is not crucial for present purposes. Instead, I focus on two key ideas that emerge in these opening chapters of Scripture: the creation of human beings in the image of God and the original destiny of human beings and the world as a whole.

At the culmination of Genesis 1's grand account of creation, God says, "Let us make man in our image, after our likeness. And let them have dominion over the fish of the sea and over the birds of the heavens and over the livestock and over all the earth and over every creeping thing that creeps on the earth" (1:26). This "man" is "male and female" (1:27). God proceeds to bless his human creation and commands them to "be fruitful and multiply and fill the earth," to "subdue" the earth, and to "have dominion" over the other creatures (1:28). The idea that God created human beings in his own image has been foundational for theological anthropology in the major Christian traditions. And since the image of God concerns a divine commission to rule in this world, as I argue, it is a fundamental issue for Christian political theology.

What it means that God made humans in his image is far from self-evident. Many older theologies understood the image to lie in certain attributes or capacities with which God endowed human nature—ordinarily, capacities that excelled those of other animals and thus capacities of soul rather than body. Rationality and moral freedom were popular candidates.

---

2. See David VanDrunen, *Divine Covenants and Moral Order: A Biblical Theology of Natural Law* (Grand Rapids: Eerdmans, 2014), 77–83.

More recently, many theologians have rejected this ancient perspective and argued that the image lies rather in certain human functions or in our relationships with God and one another.[3]

Although Genesis 1 does not present a complete theology of the image, careful exegesis indicates that being an image-bearer entails having a divine commission to exercise benevolent rule in this world as God's representative and under his authority. Recent biblical scholarship on Genesis 1:26–27 has come to a broad consensus on this point.[4] This does not mean older expositions had it entirely wrong, since being rational and morally responsible is surely a prerequisite for exercising the divine commission to rule. But possessing certain attributes is not the focus of Genesis 1:26–27. Several considerations underlie this conclusion.

To begin, Genesis 1:26 likely contains a purpose clause, suggesting a translation such as: "Let us make man in our image, after our likeness, *so that they might rule . . .*" (emphasis added). This indicates that the commission to rule is not a distant implication of image-bearing but of its essence. As a grammatical matter, this reading is likely, though not certain. But the context of Genesis 1 lends strong weight to it. Genesis 1:26–27 says that human beings are the image and likeness of *God*, which prompts us to ask what characterizes God in the surrounding text. Throughout Genesis 1, God is a God of action. Genesis 1 does not engage in any theological discussion of God's attributes—his wisdom, power, or righteousness, for example—but tells us only what God *does*. Yet readers learn important things about who God is from how the text portrays his work. In Genesis 1, being and action are inseparable for God. Who God is cannot be separated from what God does.[5] Thus, when the text states that human beings are made in God's likeness, it is not surprising, but even expected, to find that it describes the image in terms of action and thus as a moral commission. Who human beings are cannot be separated from what God calls them to do.

Buttressing this conclusion is that Genesis 1 speaks of several parts of the nonhuman creation as though their being and function were inseparable. To be created an expanse in the midst of the waters is to have a commission to separate waters from waters (1:6–7), and to be made a light in heaven is

---

3. For extensive discussion of a range of older and contemporary views of the image, see John F. Kilner, *Dignity and Destiny: Humanity in the Image of God* (Grand Rapids: Eerdmans, 2015).

4. See VanDrunen, *Divine Covenants*, 42–46. Here I also discuss the interchangability of "image" and "likeness," which I assume from here on.

5. To be clear, I am speaking only about Genesis 1, not making a general systematic-theological claim about the relationship of God's nature to his action in the world.

to separate day from night and perform several other duties (1:14–18). An expanse that did not separate waters from waters would not be an expanse, and a heavenly light that did not separate day from night would not be a heavenly light. If this God-like pattern exists among the nonhuman creation, it is all the more fitting among those made in his image. Taken together, this exegetical evidence confirms that the image of God in Genesis 1:26–27 entails a divine commission to exercise rule in this world in the likeness and under the authority of God the supreme king. To image God is to hold a royal office.[6]

Granted, the notion of human dominion over creation may not convey the best connotations. Two characteristics of God's own rule are thus worth noting. First, Genesis describes God's rule as *just*. He is a righteous legislator, giving all things their proper function (1:6, 11, 26, 28; 2:15–17). He is also a righteous judge, holding himself and human beings accountable for their actions (1:4, 10, 12, 18, 21, 25, 31; 2:17; 3:8–19). Second, God rules *bountifully* and *generously*. His creation overflows with abundance, and he empowers his creatures to enjoy and contribute to it (1:11–12, 20–22, 24–25, 28). For humans to rule in God's likeness, their own dominion must reflect these characteristics. Fittingly, God called Adam to rule justly. This is evident in the tree of the *knowledge of good and evil*, which was likely a test whether Adam would render a correct judicial verdict (2:17; 3:1–7; cf. 2 Sam 14:17; 1 Kgs 3:9, 28). Further, the tasks God gave Adam were not inward-directed but outward-focused, meant to share and expand creation's bounty. They included the self-giving of marriage (Gen 2:22–25), being fruitful, multiplying, and filling the earth (1:28), and working and guarding the Garden of Eden as a faithful priest (2:15). Human rule in God's image was thus a just and benevolent dominion, not a license for tyranny or exploitation.[7]

Another important aspect of the creation narratives is that creation had an end, a *telos*. Creation had both various subordinate ends inherent to its ongoing existence and also an ultimate eschatological goal. God made the world not to endure in its original form forever but to attain a transcendent consummation. From the outset, the first creation was destined for consummation in a new creation.

---

6. See VanDrunen, *Divine Covenants*, 46–50. To be sure, I believe that the very young, the very old, the handicapped, and others who may lack full use of ordinary human physical and intellectual capacities are image-bearers and thus worthy of all respect and protection. Although they may be able to contribute little to benevolent rule in this world, they are members of the human race that God has called corporately to this rule.

7. See VanDrunen, *Divine Covenants*, 50–67.

Although it seems speculative to some interpreters, many Christian theologians and traditions have embraced this idea in one form or another.[8] Defending it well requires a more thorough theological argument than I can offer here, but Genesis 1–2 contains several clues in this direction. The presence of the Spirit, the sabbatical pattern, and the tree of life all point to eschatological consummation, at least when interpreted in larger biblical context. Perhaps most telling is that God himself entered a triumphant rest on the seventh day after finishing his creative work in the world (2:1–3). This was, arguably, part of the pattern God created humans to imitate: just as God's rule in this world was not indefinite and aimless but meant to be completed, so also was humanity's rule in the likeness of God.[9] Hebrews 2:5–10 offers interesting confirmation of the idea that the original creation had an eschatological goal. After stating that God did not subject *the world to come* to angels (Heb 2:5), the author appeals to the account of humanity's creation in Psalm 8:4–6 (Heb 2:6–8). This reasoning indicates that God, from the very beginning of history, intended the new creation to be ruled by human beings. Although humans did not attain it then, we now see Jesus, who has already attained it and is leading many others to glory with him (Heb 2:9–10). This last point anticipates the end of the biblical story. But to conclude the present discussion, God called human beings to rule in this present world and then, after completing the work, to join him in an eschatological rest.

The Noahic Covenant

Following its creation narratives, Scripture promptly recounts humanity's failure to fulfill its divine commission (Gen 3). Adam did not attain the goal of new creation God held out for him. But while God responded by placing a curse upon humanity and upon the earth (3:16–19), he also promised that an offspring of the woman would crush the head of the serpent who seduced her (3:15). God called the first humans to exercise dominion over the other creatures, and they let the serpent rule them instead. But God would raise up another human to reverse this rebellion, to conquer evil, and to attain the original goal of new creation.

Yet God would not do so immediately. Instead, the Bible tells a lengthy and intricate narrative of how God accomplishes this work. At key turning

---

8. E.g., see Augustine, *The City of God* 12.21; John of Damascus, *The Orthodox Faith* 2.11; Thomas Aquinas, *Summa Theologiae* 1a2ae 3.8; 109.5; and Francis Turretin, *Institutes of Elenctic Theology*, 3 vols., trans. George Musgrave Giger, ed., James T. Dennison Jr. (Phillipsburg, NJ: P&R, 1992–1997), 1:583–86.

9. See VanDrunen, *Divine Covenants*, 69–74.

points along the way, readers see that God entered covenants with human beings—which I will call the Noahic, Abrahamic, Mosaic, Davidic, and new covenants. Each covenant, in its own way, advances the story as it moves toward the coming of Christ, consummation, and new creation. We begin with the Noahic covenant, which is central to the political theology of this book. I argue that the Noahic covenant is distinct from all the subsequent covenants. While the subsequent covenants are organically united with each other in bestowing the blessing of salvation, the Noahic covenant bestows only the blessing of preservation. Many theologians in my own Reformed tradition have not made this clear distinction, but I follow the line of interpretation of those who do, including prominent figures such as Herman Witsius, Abraham Kuyper, Herman Bavinck, and Geerhardus Vos.[10]

The biblical narrative of the time between the fall and the great flood is terse but establishes several crucial ideas: God is going to rectify the human fall and destroy evil through an offspring of the woman (Gen 3:15); fallen human beings (even those not of the godly line of Seth) are capable of great cultural achievements (4:20–22); and these same human beings are prone to profound wickedness (4:8, 23–24; 6:5). This last theme takes center stage at the opening of Genesis 6, when God determines to destroy the world through a flood in response to human violence. But in doing so, God does not bring world history to an end, for he saves Noah, his family, and representatives of the broader animal kingdom through the shelter of the ark. After a re-creation scene at the opening of Genesis 8 that echoes aspects of Genesis 1, Noah offers a sacrifice to God (Gen 8:20). The text that follows (Gen 8:21–9:17) records the covenant God made with the world at the headwaters of this new era in history.[11]

---

10. For these examples and others, see Herman Witsius, *The Economy of the Covenants between God and Man: Comprehending a Complete Body of Divinity*, 2 vols., trans. William Crookshank (1822; reprint, Phillipsburg, NJ: P&R, 1990), 2:239; Wilhelmus à Brakel, *The Christian's Reasonable Service*, 4 vols., trans. Bartel Elshout (Ligonier, PA: Soli Deo Gloria, 1992–95), 4:384–85; Abraham Kuyper, *Common Grace*, vol. 1.1, trans. Nelson D. Kloosterman and Ed M. van der Maas, ed. Jordan J. Ballor and Stephen J. Grabill (Grand Rapids: Christian's Library Press, 2013), 15–117; Abraham Kuyper, *Common Grace*, vol. 1.3, trans. Nelson D. Kloosterman and Ed M. van der Maas, ed. Jordan J. Ballor and Stephen J. Grabill (Grand Rapids: Christian's Library Press, 2014), 529–30, 611; Herman Bavinck, *Reformed Dogmatics*, vol. 3, *Sin and Salvation in Christ*, trans. John Vriend (Grand Rapids: Baker Academic, 2006), 218–19; Geerhardus Vos, *Biblical Theology: Old and New Testaments* (Grand Rapids: Eerdmans, 1949), 56, 62–63; Meredith G. Kline, *Kingdom Prologue: Genesis Foundations for a Covenantal Worldview* (Overland Park, KS: Two Age, 2000), 164, 244–62; Michael Horton, *God of Promise* (Grand Rapids: Baker Books, 2006), ch. 6; and J. van Genderen and W. H. Velema, *Concise Reformed Dogmatics*, trans. Gerrit Bilkes and Ed M. van der Maas (Phillipsburg, NJ: P&R, 2008), 296, 547.

11. For defense of taking the terms of the covenant as beginning toward the end of Genesis 8, although the term "covenant" does not appear until 9:9, see Steven D. Mason, "Another Flood? Genesis 9

The Noahic covenant has three crucial characteristics: it is universal, preservative, and temporary. These characteristics distinguish it from the subsequent biblical covenants.

First, the Noahic covenant is *universal*, encompassing the world as a whole and leaving nothing outside of its scope. God entered this covenant with all human beings, not only with Noah but also with his offspring and all future generations (Gen 9:1, 8, 9, 12). He also entered it with the entire animal kingdom, "every living creature" (9:9–13, 15–17). The covenant even extends to the cosmic order: the covenant is between God "and the earth" (9:13), and thus God promises never to send another great flood (8:21; 9:11) but instead to sustain "seedtime and harvest, cold and heat, summer and winter, day and night" without cease (8:22). "It is impossible to imagine a more inclusive covenant than this."[12]

Second, the Noahic covenant is *preservative*: God's purpose is not to provide salvation from evil but to sustain and maintain the world, and human society in it, despite the abiding presence of evil. The promises of preservation are evident. God will not destroy the earth again with a flood (8:21; 9:11, 15). He will sustain the uninterrupted cycles of nature (8:22) and restrain animals from harming humans (9:2–4). Furthermore, while the covenant's moral exhortations hardly constitute a grand agenda, they do address the basic requirements for human society to survive: reproduction (9:1, 7), eating (9:3–4), and administering justice (9:6). What is striking and perhaps surprising is what this covenant does *not* promise: the crushing of the serpent's head (Gen 3:15), the forgiveness of sins, everlasting life in a new creation, or any other aspect of salvation described elsewhere in Scripture. Noah was a man of saving faith, but his faith rested in God's earlier covenant to save him from the great flood (Gen 6:13–21; Heb 11:7), not in the covenant after the flood.[13] The post-flood Noahic covenant constrains evil rather than eliminates it.

---

and Isaiah's Broken Eternal Covenant," *Journal for the Study of the Old Testament* 33, no. 2 (2007): 180–83. See also VanDrunen, *Divine Covenants*, 100–102, which identifies the starting point as 8:20. In hindsight, I believe my argument actually establishes the starting point as 8:21.

12. Jonathan Burnside, *God, Justice, and Society: Aspects of Law and Legality in the Bible* (Oxford: Oxford University Press, 2011), 35.

13. The Hebrew word for "covenant" appears for the first time in Scripture in Genesis 6:18, when God calls Noah to build an ark. Although many writers argue or simply presume that this covenant and the postdiluvian covenant of 8:21–9:17 are identical, this is almost certainly not the case. The parties and promises of the two covenants could hardly be more different. For a more detailed argument, see VanDrunen *Divine Covenants*, 108–11. The distinction between these covenants explains Noah's sacrifice in Genesis 8:20. He offers the sacrifice *before* the institution of the postdiluvian covenant, not in response to it or as part of its terms. This sacrifice seems to be an offering of gratitude and consecration upon fulfillment of God's earlier covenant to rescue him from the flood.

It neither changes the human heart (8:21; cf. 6:5) nor puts an end to violence (9:6; cf. 6:11). Even the sign of the Noahic covenant is unlike the signs of later biblical covenants—such as circumcision, the Passover, baptism, and the Lord's Supper—which involve or symbolize the shedding of blood, and thus signify forgiveness of sins (see Heb 9:22). The rainbow hangs bloodless in the sky (Gen 9:12:17). The Noahic covenant highlights the value of lifeblood (9:4–6), but it provides only for retribution when someone sheds it (9:6), not atonement. In short, the Noahic covenant does not promise to rescue anyone from the final judgment. It simply promises to postpone it.

The third characteristic of the Noahic covenant is that God put it into place *temporarily*. Stating it this way may be misleading, since the biblical text indicates that the covenantal promises are enduring and that human beings can count on them indefinitely. The waters will "never again" become a great flood to destroy the world (9:15), and the covenant is "everlasting" (9:16). Yet the Hebrew word translated "everlasting" may simply mean *long-enduring* and not *without end*. And the Noahic covenant does indeed have a termination point: God promises to maintain the natural order only "while the earth remains" (8:22). From a New Testament perspective, the Noahic covenant's lease expires when Christ returns and institutes the final judgment, by fire rather than water (see 2 Pet 3:10–13). Thus God pledges to preserve human society and the broader world only until the day of judgment and new creation.[14]

These three characteristics of the Noahic covenant concern God's own actions and commitments. What about moral requirements for human beings? The Noahic covenant is not bilateral, strictly speaking. It issues no conditions that, if violated, would prompt God to terminate it. But although the covenant's continuation does not hinge on human behavior, the covenant does set forth a threefold ethic for the human community. First, through a straightforward imperative, it calls humans to "be fruitful and multiply and fill the earth" (Gen 9:1; cf. 9:7). Next, by way of gift and prohibition, it grants plants and animals for humans to eat, although they may not eat meat with its lifeblood (9:3–4). Finally, through a proverbial poem, it prescribes retributive justice for intrahuman violence (9:6). The next chapter will begin thinking through the meaning and implications of this Noahic ethic, but two brief comments are in order now.

First, the Noahic covenant presents a very modest ethic, spanning a mere

14. See VanDrunen, *Divine Covenants*, 102–7. Similarly, see Kuyper, *Common Grace*, vol. 1.3, 529–30.

seven verses and explicitly addressing only a few areas of human life. Yet this modest ethic fits the covenantal context. The purpose of the Noahic covenant is preservative, aiming not to redeem the world or create a human utopia but to maintain human society and the broader natural order. Thus its moral requirements fittingly focus upon what is necessary for human survival rather than portray a grand vision for the ideal community. If the human race is to survive, it certainly must procreate, eat, and restrain violence.

Second, the Noahic covenant is both similar to and different from the creation mandate of Genesis 1:26–28. The most evident similarity is the almost verbatim repetition of the command to be fruitful, multiply, and fill the earth (9:1, 7). Other similar themes are the concern about human-animal relations, the giving of food, and human identity as the image of God. But several differences are also conspicuous. Perhaps most notably, the Noahic covenant lacks the original command to rule and subdue the other creatures. Instead, God himself puts the fear and dread of humans in the animals (9:2). The only aspect of human rule it mentions is administering intrahuman justice (9:6). Fallen humans are evidently unable to exercise the rule of their original commission. This makes sense of another difference between the creation mandate and the Noahic covenant: in the latter, there is no indication that humans will ever complete their work and thus attain a new creation. It mentions no Spirit, no Sabbath, no tree of life, and no divine enthronement. A third difference is that the Noahic ethic unfolds against a background of evil and conflict that was prominently missing in Genesis 1–2. The human heart is evil from its youth (Gen 8:21), animals fear and dread humans, who may eat them (9:2–3), and both animals and humans kill humans (9:5–6). The best way to account for both these similarities and differences, I conclude, is to say that the original creation mandate is refracted through the Noahic covenant. In God's fallen but preserved world, human beings are not bound by the creation mandate in its original Adamic form but in its modified Noahic form.[15]

The Abrahamic Covenant

Shortly after the account of the Noahic covenant, Genesis introduces readers to Abram (11:27–32). God called him out of Ur of the Chaldeans, made a covenant with him, and changed his name to Abraham. God's promises in

---

15. For further discussion, see VanDrunen, *Divine Covenants*, 118–19; and also Burnside, *God, Justice, and Society*, 167–71.

this covenant are a principle theme in the rest of Scripture. While the Noahic covenant offered no provisions to accomplish God's plan to redeem the human race through the offspring of the woman (Gen 3:15), the Abrahamic and subsequent covenants do just this. Reformed theologians have not agreed on all the details but have traditionally viewed the Abrahamic, Mosaic, Davidic, and new covenants as constituting "administrations" of an overarching "covenant of grace."[16] To put it simply, these series of biblical covenants, although distinct in important respects, are organically united with one another. They advance a single plan of redemption through history that culminates in the coming of Christ and establishment of the new creation.

The original divine promise of rescue from sin and death pledged that an offspring of the woman Eve would crush the head of the serpent (Gen 3:15). Thus it is striking that when God initiated a redemptive covenant with Abraham, he framed its promise in terms of offspring. God would give Abraham's offspring the land where he sojourned, multiply them greatly, and be their God (Gen 12:7; 15:5, 13, 18–19; 17:7–10). He would make of them a great nation and bless other nations through them (12:2–3; 17:4–6). Paul appealed to this promise in Galatians. In a remarkable move, Paul reasons that the promises were to Abraham and his "offspring," that is, not to many offsprings, but to one—namely, Christ (Gal 3:16). Initially this seems a strange claim, since the Hebrew word for offspring (like the English "offspring") is a collective noun that can refer to a plurality even though it appears in the singular. But on further reflection, Paul's argument is not strange at all. The original promise of an "offspring" in Genesis 3:15 speaks of a single figure: "*He* shall bruise your head" (emphasis added). Since the promise of an offspring to Abraham so clearly picks up this original promise, it seems best to interpret these later words as promising *both* a single messianic offspring and a multitude of people with him. To put it another way, God promised to bring from Abraham a preeminent king, along with his people. This seems to be Paul's view. Although he identifies the offspring as the single figure of Christ in Galatians 3:16, he also describes a great community of people— Jews and gentiles—who belong to Christ by faith and thus are "Abraham's offspring" (3:26–29). The one offspring and the many offspring cannot be separated from each other, in either Genesis or Galatians.

One aspect of the promises to Abraham's offspring was that God would give them the land of Canaan where Abraham was sojourning. As with the

---

16. For a very basic summary, see *Westminster Confession of Faith*, 7.5–6.

promises about "offspring," the New Testament interprets the land promises in an initially unexpected way, given what Genesis says. According to Hebrews, Abraham by faith "went to live in the land of promise," that is, Canaan, but did so because he had eschatological hope and was "looking forward to the city that has foundations" (11:9–10). Abraham and his descendants, the text continues, did not receive what was promised, not because they never took possession of Canaan but because they "acknowledged that they were strangers and exiles on the earth" (11:13). They sought a "homeland" (11:14), a "better" and "heavenly" country, a city prepared by God (11:16). For Hebrews, then, Canaan was only the penultimate promised land. Ultimately, God promised Abraham the new creation. Hebrews 11 does say more than Genesis does but nothing contrary to it. Paul makes a similar move: God promised to Abraham and his offspring that he would be "heir of the world" (Rom 4:13)—which Genesis also never said. Paul does not deny that God promised Abraham the land of Canaan but claims that God promised him a great deal more: not just Canaan, but the world. And (per Heb 11) ultimately not the world in its present form but the world as consummated new creation.

By reading the Genesis texts in canonical context, therefore, we see that God's covenant with Abraham was a redemptive covenant that promised and advanced God's commitment to achieve his original purposes for humanity through an offspring of the woman. According to the New Testament, God's promises of an offspring to Abraham were only penultimately fulfilled in the growth of Israel as a nation. They were ultimately fulfilled through the coming of Christ and a new covenant people of Jews and gentiles. Likewise, God's promises of a land were only provisionally fulfilled through Israel's possession of Canaan and are truly fulfilled in Christ's attainment of new creation, a new creation he wills to share with his people. Thus it was fitting that Abraham responded to God's promises by *believing* (Gen 15:6). Christians look back to Abraham as the paragon of faith, who embraced his covenant blessings (Rom 4; Gal 3).

The Mosaic and Davidic Covenants

God later covenanted with Israel at Sinai (Exod 19–24) and on the plains of Moab (Deut 29)—I will refer to this as the Mosaic covenant. Interpreting the nature and purpose of this covenant is a complicated and sometimes controversial issue in Christian theology. Here we focus upon how this covenant, with the later Davidic covenant, relates to the Abrahamic covenant and continues to advance God's accomplishment of the original human destiny through the coming Christ.

The whole sequence of events concerning the appointment of Moses and the exodus from Egypt began when God heard Israel's groaning under Egyptian slavery and remembered his covenant with Abraham, Isaac, and Jacob (Exod 2:24; 6:5). He identified himself as the God of Abraham, Isaac, and Jacob when he called Moses (3:6, 15–16; 4:5). The Old Testament therefore presents the story of Israel, from Egypt to Sinai to Zion, as the continuation and advancement of Abraham's story. Thus it seems appropriate to focus upon the two aspects of the Abrahamic promises highlighted above: the offspring and the land.

God stated that Israel, already a numerous people, would be his "treasured possession among all peoples . . . and a kingdom of priests and a holy nation" if they obeyed him (Exod 19:5–6). This is an initial fulfillment of his promises to Abraham. God had promised Abraham "to be God to you and to your offspring after you" (Gen 17:7). Now to that burgeoning offspring he says, "I will take you to be my people, and I will be your God" (Exod 6:7). As argued earlier, God's promise of an offspring to Abraham referred to a single Messianic offspring with his people. That interpretation resonates with the larger story of Israel under Moses, particularly as the theme of kingship emerges. The Mosaic law presents brief but pointed regulations for the establishment of a king (Deut 17:14–20), and after the disastrous reign of Israel's first king, Saul (1 Sam 10–31), God raised up David as the king after his own heart (1 Sam 16:1–13; cf. 13:14). God made a covenant with him and his house, promising that one of his descendants would rule his people forever. The kingdom would belong to David (2 Sam 7:1–16; 1 Chr 17:1–14 cf. 23:5; Ps 89:3–4).

From this point on, Israel's history focused largely upon David's line. While the Mosaic law pronounced curse and blessing upon Israel in response to the conduct of the whole people (e.g., Lev 26; Deut 28), the conduct of the Davidic kings became the chief factor determining the nation's fate (e.g., 2 Sam 24:10–15; 2 Kgs 21:11–15). Furthermore, the famous Servant Songs of Isaiah (in Isa 42–53) seem to fluctuate between a single Servant and the nation as a whole. The Old Testament story itself thus testifies to an offspring (singular) and an offspring (plural), that is, to a royal Messianic Servant and his people. Accordingly, the New Testament announces the coming of Christ as the true Son of David (e.g., Luke 1:32–33; Rom 1:3; Rev 22:16), the Servant of the Lord (e.g., Matt 12:15–21; Acts 8:30–35). The new covenant people who are united to him, both Jew and gentile, are "a chosen race, a royal priesthood, a holy nation, a people for his own possession" (1 Pet 2:9; cf. Exod 19:5–6).

As the nation of Israel under Moses initially fulfilled the promises about Abraham's offspring, so also Israel's entrance into Canaan initially fulfilled the promises to Abraham about a land. God pledged to Moses that he would bring them into the land of other nations (Exod 3:17; cf. Gen 15:19–21), in fulfillment of his oath to Abraham (Exod 6:8). But the Old Testament also anticipates the New Testament's claim that the new creation is the ultimate fulfillment of the land promises. A number of Old Testament prophecies "describe how God's presence will break out from the holy of holies, cover Jerusalem (Isa. 4:4–6; Jer. 3:16–17; Zech. 1:16–2:11), then expand to cover all of Israel's land (Ezek. 37:25–28), and finally cover the entire earth (Isa. 54:2–3; Dan. 2:34–35, 44–45)." Israel's borders would extend to the whole world (Isa 27:2–6).[17] The prophets at times described Israel's restoration to the land after exile in terms that could not possibly be realized anywhere in the present created order (e.g., Ezek 47:1–12). These prophets looked forward to a "new heavens and a new earth," at whose center stands "Jerusalem" (Isa 65:17–25). The New Testament is therefore hardly innovative when it speaks of the new creation by using imagery of the Old Testament land—as "the Jerusalem above" (Gal 4:26), "Mount Zion," the "heavenly Jerusalem" (Heb 12:22), "the new Jerusalem," and the "holy city" (Rev 21:2).

In short, as the Abrahamic covenant promised the coming of Christ and his new creation, so also the Mosaic covenant foreshadowed them. The history and experience of Israel under Moses provided initial fulfillment of the great promise that Abraham would have an offspring and a land. But the Old Testament itself points in many ways to the coming of a King who is *the* offspring and to the coming of a new creation which is *the* promised land.

The New Covenant

That coming King was the Lord Jesus Christ, in whose blood God instituted the "new covenant" prophesied in the Old Testament (Jer 31:31–34; Luke 22:20; cf. Matt 26:28; Mark 14:24). Jesus became surety of this covenant by oath and has a better ministry than the Old Testament priests had, and thus the new covenant is a "better covenant" than the Mosaic (Heb 7:20–22; 8:6). It is indeed better, since humanity reaches its ultimate goal only in Christ.

---

17. G. K. Beale, *A New Testament Biblical Theology: The Unfolding of the Old Testament in the New* (Grand Rapids: Baker Academic, 2011), 752–53.

A "world to come" was the original human destiny, and Christ achieved that destiny (Heb 2:5–9), having "passed through the heavens" (Heb 4:14).

Jesus Christ achieved the new creation by entering the conditions of the first creation. Like everyone else, he was "born of a woman" (Gal 4:4)—in fact, born of a girl under scandalous and humble circumstances (Matt 1:18–24; Luke 1:26–38; 2:1–7). He took on human flesh and blood (John 1:14; Heb 2:14), not simply bearing physical human nature but entering the human condition generally, in its lowliness and brokenness, although he himself had no sin (Rom 8:3; Phil 2:7; Heb 2:17–18; 4:15). In this way, he could be the Last Adam, the one who would overturn the failure of the First Adam and achieve resurrection life (Rom 5:15–19; 1 Cor 15:21–22, 45–49). As God promised, no outsider would rescue humanity from sin, death, and the devil, but an offspring of the woman (Gen 3:15).

By calling Jesus the Last Adam, Paul identified him as a representative figure. He was one of the human race, to be sure, but also stood in its place, and did so in two primary ways. For one thing, he endured the consequences of human rebellion. He was tempted by the devil (Matt 4:1–11; Mark 1:12; Luke 4:1–13; Heb 2:18; 4:15), drank the cup of God's wrath (Matt 26:39; Mark 10:38; 14:36; Luke 22:42; cf. Ps 75:8), and bore the sins of his people in his body upon the cross (1 Pet 2:24), giving his life a ransom for many (Mark 10:45). He also fulfilled the human responsibilities God had placed upon the human race. He was born under the law (Gal 4:4), which entailed an obligation to obey the law in its entirety (Gal 5:3). Christ thus fulfilled all righteousness (Matt 3:15), learned obedience through suffering (Heb 5:8) and was faithful to his calling precisely where the First Adam had failed (Rom 5:18–19). As God tested the First Adam's obedience through a time of probation and temptation (2:17; 3:1–7), so too with Christ, who overcame the devil and passed the test (Matt 4:1–11; 26:36–46; Col 2:14–15; Heb 2:14).

God glorified Christ because he bore the burden of sin and persevered in obedience through trial. Christ was "obedient to the point of death, even death on a cross. *Therefore* God has highly exalted him and bestowed on him the name that is above every name" (Phil 2:9–10; emphasis added). This exaltation involved, first, resurrection from the dead (Matt 28:5–6; Mark 16:6; Luke 24:5–7), not a mere bodily resuscitation but a Spirit-worked transformation to make his body fit for eschatological glory (Rom 8:11; 1 Cor 15:35–49; Phil 3:21). As one raised according to the Spirit with a new-creation body, Christ did not remain in the present world. He ascended into the glory of heaven, and God seated him at his right hand (Dan 7:13–14; Luke 24:51; Acts

1:9; 2:32–33; Eph 4:8–9; Heb 1:3). Through this ascension and session, Christ entered the new creation. The new creation already exists in some form, and Jesus Christ in his glorified human nature already rules there. He has attained the original human goal.

In another sense, the new creation is currently under construction. The new creation is the destiny of the whole human race (Heb 2:5–8), not Christ's alone, and he will bring many to glory with him (Heb 2:10). He is now preparing the new creation as a fit dwelling for his people (John 14:2–3), until the first creation undergoes its final judgment and finds its consummation in the new heavens and new earth (2 Pet 3:7, 10–13), which will then be fully revealed and inhabited (Rev 21:1–5). In the meantime, Christ gives his people a foretaste of the new creation even while they sojourn in the first creation with mortal bodies. He does so chiefly by pouring out his Holy Spirit upon them (Acts 2:33). He bestows the Spirit of resurrection as the firstfruits of what is to come, for their justification, adoption, sanctification, sealing, and encouragement (Rom 8:3–27; 2 Cor 5:5; Gal 3:2–9; 4:6–7; Eph 1:13–14; 4:30).

In this summary of the new covenant, we can see the fulfillment of the Abrahamic promises, which the Mosaic and Davidic covenants only provisionally realized. God promised an offspring (singular), and the Lord Jesus Christ is this offspring (Gal 3:16), the perfect king-priest (Heb 7). God also promised an offspring (plural), and the Lord Jesus Christ has redeemed a great multitude to be a royal priesthood with him (1 Pet 2:9). And God promised a land—a new creation which Christ purified through his cross and entered through his ascension (Heb 9:18–26). In thus fulfilling these Abrahamic promises, Christ has also fulfilled the primordial gospel promise that God would provide an offspring of the woman to defeat the one who had defeated Adam, the original king-priest. As this offspring of the woman, Christ has accomplished the original destiny God set before the human race.

The Biblical Covenants: Conclusion

In summary, the Abrahamic, Mosaic, Davidic, and new covenants are united in achieving the original goal of the human race. Together, these covenants bring the first creation to consummation in a new creation through the Lord Jesus Christ. The Noahic covenant, in comparison, provides a sort of prerequisite for the work of these other covenants but does nothing directly to achieve their goal of new creation. The Noahic covenant *preserves* the first creation so that the subsequent covenants can bring it to *consummation*—although the latter would hardly be possible without the former.

Therefore, a twofold conclusion is appropriate. First, while the Abrahamic, Mosaic, Davidic, and new covenants are organically united with each other, the Noahic covenant does not share in this organic unity. In other words, the later covenants do not grow organically out of the Noahic covenant in the way the Mosaic covenant grows out of the Abrahamic covenant or in the way that the new covenant grows out of the Abrahamic, Mosaic, and Davidic covenants. In comparison with these later covenants, the Noahic covenant has different parties, different promises, and a different destiny. As to parties, God entered the later covenants with a particular people chosen out of the broader human race, while he entered the Noahic covenant with the whole of humanity and the rest of creation. With respect to promises, God pledged salvation in the later covenants but pledged only preservation in the Noahic. That is, the former promised the conquest of sin and evil, while the latter promised only to keep sin and evil in check. And as for destiny, the later covenants come to fulfillment in the new creation, while the Noahic covenant will expire at Christ's return. In the new Jerusalem, God will repeat the great divine promise of the Abrahamic, Mosaic, and new covenants—I will be your God, you will be my people (Rev 21:3; see, e.g., Gen 17:7; Exod 6:7; Jer 31:33). But the "first heaven and first earth" upheld by the Noahic covenant will have passed away (Rev 21:1).

Second, although the Noahic covenant is not organically united to the subsequent covenants, it is ultimately harmonious with them as together they bring glory to God in the unfolding of his comprehensive plan for human history. They are not united in party, purpose, or destiny, as outlined above, but they enjoy an ultimate harmony in God's own infinite mind as he "works all things according to the counsel of his will" (Eph 1:11). A few aspects of their harmony are worth mention. Both the Noahic covenant and the subsequent covenants represent responses of God to the plight of his original creation. Furthermore, the later covenants would never have been established had it not been for the Noahic covenant, and thus the Noahic covenant does serve the purpose of the later covenants indirectly. If God did not preserve the world and human society, there would be no people to be saved and no first creation to be consummated in new creation. Finally, when civil government and other institutions emerging from the Noahic covenant do their job, it affords a measure of peace and protection for the church to do its job.

NATURE AND GRACE

The preceding discussion of the covenants provides a summary of the biblical story that undergirds the treatment of political theology in subsequent chapters. The following discussion of the nature-grace relationship provides a summary of the broader theological doctrine that undergirds this political theology. Defining the relationship of nature and grace requires theologians to integrate their views of human nature, sin, Christ, salvation, the church, and eschatology. Thus how someone formulates the relationship provides insight into that person's fundamental theological commitments.

The nature-grace formulation I suggest below corresponds to the covenant theology developed above. It has sympathies with the famous Thomistic formula, "grace perfects nature," and with the more recent neo-Calvinist proposal, "grace restores nature," but presents a more nuanced alternative to both.[18] Before presenting my formula, however, I should offer a brief defense of the necessity and priority of nature.

The Necessity and Priority of Nature

Classical Christian theology ordinarily affirms that *nature* is a necessary concept and that it has a certain priority to the concept of grace—"priority" in the sense that grace presupposes nature whereas nature does not presuppose grace. This necessity and priority is in one sense historical, in that God's work of creation preceded his work of redemption, and in another sense theoretical, in that a theology of redemption presupposes a theology of creation. This classical Christian conviction is important background for the exploration of political theology in subsequent chapters. I now summarize why this conviction is worth maintaining, over against the tendency in some circles to portray grace as such an expansive reality that it effectively swallows up nature,[19] and over against the tendency in other circles to reverse or relativize the nature-grace relationship.[20]

First, the necessity and priority of nature follows from the idea that natural revelation is necessary and has priority to special revelation.[21] A moment's

---

18. By "neo-Calvinist," I refer to a school of thought popular in many Reformed circles over the past century or so, whose practitioners seek to develop the thought of Dutch theologians Abraham Kuyper and Herman Bavinck. For my own perception of the relationship between my natural-law theology and common neo-Calvinist convictions, see VanDrunen, *Divine Covenants*, 525–33.

19. A danger, I believe, in the work of Henri de Lubac, SJ; see, e.g., *The Mystery of the Supernatural*, trans. Rosemary Sheed (New York: Herder & Herder, 1967).

20. A tendency illustrated, e.g., in Karl Barth, "Gospel and Law," in *Community, State, and Church: Three Essays* (Gloucester: Peter Smith, 1968).

21. In Reformed theology, natural revelation refers to God's revelation through the natural order,

thought demonstrates why this must be the case. Biblical (and other forms of special) revelation come to already-existing people who have human natures and are immersed in the world, not to nature-less blank slates living in a vacuum. Before people can even begin to understand a word of special revelation, they have already encountered God's natural revelation. In addition, biblical revelation presupposes that its recipients are familiar with the world in which they live. Scripture assumes they know a language, the geography of the Mediterranean world, the character of certain animals, the difference between day and night, and thousands of other facts it would be impossible to list. The Reformation doctrine of the sufficiency of Scripture (*sola scriptura*), which I affirm, does not claim that Christians need only Scripture and not natural revelation, but that Christians need only Scripture and not other kinds of special revelation.[22] Conversely, natural revelation does not presuppose that its recipients know the Scriptures. It leaves all people without excuse before God, whether they know the Scriptures or not (Rom 1:18–32).

Second, nature is necessary and has priority to grace because the message and power of redemption presuppose the natural human condition. In classical Reformation terms, the gospel presupposes the law. The gospel presumes that people have a problem they cannot resolve themselves, a problem only God's grace can heal. The proclamation and administration of this gospel therefore presumes an already-existing relationship with God, an already-existing knowledge of God's expectations, and an already-existing sense of the misery and curse of sin. Without God's law already a reality, the gospel makes little sense.[23]

Part of that legal foundation for the gospel is the natural law. The idea of natural law enables Christian theology to explain why the church proclaims the gospel as good news for *all* people—and not just for Jews, who have been trained in God's law under Moses. Romans 1:18–3:20 is probably the biblical text that makes this point most clearly.[24] This first major section of Romans

---

while special revelation refers to God's revelation through Christ, the prophets, and Scripture; e.g., see Bavinck, *Reformed Dogmatics*, 1:301–85.

22. See VanDrunen, *Divine Covenants*, 488–89. This is illustrated in important Reformed confessional documents: e.g., see *Westminster Confession of Faith*, 1.1, 1.6; and *Belgic Confession*, Articles 2, 7. See also Matthew Barrett, *God's Word Alone—The Authority of Scripture* (Grand Rapids: Zondervan, 2016), 337–39.

23. Reformation theology also speaks of a "third use" of the law, by which the law guides the grateful obedience of those who have believed the gospel. In this sense, the law follows and presupposes the gospel.

24. My comments on this text reflect traditional Reformed exegesis. I am aware that many prominent New Testament scholars have challenged this exegesis in recent decades. For example, the "New Perspective on Paul" has raised important issues, especially pertaining to the relationship of first-century Judaism and Pauline theology, that challenge traditional readings of Paul's understanding of sin and salvation. Among influential works see E. P. Sanders, *Paul and Palestinian Judaism: A Comparison of*

indicts the whole human race. Both Jews and gentiles sin and are unable to meet the high standards of God's law, and hence all alike are unable to be justified by works of the law and are liable to divine judgment. But beginning in Romans 3:21—"But now"—Paul sets forth good news for the human race. In Christ, God has provided justification for the ungodly, who do not work but believe (4:4–5). Natural law is a crucial piece of the theological puzzle Paul constructs in Romans. The Mosaic law does play an important role in how Romans 1:18–3:20 lays foundation for the gospel, but the natural law is also prominent. Through the natural law, all people know God's moral requirements and their own sin, and thus God is just in holding all people accountable before his judgment. Natural law is thus foundational for the gospel. It explains why the gospel is good news for all people. It makes the gospel coherent.

Third, the first two points imply that Thomas Aquinas was correct to affirm the reality of *praeambula fidei*, preambles of the Christian faith: "The existence of God and other like truths about God, which can be known by natural reason, are not articles of faith, but are preambles to the articles; for faith presupposes natural knowledge, even as grace presupposes nature, and perfection supposes something that can be perfected."[25] Reformed theology should happily join Thomas in this basic affirmation.[26] But this begs the question whether Thomas's familiar aphorism, "grace does not destroy nature, but perfects it," is a good summary of the relationship of nature and grace.[27] Early Reformed theologians used this language,[28] and it is not a bad way to put it. But I believe we can do better.[29]

Patterns of Religion (Philadelphia: Fortress, 1977); N. T. Wright, *What Saint Paul Really Said: Was Paul of Tarsus the Real Founder of Christianity?* (Grand Rapids: Eerdmans, 1997); and James D. G. Dunn, *The Theology of Paul the Apostle* (Grand Rapids: Eerdmans, 1998). Another recent attempt to rework the interpretation of Paul in a way at odds with traditional Protestant understandings of law and gospel is Douglas A. Campbell, *The Deliverance of God: An Apocalyptic Rereading of Justification in Paul* (Grand Rapids: Eerdmans, 2009). I have offered more detailed defense of traditional Reformed exegesis of Romans 1:18–3:20, in interaction with some of these scholars, in VanDrunen, *Divine Covenants*, 211–57.

25. *Summa Theologiae*, 1a 2.2 ad.2. English translations of this work are taken from *Summa Theologica*, 5 vols., trans. Fathers of the English Dominican Province (Allen, TX: Christian Classics, 1981).

26. For a Reformed treatment similar to Thomas's, see, e.g., Turretin, *Institutes*, 1:29–30. And see Paul Helm, "Nature and Grace," in *Aquinas among the Protestants*, ed. Manfred Svensson and David VanDrunen (Hoboken, NJ: Wiley-Blackwell, 2018), 229–47.

27. *Summa Theologiae*, 1a 1.8 ad.2.

28. E.g., see Franciscus Junius, *The Mosaic Polity*, trans. Todd M. Rester, ed. Andrew M. McGinnis (Grand Rapids: Christian's Library Press, 2015), 38: "Grace perfects nature; grace does not, however, abolish it."

29. In *Divine Covenants*, 28–36, I discussed the Thomistic formula, the neo-Calvinists' critique of it, and my own preferred paradigm. My view of the subject has not changed, so here I simply summarize my earlier argument.

Defining the Relationship of Nature and Grace

The Thomist tradition has had plenty of internal debates about nature and grace, but its basic perspective is as follows: God has created human beings with certain natural and penultimate ends. Yet God also endowed them, both at creation and through Christ after the fall, with supernatural gifts of grace that enable them to do works meritorious of a supernatural end, which is the beatific vision. Hence, grace does not cancel out or nullify what is natural but brings it to its perfection, its ultimate destiny. Many prominent neo-Calvinists over the past century have strongly critiqued the Thomistic grace-perfects-nature paradigm, believing that the paradigm communicates too negative a view of created nature and too weak a view of the fall into sin.[30] In my judgment, neo-Calvinist critiques raise important considerations but rely upon caricatured portrayals of the Thomist view—or at least of the views of Thomas himself.[31] As an alternative to Thomism, neo-Calvinists propose that grace *restores* nature. In my judgment, what neo-Calvinists mean by this is not nearly as different from the Thomist position as they suggest. Furthermore, the neo-Calvinist alternative has the distinct disadvantage of suggesting that redemption simply puts people back into Adam's original shoes (although neo-Calvinists in fact believe that Christ does much more for believers than "restore" them). The Thomist formula does not have this disadvantage.

At best, the neo-Calvinist alternative fights the Thomist formula to a draw. After all, Scripture speaks of redemption in terms of *both* perfection (e.g., Heb 12:23) *and* restoration (e.g., Acts 3:21). The shortcoming of both paradigms, in my view, is that they attempt to capture what grace does to nature with a single verb, whereas Scripture speaks of a twofold response of divine grace to (fallen) nature, thus requiring a paradigm with two verbs. Accordingly, I suggest a better formula: *(common) grace preserves nature, and (saving) grace consummates nature.*

The idea of *common grace preserving nature* draws upon my previous argument that God preserves the present fallen world through the Noahic covenant. Ironically, neo-Calvinists have long recognized common grace as a distinct theological category, although their grace-restores-nature formula does not utilize it.[32] The idea that *saving grace consummates nature* draws

---

30. For a prominent example, see Herman Bavinck, *Reformed Dogmatics*, 4 vols., trans. John Vriend, ed. John Bolt (Grand Rapids: Baker Academic, 2003–2006), 2:546–47, 3:43.

31. For excellent discussion of these caricatures, along lines similar to my analysis, see John Bolt, "Doubting Reformational Anti-Thomism," in *Aquinas among the Protestants*, 129–47.

32. Abraham Kuyper's own view seems very close to what I am defending. E.g., see Kuyper, *Common Grace*, vol. 1.3: "First, his [God's] common grace has restrained the full effect of sin and destruction in

upon the previous discussion of the Abrahamic, Mosaic, Davidic, and new covenants: God not only preserves this world but also brings it to consummation.[33] God's work of preservation is distinct from his work of redemption, and thus we need two verbs rather than one to describe the relationship of nature and grace.

CONCLUSION

This chapter has made distinctions between the Noahic covenant and subsequent biblical covenants, and between common grace and saving grace. In so doing, it appropriates and refines a classical Reformed conception of the Two Kingdoms, as suggested in chapter 1. God rules this present world through two kingdoms, I propose, insofar as he rules through the Noahic covenant and new covenant, and through common grace and special grace. Some people accuse such paradigms of promoting improper dualism or unhelpful bifurcation of God's unified work.[34] In most cases, such accusations are merely assertions rather than demonstrated claims. How, after all, is one to prove that a theological distinction is in fact an unwarranted dualism? A given distinction may *appear* dualistic to certain writers because of their other theological convictions. But there is nothing more inherently dualistic about claiming a distinction between God's two kingdoms than there is in claiming a distinction between justification and sanctification in Reformation theology or in claiming a distinction between nature and person in Chalcedonian Christology. Each of these formulas attempts to distinguish one thing from another while also affirming their relation and harmony. Most Christian traditions affirm the nature-person distinction as a hallmark of orthodoxy, while monophysites, presumably, regard it as an unwarranted

---

our nature, in our race, and in our human life. And second, he has prepared, worked out, and completed his particular grace within a separate sphere" (434); "the eternal Word stands in twofold relationship or connection with the world" (498).

33. One reason I prefer "consummate" to "perfect" is that the former conveys the biblical sense of historical movement and destination in a way that the latter does not.

34. This is evident in several recent comments from critics of my work. Even Jonathan Leeman, who is "very sympathetic" to my project, thinks my Two Kingdoms distinction maintains an undue "separation" in the unified work of God; see *Political Church: The Local Assembly as Embassy of Christ's Rule* (Downers Grove, IL: IVP Academic, 2016), 176–80. Among the unsympathetic, James Skillen judges that my view of the Two Kingdoms does not account for the "genuine unity of his [God's] kingship"; see *The Good of Politics: A Biblical, Historical, and Contemporary Introduction* (Grand Rapids: Baker Academic, 2014), 200n2. William Edgar finds in my work "a profoundly disturbing dichotomy"; see *Created and Creating: A Biblical Theology of Culture* (Downers Grove, IL: IVP Academic, 2017), 97. I apologize to Edgar for the emotional stress I have caused him—completely unintended.

dualism. Reformation Christians see the justification-sanctification distinction as essential for preserving biblical teaching on salvation, while it strikes Roman Catholics as an undue bifurcation of Christ's saving work.

Accusations of dualism or dichotomy prove nothing in and of themselves. One can make such accusations against any proposed distinction. The question is whether a proposed distinction clarifies or distorts theological truth. In my judgment, the distinctions explored here rightly distinguish without separating, and thus I employ these distinctions to formulate the political theology of this book. To this political theology we now turn.

CHAPTER 3

THE NOAHIC ORIGINS OF
POLITICAL COMMUNITY

The Old Testament

Having considered the biblical covenants and the relationship of nature and grace, we now return to our main concerns. Any political theology must answer some key questions, such as why political communities and their governments exist at all and why they are legitimate in the sight of God. Only when we answer these questions can we accurately explain the proper character and purpose of political life. This chapter and the next contend that the Noahic covenant ought to play a foundational role in Christian political theology. This is because the political communities and civil governments of the world, including those in which Christians live today, are rooted in the Noahic covenant. This covenant explains why these communities are legitimate and why their governments are divinely authorized.

The Noahic covenant receives relatively little attention in Christian political theology.[1] The proposal in these next two chapters presents a challenge to many contemporary political theologies, since it claims that the Noahic

---

1. As an exception to the general rule, Jonathan Leeman has recently utilized the Noahic covenant to productive effect in his political theology; see *Political Church: The Local Assembly as Embassy of Christ's Rule* (Downers Grove, IL: IVP Academic, 2016), 182–208. The idea of the "Noahide laws" in the Jewish tradition is interesting to compare with my use of the Noahic covenant, although Jewish theology does not ordinarily connect the Noahide laws strictly to the Noahic covenant; see David VanDrunen, *Divine Covenants and Moral Order: A Biblical Theology of Natural Law* (Grand Rapids: Eerdmans, 2014), 543–45; cf. Daniel J. Elazar, *Covenant and Polity in Biblical Israel: Biblical Foundations and Jewish Expressions* (New Brunswick, NJ: Transaction, 1995), 111. Among Jewish theologians, the views of David Novak are perhaps the closest to mine on these issues; see, e.g., David Novak, *The Jewish Social Contract: An Essay*

covenant is not simply an underutilized detail useful in political-theological reflection but a foundational element that illumines the whole enterprise of political theology. While we need other biblical material to understand the implications of the Noahic covenant, my central argument is that the Noahic covenant makes sense of what the rest of Scripture says about political community and civil government. Without the Noahic covenant, we lack a good explanation for why such communities and governments exist and why Scripture treats them as legitimate and authoritative. With this covenant, we have a light that illuminates the political teaching of Scripture as a whole.

The chief theological issue of chapters 3 and 4 can be stated simply: Are the political communities and civil governments of this world in covenant with God, and if so, which covenant? The following two chapters argue that these communities and their governments are in covenant with God through the Noahic covenant, which thus determines their character and purpose.

This chapter explores the Noahic roots of political community with focus on the Old Testament. The next chapter examines the same theme in the New Testament. Here I begin by expanding the discussion of the moral requirements of the Noahic covenant initiated in chapter 2. I argue that for the human race to pursue these moral requirements they must inevitably form *common* political communities, and thus the Noahic covenant implicitly authorizes and governs these communities. Then we consider whether the subsequent Old Testament covenants also authorize and govern common political community. I conclude that they do not, because the communities these covenants establish and govern are not common but *holy*.[2] Finally, we consider how the Old Testament actually does speak of common political community and civil government, and I argue that this evidence points compellingly to their Noahic origin.

THE NOAHIC ORIGINS OF COMMON POLITICAL COMMUNITY

The Noahic covenant calls the human race to be fruitful, multiply, and fill the earth (Gen 9:1, 7), authorizes it to eat plants and animals, though not animals

---

in Political Theology (Princeton: Princeton University Press, 2005), ch. 2. I discuss the Noahide laws in connection with Romans 13:1–7 in the next chapter.

2. Let it be noted that the distinction between common and holy is *not* a simplistic distinction between *religious* and *political*. *Both* common and holy communities are in covenant with God and responsible to him, and both can be political.

with their lifeblood (9:3–4), and grants it responsibility to enact retributive justice against murderers (9:6). This is what lies on the face of the text. It is a modest ethic, although that seems appropriate given the limited, preservative purpose of the covenant: this ethic deals with things that are absolutely necessary for the human race to survive. But if we probe a little deeper, we discover that this threefold Noahic ethic implies a number of activities beyond what the text says explicitly. This opening section of the chapter begins to think through some of these implications. I propose that the Noahic covenant commissions human beings to form a variety of institutions and that common political communities properly arise as they carry out this commission.

Initial Implications of the Noahic Ethic

The first aspect of the Noahic ethic is to be fruitful, multiply, and fill the earth. That is, procreation should lead to a great increase in the human population, and the increase in population should lead to people spreading out through the world. The goal of increased population implies that people cannot simply be concerned about *having* children but also must *nurture* them, so that they survive into responsible adulthood and can have children of their own. The goal of spreading through the world implies that people will have to be on the move and will need to adapt to new conditions that coastlands, forests, steppes, deserts, and mountains present. They will need to develop the right kinds of clothing, housing, and tools. All of this, in turn, requires creativity and technological innovation.[3]

The second aspect of the ethic involves God's giving plants and animals for humans to eat—with a caveat: no eating meat with its lifeblood. On the face of it, the fact that God *gives* animals and plants for food makes it sound as though it promulgates no moral requirement at all. But this divine gift of food obviously does not come in premade packages ready to be taken out of the refrigerator. Eating requires work. Animals need to be hunted. Plants at least need to be found and collected. And once people find food, they have to prepare it. If nothing else, they ought to cook their meat in order to observe the prohibition of lifeblood. Furthermore, as human populations grow and spread (in obedience to the first aspect of the ethic), the increasing number of mouths to feed will require cultivation of crops. This is easy for people in contemporary wealthy societies to take for granted, but it has been arduous

---

3. Compare similar ideas in Abraham Kuyper, *Common Grace*, vol. 1.3, trans. Nelson D. Kloosterman and Ed M. van der Maas, ed. Jordan J. Ballor and Stephen J. Grabill (Grand Rapids: Christian's Library Press, 2014), 604.

and time-consuming work for most humans through most of history.[4] Again, the Noahic ethic calls for creativity and technological innovation.[5]

The final aspect of the ethic calls human beings to shed the blood of those who shed human blood. It is not immediately clear whether this requires the shedding of blood when someone sheds another's blood without killing him, or when someone kills another without shedding blood in the process, or whether capital punishment is the only just response to murder. For now, it is sufficient to note that Genesis 9:6 is formulaic: it expresses the *lex talionis*. Genesis 9:6 states the formula in terms of *blood for blood*. Elsewhere Scripture speaks of eye for an eye, tooth for tooth, wound for wound (e.g., Exod 21:23–25; Lev 24:19–20; Deut 19:21). As chapter 9 will argue in detail, the *lex talionis* is designed to express a fundamental principle of justice: the person who harms another person deserves a *proportionate* penalty. It thus seems proper to conclude that this third aspect of the Noahic ethic implies a general human responsibility to administer proportionate retributive justice in response to the harm that one person inflicts upon another, whether or not that harm involves literal bloodshed.

These reflections on the implications of the threefold Noahic ethic suggest that though this ethic is modest, there is more to it than initially meets the eye. If human beings are simply to do the things lying on the surface of the text, they must pursue a range of supporting activities, including nurturing children, exploring new places, working hard, developing technology, and instituting a system of justice.

Institutions and Authority Structures

This Noahic ethic requires communal activity. Procreation, spreading through the earth, and establishing a justice system are obviously not individual endeavors. Procuring and preparing food usually involves cooperation too, and cooperation is necessary to meet the broader range of humanity's material needs, including housing, clothing, and medical care. When human beings coordinate their activities, they achieve exponentially more than when they just pursue their own autonomous projects. Since the Noahic covenant thus requires communal activity, the question arises as to how this cooperation and coordination should occur in a way consistent with the Noahic ethic.

---

4. E.g., see Colin Tudge, *Neanderthals, Bandits and Farmers* (New Haven: Yale University Press, 1999).

5. With respect to issues mentioned in the preceding two paragraphs, I am grateful for the intellectual stimulation provided by Jared Diamond, *Guns, Germs, and Steel: The Fates of Human Societies* (New York: W. W. Norton, 1997).

One crucial part of the answer must be that people form *institutions* and *associations*.[6] That is to say, people establish practices and organizations in order to pursue mutual goals in cooperative fashion. Strangers who meet wandering in the wilderness can cooperate briefly without developing expected patterns of conduct or forming a corporate body, but this is not how humans typically interact. To bring one another together to plan and act in coordinated ways toward mutually shared goals, people have had to form practices and organizations whose purpose transcends that of any single participant. These practices and organizations can develop and gain recognition either formally or informally, although what is informal seems to become more formal as particular communities expand, interact with other communities, and deal with internal and external disputes. It is difficult to conceive of any productive human life without such practices and organizations.

With respect to the first aspect of the Noahic ethic, then, what sort of institutions or associations are necessary to promote the task of being fruitful, multiplying, and filling the earth? The answer is easy: *familial* institutions. To be fruitful, multiply, and fill the earth demands an interconnected set of activities, particularly the procreation, nurture, and training of children. What is needed is not just a proper context for sexual intercourse but also a setting in which adults can care for the children procreated and teach them how to live productively in the world. These institutions that serve as forums for sexual intercourse, procreation, and the nurture and training of children are precisely what we call families.

With respect to the second aspect of the Noahic ethic, what institutions or associations are required to feed a growing population and to provide for its other material needs? In the absence of an obvious term such as *family*, I will call them *enterprise* associations.[7] These associations fulfill the tasks just identified, as people coordinate efforts in exploring, farming, building, and technological innovation, and as they develop a variety of intellectual disciplines that promote such activities. Obviously, these associations must take a variety of forms to accomplish different sorts of purposes. But "enterprise" seems to be a unifying characteristic, since these associations require initiative and energy in the promotion of fruitful human commerce.

---

6. I do not use these terms in a technical way but take them as related terms with overlapping meaning. I use both of them, rather than one, simply to avoid the impression that I have something overly narrow in mind.

7. Michael Oakeshott uses this term in a way similar to how I use it here; see *On Human Conduct* (Oxford: Clarendon, 1975), 114–18.

Enterprise associations presumably need to be fewer and simpler in earlier stages of human civilization, focused upon the bare necessities of human survival. Families could provide many of these necessities for themselves. But the advantages of sharing skills, dividing up labor, and trading products across families and small communities become evident over time, and to do such things people must form enterprise associations, however informally at first. As the population expands, develops knowledge and skills, and grows wealthier, enterprise associations can multiply, specialize, and become more complex and interrelated.

Finally, what institutions or associations are necessary to fulfill the third aspect of the Noahic ethic, that is, to bring justice against destructive people who harm fellow human beings and thus hinder the work of familial and enterprise associations? It seems fitting to call these *judicial* institutions. Familial and enterprise associations can develop their own ways of resolving internal disputes, but many human conflicts require outside parties to bring resolution. Thus judicial institutions become necessary to determine what sorts of harmful conduct require redress, to resolve conflicts, and to enforce appropriate penalties and remedies. These judicial institutions need not be arms of the state, since private organizations can provide security, mediation, arbitration, and related services. But the need for such institutions presents a context in which civil government, arguably, becomes a morally plausible idea.

The preceding paragraphs have suggested what sorts of institutions and associations are necessary for human beings to pursue the Noahic ethic. As these corporate bodies emerge, they surely require *authority structures*. This is because institutions, by nature, involve united action undertaken by a multiplicity of individuals, all of whom have their own opinions and insights. There must be some way for the many to act as one. A great deal of coordination emerges spontaneously, apart from explicit plans or decisions.[8] But sometimes there need to be formal ways to harmonize the various insights of individual members and resolve their differences of opinion. This is what authority structures provide. Such structures can obviously take a variety of shapes, but they often involve the establishment of *office*. That is, an association's authority structures regularly confer a special status on some of its

---

8. The spontaneous development of customs and laws will be an important topic in chapter 10. Among notable works on this topic, see Friedrich A. Hayek, *Law, Legislation and Liberty*, vol. 1, *Rules and Order* (Chicago: University of Chicago Press, 1973); James C. Scott, *Seeing like a State: How Certain Schemes to Improve the Human Condition Have Failed* (New Haven: Yale University Press, 1998); and Randy E. Barnett, *The Structure of Liberty: Justice and the Rule of Law*, 2nd ed. (New York: Oxford University Press, 2014).

members that entails authority to do certain sorts of things and to make certain sorts of decisions. For authority structures and offices to be legitimate rather than usurpations of power, they must at least advance the ends of the institutions they serve. Thus familial institutions require parental authority and offices that correspond to the purpose of families to procreate, nurture, and train the next generation. Enterprise associations require authority structures that correspond to their respective purposes and needs. And judicial institutions require judicial authority and offices that render just judgments about disputes before them.

Common Political Community

Thus far, this section has considered the broader Noahic moral commission entailed in the modest ethic lying on the surface of the text, as well as the kinds of institutions, associations, and authority structures that necessarily emerge from pursuing this commission. It is now time to turn to our main concern, the origin of common political community in the Noahic covenant.

In chapter 1, I defined "political community" as the life of the *polis*, that is, the larger community in a given geographical region in which smaller institutions and associations interrelate. It seems fair to conclude that forming political communities of this sort is another implication of the Noahic ethic described in Genesis 9:1–7. This is because familial, enterprise, and judicial institutions cannot exist in isolation. A particular family might be able to live self-sufficiently for a time, but pursuing the range of tasks the Noahic covenant requires demands more than just independent family units. Families (plural) need a forum in which to relate to one another. Furthermore, enterprise associations are parasitic, for they rely upon the existence of families to produce the people who will establish and participate in them. Of course, families also come to rely on enterprise associations to supply many of their needs. And one enterprise association depends upon other enterprise associations to supply goods and services necessary for its own work. In addition, a single individual will often have to participate in multiple institutions and associations—and the set of institutions in which one person claims membership will differ from the set of institutions in which another has membership. Families and enterprise associations thus exist in symbiotic relationship and need some context in which to interrelate. The presence of judicial institutions, which resolve conflicts among families and enterprise associations, adds additional layers to this interdependence.

When we speak about a context for these interrelationships, I suggest, we are talking about the *polis*—the political community. Thus *political* here does not mean "governmental" or disputes about affairs of state. Political community is simply the larger community in a particular place in which many smaller institutions and associations work out their symbiotic relationships. Civil government is just one aspect of political community. The Noahic covenant does not specify how large a political community ought to be or exactly what government institutions ought to look like, but as people pursue the Noahic ethic they will inevitably form political communities sooner or later.

One final point completes this initial argument. The political communities whose origins lie in the Noahic covenant are *common* in nature. By "common," I mean common to human beings as human beings. As discussed in chapter 2, God did not establish the Noahic covenant for any particular people, whether of a special ethnic identity or religious profession, but for all those who bear the divine image. As we will soon consider, it is possible for political community to be something other than common. But given the nature and purposes of the Noahic covenant, the political communities originating in this covenant are (or at least *ought* to be) of common character.

POLITICAL COMMUNITY AND HOLY COMMUNITIES

The previous section drew a basic but important conclusion: the implications of the Noahic covenant require the formation of political communities, and thus common political communities are implicitly authorized by this covenant. Since the Noahic covenant marks the beginning of the present world (that is, the world following the great flood—2 Pet 3:7), we thus have initial evidence that common political community has Noahic origins. But since a Christian political theology should account for the whole of Scripture, we wonder whether later biblical texts that speak of political community and civil government confirm this initial evidence or contradict it. If the former, it strengthens and clarifies the case for the Noahic origins of political community. If the latter, we have good reason to reconsider the conclusions above.

In the rest of this chapter and the next, I argue that the larger teaching of Scripture about political community and civil government strongly confirms that their origins and legitimacy lie in the Noahic covenant. This chapter continues to focus on the Old Testament. First, in this section, we consider whether the subsequent Old Testament covenants also in some way authorize political community, such that the origin of common political community and civil government lies in these covenants too. After refuting this idea, I argue, in the final section, that the way the Old Testament does speak about common political community points decisively to Noahic origin.

The Abrahamic Covenant

Following its account of the Noahic covenant, the Old Testament also describes the Abrahamic and Mosaic covenants. The question before us now is whether these subsequent Old Testament covenants authorize or establish common political community. My answer is negative. These subsequent covenants did institute communities, but the Abrahamic covenant community was not *political* (in the sense defined above), and both the Abrahamic and Mosaic communities were *holy* rather than *common*. Let us consider each of these covenants in turn.

The Abrahamic covenant instituted a community: the *household* of Abraham, which was meant to grow into a *nation*. God called Abraham out of Ur of the Chaldeans and promised to bless him (Gen 12:1–3). God later entered covenant with him in Canaan (Gen 15). The latter text has a corporate focus: "On that day the Lord made a covenant with Abram, saying 'To your offspring I give this land'" (Gen 15:18). When God later ratified and clarified the covenant's terms, he emphasized that the covenant was with Abraham and his offspring after him (17:7–10). The covenant thus marked out a community of some sort. Genesis 17 describes this community as a "house." Circumcision was the sign of the covenant, to be administered to every male born in Abraham's house or brought into it as a purchased servant (17:10–14, 27). Another way to put it is that God set apart an already-existing family (with its servants) to constitute the Abrahamic covenant community at its inception. Although the surrounding narratives suggest that this household enjoyed a certain self-sufficiency at times, it was not a political community in the sense defined above.

Nevertheless, the account of the Abrahamic covenant promised that this household would become a nation in the course of time. In a way, this seems to be the inevitable outcome of God's covenant promise that Abraham would "multiply . . . greatly" (17:2) and be "exceedingly fruitful" (17:6). Such a community could not remain a mere household for long. Scripture also states this explicitly. God's very first promise to Abraham was to make of him "a great nation" (12:2; cf. 18:18). Later, he promised to give Abraham and his offspring the land of Canaan "to possess," as their "possession," following their sojourn in Egypt (15:7, 13 18–21; 17:8). A household might lease or buy property, but a nation is the sort of community that claims territorial boundaries.[9] Later Old Testament narratives identify Israel as this nation, which God brought out of Egypt and into the promised land. The New Testament identifies the New Jerusalem and its inhabitants as the ultimate fulfillment of the promise (e.g., Rev 21:3).

This evidence indicates that the Abrahamic covenant community was not initially a political community, although it would grow into one. Focusing for now on its early days as a household, we see that this community was not common in character. It was not open to human beings simply as human beings, but to people with certain distinguishing characteristics. Among those that stand out are faith in God's promises (Gen 15:6), worshiping the true God and relinquishing idols (12:7–8; 13:18; cf. Josh 24:2–3), and the mark of circumcision (17:10–14). Although Genesis does not use the terminology of holiness to describe the Abrahamic community, holiness seems to be a good way to explain its noncommon character. This community was not for human beings generally but for a people set apart by faith, worship, and a blood-shedding ritual.

As portrayed in Genesis, therefore, the Abrahamic covenant did not authorize, establish, or otherwise regulate a common political community. It instituted a community, but not one that was common, and not even one that was political at first. The Abrahamic covenant community did not replace, displace, or challenge the legitimacy of the common political communities of Abraham's day but existed alongside them. In fact, Abraham and other members of his covenant community freely participated in the life of neighboring common political communities. They waged war in alliance with them (Gen 14:1–16), participated in their judicial procedures (Gen 20:8–13), bought real estate from them (Gen 23; 33:19), and even entered covenants with them (Gen 14:13; 21:22–32; 26:26–31).

The Mosaic Covenant

It is impossible to say precisely when the Abrahamic covenant community ceased being a household and became more like a nation instead. But Exodus opens by telling readers that over the centuries Abraham's offspring had been fruitful, multiplied, and filled the land of Egypt (Exod 1:7), where they went to live in the days of Joseph. It may not be quite accurate

---

9. The covenant also promised to make Abraham the father of "a multitude of nations" (Gen 17:4–6), referring at least in part to the many children other than Isaac that Abraham sired and the various peoples they became (25:1–18).

to call them a political community while they lived as slaves in Egypt, but they unambiguously became one when God brought them out of bondage, entered a covenant with them at Mount Sinai, gave them the law, and sent them to the promised land of Canaan as their possession. Israel was a political community; that much is clear. But what sort of political community?

God informed them when they arrived at the foot of Sinai: "If you will indeed obey my voice and keep my covenant, you shall be my treasured possession among all peoples, for all the earth is mine; and you shall be to me a kingdom of priests and a holy nation" (Exod 19:5–6). Israel was therefore not a *common* political community. God did not covenant with them as human beings generally but as a special people who would be his treasured possession in distinction from all other people. Israel was not a common political community, because they were a "holy" political community. Accordingly, God made them a kingdom of *priests*. While the Noahic covenant gave humanity a royal commission but no priestly commission, the Mosaic covenant united the royal and priestly. While the Noahic ethic gave no instructions about worship, the law of the Mosaic covenant dealt with worship thoroughly.

To inquire about the covenant at Sinai is to inquire about the law. Exodus 19–24 (cf. Deut 5) makes clear that the Sinaitic covenant and the giving of the law were inseparable, as were the covenant renewal on the plains of Moab and the Deuteronomic law (Deut 29).[10] Since the covenant established Israel as a holy nation, the law naturally prescribed the way for Israel to honor and protect its holiness. The law's focus on holiness is most intense in Leviticus, but it permeates the whole. The Mosaic law deals with many matters that are common to the human race, including Noahic concerns about sex and family, eating, and retributive justice against the violent. But it deals even with these in ways that reflect Israel's unique holiness. For example, childbirth required purification (Lev 12), farms were not to be sown with two kinds of seed (Lev 19:19), and the *lex talionis* was intertwined with punishment for blasphemy (Lev 24:10–23). Laws against sorcery, idolatry, and blasphemy found their way into the midst of the predominantly common laws of the Covenant Code (Exod 22:18, 20, 28), and the common command to do justice was sandwiched between regulations about festivals and idolatrous worship (Deut 16:18–20). While the ethic of the Noahic covenant reflected that covenant's purpose to preserve political community for the human race in common,

---

10. As noted in chapter 2, I take the covenants at Sinai and at Moab as two aspects of what I am calling the Mosaic covenant.

the law of the Mosaic covenant reflected that covenant's purpose to constitute Israel as a holy political community.

Perhaps the most poignant illustration of the holy, noncommon character of the Mosaic covenant is the law's requirement that Israel exclude all other peoples from their land (e.g., Num 33:50–56). Israel eliminated many of them when they entered the land under Joshua, although God rebuked them for various failures to complete the work (e.g., Josh 7; 9; Judg 1:27–2:5). The Abrahamic covenant community was holy, but as a household it lived alongside the political communities inhabiting the land. In contrast, the Mosaic covenant community, as a holy *political* community, was to claim the whole land as its own. Sojourners were permitted and protected (e.g., Exod 22:21; 23:9)—although they too were obligated to adhere to the Mosaic laws (Lev 18:26)—and the occasional gentile could become part of Israel (e.g., Ruth; but cf. Deut 23:3–6). Yet other political communities were not welcome within its borders. The Abrahamic household could make covenants with the political communities in the land, but God did not permit the Israelite nation to do so (e.g., Exod 23:32).

These considerations make it doubtful that Christians should "regard the society and laws of Israel as a *paradigm*," or as "a model . . . *for* the nations," as Christopher Wright suggests.[11] To be sure, Christians should affirm that the Mosaic law is "profitable for teaching, for reproof, for correction, and for training in righteousness" (2 Tim 3:16). How Christians should interpret and apply this law today is a very complicated issue, and Wright properly rejects some unhelpful ideas.[12] But viewing Israel as a paradigm "of the kinds of social values God looks for in human life generally" and "as a showcase of the way God longs for human society as a whole to operate"[13] only works if God wills all societies now to be *holy* communities, since the call to holiness permeated the Mosaic law. As the next chapter discusses, God has established *the church* as a holy community in the present age, after Christ's first coming (e.g., 1 Pet 2:9; cf. Exod 19:5–6), but God does not will political communities and civil governments of the present age to be holy. Thus for all that the

---

11. Christopher J. H. Wright, *Old Testament Ethics for the People of God* (Downers Grove, IL: InterVarsity Press, 2004), 63–64. Jonathan Burnside also uses *paradigmatic* to describe Israel, although he does not emphasize the term. See *God, Justice, and Society: Aspects of Law and Legality in the Bible* (Oxford: Oxford University Press, 2011), 82. Many of my comments here about Wright's work also apply to Burnside's.

12. Wright mentions those who seek to "replicate Israelite society in our own age" through "heavily literal adherence to Old Testament laws" and those who "dismiss the Old Testament as ethically irrelevant altogether." See *Old Testament Ethics*, 62–63.

13. Wright, *Old Testament Ethics*, 65, 74.

Mosaic law and covenant can teach the world about God, righteousness, sin, and grace, they do not provide a model or paradigm of *political community*.[14]

I believe the *Westminster Confession of Faith* (19.4), following a prevalent line of Christian interpretation, is correct to say that the "judicial laws" of Moses bound Israel "as a body politic" and thus "expired together with the State of that people." Therefore, they are "obliging" no longer, "further than the general equity thereof may require."[15] This implies that determining the "general equity" underlying the Mosaic provisions is key to determining the relevance of the Mosaic law for contemporary law and government. The Mosaic law itself does not specify what its general equity is; determining this requires attention to the Noahic covenant and natural law.[16] The present volume might therefore serve as a prolegomenon to a study of the legal-political use of the Mosaic law today. But the present volume itself does not provide such a study of the Old Testament law.

It is worth noting that although the Mosaic law required Israel, as a holy political community, to exclude all other political communities from the bounds of the promised land, it did not call Israel to eliminate political communities outside the land. In fact, Israel ought *not* to have treated nations outside their boundaries in the way they were to treat those inside. Deuteronomy 20:10–20, for example, lays down rules for warfare against cities far away that are different from the rules for fighting cities nearby. Likewise, Kings David and Solomon, in the days when the Israelite theocracy was flourishing in relative righteousness, had peaceful relations with foreign rulers (e.g., 1 Kgs 5; 10:1–13). They even entered covenants with them (1 Kgs 5:12), which was strictly forbidden with respect to nations within the land. This continuing and uninterrupted existence of political communities throughout most of the world, even during Israel's tenure in Canaan, has important implications for discussion below.

All of these considerations indicate that the Mosaic covenant, like the Abrahamic covenant, did not authorize, establish, or otherwise regulate common political community. Unlike the Abrahamic covenant, the Mosaic

---

14. I do not believe Deuteronomy 4:6–8 provides counter evidence to this claim. For explanation, see VanDrunen, *Divine Covenants*, 319–26.

15. This statement presumes the ancient Christian distinction among the moral, ceremonial, and judicial aspects of the Mosaic law; see *Westminster Confession of Faith*, 19.1–3. Among earlier Christian theologians taking a similar view of the judicial law, see Thomas Aquinas, *Summa Theologiae* 1a2ae 104.3; and John Calvin, *Institutes of the Christian Religion*, 4.20.14–16.

16. On the natural law background of "general equity," see David VanDrunen, *Natural Law and the Two Kingdoms: A Study in the Development of Reformed Social Thought* (Grand Rapids: Eerdmans, 2010), 169–71.

covenant did institute a *political* community, but as a holy rather than common one. Therefore, we have no reason thus far to question the conclusion that the origins of common political community lie in the Noahic covenant and do not lie in the subsequent biblical covenants.

OLD TESTAMENT POLITICAL COMMUNITIES UNDER THE NOAHIC COVENANT

To this point, I have argued that the Abrahamic and Mosaic covenants established communities, but not the kind of *common political* communities that the Noahic covenant implicitly authorizes. Thus we need to look elsewhere if we wish to answer the question posed above: what insight does the rest of Scripture provide as to how to understand common political community and the formation of civil government? The Old Testament provides quite a bit of information. We do not find any text that authorizes the *creation* of political community in general or of civil government in particular. But as we read on from Genesis 9, we find the peoples of the earth forming political communities and civil governments in various locales. These political communities and governments were *common*, because they emerged among human beings of all sorts and because God had not declared any of them holy. At least some of them evidently viewed themselves as holy, in that they combined the royal and priestly by making (idolatrous) religious profession and worship into affairs of state, but they did so on their own initiative, not God's.[17]

In seizing priestly responsibilities and in many other matters, the peoples of the earth showed their sinfulness. Nevertheless, the Old Testament portrays their political communities as morally mixed. They displayed some concern about marriage and children but also condoned sexual violence. They showed some concern for justice but also perverted it. They showed some concern for aliens within their gates but also treated them brutally. In both their formation of political communities which achieved genuine goods and their sinful perversion of these goods, we see exactly what the Noahic covenant leads us to expect. For God called the human race to be fruitful,

---

17. This would have been a helpful point for James K. A. Smith to make in *Awaiting the King: Reforming Public Theology* (Grand Rapids: Baker Academic, 2017), 20–23; cf. 120–22. In his enthusiastic polemic against a penultimate/ultimate distinction, which roughly tracks my common/holy distinction here, he correctly points out that earthly political societies usually do not consider themselves penultimate. Christians indeed should be alert to this. But the point here is that such communities *are* penultimate by God's appointment, and Christians should act accordingly in the public square.

multiply, fill the earth, and do justice (Gen 9:1, 6–7) and also declared that the human heart is sinful from its youth (8:21). Accordingly, the Old Testament treats these political communities and governments as legitimate, despite their serious flaws, and describes how God held them accountable for their injustice.

In this final section of the chapter, we consider what the Old Testament says about these political communities and civil governments of the world. We have already seen they did not arise out of the Abrahamic or Mosaic covenants. I argue now that these communities and governments emerged as the human race lived under the Noahic covenant. I also argue that God both recognized their legitimacy and held them accountable for injustice on the basis of their Noahic origins.

The Genesis Narratives

Although the text of Genesis (from chapter 12 on) focuses on the Abrahamic covenant community, it also refers to many cities and nations of the ancient Near Eastern world. Even before readers meet Abraham, they learn about the famous Babel whose tower arose on the plains of Shinar. Abraham and his family sojourned in or near Egypt, Sodom, Gerar, and Shechem, among other places, and they interacted with Canaanites, Perizzites, Hittites, and many others. These places and peoples often play important supporting roles as the main storyline of Genesis unfolds. The regions in which Abraham's family sojourned teemed with political communities.

What are we to make of this? Where did they come from and how are readers to evaluate them? Genesis 10 indicates where they came from. "Sons were born" to Noah's sons Shem, Ham, and Japheth (10:1). They developed into "clans" and "nations" and "spread abroad on the earth after the flood" (10:32). In other words, none of the cities or peoples mentioned later in Genesis owed their origins to a brand new act of divine authorization, but they emerged in the course of time as human beings did exactly what God commissioned them to do under the Noahic covenant. They were fruitful, multiplied, and filled the earth. As they did, they paid much attention to securing enough food and other material needs (e.g., 13:2–11; 21:25–27; 41:46–49; 42:1–2; 43:11), and they recognized rulers who oversaw the defense of their peoples and the administration of justice (e.g., 14:1–7; 20:8–10; 42:6–25). In these matters, too, they did what the Noahic covenant commissioned—at least in part, for even these actions were corrupted by sin. The Noahic covenant issued its moral commission while recognizing the depth of human corruption (8:21), and thus it is no surprise that the political communities of Abraham's world were a mixed lot. Injustice was rampant in some of them, most egregiously in Sodom (18:20–19:22). In other communities, the people displayed some genuine concern for justice. Gerar was perhaps the best of them (20:8–18).[18]

Three noteworthy characteristics of these political communities and their civil officials are implicit in the Genesis narratives. First, the narratives presume that their existence and authority are *legitimate*. Abraham submitted to their judicial proceedings (20:8–13), Abraham and Isaac made covenants with them (14:13; 21:22–32; 26:26–31), Joseph accepted appointment to civil office (41:37–46), and Jacob blessed Pharaoh (47:7–10). Second, the narratives speak of these political communities and their civil officials as *accountable* before the divine judgment. This is clearest in the destruction of Sodom and Gomorrah (19:23–29), but it is also evident in God's dealings with the relatively just Abimelech, king of Gerar (20:3–7, 17–18). Third, the narratives suggest that these political communities were *common* in nature, in the sense that they were not holy but existed for human beings in general. The text reveals little about the religious convictions and practices of the cities among whom Abraham and his family sojourned or about the ethnic unity or diversity of particular places. But one relevant fact is that these political communities were obligated to treat strangers justly. When Genesis describes injustice, it often involves mistreatment of foreigners. Sodom's attempted gang rape is again the prime example (19:4–11), although Shechem's abuse of Jacob's daughter Dinah was also "an outrageous thing" (34:1–2, 7). Conversely, readers recognize that Gerar and its king Abimelech are of much higher moral quality. The text portrays this city as the kind of place that would not harm a foreign man on account of his wife, due to its "fear of God" (20:11).[19] Abraham wronged the people of Gerar by not reciprocating their decency across cultural divides. Many of these cities probably thought of themselves as having distinctive religious and ethnic identities, but God considered them the kind of community in which people of different religious and ethnic identities should live in peaceful coexistence.[20]

---

18. For detailed discussion of the narratives about Sodom and Gerar, see VanDrunen, *Divine Covenants*, ch. 3.

19. To put things in context, matters were far from wonderful even in Gerar. Abimelech was not the sort of king who would kill a man for his wife, but he still "took" Sarah when he believed she was Abraham's sister (Gen 20:2). This hardly sounds good, yet it is better than with the kings before the flood who "took as their wives any they chose" (6:2).

20. It is true that Israel under the Mosaic law, as a *holy* political community, was also obligated

Thus, while the Abrahamic covenant did not establish or govern a common political community, many common political communities existed in the regions where Abraham's household sojourned. As far as the text indicates, these communities were legitimate and divinely accountable, for they had emerged as human beings (imperfectly) carried out their Noahic moral commission. This confirms the prior argument that the origins of common political community lie in the Noahic covenant.

COMMON POLITICAL COMMUNITIES IN THE DAYS OF ISRAEL'S NATIONHOOD

As considered above, Israel under the Mosaic covenant was a political community, but not a *common* one. Their law required them to be hospitable to strangers and permitted foreign converts, but it did not allow the land of Israel to be a place of peaceful coexistence among peoples of all sorts. The land was to be characterized by pervasive holiness, from which all idolatry and idolaters were expunged. The cities and peoples considered in the previous section emerged legitimately from the Noahic covenant yet met their end at the hands of Joshua under the Mosaic law. Within the boundaries of their promised land, there was to be one *holy* political community.

But as any world map shows, Canaan is a small place. And Scripture makes clear that even while God required Israel to maintain pervasive holiness within its borders, the rest of the world continued to carry on its ordinary business. Beginning in Exodus, the Old Testament canon focuses on the fortunes of Israel, but it also gives many insights about gentile political communities. Outside Israel's borders, what we observed in Genesis continues and develops as history moves forward. Among the developments are the rise of multinational empires, such as Assyria, Babylon, and Persia. As evident in many texts, political communities rose and fell, they displayed varying degrees of justice and injustice, and Scripture treats them and their rulers as legitimate, divinely accountable, and common. Scripture also provides no explanation for these things other than the one already identified, the Noahic covenant.

---

to treat strangers decently. The main difference, as I see it, is that Israel was not to tolerate idolatrous or blasphemous activity from the sojourners within the land, while the cities within which Abraham sojourned obviously were obligated to tolerate Abraham's religious worship and profession, or else they would have prohibited what God demanded of him. Thus Scripture presents the cities of Abraham's sojourn as places that should have tolerated religious coexistence, but it presents Israel as a place that should not have tolerated such coexistence.

To begin, Israel's most famous kings, David and Solomon, carried on peaceful relations with many nations outside their land. Granted, the Old Testament historical books record God's displeasure with Israelite kings who collaborated with gentile nations in ways that compromised their allegiance to him. But David and Solomon were relatively righteous. They reigned during years when God prospered Israel, and Scripture does not condemn their collaboration with Hiram, king of Tyre (1 Kgs 5; 10:11, 22), Solomon's hospitality to the Queen of Sheba (1 Kgs 10:1–13), or his extensive commerce with many peoples (1 Kgs 10:15, 22–29). These texts imply that these nations outside Canaan and their civil officials were legitimate.

In addition, two kinds of Old Testament texts are particularly relevant for understanding these communities beyond Israel's borders. One kind are the prophetic oracles against gentile nations. These oracles indicate how God evaluated gentile communities and their rulers and thus reveal something of their proper character. The other kind of text are those that describe Israel's exile in Babylon and instruct Israel how to live within it. These also indicate something of the proper character of political communities existing outside Israel's boundaries. Let us consider these two kinds of texts in turn.

Oracles directed to gentile nations appear in the three major prophets and in several minor prophets. Some of these texts promise that God's redemptive grace will extend to these peoples in years to come, anticipating the church's worldwide mission under the new covenant. Our interest here is in the oracles that pronounce judgment, since here we learn what God expected from these communities and, at least indirectly, what their proper character was. Two kinds of wrongs seem to trigger God's judgment in these oracles. The first are egregious acts of injustice. In the trenchant oracles of Amos, for example, God decried various foreign communities for slave-trading, treaty-breaking, ripping open pregnant women, and desecrating the dead (1:6, 9, 13; 2:1). The oracles often give special attention to unjust deeds that were excessive or over-the-top (evident in Amos 1:11). In many of the oracles, God condemned the gentile nations for mistreating his covenant people Israel, although intragentile wrongs were also within his purview (as in Amos 2:1). The second sort of wrong that triggered God's judgment was hubris, a self-deifying pride. The judgment against Babylon in Isaiah 14 provides a vivid illustration. The king of Babylon sought to ascend to heaven, set his throne on high, and sit "on the mount of assembly in the far reaches of the north" in order to be "like the Most High." In response, God promised to bring him down to the far reaches of the pit of hell (14:13–15).

Reflection on these texts yields similar conclusions to the ones I drew about the political communities described in Genesis. First, the oracles imply the *legitimacy* of these communities and their rulers. God never condemned their existence but only their abuse of power. Second, the oracles show the *accountability* of these nations before the divine judgment. This is the main point of these texts and hardly needs further comment. Third, more subtle yet important, the oracles show that these political communities were properly *common* in character. God held them accountable for egregious acts of injustice and hubris, but he did not pronounce judgment for their idolatry. This is striking. When prophets condemned Israel throughout the Old Testament, idolatry was of chief concern. Yet this issue drops almost completely out of sight when the prophets turn to the gentile nations. This makes good sense since Israel was a holy community devoted to the right worship of God while no gentile nations was such a community. Although God ultimately holds all people liable for their idolatrous rebellion (Rom 1:18–25), these ancient gentile political communities and their civil officials apparently were not supposed to purge out idolatry and thus make their societies holy.[21]

These conclusions further support the idea that the origin of the world's political communities lies in the Noahic covenant. The Noahic covenant implies that political communities and authority structures should emerge in the course of history and that they should be of common rather than holy character. That is, they should be open and just toward human beings of whatever religious and ethnic identity. Injustice (Gen 9:6) and arrogant refusal to recognize any higher authority (9:5) strike at the heart of the covenant. Just as such communities emerged in the days of Abraham without any need for additional divine authorization, so they continued to emerge and develop in the days of Israel as a nation, again without any additional authorization from on high.

The second kind of Old Testament text that provides important insight into the world's political communities are those describing and regulating Israel's exile in Babylon. As described in 2 Kings and 2 Chronicles, as well as in Jeremiah and Ezekiel, Nebuchadnezzar conquered Jerusalem in the late seventh and early sixth centuries before Christ and sent exiles to Babylon in several waves. This exile was a calamity for Israel from which it never truly recovered. It signaled the ultimate curse of the Mosaic covenant

---

21. For detailed discussion of the prophetic oracles against gentile nations, see VanDrunen, *Divine Covenants*, ch. 4.

(e.g., Lev 18:26–28; Deut 28:63–68; Lam 1–5) and prompted the need for a new covenant (Jer 31:31–34). These matters shape the main storyline of the latter phases of Old Testament history. But alongside the main action, several biblical books speak of Babylon as a legitimate and common political community, despite its brutality and arrogance as a conquering power that would provoke God's judgment in due time.

We may consider this in terms of the three ideas utilized above. First, Babylon was a *legitimate* political community. Jeremiah 29 records a letter the prophet sent to the early exiles directing them how to live in their new place. The letter instructed the exiles to build houses, plant gardens, eat their produce, get married, have children, and multiply (29:3–6). It also commanded them to seek the welfare of Babylon and to pray for it (29:7). This is remarkable. Nebuchadnezzar had absolutely no authority under the Mosaic law to exert his power in the holy land. But in Babylon life had been going on. When the Israelites found themselves outside their land and in another's country, they were to pursue strikingly normal things. In fact, the call to have children and multiply, to plant gardens and eat from them, and to seek the peace of the city has an unmistakably Noahic character. Babylon is a legitimate political community, a place for pursuing ordinary human activities, whose peace should be promoted. The biblical stories of how Daniel, Shadrach, Meshach, Abednego, Nehemiah, Esther, and Mordechai assumed civil office in Babylon and later Persia confirms the legitimacy of these communities. Daniel even abided so carefully by the laws of the Medes and Persians that his fellow civil servants, when jealous, could find no legal basis for accusing him (Dan 6:4).

Second, Babylon was *accountable* before God for its injustice and hubris. Several of the Old Testament prophets included oracles condemning Babylon for these very sins (e.g., Isa 13:1–14:23; Jer 50–51). Daniel also records divine judgments against the city, both a temporary curse upon Nebuchadnezzar (Dan 4) and the final verdict delivered to King Belshazzar on the eve of its fall to the Persians (Dan 5; cf. 2:34–45).

Third, Babylon was properly *common* in character. The city was obviously an idolatrous place. One of the most memorable parts of the book of Daniel records Nebuchadnezzar's construction of an idol nearly one hundred feet tall (Dan 3). Yet God did not bring judgment upon him for this but for lack of justice and mercy (4:27) and for his hubris in taking all the credit for building Babylon (4:30). Nebuchadnezzar did come to learn that he should honor the true God (4:34–37), but he never required the people to worship this God exclusively. And neither Daniel nor the other Israelites who held office in Babylon or Persia attempted to establish these nations as holy communities thoroughly devoted to worship of the living God. The biblical texts recognize Babylon's legitimacy but not its holiness. Babylon was legitimate as a common political community.

This biblical material about Babylon, therefore, further confirms that common political community originates in the Noahic covenant. Babylon obviously had a special place in God's plan for his people that cities such as Gerar did not, for Babylon was an agent of divine judgment for Israel's gross violation of the Mosaic covenant. But though God gave Jerusalem (and many other places) over to the harsh hand of Nebuchadnezzar (Jer 28), Babylon itself came into existence as part of the same process that produced all the other political communities of the earth (except Israel). Babylon needed no special act of divine authorization to make it a legitimate and common political community in the ancient Near East. It too emerged from human beings' sinfully tainted pursuit of the Noahic moral commission, and that was sufficient.

CONCLUSION

This chapter has argued that several lines of evidence from the Old Testament indicate that the origin of common political community lies in the Noahic covenant. The explicit terms of the Noahic covenant imply that common political communities ought to emerge in the course of time, as human beings multiply and fill the earth. The Old Testament amply documents that this is exactly what happened. The Abrahamic and Mosaic covenants established holy communities, but these covenants played no role in authorizing or governing common political communities. Nor does the Old Testament record any other brand new act of divine authorization that legitimates these communities. The Noahic covenant alone explains the divinely authorized formation and legitimacy of common political communities in the post-flood world.

That leaves a major question before us: should this conclusion about political communities be any different when viewed from New Testament perspective? Christ has come, died, risen, and ascended. He has established the new covenant. What difference, if any, does this make for the way Christians understand the character and purpose of the political communities in which they live in these last days? To this we now turn.

CHAPTER 4

THE NOAHIC ORIGINS OF POLITICAL COMMUNITY

The New Testament

The previous chapter began an argument that the origins of common political community lie in the Noahic covenant and thus that the Noahic covenant should be foundational for Christian political theology. For the human race to carry out the modest ethic commissioned in Genesis 9:1–7, I argued, it has to pursue a number of other activities as well, such as forming institutions, associations, and authority structures. As people do so, they inevitably establish political communities—the *polis*—in which these many institutions and associations can interrelate. The rest of the Old Testament indicates that this is exactly what happened among the peoples of the world. Therefore, I concluded, the Noahic covenant explains why the common political communities of the world before Christ's coming were legitimate and why their rulers possessed authority.

But we now ask: What about *after* Christ's coming? In this chapter, I argue that the political communities in which Christians now live have the same nature and purpose as Gerar, Babylon, and other cities we examined in the Old Testament. Like them, our contemporary political communities are in relationship to God through the Noahic covenant and are bound by its terms. The new covenant, like the Abrahamic and Mosaic covenants, established and governs a holy community, the church, but not common political communities. Alongside their non-Christian neighbors, Christians are obligated to participate in the political communities in which they find themselves and to honor their civil officials. Yet they do so with the assurance that God now rules these communities through his incarnate and exalted Son, and this Son will defend his people and avenge the injustices these communities inflict upon them.

The chapter begins by discussing what sort of community the new covenant establishes. Then it considers how the New Testament speaks about political community and civil government, and it contends that this evidence strongly supports my thesis about the Noahic covenant. Following this, I seek to integrate this conclusion with New Testament teaching that God now rules the entire world through Jesus Christ, his incarnate and exalted Son.

THE NEW COVENANT HOLY COMMUNITY

To continue the study begun in chapter 3, it is fitting to inquire first whether the new covenant authorizes common political community. If so, this will require us to reconsider the provisional thesis that the origin of common political community lies in the Noahic covenant alone and thus that such communities are obligated by its terms. If not, it clears the way for us to see whether the New Testament speaks of political community in ways consistent with Noahic origins.

Like the Abrahamic and Mosaic covenants, the new covenant clearly established a community. The Old Testament prophesied that God would make this covenant with "the house of Israel and the house of Judah," and it repeated the Abrahamic promise, "I will be their God, and they shall be my people" (Jer 31:31–33). The New Testament announces the arrival of the new covenant at Jesus's institution of the Lord's Supper (e.g., Luke 22:14–20), a communal meal that foreshadowed the fellowship of his Father's kingdom (Matt 26:28–29).

The broader New Testament speaks of *the church* as this community established by the new covenant. Following Peter's famous confession of Jesus as the Christ, Jesus declared him blessed and said, "You are Peter, and on this rock I will build my church, and the gates of hell shall not prevail against it. I will give you the keys of the kingdom of heaven, and whatever you bind on earth shall be bound in heaven, and whatever you loose on earth shall be loosed in heaven" (Matt 16:16–19). In this way, Jesus gave to the church the power and ministry of his kingdom. This is the first appearance of "church" in the New Testament, and the Greek *ekklēsia* was the Greek Old Testament's (Septuagint) translation of the Hebrew *qahal*, which described the assembly of Israel as it traveled out of Egypt toward Canaan.[1] Thus Jesus portrayed his ("my") community of followers as in continuity with Israel of old—as expected, if the new covenant was to be with the houses of Israel and Judah (Jer 31:31–33). Yet Matthew (and the New Testament generally) also makes clear that this new covenant, while organically continuous with Old Testament Israel, established a *new* community characterized by self-denial and following Jesus (Matt 16:24–25). Unfaithful members of the old community were excluded and new faithful members welcomed (Matt 21:41–43; cf. Rom 11:11–24). Jesus required this community to make disciples of all nations (Matt 28:19), and thus it is open to Jews and gentiles alike (e.g., Gal 3:28). This Jew-gentile body, reconciled to God and to one another, is the new "household of God" and "holy temple" (Eph 2:11–22). It fulfills God's promise to Abraham that all nations would be blessed through him (Gal 3:7–14, 26–29; cf. Gen 12:2–3).

Is the new covenant community *common* and *political*? It is clearly not common, in the sense defined in chapter 3. Jesus did not establish this community universally, with human beings simply as human beings, but with those who have faith in him, deny themselves for his sake, and are baptized (see Matt 16:18, 24; Gal 3:26–29). Furthermore, this community is not common because, instead, it is *holy*: "You are a chosen race, a royal priesthood, a holy nation, a people for his own possession" (1 Pet 2:9; cf. Rev 1:6). This statement incorporates the Old Testament description of Israel at Sinai (Exod 19:5–6). Israel was a holy community, and so is the church. The church is to be holy as God is holy (1 Pet 1:16; cf. Lev 11:44). It is to "cleanse out the old leaven" and "purge the evil person from among you" (1 Cor 5:7, 13)—although not by the sword, and with the ultimate goal of repentance and reconciliation (e.g., Matt 18:15–20; 1 Cor 5:5; Gal 6:1–2).

The new covenant community is also not political in the sense defined in chapter 3. The New Testament uses many terms to describe the church that have political overtones. It calls the church a "nation" and "people" (e.g., 1 Pet 2:9) and describes it as the present manifestation of the "kingdom" (e.g., Matt 16:18–19; Rom 14:17). But the church is not a community with territorial borders, within which a host of familial, enterprise, and judicial institutions interrelate and civil governments emerge. In this sense, the church is like the Abrahamic rather than Mosaic covenant community. The church does not

---

1. As noted by many commentators. E.g., see W. D. Davies and Dale C. Allison, *A Critical and Exegetical Commentary on the Gospel according to Saint Matthew*, vol. 2 (Edinburgh: T&T Clark, 1991), 629.

replace, displace, or absorb the political communities of the world but exists alongside them and operates within their territories. Its members can experience dual citizenship, enjoying rights and privileges in temporal political communities (e.g., Acts 16:37; 22:25–29) while claiming ultimate membership in the church and a heavenly kingdom (e.g., Gal 4:26; Eph 2:19; Phil 3:20).

This evidence indicates that the new covenant has established a community, the church, but it has not established common political communities. Thus far, we have no evidence against the idea that the origin of common political community lies in the *Noahic* covenant. We must now consider what the New Testament says about political communities themselves and thereby put my thesis about Noahic origins to further test.

NEW TESTAMENT POLITICAL COMMUNITIES AND THE NOAHIC COVENANT

If the argument in chapter 3 is correct that gentile political communities mentioned in the Old Testament originate in the Noahic covenant, the idea that gentile political communities mentioned in the New Testament have the same origin is immediately plausible. After all, Rome and its empire emerged through the same process that produced Gerar, Babylon, and countless others. Generation after generation, the peoples of the world migrated, traded, intermarried, fought wars, and made peace. Cities, nations, and empires rose and fell. It all started, the Old Testament explains, as the sons of Noah had children of their own and they spread out over the earth after the flood (Gen 10:1, 32). In the course of time, Rome was settled and later gained an empire. The same process has continued over the two millennia since.

But we wonder whether anything in the New Testament specifically confirms this plausible idea that present political communities are of the same character and origin as common political communities in the Old Testament. The four Gospels and Acts provide no theoretical discussions of political community or civil government. The Gospels on occasion acknowledge the divinely ordained legitimacy and authority of civil magistrates (Matt 22:21; John 19:11), but these texts teach nothing about their purpose or historical origins. Acts offers more material for reflection. It often portrays the apostles as recognizing the legitimate authority of both the Roman laws and the various magistrates they encounter (e.g., Acts 16:37; 22:25; 24:10; 25:11).

The New Testament epistles supply some of the theological commentary lacking in the Gospels and Acts, although here too the material is limited.

Romans 13:1–7 and 1 Peter 2:13–17 have the two most extensive discussions. Both texts speak of civil magistrates as instituted by God, say that magistrates are to punish evildoers and praise the good, and exhort Christians to honor and submit to their magistrates. Of the two, Romans 13:1–7 is more detailed, and thus seems to be the most promising place to find evidence confirming or challenging my claim that contemporary political communities originate in the Noahic covenant. The fact that this text has traditionally played an important role in Christian reflection about political authority further justifies a detailed examination of it.

One thing Romans 13 states that 1 Peter 2 does not is that civil magistrates "have been instituted by God" (13:1). God has "appointed" them (13:2), and thus they are his "servants" and "ministers" (13:4, 6). This is a strong statement of the divinely backed legitimacy and authority of these officials, but it raises questions about *how* God instituted and appointed them. Romans 13 itself does not say. Neither this text nor any other in the New Testament speaks about a particular decree by which God brought political communities into existence. The argument I have been developing—that common political community originates in the Noahic covenant—suggests that this New Testament silence is no problem and may even be expected. But there is also extensive positive evidence from Romans 13:1–7 that confirms my thesis about the Noahic covenant. To show this, I first argue that Paul probably had the Noahic covenant in mind when he wrote Romans 13:1–7. But even if he did not, I explain why the Noahic covenant is still important background for understanding the political-theological implications of this Pauline text.

Romans 13:1–7 and the Noahide Laws

The first part of the argument is this: Paul most likely knew about the Jewish tradition concerning the "Noahide laws," such as that tradition was in his day. Thus it is probable (though not certain) that Paul associated his teaching in Romans 13 with Noah and, by extension, with the Noahic covenant of Genesis 8–9.

The Noahide laws refer to seven general moral obligations that bind gentiles and form the basis for relationships between gentiles and Jews. According to Jewish theology, Jews alone are bound by the laws of Sinai, but God holds gentiles morally accountable through the Noahide laws. Noahide laws prohibit six things: worship of idols, taking God's name in vain, murder, sexual immorality, theft, and eating flesh torn from a living animal.

And they require one thing: the enforcement of just laws through a legal system.[2] The rabbis who developed this tradition believed that God imposed moral requirements upon the human race before the covenant at Sinai. They called them the *Noahide* laws because Genesis portrays Noah as a righteous man and the father of humanity after the great flood, and thus makes him the paradigmatic gentile in moral relationship with God. Jewish tradition did not assert that God directly commanded all seven laws in Genesis 8:21–9:17, although this text does touch on several of them.[3]

Paul's teaching that God has ordained civil authorities (Rom 13:1–2) to administer justice (13:3–4) corresponds to one of the Noahide commands, the notion that gentiles should enforce just laws.[4] As Markus Bockmuehl puts it, Romans 13 reflects "a point of view that is remarkably compatible with later rabbinic ideas of the legitimacy of gentile government—along with the Noachide obligation to establish and honor civil authorities and lawcourts."[5]

Was Paul consciously promoting this Noahide law? This could only be true if the Noahide law tradition already existed in his day. Unfortunately, it is impossible to say exactly when the tradition originated. Among extant sources, the first explicit reference to it appears in the *Tosefta*,[6] commonly dated to the late second century AD, although there is good reason to think that the pertinent text in the *Tosefta* (*Abodah Zarah* 8.4) originates from no later than the early second century.[7] Thus perhaps only half a century separates the writing of Romans from an explicit statement about the seven Noahide laws. But rabbis must have been talking about the idea of seven

---

2. E.g., see Michael J. Broyde, "The Obligation of Jews to Seek Observance of Noahide Laws by Gentiles: A Theoretical Review," in *Tikkun Olam: Social Responsibility in Jewish Thought and Law*, ed. David Shatz, Chaim I. Waxman, and Nathan J. Diament (Northvale, NJ: Jason Aronson, 1997), 109–10; and Markus Bockmuehl, *Jewish Law in Gentile Churches: Halakhah and the Beginning of Christian Public Ethics* (Grand Rapids: Baker Academic, 2000), 150, 160. Generally, see David Novak, *The Image of the Non-Jew in Judaism: An Historical and Constructive Study of the Noahide Laws* (New York: Edwin Mellen, 1983).

3. For relevant discussion, see Bockmuehl, *Jewish Law*, 150–51; Novak, *The Image of the Non-Jew*, 151; and David Novak, *The Jewish Social Contract: An Essay in Political Theology* (Princeton: Princeton University Press, 2005), 50.

4. On the obligation of gentiles to administer justice through courts of law, see especially Nahum Rakover, *Law and the Noahides: Law as a Universal Value* (Jerusalem: The Library of Jewish Law, 1998).

5. Bockmuehl, *Jewish Law*, 137.

6. See Novak, *The Image of the Non-Jew*, 3. The relevant part of the *Tosefta* begins in this way: "Concerning seven religious requirements were the children of Noah admonished." See Jacob Neusner, *The Tosefta: Translated from the Hebrew with a New Introduction*, 2 vols. (Peabody, MA: Hendrickson, 2002), 1291–92.

7. See Klaus Müller, *Tora für die Völker: Die noachidischen Gebote und Ansätze zu ihrer Rezeption im Christentum*, 2nd ed. (Berlin, Institut Kirche und Judentum, 1998), 47–48; and Bockmuehl, *Jewish Law*, 159.

Noahide laws for quite some time before they began recording it as part of their oral tradition. We cannot know for just how long they were talking about it, but the book of *Jubilees*, written some two centuries before Romans, says that Noah passed along moral commands to his children after the great flood. Several of the commands it mentions correspond to the seven Noahide laws.[8] Jewish teachers, therefore, were associating Noah with a universal human morality for quite some time before the birth of Saul of Tarsus. And if this idea was circulating for so long, Paul, born in the Diaspora and trained by elite teachers in Jerusalem, almost certainly knew about it.[9]

Romans 13:1–7 and the Noahic Covenant

Thus it is quite likely that Paul associated gentile morality, and specifically the obligation to enforce just laws through a legal system, with the Old Testament figure of Noah. But would he have associated this obligation with *the Noahic covenant* as recorded in Genesis 8:21–9:17? It seems unlikely that a learned rabbi, when thinking about Noah, would not have thought simultaneously about the biblical texts that narrate Noah's story. But we should compare the texts in Genesis and Romans to see whether an affirmative answer is justified. In what follows, I point out extensive substantive similarities of Romans 13:1–7 to the text of the Noahic covenant, and especially to Genesis 9:5–6. I argue that these similarities make it probable, though not certain, that Paul had the Noahic covenant in mind as he wrote Romans 13.

To appreciate the following argument, readers should keep in mind that Paul must have known the Hebrew Bible extraordinarily well. As N. T. Wright has put it, "Israel's scriptures were as familiar to Paul, and as readily available in his well-stocked mind, as Beethoven's sonatas to a concert pianist."[10] Furthermore, many New Testament scholars commenting on

---

8. The relevant section is *Jubilees* 7.20: "During the twenty-eighth jubilee . . . Noah began to prescribe for his grandsons the ordinances and the commandments—every statute which he knew. He testified to his sons that they should do what is right, cover the shame of their bodies, bless the one who had created them, honor father and mother, love one another, and keep themselves from fornication, uncleanness, and from all injustice." See *The Book of Jubilees*, trans. James C. Vanderkam (Louvain: Peeters, 1989), 46–47.

9. Jewish communities' perception of Noah and their interpretation of the Noah stories during this time period are complicated subjects. For general discussion, see, e.g., Jack P. Lewis, *A Study of the Interpretation of Noah and the Flood in Jewish and Christian Literature* (Leiden: Brill, 1968); and Dorothy M. Peters, *Noah Traditions in the Dead Sea Scrolls: Conversations and Controversies of Antiquity* (Atlanta: Society of Biblical Literature, 2008). Such studies indicate that Noah was a pervasive topic of conversation in Jewish circles, which seems to confirm the unlikelihood of Paul not being aware of the developing tradition of the Noahide laws.

10. N. T. Wright, *Paul and the Faithfulness of God* (Minneapolis: Fortress, 2013), 13. Cf. Bryan D. Estelle, *Echoes of Exodus: Tracing a Biblical Motif* (Downers Grove, IL: IVP Academic, 2018), 270–71.

Romans 13:1–7 remark that Paul was evidently drawing on old Jewish beliefs embedded in the Old Testament, and these scholars are surely correct.[11] Therefore, if we can identify an Old Testament text that is relevant to civil law and government and that makes numerous claims substantively similar to Romans 13:1–7, it would be compelling to conclude that Paul was not oblivious to this text while writing Romans 13:1–7. As I now argue, Genesis 8:21–9:17 (and especially 9:5–6) is such a text. What is more, it displays many more points of substantive similarity to Romans 13:1–7 than any other single text in the Old Testament I can think of. Seven substantive similarities stand out.

A first and striking point of similarity is that both texts describe judicial authority as delegated from God: God holds ultimate judicial authority but also commissions human beings to exercise this power on his behalf. In the Noahic covenant, God asserted his ultimate authority: "For your lifeblood I will require a reckoning: from every beast I will require it and from man. From his fellow man I will require a reckoning for the life of man" (9:5). But God immediately proceeded to delegate authority: "Whoever sheds the blood of man, by man shall his blood be shed, for God made man in his own image" (9:6). Contrary to popular assumption, the reason this text appeals to the image of God is probably not to highlight why murder is so bad but to explain why God delegates such a profound authority to human beings. That is, human beings can administer justice on God's behalf because they *bear his image*.[12] Romans 13:1–7 also emphasizes God's delegation of authority. In the text immediately preceding, Paul commands Christians not to repay evil

---

11. E.g., see James D. G. Dunn, "Romans 13.1–7—A Charter for Political Quietism?" *Ex Auditu* 2 (1986): 64–65, 67; James D. G. Dunn, *Word Biblical Commentary*, vol. 38B, *Romans 9–16* (Dallas: Word, 1988), 764, 770; Douglas J. Moo, *The Epistle to the Romans* (Grand Rapids: Eerdmans, 1996), 794, 798; Ben Witherington, with Darlene Hyatt, *Paul's Letter to the Romans: A Socio-Rhetorical Commentary* (Grand Rapids: Eerdmans, 2004), 309, 311; Arland J. Hultgren, *Paul's Letter to the Romans: A Commentary* (Grand Rapids: Eerdmans, 2011), 467; Seyoon Kim, *Christ and Caesar: The Gospel and the Roman Empire in the Writings of Paul and Luke* (Grand Rapids: Eerdmans, 2008), 37–38; N. T. Wright, "The Letter to the Romans: Introduction, Commentary, and Reflections," in *The New Interpreter's Bible*, vol. 10 (Nashville: Abingdon, 2002), 717, 718; N. T. Wright, *Paul: In Fresh Perspective* (Minneapolis: Fortress, 2005), 65–66; Robert Jewett, *Romans: A Commentary* (Minneapolis: Fortress, 2007), 789; Thomas R. Schreiner, *Romans* (Grand Rapids: Baker, 1998), 682; Leander E. Keck, *Romans* (Nashville: Abingdon, 2005), 314; Thomas H. Tobin, SJ, *Paul's Rhetoric in Its Contexts: The Argument of Romans* (Peabody, MA: Hendrickson, 2004), 397; Christopher Bryan, *Render to Caesar: Jesus, the Early Church, and the Roman Superpower* (Oxford: Oxford University Press, 2005), 79, ch. 5; and Bockmuehl, *Jewish Law*, 136–37.

12. For arguments in favor of this view, see, e.g., W. Randall Garr, *In His Own Image and Likeness: Humanity, Divinity, and Monotheism* (Leiden: Brill, 2003), 163; Stephen D. Mason, "Another Flood? Genesis 9 and Isaiah's Broken Eternal Covenant," *Journal for the Study of the Old Testament* 32, no. 3 (2007): 192–93; and David VanDrunen, *Divine Covenants and Moral Order: A Biblical Theology of Natural Law* (Grand Rapids: Eerdmans, 2014), 116–17.

for evil or to take vengeance (12:17, 19) but instead to "leave it to the wrath of God, for it is written, 'Vengeance is mine, I will repay, says the Lord'" (12:19). But then Paul explains that civil magistrates are "instituted" (13:1) and "appointed" (13:2) by God; they are God's "servant[s]" (13:4) and "ministers" (13:6). They avenge and carry out God's wrath on wrongdoers (13:4), the very task that belongs to God (12:19). Thus both Paul and the Noahic covenant describe God delegating judicial authority to his human servants.

A second point of similarity between Romans 13 and the Noahic covenant is that coercion undergirds judicial authority. The Noahic covenant speaks of judicial authority as exercised through *bloodshed*: "whoever sheds the blood of man, by man shall his blood be shed" (Gen 9:6). Paul writes that civil officials "bear the *sword*" (Rom 13:4, emphasis added). As discussed next, these texts authorize coercion only in pursuit of justice, yet both texts highlight the threat of violence that lies behind legitimate judicial authority.

A third point of similarity is that both Romans 13 and the Noahic covenant portray judicial authority as delegated from God for the purpose of enforcing retributive justice. The Noahic covenant states, "Whoever sheds the blood of man, by man shall his blood be shed." As noted in chapter 3 (and explored in detail in chapter 9), this expresses the *lex talionis*, the law of retribution, and communicates the principle of proportionality: a wrong merits a proportionate penalty in response. Likewise, Romans 13 speaks of civil magistrates' duties in retributive terms.[13] Paul's terminology in 13:4 alludes back to what he says at the end of Romans 12. While Christians should "repay no one *evil* for *evil*" (12:17, emphasis added), should not "*avenge*" themselves, and should "leave it to the *wrath* of God" (12:19, emphasis added), Romans 13:4 says the magistrate "is the servant of God, an *avenger* who carries out God's *wrath*" on the one who does *evil* (emphasis added). Civil authorities, according to Paul, are responsible for doing what Christians (in their private capacity as Christians) are not to do.[14] Entrusted by God with the task withheld from private Christians, magistrates must administer retributive justice. The nature of the justice God commissions human beings to pursue is therefore the same in Genesis 9:6 and Romans 13:4.

Fourth, both the Noahic covenant and Romans 13:1–7 describe God as

---

13. Nicholas Wolterstorff argues that this is not the case. See *The Mighty and the Almighty: An Essay in Political Theology* (Cambridge: Cambridge University Press, 2012), 85–87; and *Justice in Love* (Grand Rapids: Eerdmans, 2011), 198. I interact with his argument in more detail in chapter 9.

14. Among New Testament scholars who see a similar connection between Romans 13:3–4 and these earlier verses in Romans 12, see Dunn, *Romans 9–16*, 759; Moo, *Romans*, 792, 802; Wright, "The Letter to the Romans," 717–18; and Jewett, *Romans*, 796.

delegating coercion-backed authority to pursue *protectionist* ends, but not *perfectionist* ends. Here I borrow terms sometimes employed in political theory to discuss the purpose of civil law and government. Perfectionism claims that the "task of the state is to promote virtue in the citizens," while protectionism holds that the "task of the state is to protect citizens from being wronged."[15] The point here is an extension of the previous one. The responsibility to pursue retributive justice presented in Genesis 9 and Romans 13 is protectionist in nature.[16] The use of coercion to promote the virtue of citizen or community is absent in both texts.[17] Whether either text should be read as prohibiting governments from pursuing perfectionist functions altogether is another question, which I consider in chapter 11.

A fifth point of substantive similarity is that both Genesis 8:21–9:17 and Romans 13:1–7 embed their instructions about judicial authority in the context of a general, sparse moral structure. Neither text is morally vacuous or relativistic, but each is morally modest. Chapters 2 and 3 discussed this idea in the Noahic covenant. To see it in Romans 13:1–7, it is helpful to compare it with the texts that come before and after. The whole of Romans 12 unfolds against the background of Paul's exhortation for Christians to present their bodies as living sacrifices to God and to be transformed by the renewal of their minds (12:1–2). He proceeds to describe the love, humility, joy, patience, and generosity that should mark the Christian community (12:3–21). Paul resumes this line of thought in 13:8–14, urging believers to show the love that fulfills the law and to pursue a life that abhors all "works of darkness," in view of the immanent coming of Christ. Romans 12:1–21 and 13:8–14 present a rich, christocentric morality. In comparison, what comes in between is strikingly modest. In 13:1–7, Paul uses only generic moral terms: "good" (*agathos*) and "bad" (*kakos*). Civil magistrates are to punish those who do bad works and praise those who do good works. Christians, therefore, should "do what is good," submit to their magistrates, honor them, and pay taxes.

---

15. Wolterstorff, *The Mighty and the Almighty*, 101.

16. Wolterstorff offers an explicitly protectionist interpretation of Romans 13:1–7 in *The Mighty and the Almighty*, ch. 8. N. T. Wright does not use the language of "protectionism," but he seems to make a similar point in remarking that the "appointed task" of the "temporary subordinates" is "to bring at least a measure of God's order and justice to the world." See "The Letter to the Romans," 719.

17. Perhaps the only statement in 13:1–7 that sounds remotely perfectionist is Paul's comment that the one who does what is good will receive praise from the magistrate. This comment is enigmatic. The most thoroughly documented study of it I know argues that Paul referred to the honor that Roman officials rendered to wealthy public benefactors, not to the promotion of community virtue. See Bruce W. Winter, "The Public Honouring of Christian Benefactors: Romans 13.3–4 and 1 Peter 2.14–15," *Journal for the Study of the New Testament* 34 (1988): 87–103.

Many commentators recognize the striking difference in moral depth between 13:1–7 and what precedes and follows, although they often differ about the implications for Christian ethics.[18] At present I simply observe again the close similarity between Romans 13:1–7 and the Noahic covenant.

The sixth similarity is the universal—rather than particular or parochial—flavor of both texts. Chapters 2 and 3 explored this aspect of the Noahic covenant. In Romans 13:1–7, Paul too has the whole human race in view. Although Paul wrote this letter to the church at Rome, and thus addressed Christian believers particularly, he makes clear that duties toward civil authorities apply to all people. He begins by exhorting "every person" to be subject to the governing magistrates (13:1). In the latter part of 13:1, Paul also says that there is "no authority" that is not ordained by God. Put positively, God ordains every existing authority. Paul motivates obedience by appealing both to the widespread fear people experience when they run afoul of sword-bearing magistrates (13:4) and to the pangs of conscience (13:5), another universal human attribute, which Paul mentioned earlier in Romans when showing that Jew and gentile alike are accountable to God (2:14–15). Thus both the Noahic covenant and Romans 13:1–7 describe God's delegation of judicial authority as matters relevant to the whole of humanity.

The seventh and final similarity is that both the Noahic covenant and Romans 13:1–7 lack a redemptive element. Both biblical texts present God as creator and sustainer, but not as redeemer. We considered this aspect of the Noahic covenant in chapter 2. And while Romans as a whole contains one

---

18. From a Mennonite perspective, John Howard Yoder recognizes the clear differences between Romans 13:1–7 and what precedes and follows, concluding, "The function exercised by government is not the function to be exercised by Christians." See *The Politics of Jesus* (Grand Rapids: Eerdmans, 1972), 199. For Yoder, this means that Christians should not participate in these government functions. Other writers, sympathetic to a liberationist perspective, also see 13:1–7 as very different from the surrounding material, and believe Paul's conservative posture here exposes contradictions in his thought. See, e.g., Neil Elliott, "Romans 13:1–7 in the Context of Imperial Propaganda," in *Paul and Empire: Religion and Power in Roman Imperial Society*, ed. Richard A. Horsley (Harrisburg, PA: Trinity, 1997), 186, 203; Neil Elliott, "The Letter to the Romans," in *A Postcolonial Commentary on the New Testament Writings*, ed. Fernando F. Segovia and R. S. Sugirtharajah (New York: T&T Clark, 2009), 210; and Jewett, *Romans*, 803. A different approach, to which I am sympathetic, defends a "minimalist reading of Romans 13," but not in a way that makes Paul's thought internally inconsistent or makes the Bible politically irrelevant; see Gerrit de Kruijf, "The Function of Romans 13 in Christian Ethics," in *A Royal Priesthood? The Use of the Bible Ethically and Politically: A Dialogue with Oliver O'Donovan*, eds. Craig Bartholomew, Jonathan Chaplin, Robert Song, and Al Wolters (Grand Rapids: Zondervan, 2002), 233–35. Among other scholars commenting on the distinctiveness of the Romans 13:1–7 ethic in comparison with surrounding texts, see Robert H. Stein, "The Argument of Romans 13:1–7," *Novum Testamentum* 31, no. 4 (1989): 326; and Troels Engberg-Pedersen, "Paul's Stoicizing Politics in Romans 12–13: The Role of 13.1–10 in the Argument," *Journal for the Study of the New Testament* 29, no. 2 (2006): 163–72. Among scholars noting the lack of anything distinctively Christian in 13:1–7, see Keck, *Romans*, 324; and Dunn, *Romans 9–16*, 771.

of the most detailed discussions of salvation in Scripture, Romans 13:1–7 is like an island, without reference to Christ or any redemptive benefit in him. As many New Testament scholars comment, this text is theological rather than christological, practical rather than soteriological.[19] It deals with how God has ordered this present creation but does not describe or anticipate a coming new creation. This corresponds to the previous point. If God's work of delegating authority to do justice is for the human race universally rather than for the Christian community particularly, it makes sense that Paul roots this work in God's identity as universal creator and sustainer.

These seven points of similarity between Genesis 8:21–9:17 and Romans 13:1–7 are not incidental or vacuous but theologically and morally substantive. I close this section by making one more claim: Genesis 8:21–9:17 appears to have more extensive similarity to Romans 13:1–7 than does any other Old Testament text. Such a claim is difficult to prove, but to test its accuracy I propose a brief comparison with the Old Testament texts that are its most likely competitors. As mentioned above, commentators on Romans often note that Paul's teaching about civil government picks up on themes common to an established Jewish tradition. These commentators cite numerous Old Testament texts in which they see this tradition grounded. Most of the repeatedly cited texts teach that God raises up political rulers for his own purposes (e.g., Isa 42:2–4; 45:1–7; Dan 2:21, 37–38, 5:21). This is an important claim, to be sure, but gets at only one of the many things Romans 13:1–7 teaches. Jeremiah 27:5–17 makes the same point, and adds that the people (in this case, exiled Jews) ought to submit to the ruler God placed over them. Daniel 4:17, 25, 31 also affirms that God raises up political rulers for his own purposes but adds that these rulers ought to do justice. Commentators sometimes also cite Proverbs 8:15–16, which highlights rulers' task of doing justice, communicates the theme of universality, and lies embedded in a creation-order rather than redemptive context.

I agree that these Old Testament texts provide important background for understanding Paul's claims in Romans 13:1–7. But this brief survey suggests that my conclusion is sound: the Noahic covenant has a far more extensive range of similarities to Romans 13 than does any other Old Testament text. It is thus improbable that Paul, a rabbi with elite training in

19. E.g., see Dunn, "Romans 13.1–7," 65; Dunn, *Romans 9–16*, 771; Stein, "The Argument of Romans 13:1–7," 329–30; Hultgren, *Romans*, 467; Wright, "The Letter to the Romans," 717, 721; Keck, *Romans*, 319, 321; Tobin, *Paul's Rhetoric*, 396; and Stanley E. Porter, "Romans 13:1–7 as Pauline Political Rhetoric," *Filologia Neotestamentaria* 3, no. 6 (1990): 131–32.

the Hebrew Scriptures, was oblivious to the Noahic covenant when thinking about civil magistrates. And this conclusion supports the larger point of the section: it is probable that Paul had Genesis 8:21–9:17 in mind when writing Romans 13:1–7.

Of course, this conclusion is impossible to prove with certainty, so I have spoken merely of what is probable and likely. But what if Paul did not in fact have the Noahic covenant in mind when writing to Rome? Even so, I argue briefly now, Genesis 8:21–9:17 is still important background for interpreting Romans 13:1–7.

In this text, Paul writes to the Roman church while signaling in many ways that he presents general truths of universal applicability, as argued above. He begins by exhorting "every" person to be subject to civil officials, since there is "no authority" except those God has instituted (13:1). He goes on to describe the exercise of authority and submission to it in generic moral categories of "good" and "bad" (13:3–4) and to motivate his readers through appeal not to any parochial knowledge but to the universal human "conscience" (13:5; cf. 2:14–15).

By speaking in these universal and general terms, Paul communicates that he means to teach nothing new or hidden. He wants his readers to live according to what they already know, or at least should know. Evidently, he feels no need to elaborate the specific content of the "good" and "bad" in political life. The basic idea that it is right to submit to civil magistrates, who punish evildoers and praise the good, would have been familiar to Paul's gentile readers living in Roman culture,[20] as it would have been to his Jewish readers who found this and other aspects of Romans 13:1–7 in the Old Testament. Many Christians in the Roman church probably wondered whether the new and radical message about Jesus Christ and his coming kingdom had rendered the existing authority structures irrelevant. It is completely understandable that they might have suspected this, but Paul explains that this is not the case, as he did in epistles to other churches too (e.g., see 1 Cor 7). Paul indicates that they should not expect innovative political obligations to arise from the Christian gospel. They need to stay the course and not neglect their ongoing responsibilities, which they know through the testimony of conscience. Paul, in effect, instructs them not to find a secret political theory embedded in Romans but to look to those ordinary and recognizable sources readily available to them.

---

20. See, e.g., the discussion in Engberg-Pedersen, "Paul's Stoicizing Politics," 167–69.

These instructions imply that Paul thought God had structured the world in an orderly way and established a natural moral law accessible to all people and known by them. That Paul did believe these things is evident from many things he wrote, not least of which is an extended discussion earlier in Romans (1:18–2:16).[21] From where did Paul derive such convictions? Surely the theology of creation and providence that he learned from the Old Testament was as important as anything. And where in the Old Testament would he have imbibed this theology? Genesis 8:21–9:17 is one of the most important, if not *the* most important, source for the idea that God has structured the world in an orderly way and established a natural moral law.[22] The next chapter will consider this topic in more detail.

Thus, even if Paul was not thinking explicitly about the Noahic covenant when writing Romans 13:1–7, the Noahic covenant is still important background, for Genesis 8:21–9:17 would have shaped the theological ideas that enabled Paul to say what he did. It is likely that Paul was thinking about the Noahic covenant when writing Romans 13:1–7, but, even if he was not, Paul's words ought to be read in light of this Old Testament covenant.

This extended study of Romans 13:1–7 indicates that the Noahic covenant is neglected but crucial background for interpreting this text. Paul does not specifically say how God instituted and appointed the existing civil magistrates, but the Noahic background makes perfect sense of what he does say. Thus Romans 13:1–7 confirms my thesis that political communities existing after Christ's coming and exaltation originated in the Noahic covenant, as did those political communities that existed before, with the exception of Israel under the Mosaic law. Contrary to the views of some political theologians, one of whom we consider below, our findings thus far indicate that the climactic events surrounding Christ's incarnation, death, and exaltation did not change the nature and purpose of political communities or modify the legitimacy and authority of their civil governments.

CHRIST, RULER OF THE NATIONS

The evidence thus far gives good reason to believe that political communities and civil governments have the same Noahic origins, nature, and purpose after Christ's coming as they did before. But one aspect of New Testament

---

21. See VanDrunen, *Divine Covenants*, ch. 5.
22. For discussion of natural law in the Noahic covenant, see VanDrunen, *Divine Covenants*, ch. 2.

teaching raises questions about this conclusion. Several texts speak of Christ's death, resurrection, and ascension as a conquest of the powers of this world or declare that God now rules all things through this incarnate and exalted Son. This indicates that something about God's rule over the world changed in the first century. The first part of this section considers how to integrate this part of Christian doctrine with my previous exegetical study that highlighted the continuity throughout biblical history in how God oversees political community. After this, I examine two implications of my proposed integration.

The Incarnate Son Ruling through the Noahic Covenant

The conclusion to which the following discussion points is this: after Christ's death and exaltation, God continues to ordain and govern common political communities by means of the Noahic covenant, but he does so now through his incarnate and glorified Son, which he did not do before Christ's coming. Although affirming only one of these ideas would be simpler, this more nuanced conclusion better captures the full picture of New Testament doctrine.

The New Testament calls Christ's death and resurrection a triumph over Satan and the power of death. "Through death," the Epistle to the Hebrews states, Christ destroyed "the one who has the power of death, that is the devil" (2:14). Other texts speak more generally of a victory over the ruling powers. For example, Colossians 2:15 states that Christ "disarmed the rulers and authorities and put them to open shame, triumphing over them in him" (Col 2:15). Perhaps these rulers and authorities are angelic, or both angelic and human. Yet other texts make clear that the exalted Christ now exercises authority over all things. Perhaps most familiar is the opening of the Great Commission: "All authority in heaven and on earth has been given to me" (Matt 28:18). More expansively, Paul comments that when God raised Jesus from the dead, he "seated him at his right hand in the heavenly places, far above all rule and authority and power and dominion, and above every name that is named" (Eph 1:20–21). Hence, Christ is "the head of all rule and authority" (Col 2:10) and "the ruler of kings on earth" (Rev 1:5).

These declarations are striking in comparison with the New Testament texts that concretely describe the appointment, purpose, and functions of civil authority. As considered above, Romans 13:1–7 treats these topics theologically rather than christologically, with reference to creation and not redemption, and in terms of the Noahic covenant rather than new covenant. Conversely, when the biblical writers discuss Christ's rule of the nations, they do not reflect on the origins or functions of civil authority. Taken together, these various texts indicate that the incarnate and exalted Christ rules the political communities of the world and their rulers. But, apparently, a person does not need to comprehend *this* doctrine in order to understand how God has appointed these rulers or the basic things he expects them to do.

If we are not to jettison one aspect of New Testament teaching for the other, therefore, it seems necessary to say that the covenant by which God rules the nations has not changed, but his appointed agent for ruling the nations has. God ruled common political communities by means of the Noahic covenant before Christ's coming, and after Christ's coming God rules common political communities by means of the same Noahic covenant. But he does so through his incarnate and exalted Son. A glorified human being is now God's agent for sustaining the world and its institutions.

Putting things in these terms is different from some other ways of explaining them that may be attractive if we take only one side of New Testament doctrine into account. On the one hand, the idea that God rules his church through the Son as glorified God-Man and rules political communities through the Son as creator and sustainer, as taught by many early Reformed theologians, does not state matters quite correctly. On the other hand, the recent proposal of Oliver O'Donovan, who argues that God has instituted a new kind of civil authority through Christ's death and resurrection, moves far too much in the other direction.

The first of these reflects a version of the Two Kingdoms doctrine, as understood by many Reformed Orthodox theologians. Francis Turretin, for example, when distinguishing Christ's universal kingship over all creatures from his mediatorial kingship over his church, says that Christ possesses the former as "God" and "Logos" (with the Father and Spirit) and the latter "as God-Man."[23] He grounds political authority in the former and ecclesiastical authority in the latter.[24] As indicated in chapter 1, I embrace the Reformed Two Kingdoms tradition and find Turretin's expression of it very helpful, on the whole. The political theology of this book stands in this tradition. But if indeed the *resurrected and ascended* Christ rules all things now, it suggests some modification in the way Turretin expresses matters. Insofar as he says that political authority has its "origin" in Christ as eternal God and Logos, rather than in Christ as God-Man, he speaks accurately. Political authority in

23. Francis Turretin, *Institutes of Elenctic Theology*, 3 vols., trans. George Musgrave Giger, ed. James T. Dennison Jr. (Phillipsburg, NJ: P&R, 1992–97), 2:486.
24. Turretin, *Institutes*, 3:278–80.

the present, post-flood world originated in the Noahic covenant, and the Son did not establish this covenant as God incarnate. But insofar as we consider political authority after Christ's death and resurrection, and hence political authority today, it seems proper to say that the Son continues to oversee it not simply as God but as the God-Man. Neither the nature of the political authority itself nor its covenantal grounding has changed, but God's identity in ruling it has.

Oliver O'Donovan's proposal regarding the nature of political authority also differs from the way I have put it, but in the other direction: while Turretin's scheme does not account for the incarnate and exalted Christ's present rule over political communities, O'Donovan's scheme does not recognize the historical continuity of divine rule over political communities through the Noahic covenant.[25] O'Donovan argues that the exaltation of Christ has effected a fundamental change in the nature of political authority. He points to the idea that civil government's authority now resides in the practice of *judgment*. Rulers of old exercised judgment, but it was not their essential role. Upon God's triumph in Christ, the authority of rulers has been "stripped down" and "reduced" to the exercise of judgment.[26] Hence, there must be a "change" in the ruling power's "self-understanding and its manner of government to suit the dawning age of Christ's own rule." It now must be a "humble state." It is "responsible" and exists "provisionally." It "gives judgment *under law*, never as its own law."[27] According to O'Donovan, Christendom also becomes possible following Christ's exaltation. This is "the idea of a professedly Christian secular political order" or a "Christian state." It confesses "Christ's victory," although it does not achieve or maintain this confession by coercion but as a free response to the church's mission. O'Donovan hence emphasizes that a Christian state is never permanent but "may be disclosed from time to time as a sign of the Kingdom, disappearing at one moment to return at another."[28]

I will critique the idea of a confessional state in chapter 7. Here I simply

---

25. In light of where each differs from my paradigm, however, it may seem ironic or even incoherent that Turretin supports the coercive enforcement of civil laws against blasphemy and heresy while O'Donovan stresses that Christendom (the Christian state) is not achieved or maintained by coercion. This is a reminder of the complexity of these political-theological issues and of how historical context can influence interpretation.

26. See Oliver O'Donovan, *The Desire of the Nations: Rediscovering the Roots of Political Theology* (Cambridge: Cambridge University Press, 1996), 146–51; and Oliver O'Donovan, *The Ways of Judgment* (Grand Rapids: Eerdmans, 2005), 3–5.

27. See O'Donovan, *The Desire of the Nations*, 219, 231, 233 (emphasis original).

28. O'Donovan, *The Desire of the Nations*, 195, 219, 224.

wish to challenge O'Donovan's conception that the nature and authority of civil government changed when Christ was glorified. Most of the characteristics O'Donovan attributes to the contemporary state are proper, it seems to me, and consistent with the claims of the present volume. But these characteristics are hardly unique to civil governments *after* Christ's resurrection. O'Donovan says the state is now "responsible," but political authority arising out of the Noahic covenant was also responsible because it was divinely delegated (Gen 9:5). O'Donovan claims that the state's essential work is to exercise judgment, but this is precisely what the Noahic covenant authorized (Gen 9:6). O'Donovan says that the state should be humble, but hubris was one of the prime charges the Old Testament prophets brought against gentile political communities of their day—as well they should have, if these communities were in covenant with the Almighty. And O'Donovan asserts that the state exists provisionally, but political communities have always been provisional, rooted as they are in a covenant established only "while the earth remains" (Gen 8:22). In short, O'Donovan is correct to recognize these important limitations upon the state and its authority, but God put these limitations in place long ago. Christ has conquered the evil powers of this age, but the scope of legitimate political authority has not changed.

THE REDEMPTION OF POLITICAL COMMUNITY AND CIVIL GOVERNMENT?

I have been arguing that after Christ's exaltation God continues to ordain political communities and their civil governments by means of the Noahic covenant but that he now does so through his incarnate and glorified Son. I now consider two initial implications of this conclusion. The first derives especially from the Noahic origin of political communities, while the second derives especially from Christ's present rule of them.

The first implication is that popular claims about the redemption of political communities and their governments ought to be rejected. Chapter 1 discussed several theologians, from various traditions, who argue that legitimate political institutions participate in the redemptive work of Christ and are part of the realization of his eschatological kingdom. I offered their work as examples of political theology that fails to recognize sufficiently the provisionality of civil government. But I did not explain precisely what is wrong with viewing political community through a redemptive and eschatological lens. Here I seek to do so through three interrelated claims.

First, Christ does not save or redeem political institutions. This claim is not meant to deny that salvation is holistic in some very important sense. Scripture sometimes speaks of redemption in universal terms: for example, God through Christ was pleased "to reconcile to himself all things, whether on earth or in heaven" (Col 1:19–20). Scripture also portrays the new creation as the consummation of the original creation. But it is a different thing to claim that each *particular* part of this first creation will be redeemed. In fact, this cannot be what Scripture means when it speaks of redemption in universal terms. New Testament and traditional Christian teaching about hell surely offers the clearest proof of this.[29] I will not defend the traditional doctrine here, although I note that the New Testament speaks about hell more frequently than it speaks about redemption in universal terms. In any case, those who affirm the traditional doctrine (and anyone else who does not believe every individual creature will enjoy everlasting new-creation blessing) should conclude that the first creation *as a whole* is redeemed and consummated, but not every particular thing within it.

Are political institutions among the particular things Christ redeems? Scripture never speaks in this way. The biblical writers ordinarily speak of *individual people* being saved. And the only institution to which Scripture applies redemptive language is *the church*. Christ "loved the church and gave himself up for her" that she might be "holy and without blemish" (Eph 5:25–28). "The church of God" was "obtained with his own blood" (Acts 20:28). Even this language must be somewhat metaphorical, since the church, unlike individual people, did not exist in a fallen state apart from Christ's work but was brought into existence through it (Matt 16:18). The idea that Christ redeemed his church must mean that he established the church as an institution that gathers and nourishes redeemed people. As for political institutions, Scripture never says that Christ gave himself up for them and purchased them with his blood. This is consistent with the arguments developed so far. God has established political institutions and their authority

---

29. I recognize that a number of theologians have disputed the traditional doctrine of hell in recent years, and the doctrine is sobering to contemplate even for those who affirm it. I also recognize that many who are most attracted to a redemptive-transformationist view of political institutions are also attracted to a universal-salvation view that revises the notion of hell. E.g., H. Richard Niebuhr saw universalism as part of a consistent expression of his "Christ the Transformer of Culture" paradigm; see *Christ and Culture* (New York: Harper, 1951), ch. 6. I do not know the view of David Schindler (my Roman Catholic interlocutor at the end of chapter 1), but his work is deeply indebted to Hans Urs von Balthasar, a notable revisionist on the doctrine of hell; see Schindler's reliance on Balthasar in many places throughout *Heart of the World, Center of the Church:* Communio *Ecclesiology, Liberalism, and Liberation* (Grand Rapids: Eerdmans, 1996).

structures through the Noahic covenant, and thereby has appointed them to promote ends that are common, preservative, and temporal in nature. The roots of political authority do not grow in the soil of the Abrahamic, Mosaic, Davidic, or new covenants. Political authority is thus not redeemed, and does not need to be redeemed to be legitimate.

Second, Christians are not to seek the transformation of political institutions according to the moral pattern of Christ's kingdom.[30] The Noahic covenant, *not* the kingdom of Christ, provides the normative vision to guide Christians' political activity. The ethic of Christ's kingdom is the *fulfillment* of the ethic of the Noahic covenant, and thus there is substantive continuity between them, as chapters 8–10 will discuss. But political institutions arise out of the Noahic covenant, not the Abrahamic, Mosaic, Davidic, or new covenants, through which God brings the kingdom of Christ, with its promises of forgiveness, life, and new creation.

The church is the institutional manifestation of Christ's kingdom now (Matt 16:18–19). Thus, when Paul tells the church how to conduct its affairs, he appeals to the moral pattern of this kingdom: "the kingdom of God is not a matter of eating and drinking but of righteousness and peace and joy in the Holy Spirit" (Rom 14:17; cf. 1 Cor 6:9–10). Scripture never makes such an appeal when speaking about common political community. Furthermore, the crux of what political institutions do, as authorized in the Noahic covenant and confirmed in Romans 13 and 1 Peter 2, is to promote justice by punishing wrongdoers, a task entirely foreign to the kingdom of Christ. Christ's mission does not advance by earthly weapons (2 Cor 10:3–4). The ethic of Christ's kingdom requires turning the other cheek to wrongdoers rather than seeking retributive punishment (Matt 5:38–42), and the church manifests Christ's kingdom by seeking reconciliation, restoration, and forgiveness for the sinner rather than imposing the claims of retributive justice (e.g., Matt 18:15–20; 1 Cor 5:4–5; Gal 6:1–2).

To impose the pattern of Christ's kingdom upon political institutions is to impose the pattern of a kingdom to which these institutions do not belong. These institutions cannot coherently manifest the peaceable vision of Christ's kingdom while fulfilling their responsibility to enforce coercion-backed justice.

Third, political institutions do not find their perfect expression in the new creation. When the New Testament speaks about the eschatological

---

30. As advocated by Skillen, *The Good of Politics*, 122–23, for example.

consummation, it points to the *church* as coming to perfect expression. Paul writes that Christ gave himself for his church as a husband loves his wife, that she might be presented to him "in splendor, without spot or wrinkle or any such thing, that she might be holy and without blemish" (Eph 5:25–27). Accordingly, Revelation characterizes the new creation as a wedding banquet, the marriage of the Lamb to his radiant Bride (19:7–9; 21:1–2, 9–10). But Scripture does not assign this privilege to any other institution. The origin, nature, and purpose of common political communities lie in the provisional Noahic covenant, and thus they serve to advance the preservation of the present world for a time. When Christ returns and reveals the new Jerusalem, the services of Noahic political institutions will no longer be needed—thanks be to God.

One might object that the new Jerusalem portrayed at the end of Revelation is a *city*, "the embodiment of a just political community," the fulfillment rather than the termination of government.[31] It is true that Revelation 21:2 describes the new creation as a *polis*, a "city" (although this must be metaphorical, since the same verse also calls it a "bride"), and its inhabitants will obviously live in community. The New Jerusalem will thus be a "political community" of a certain sort. But is it the perfect expression of the common political communities that presently exist? Noahic political communities are places where familial, enterprise, and judicial institutions interrelate. The core responsibility of these communities' governments is to enforce retributive justice (Rom 13:3–4; 1 Pet 2:14). The New Jerusalem will be a city of a very different sort, a place where there is no more marriage and procreation (Luke 20:34–35) and no more evildoers to punish (Rev 22:14–15). The work of civil government may well anticipate the *final judgment*—when God will wield the sword with the most pure and complete justice—but it does not anticipate the serene and sinless life of the heavenly city.

The new creation is a *polis*, but Scripture portrays it as the perfect expression of a different kind of commonwealth: the church. The church is an institution with authority structures, built upon the apostles and prophets and governed now by its overseers or elders (e.g., Eph 2:19–20; 4:11–12; 1 Tim 3:1–7; Tit 1:5–9). The church is a kingdom of righteousness, peace, and joy in the Holy Spirit (Rom 14:17), and it thus anticipates the heavenly reign of God. Here there is no need for a sword to bring justice, since the word of Christ declares believers fully justified before God's throne (e.g., Rom 3:21–5:21).

---

31. See Skillen, *The Good of Politics*, 36–37.

Thus it seems best to say that the new Jerusalem will be the perfection of an earthly institution, even of a "political" community of sorts: the humble assembly of the saints, not the Noahic institutions of this present age.

Christ, Defender of His Church

We have just reflected on one implication of the doctrine that God rules present political communities through his incarnate and exalted Son by means of the Noahic covenant. Now we consider a second: due to the exalted Christ's rule of these communities, he holds them especially accountable for their mistreatment of his new covenant community, the church.

The end of Ephesians 1 encapsulates this idea. After speaking of Christ's exaltation to God's right hand over all rule, authority, power, and dominion, Paul writes that God "put all things under his feet and gave him as head over all things to the church, which is his body, the fullness of him who fills all in all" (1:22–23). The exalted Christ carries out his rule over the nations under the Noahic covenant with a special view *to the church*.[32] This is presumably a specific manifestation of a general truth: God exercises his common providence with a particular eye for the well-being of his redeemed people. As Paul writes, "For those who love God all things work together for good, for those who are called according to his purpose" (Rom 8:28). These are not altogether new realities following Christ's ascension. The previous chapter considered how Old Testament prophetic oracles often condemned gentile nations for their unjust acts toward Israel. God cared about all injustice, but mistreatment of his old covenant people, "the apple of his eye" (Zech 2:8), piqued his interest. Common political communities were not holy communities and God never judged them for failing to act in this capacity, but they were not to set themselves up against God, his people, and their anointed ruler, lest they trigger God's wrath (e.g., Ps 2:1–5).

But Christ has now shed his blood and thereby established a new covenant (Luke 22:20), and he is building a new assembly of his people (Matt 16:18). Thus it is fitting that as the incarnate, crucified, and exalted Lord, he now rules the nations with particular concern for this church. These nations, like those before Christ's coming, are not holy communities and will not be

---

32. For helpful discussion of this text and its implications, see A. Craig Troxel, "The World Is Not Enough: The Priority of the Church in Christ's Cosmic Headship," in *Confident of Better Things: Essays Commemorating Seventy-Five Years of the Orthodox Presbyterian Church*, eds. John R. Muether and Danny E. Olinger (Willow Grove, PA: The Committee for the Historian of the Orthodox Presbyterian Church, 2011), 337–65.

judged for failing to act as though they were. But when their governments properly maintain justice, they provide protection for the church and enable Christians to live the peaceful and godly lives to which God calls them. The New Testament instructs Christians to pray for their civil authorities accordingly: "that we may lead a peaceful and quiet life, godly and dignified in every way" (1 Tim 2:2). When political communities and their governments mistreat the church instead, they can expect God's judgment—on the last day, at least. Accordingly, in Revelation, God does not judge the nations for failing to act as though they were the kingdom of Christ on earth, but for inflicting violence rather than punishing it, especially with respect to Christians. In "Babylon the great city" (18:21), Revelation proclaims, "was found the blood of prophets and of saints, and of all who have been slain on the earth" (18:24).

God rules contemporary political communities and their governments through his incarnate Son by means of the Noahic covenant. This entails that Christians should relinquish aspirations to transform these communities according to the pattern of Christ's kingdom. But it also gives Christians great hope in the midst of the injustice of the present age, especially when directed at them as followers of Christ. Their incarnate and exalted Lord will avenge their blood. For "God considers it just to repay with affliction those who afflict you, and to grant relief to you who are afflicted as well as to us, when the Lord Jesus is revealed from heaven" (2 Thess 1:6–7).

CONCLUSION

At the beginning of the previous chapter, I set out to establish, contrary to conventional wisdom, that the Noahic covenant ought to be foundational for Christian political theology. The basic case is now complete. The text of the Noahic covenant sets forth only a sparse set of requirements for the human race, but its implications are considerably more extensive. For human beings to carry out this covenant's modest ethic, they must form familial, enterprise, and judicial institutions, and for these institutions to function well, they must interrelate within political communities. In the Noahic covenant, therefore, God indirectly authorizes the formation of common political communities and their authority structures.

Scripture nowhere else describes God authorizing common political communities, either through a covenant or another divine decree. Rather, in both Old and New Testaments, Scripture recognizes and confirms the legitimacy of existing political communities and the authority of their governments to pursue justice. Instead of establishing political communities and their governments through special decrees, Scripture speaks about them as we would expect if their origins lie in the Noahic covenant. The Noahic covenant thus makes sense of what subsequent texts say (and do not say) about political community and civil government. These subsequent texts also clarify how God evaluates them under the Noahic covenant, and how we should too.

If this is true, the Noahic covenant must indeed be foundational for Christian political theology. Christians properly evaluate their political communities and authorities according to the normative pattern established by this covenant, not (for example) by the Mosaic law, the *shalom* of the Old Testament prophets, the Sermon on the Mount, or the vision of new creation. The Noahic covenant indicates what ends Christians should seek from their political communities and what expectations they rightly have of them. This fundamental commitment underlies the political theology and ethics developed in the rest of this volume.

CHAPTER 5

NATURAL LAW AND POLITICAL COMMUNITY

The previous chapters have argued that common political communities originated in the Noahic covenant, and thus these communities are bound by this
covenant's terms. If this argument is sound, it raises an important question:
How do common political communities know about their relationship to God
through the Noahic covenant? How do they know their responsibilities under
it? It is not sufficient simply to point to Genesis 8:21–9:17. This text is part of
the Old Testament, the sacred book of old-covenant Israel and now also of the
New Testament church. Most common political communities through history
have lived in ignorance of the Old Testament, and even those communities in
which Scripture is accessible cannot claim it as *their* sacred book.

God is just. He will not hold people accountable for what they cannot
know (see Rom 2:12). For my claims about political theology and the Noahic
covenant to work, therefore, common political communities must have some
way of knowing their obligations under this covenant apart from Genesis
8:21–9:17. Perhaps they do not know that there is something called the "Noahic
covenant," but they must know the basic terms of their relationship to God. Of
course, this is not a challenge unique to the present project. Every Christian
political theology has to explain how God holds all people responsible to himself, even though Scripture does not reach all people universally.

I propose a classical Christian answer: all human beings know their
moral responsibilities before God through the *natural law*. I argue, furthermore, that since God now sustains and governs the created order through

the Noahic covenant, God's communication of the natural law in the present world is a covenantal act. Because of this, the moral requirements of the Noahic covenant are not unfamiliar to human beings or political communities. Rather, they resonate with what human beings are by nature, as they live in the kind of world they do. The natural law, therefore, ensures the just accountability of common political communities under the Noahic covenant. This natural law is necessary even for people and political communities who have access to the Scriptures, in fact, because they need knowledge of the world and its moral structure if they are to carry out even the basic implications of the modest ethic stated in Genesis 9:1–7, as explored in chapter 3.

This chapter does *not* construct a natural law *theory* from scratch. That is, it does not provide a philosophical explanation or proof of how exactly we know particular moral obligations from nature. I am not sure natural-law obligations are the kinds of things that can be *proven*, at least on certain understandings of what constitutes "proof." But since the natural order testifies to God's existence and to humanity's obligations before God, Christians ought to explore and present this testimony as an exercise in faith seeking understanding. This chapter pursues such an exercise. But it makes no claim to build a comprehensive natural-law theory and to prove it to an unbelieving world. As far as natural law theory goes, I am generally content with Thomas Aquinas's understanding of natural law, as have been many eminent theologians of my own Reformed tradition.[1] But I believe there are several ways in which this tradition might be improved or enriched, as reflected in the pages below.[2]

In short, this chapter intends to offer some reflections on a large and controversial topic, in light of Scripture, Christian theology, and human experience. These reflections do not seek to address every issue related to natural law but rather a few issues necessary to support the broader political theology of this book. This lays foundation for part 2, which considers a series of perennially important topics in political and legal theory in light of

---

1. E.g., see Girolamo Zanchi, *On the Law in General*, trans. Jeffrey J. Veenstra (Grand Rapids: Christian's Library Press, 2012); Franciscus Junius, *The Mosaic Polity*, trans. Todd M. Rester, ed. Andrew M. McGinnis (Grand Rapids: Christian's Library Press, 2015); and Francis Turretin, *Institutes of Elenctic Theology*, 3 vols., trans. George Musgrave Giger, ed. James T. Dennison Jr. (Phillipsburg, NJ: P&R, 1992–1997), 2:2–7.

2. For other critically appreciative reflection on Aquinas's thought on related issues, see David VanDrunen, "Natural Knowledge of God," in *Oxford Handbook of the Reception of Aquinas*, ed. Matthew Levering and Marcus Plested (Oxford: Oxford University Press, forthcoming); and David VanDrunen, *Divine Covenants and Moral Order: A Biblical Theology of Natural Law* (Grand Rapids: Eerdmans, 2014), 22–36.

the Noahic covenant. As I understand it, these later discussions will be, in part, an exercise in natural-law reasoning.

This chapter begins with a brief explanation of why Christians need some conception of natural law to make sense of what Scripture says on numerous occasions. I will then defend the idea that God's present communication of the natural law is covenantal and that this natural law is a *moral order* rather than a code or a collection of discrete rules. Finally, I discuss why *wisdom* is the proper human faculty for perceiving the natural law, and thus why learning the natural law is essentially a process of maturing in wisdom.

THE PERVASIVE PRESENCE OF NATURAL LAW IN SCRIPTURE

The claim of this section is simple: those who wish to take Scripture seriously and to make sense of it must have *some* conception of natural law. Although it does not use the term "natural law," Scripture presupposes that there is a natural law, and therefore biblical teaching is coherent only if natural law exists. There are various ways to describe exactly what natural law is, how people know it, and what role it plays in human life, and Scripture has something to say about such things. But apart from these details, which will probably always remain matters of debate, Christians at least ought to affirm that there is a natural law. Otherwise, their Scriptures become incoherent. By "natural law," I refer to the idea that God makes known the basic substance of his moral law through the created order itself. Human beings therefore know this law simply by virtue of being human, even apart from access to Scripture or other forms of special revelation.[3] They know it through their natural capacities as they live in this world.[4]

Where, then, do we see evidence that Scripture affirms the reality of natural law? Perhaps the most basic evidence is that biblical texts often describe people who are not members of Israel or the church as though they have genuine moral knowledge. Such people had no exposure to Israel's or the church's sacred texts and prophetic revelation. They just knew that certain things were right and others wrong. We observed this with Abimelech of Gerar in chapter 3. Although Abraham was God's covenant partner, Abimelech stood on the

---

3. As noted in chapter 2, natural revelation refers to God's revelation through the natural order, while special revelation refers to God's revelation through Christ, the prophets, and Scripture.

4. For more detailed discussion of almost all the texts considered below and interaction with many other scholars about them, see VanDrunen, *Divine Covenants*.

higher moral ground, chiding Abraham for doing to him "things that ought not to be done" and provoking Abraham to admit that Gerar had a certain "fear of God" (Gen 20:9, 11; cf. 34:7). Later, the Egyptians who served as midwives to Hebrew women practiced civil disobedience against Pharaoh and refused to kill the newborn baby boys.[5] They too "feared God" (Exod 1:15–21). Even the Mosaic law testifies to the moral understanding of gentile peoples. The "Covenant Code" of Exodus 20:23–23:19, for example, has many similarities to other legal material of the ancient Near East, most notably the Babylonian Laws of Hammurabi. This is hardly comprehensible unless these other legal codes were of value and got many things right. The exhortation and questions of Deuteronomy 4:1–8 also indicate that gentile nations had moral insight, but from a different direction. These verses indicate that if Israel would obey God's law and thus receive his blessing, the surrounding nations would recognize the Israelites' wisdom and righteousness. Elsewhere, the Old Testament acknowledges the wisdom of gentile peoples (e.g., 1 Kgs 4:30; Prov 8:15–16; Jer 49:7; Ezek 14:14, 20; 28:3; Obad 8; and probably Prov 30:1–9; 31:1–9).

The New Testament also speaks of the moral understanding of people who are outside the church and lack exposure to biblical revelation. The Pauline epistles provide a number of examples. Paul exhorts believers to conduct themselves in ways that meet the approval of non-Christians (e.g., Col 4:5; 1 Thess 4:12; 1 Tim 3:7). While these are obviously not exhortations simply to conform to pagan practices, they do presume that non-Christians can make valid judgments about moral behavior. Paul also calls Christians to honor patterns of authority in their households that reflect longstanding Greco-Roman ethical traditions (Eph 5:22–6:9; Col 3:18–4:1), and he urges them to adhere to contemporary notions of public decorum and social propriety (Phil 4:8). While Paul would not have wanted Christians to do this uncritically, the fact that he can offer such instructions at all indicates that there was moral value in these non-Christians' practices and habits. Such texts, with their Old Testament counterparts, are only coherent if they presuppose the existence of some natural knowledge of right and wrong.

This conclusion is bolstered by the fact that Scripture often speaks about God holding people outside Israel and the church responsible for their misdeeds. This means that the moral insights such people exhibited, as described in the previous paragraphs, were not the luck of a blind squirrel finding a

---

5. For a persuasive argument that "Hebrew midwives" refers to Egyptians who were midwives to Hebrews, see David Novak, *Natural Law in Judaism* (Cambridge: Cambridge University Press, 1998), 49–50.

nut. God designed them to gain such insight and put it into practice, and he called them to account when they failed to do so.

This is illustrated throughout the Old Testament when God pronounces or carries out judgment against gentile peoples without having previously instructed or warned them through special revelation. Most famously, God destroyed Sodom and Gomorrah for their wickedness (Gen 19:23–29). The Mosaic law also teaches that God threw the gentile inhabitants out of Canaan as punishment for their "abominable customs"—in fact, the same sort of customs God prohibited Israel from following (Lev 18:24–30; cf. 20:23). These gentiles were liable apart from any prophetic warning. And as chapter 3 discussed, many of the Old Testament prophets issued oracles pronouncing judgment against foreign nations, who did not receive God's law at Sinai.

One of the ways Scripture helps readers make sense of such material is by speaking of the natural world as well-ordered, intelligible, and morally instructive. In other words, at least part of the reason why human beings have moral knowledge apart from special revelation and are accountable to God for how they use it is because creation itself communicates moral truth to them. Three examples illustrate this point.

First, the book of Proverbs treats the natural order as morally charged and teaches that people gain wisdom, in part, through experience and contemplation of it. God created the world by his own wisdom (Prov 3:19–20; 8:22–31), which helps to explain why the world, in turn, communicates wisdom to humans. Proverbs views the cosmic and human social realms as interconnected. As there is cause-and-effect regularity in the natural world, so there is in human interaction (e.g., 30:33). As some things are unfitting in the natural world, so also in humanity's moral world (e.g., 26:1). As some things are bad or ominous in the natural world, so also in human relations (e.g., 6:27–29; 25:14, 19). One can study the behavior of ants and gain wisdom (6:6–11).

Second, the Old Testament prophets sometimes appeal to what one scholar has called "cosmic nonsense."[6] That is, the prophets do not simply condemn Israel for breaking God's commandments but also seek to show that there is something bizarre and stupid about their sin. Sin bends against the order of reality. It cuts against the grain of the universe. Israel was violating God's specially revealed decrees, indeed, but in doing so they were living out of accord with the structure of an intelligible universe. Amos mused,

---

6. See John Barton, *Understanding Old Testament Ethics: Approaches and Explorations* (Louisville: Westminster John Knox, 2003), 38.

for example, "Do horses run on rocks? Does one plow there with oxen? But you have turned justice into poison and the fruit of righteousness into wormwood" (6:12). Isaiah especially loved such reasoning. "The ox knows its owner, and the donkey its master's crib, but Israel does not know, my people do not understand" (1:3; cf. Jer 8:7). "Woe to those who call evil good and good evil, who put darkness for light and light for darkness, who put bitter for sweet and sweet for bitter!" (Isa 5:20; see also 10:15; 29:15–16). As Isaiah explains, "You turn things upside down" (29:16).

Third, Romans 1 grounds universal accountability before God in humans' moral knowledge gained through the world itself. Paul explains first that all people know *God* through creation. What can be "known about God is plain to them, because God has shown it to them" (Rom 1:19). What can be known includes God's "invisible attributes, namely, his eternal power and divine nature," and these things are "clearly perceived . . . *in the things that have been made*" (1:20; emphasis added). And this natural knowledge of God entails natural knowledge of moral responsibility. People are left "without excuse" for failing to honor and worship God (1:20–25) and for falling into a multitude of other wrongs (1:26–31). They "know God's decree that those who practice such things deserve to die" (1:32).

Another way Scripture helps readers make sense of human beings' moral insight and accountability apart from special revelation is through appeal to certain internal human attributes that enable all people to engage in fallible but relatively trustworthy moral reasoning. For example, the Old Testament often refers to the "heart" (*leb*) as the human faculty that makes moral self-judgments and is also aware of God's judgment (e.g., 1 Sam 24:6; 2 Sam 24:10; Job 27:6; Eccl 3:17). Similarly, the "kidneys" (*kelayot*) provide moral instruction and reveal a person's character before God (e.g., Ps 7:9; 16:7; 26:2; Jer 11:20; 17:10; 20:12).[7] The New Testament uses the term "conscience" (*suneidesis*) to describe the same sort of human faculty that the Old Testament "heart" and "kidneys" were getting at. Paul indicates that the conscience is a universal faculty (Rom 2:15; 2 Cor 4:2) and that its chief work is to render judgment about good and evil (e.g., Rom 2:15; 9:1; 13:5; 2 Cor 1:12).[8]

---

7. On the moral activity of the heart and kidneys in the Old Testament, see, e.g., Hans Walter Wolff, *Anthropology of the Old Testament* (Philadelphia: Fortress, 1974), 40–58, 65–66; and David VanDrunen, "Conscience and Natural Law in Scripture," in *Christianity and the Laws of Conscience*, eds. Jeffrey Hammond and Helen Alvaré (Cambridge: Cambridge University Press, forthcoming).

8. For discussion of conscience in the New Testament, see, e.g., Philip Bosman, *Conscience in Philo and Paul* (Tübingen: Mohr Siebeck, 2003); C. A. Pierce, *Conscience in the New Testament* (London: SCM, 1955); and VanDrunen, "Conscience and Natural Law."

In Romans 2:14–15, Paul explicitly credits the conscience with making moral judgments apart from knowledge of biblical law: "For when Gentiles, who do not have the law, by nature do what the law requires, they are a law to themselves, even though they do not have the law. They show that the work of the law is written on their hearts, while their conscience also bears witness, and their conflicting thoughts accuse or even excuse them."[9]

This section has not presented a detailed explanation of what natural law is or how people know it, but it has offered a précis for why Christians need some conception of natural law in order to make sense of the Scriptures. Even apart from special revelation, human beings have genuine moral knowledge and are accountable to God for how they use it. They know God's law through the objective testimony of the world and the subjective judgments of their heart or conscience.

NATURAL LAW AND THE NOAHIC COVENANT

This chapter faced an important question at the outset: How can God govern common political communities and hold them accountable through the Noahic covenant if he did not deliver Scripture to these communities and if most of them through history have not had access to Scripture at all? If there is a natural law that provides universal knowledge of God's moral will, as the preceding discussion indicates, we are on our way to an answer. But does the natural law really explain how God governs political communities through the *Noahic covenant*? In this section, I offer a concise case for linking these two things. I contend that in the present world, God communicates the natural law by means of the Noahic covenant, and thus human beings know their moral obligations under the Noahic covenant through the natural law.[10] To clarify, I am not claiming that God communicates the natural law simply by means of Genesis 8:21–9:17 itself, the *text* that records the Noahic covenant. That would imply that Scripture is the only mode of divine moral instruction after all. Rather, God communicates the natural law through the created order, but the created order only continues to exist because God maintains it through the Noahic covenant. Thus, when God makes his natural law

---

9. Most Christian theologians have believed these verses refer to natural law. A minority has thought that Paul instead refers to *Christian* gentiles who "do not have the law by nature." I believe the former view is correct and have presented a thorough argument for it, in interaction with many biblical scholars, in *Divine Covenants*, 231–57.

10. See also the defense of this in VanDrunen, *Divine Covenants*, 123–28.

known through the created order, it is an act of covenantal commitment on God's part. And when human beings respond to the testimony of natural law, they offer a covenantal response. If this is true, then the reality of natural law provides a satisfying response to the question at the beginning of the chapter.

Before presenting a case for linking natural law and the Noahic covenant, I should explain that though there are some real advantages of describing natural law in a covenantal framework, this does not require one to reject the traditional Thomistic idea linking natural law to the eternal law. Thomas Aquinas understood eternal law as the "Divine Reason" that governs "the whole community of the universe," and he understood natural law as "the rational creature's participation of the eternal law."[11] Eminent early Reformed theologians took a similar view. Franciscus Junius, for instance, defined eternal law as *the immutable concept and form of reason existing before all time in God the founder of the universe*" and wrote that the natural law "*adumbrate[s] the eternal law by a certain participation.*"[12]

The terminology of "participation" carries philosophical connotations that are not obvious to most people today, and there is no need for Christians to embrace a particular philosophical system. But it is compelling to conclude that human moral reasoning about what is just and good is somehow grounded in God's own reasoning about these things. God made human beings in his image and likeness and designed them to pursue a moral commission in this world that reflects his own righteous work in making and ruling the world, as discussed in chapter 2. Humans have a genuine share in the government of creation, doing works that are truly their own but which always stand under God's sovereign authority. As theologians have long argued, many of God's attributes are "communicable": their infinite perfection is reflected in finite human beings. These attributes are both intellectual and moral in nature. They include knowledge, wisdom, goodness, and justice.[13] In fact, possessing and practicing these attributes is at the heart of bearing God's image (see Eph 4:24; Col 3:10). Thus it is compelling to conclude that insofar as the natural law communicates God's law, human beings who know it and follow it are echoing, on a creaturely level, what God does eternally. They analogically

---

11. Thomas Aquinas, *Summa Theologiae* 1a2ae 91.1–2. English translations are taken from St. Thomas Aquinas, *Summa Theologica*, 5 vols., trans. Fathers of the English Dominican Province (Allen, TX: Christian Classics, 1948).

12. Junius, *The Mosaic Polity*, 42, 44.

13. For a detailed Reformed discussion of God's communicable attributes, see, e.g., Herman Bavinck, *Reformed Dogmatics*, 4 vols., ed. John Bolt, trans. John Vriend (Grand Rapids: Baker Academic, 2003–2008), 2:178–255.

think God's thoughts after him. In this sense, at least, the natural law is a participation in eternal law.

While we need not abandon this perspective, there are advantages of understanding natural law in covenantal terms as well. For one thing, generally, covenant is a central theme uniting the grand biblical story. Many natural lawyers in recent years have called for a more robust connection between biblical ethics and Christian natural law theory,[14] and a successful attempt to link natural law to the covenants could advance discussion a good way toward that goal. For another thing, linking natural law to the covenants could also help to make discussions about natural law less abstract and more concrete. Natural law is not some impersonal force about which smart people can develop rational theories. Rather, natural law represents the moral obligations of human individuals and communities toward the living God, who has entered a solemn relationship with them. To respond to the natural law is to respond to God.

Although the word *covenant* does not appear in Genesis 1–2, there are good reasons to believe that God established a covenant with creation when he made it.[15] If so, then the created order exists by God's covenantal decree, and when human beings are confronted with the testimony of that created order, their only two options are to respond with covenant fidelity (obedience) or covenant rebellion (disobedience).

But whether or not the original creation is understood in this covenantal manner, Scripture explicitly declares that God, since the great flood, maintains and governs the human race and the broader natural order through the Noahic covenant. The Noahic covenant did not re-create the world out of nothing but reestablished the regular rhythms of creation that the flood interrupted. Thus God did not issue the natural law for the first time when he entered the Noahic covenant. But this covenant did become God's means for communicating natural law in the fallen, post-flood world. Since God maintains the created order through the Noahic covenant, the natural law communicated by the created order must be God's covenantal law. To put it another way, one of the things God does by upholding the created order through the Noahic covenant is to make himself known "in the things that have been made" and thereby to hold human beings "without excuse" (Rom 1:20).

---

14. E.g., see Jean Porter, *Natural and Divine Law: Reclaiming the Tradition for Christian Ethics* (Grand Rapids: Eerdmans, 1999); Russell Hittinger, *The First Grace: Rediscovering the Natural Law in a Post-Christian World* (Wilmington, DE: ISI, 2003); and Matthew Levering, *Biblical Natural Law: A Theocentric and Teleological Approach* (Oxford: Oxford University Press, 2008).

15. This is a common view among Reformed theologians. I have defended it in *Divine Covenants*, 77–86.

As noted above, this claim that God communicates the natural law through the Noahic covenant is *not* saying that God communicates the natural law merely through the *text* that records the Noahic covenant (Gen 8:21–9:17). But this text may nevertheless be valuable for theological reflection on natural law. It provides, I propose, a summary of the natural law—not the only possible summary of it, but one that is fitting in context. This proposal should be plausible in light of the argument above. If all human beings know their responsibilities under the Noahic covenant through natural law, then the commands of Genesis 9:1–7 and the natural law must have the same basic moral content.

A couple of other points also suggest that Genesis 9:1–7 summarizes the natural law. First, consider the biblical texts relevant to natural law that I discussed above. A great many of these texts have to do with themes that are prominent in Genesis 9:1–7, specifically, justice and/or sex and family. For example, the incidents in Genesis 19; 20; and 34 (regarding Sodom, Gerar, and Shechem, respectively), which raise such important natural-law issues, all concern acts of injustice about sex or family matters. Justice, sex, and family are also pervasive themes in Proverbs' description of natural wisdom.[16] Furthermore, chapter 4 noted that injustice was one of the prime grounds for the prophets' condemnation of gentile nations. And in Romans 1, Paul famously referred to certain sexual actions as sins "contrary to nature" (1:24–27) and decried the fact that people not only practice a range of wrongs against the natural order but also "give approval to those who practice them" (1:32), that is, fail to make proper judgments. In short, given how Scripture generally speaks about natural law, it makes sense that a summary of natural law would highlight issues of justice and sex/family, as Genesis 9:1–7 does.

Second, the fact that the Noahic covenant deals with human beings as *divine image-bearers* also supports a natural-law reading of Genesis 9:1–7. In this covenant, God does not give human beings arbitrary commands but commands fitting for the kind of creatures they are. The one who sheds human blood should receive retribution at the hands of a human being, "for God made man in his own image" (Gen 9:6). Exercising dominion is what image-bearing human beings are made to do (Gen 1:26), and administering rectifying justice is a necessary aspect of dominion in this (fallen) world. Furthermore, the Noahic exhortation to be fruitful, multiply, and fill the earth (9:1, 7) is also fitting for the kind of creatures that human beings

---

16. See VanDrunen, *Divine Covenants*, 399–406.

are, given how closely Genesis 1:27–28 associates procreative fruitfulness and bearing God's image. In short, Genesis 9:1–7 is plausibly a summary of the natural law because it calls human beings to do exactly the kinds of things God designed and commissioned them to do when he created them in his likeness.

A question that remains is why the Noahic covenant summarizes the natural law in *this* way. The Christian tradition has often viewed the Ten Commandments and the commandments to love God and neighbor as summaries of the natural law. If these are good summaries, why does Genesis 9:1–7 summarize it differently? Perhaps for the following reason. According to classical Christian theology, God gives the natural law both to govern the world presently and to enable him to judge the world justly on the last day. The Noahic covenant, however, only has to do with the former. It is a covenant of preservation, put into effect for as long as this world endures, and its moral exhortations correspond to this limited purpose. In contrast, Romans 1:18–2:15, whose discussions of natural law point ultimately to the final judgment (2:16), presents a much more penetrating, heart-unveiling account of the sins against the natural order into which human beings have plunged (see especially 1:29–31). Are love of God (the first love commandment; Rom 1:30) and coveting (the tenth commandment; Rom 1:29) natural-law issues? Yes. All human beings must answer to God on the last day about these things. But the Noahic covenant summarizes the natural law merely by pointing to matters absolutely essential for the preservation of the human community here and now.

THE NATURAL LAW AS MORAL ORDER

This section advances our study of natural law a bit further by considering how best to describe natural-law morality. I argue here that natural law is best understood not as a collection of rules but as a holistic moral system, or perhaps better, a *moral order*. By this, I mean that natural law directs human beings toward ways of life that promote proper goods and purposes. According to this conception, there is still an important place for identifying rules or precepts of the natural law. But the precepts themselves do not simply equal the natural law, but rather serve to summarize or point to a much broader and more complex moral order that advances the purposes of human existence.

This way of thinking about the natural law is another point of similarity with a classical Thomistic view, although I will again try to put things in more concretely biblical terms than the Thomist tradition typically has. As Aquinas put it, God not only made all things but moves "all things to their due end," and "the eternal law is nothing else than the type of Divine Wisdom, as directing all actions and movements."[17] Insofar as natural law is a participation in the eternal law, as considered above, the natural law directs people toward these proper ends, or goals.[18] Thus the natural law, so conceived, has a teleological character. But Thomas also affirmed that there are "precepts of the natural law," both primary precepts that are general and easily understood and secondary precepts that are more specific and more difficult to understand.[19] Taken together, this presents the natural law as a holistic moral system, or moral order, not as a code. The natural law orients or directs people toward proper human goals. Its precepts describe this orientation or direction but do not themselves constitute the natural law.

This perspective seems consistent with biblical teaching. Scripture does not portray God as creating human beings to execute a bunch of specific, atomistic rules. Instead, God designed humans to accomplish certain good purposes. God made them in his image to occupy the whole world and to have benevolent dominion over it (Gen 1:26–28), and ultimately to rule the world to come (Heb 2:5). God also made people in his image to *be* a certain sort of creature—righteous, knowledgeable, and holy (Eph 4:24; Col 3:10)—that is, to be virtuous. In other words, God designed human beings as image-bearers for the goal of virtuous dominion over the whole earth now and over the new creation to come. This is the natural human moral vocation. As we view things in this way, it makes sense to describe many common moral rules as "precepts of the natural law." "Do not kill," "do not commit adultery," and "do not steal" helpfully prohibit kinds of conduct that fail to honor other humans as fellow image-bearers and hinder the human community from attaining its goal of virtuous dominion. Conversely, positive versions of such precepts ("protect life," "honor marriage," and "respect property") point to conduct that promotes this goal. The natural law, then, is a moral order directing people to ways of life that promote and attain the purposes for which God designed them. Rules cannot exhaust the content of this natural law, but they do help us learn and describe it in concrete ways.

As we continue to think along these lines, another appropriate conclusion is that the precepts of natural law are relatively indeterminate: although they

---

17. Thomas Aquinas, *Summa Theologiae* 1a2ae 93.1.
18. E.g., see Thomas Aquinas, *Summa Theologiae* 1a2ae 91.2; 94.2.
19. E.g., see Thomas Aquinas, *Summa Theologiae* 1a2ae 94.2, 4, 6.

describe important features of proper moral conduct, they do not specify in detail how to live a holistically good life, either as individuals or communities.[20] For one thing, there are many possible ways to live consistently with the natural law, if what natural law does is direct human beings toward virtuous rule over the whole world. Pursuing and achieving that goal requires people to take up a variety of tasks, to develop a range of institutions and associations, and to stand in a variety of relationships to one another, as considered in chapter 3. No set of rules can both be general enough to apply to every person and be specific enough to direct every person in the concrete details of his or her life. "Do not commit adultery" is an important universal rule, but there is a lot more to a successful, lifelong marriage relationship and to training children toward responsible adulthood. And since every husband-wife and parent-child relationship is unique, there is no set of detailed rules for a good family life that apply equally well to everyone.

There is another good reason to think that the precepts of the natural law are relatively indeterminate: these precepts themselves presuppose a cultural context, and cultural contexts differ. Putting "do not steal" into real-life practice, for example, depends upon a legal and economic system that defines what property is. People disagree about what exactly can be owned (ideas? airspace?), who can own it (trusts? corporations?), and on what terms. While people make serious moral arguments for and against certain property laws, sometimes there is no clear moral answer whether something should really be deemed property, and a community simply has to decide one way or another. Therefore, "do not steal" tells us something very important morally, but all by itself it does not tell each individual precisely how to use her own property or respect other people's.

This has important implications for thinking about the civil laws of political communities. If the arguments of this book thus far are sound, and the

---

20. Although I think she overstates her case, I have sympathy with Porter when she writes, "I am not persuaded that the natural law as Aquinas understands it is tantamount to, or can be made to yield, normative precepts that are both specific enough to be put into practice and valid and binding in all times and places"; and "any attempt to specify the general precepts of the natural law will remain indeterminate and incomplete, apart from the traditions and practices of some specific community." See Jean Porter, "Does the Natural Law Provide a Universal Morality?," in *Intractable Disputes about the Natural Law: Alasdair MacIntyre and Critics*, ed. Lawrence S. Cunningham (Notre Dame: University of Notre Dame Press, 2009), 55, 91. Porter develops this idea at length in both *Nature as Reason: A Thomistic Theory of the Natural Law* (Grand Rapids: Eerdmans, 2005) and *Ministers of the Law: A Natural Law Theory of Legal Authority* (Grand Rapids: Eerdmans, 2010). Cf. John Bowlin, "Notes on Natural Law and Covenant," 143–44. For a critical Roman Catholic response to Porter's claims, see Alasdair MacIntyre, "From Answers to Questions: A Response to the Responses," in *Intractable Disputes*, 314–22.

Noahic covenant is both the foundation of political communities and God's means for communicating the natural law, then the traditional Christian teaching that civil laws ought to be grounded in the natural law is correct.[21] This does not imply that civil laws should attempt to enforce *all* aspects of natural-law morality, which the Christian tradition has always denied.[22] But since a political community's laws ought to promote the proper goals for which that community exists, its laws must be grounded in the natural-law morality that orients people toward these goals. Insofar as the natural law itself is relatively indeterminate, then, political communities have to exercise prudence and discretion as they develop their laws. These laws ought to be just and advance the purposes for which the community exists, but there is no single way for them to accomplish this. We cannot expect to find a detailed civil code hidden within the natural law. The natural law provides certain boundaries and orients in certain directions, but cannot provide a comprehensive public policy. This idea will shape the ambitions and limitations of part 2 below.

LEARNING THE NATURAL LAW

One major topic remains to consider: how do people learn what the natural law is? It is one thing to assert that the natural law obligates all people and that all people know it at some basic level. It is another thing to explain how people come to recognize what those obligations are as they experience the world around them. In a previous book, I concluded that although Scripture says a great deal about the existence and purpose of the natural law, it provides little information about how people come to know the natural law. But I also suggested that Proverbs is where Scripture may address this issue most helpfully.[23] Expanding on that thought, I will now utilize Proverbs but also draw upon the broader Western moral tradition and contemporary psychology, philosophy of science, and complexity theory. I argue that learning the natural law can be viewed as a sapiential process—that is, a process of maturing in wisdom. What follows is not a comprehensive epistemology of natural law, but if true it has important implications for natural law theory.

Many discussions of natural law operate at a high level of rational discourse, often contending for controversial moral positions through sophisticated

---

21. Thomas expresses this view in *Summa Theologiae* 1a2ae 91.2; 95.2. Reformed theologian Junius expressed things very similarly in *The Mosaic Polity*, 54–57.

22. E.g., see Thomas Aquinas, *Summa Theologiae* 1a2ae 96.2; and Junius, *The Mosaic Polity*, 56–57.

23. See VanDrunen, *Divine Covenants*, ch. 8.

philosophical arguments.[24] These arguments can have value, and it is difficult to imagine natural lawyers giving up this mode of discourse altogether. But there are reasons to suspect that those who actually understand and practice natural-law morality do not do so because they were persuaded by a technical philosophical argument. Most of them are not intellectuals at all but ordinary people who live well in their homes, neighborhoods, and workplaces. They may not be learned, but we probably consider them wise. The discussion that follows helps to explain this.

The idea that learning the natural law is a process of maturing in wisdom fits the conception of natural law defended thus far in the chapter. Natural law is a moral order that directs people to proper human goals corresponding to the purposes for which God made them. As such, it is relatively indeterminate concerning detailed moral rules and can be put into concrete practice in a variety of ways. It thus seems unlikely that one can learn the natural law (merely) through theoretical reasoning. Experience in the world and a keen eye for circumstances must also be crucial, and this is the stuff of wisdom, as we shall consider.

Many writers in the Christian natural law tradition have observed a connection between natural law and wisdom, even if recent literature has often missed it. Aquinas understood the eternal law as "the type of Divine Wisdom, as directing all actions and movement."[25] Thus, according to Aquinas's logic, our knowledge of the natural law, as participation in the eternal law, must be a participation in God's wisdom. Several contemporary writers have explored this theme.[26] But I believe there is more to say.

The kind of wisdom we consider here is attainable, at least in part, through experiencing and reflecting upon the natural order of this world. To use traditional Reformed theological categories, this wisdom is rooted

---

24. For a recent example, see Sherif Girgis, Ryan T. Anderson, and Robert P. George, *What Is Marriage? Man and Woman: A Defense* (New York: Encounter, 2012).

25. Thomas Aquinas *Summa Theologiae* 1a2ae 93.1. Junius says the same thing in *The Mosaic Polity*, 42; cf. Turretin, *Institutes,* 2:2. Porter comments that for the medieval scholastics, "natural law . . . broadly understood does include specific moral norms as well as a fundamental capacity for moral judgment"; see *Nature as Reason*, 14.

26. E.g., see International Theological Commission, "In Search of a Universal Ethic: A New Look at the Natural Law," in *Searching for a Universal Ethic: Multidisciplinary, Ecumenical, and Interfaith Responses to the Catholic Natural Law Tradition*, ed. John Berkman and William C. Mattison III (Grand Rapids: Eerdmans, 2014), 25–92, especially 31–34; Celia Deane-Drummond, "Plumbing the Depths: A Recovery of Natural Law and Natural Wisdom in the Context of Debates About Evolutionary Purpose," *Zygon* 42, no. 4 (December 2007): 981–98; Susan F. Parsons, "Wisdom and Natural Law: A Christian Feminist Inquiry," in *Where Shall Wisdom Be Found? Wisdom in the Bible, the Church and the Contemporary World*, ed. Stephen C. Barton (Edinburgh: T&T Clark, 1999), 279–93; and VanDrunen, *Divine Covenants*, 367–414.

in *natural revelation*, although *special revelation* (especially Proverbs) also discusses and promotes it.[27] In addition to this kind of wisdom, special revelation also speaks of a wisdom known only through Christ crucified, and not accessible through the natural order (e.g., 1 Cor 1:18–3:23; Col 2:2–3). The former might be called a "proximate" or "natural" wisdom and the latter an "ultimate" or "Christian" wisdom. The latter transcends without cancelling out the former.[28] How Christ is the highest expression of divine wisdom is an important topic in its own right, but is not our topic here. We will consider first the idea that wisdom perceives the natural law, and then I will argue that learning the natural law is a process of maturing in wisdom.

Wisdom as Perception of the Natural Law

What is wisdom? Specifically, what is the proximate wisdom attainable through experience and reflection upon the natural order of the world? In Proverbs as well as in popular parlance, wisdom is a moral and intellectual power by which people understand which courses of conduct are good and bad and become able to put this knowledge into skillful practice. To unpack this idea and to demonstrate wisdom's relation to natural law, it is helpful first to identify what wisdom is not.

First, wisdom does not consist in the memorization of moral rules. Most people recognize a difference between a wise person and someone who can recite a list of commandments. Proverbs confirms this intuition. Most of Proverbs, beginning in 10:1, proceeds by way of short sayings. These sayings are not rules but observations about life and counsel for conduct. What they observe and advise holds true generally but not universally. Many observations prove to be inaccurate in particular circumstances. For example, the proverb that states "a gracious woman gets honor, and violent men get riches" (11:16) may describe how things often work but obviously not how they always turn out. Likewise, sometimes proverbs give mutually contradictory counsel. For example, Proverbs 26:4 advises, "Answer not a fool according to his folly," while the following verse (26:5) advises, "Answer a fool according

---

27. On the universal accessibility of wisdom in Proverbs, see VanDrunen, *Divine Covenants*, 393–98. Proverbs, of course, is addressed specifically to Old Testament Israel, and interpretation of this book needs to be attentive to both the universal and the particular aspects of its teaching.

28. The International Theological Commission reflects on the Old Testament wisdom literature in several ways similar to my understanding of "proximate" wisdom; see "In Search of a Universal Ethic," 41. Its treatment of matters pertaining to Christology, soteriology, and the New Law, however, manifest some fundamental differences, rooted in Reformation-era debates, with my understanding of "ultimate" wisdom (84–90).

to his folly." Since only one of these options can be followed in a particular situation, neither can be interpreted as a universal rule.[29]

Wisdom thus does not consist in the memorization of rules, but neither does it consist in the *application* of rules to particular circumstances. Here, following Proverbs, I wish to challenge the conventional opinion that wisdom kicks in to fill gaps that moral rules do not clearly cover.[30] To see that this is not a correct way to understand wisdom, we might consider the fact that wisdom is manifest in part by observing moral rules that are basic and obvious. For example, the extended prologue of Proverbs (chapters 1–9) repeatedly emphasizes the folly of adultery (5:1–23; 6:20–35; 7:4–27). Wisdom keeps a young man "from the forbidden woman, from the adulteress with her smooth words" (7:5). "Do not commit adultery" is a straightforward precept likely to make it into most short lists of essential moral rules, and yet, according to Proverbs, observing this precept exemplifies wisdom. Here wisdom does not apply a clear rule to a borderline case but grasps the gravity of an unambiguous act of adultery and knows how to avoid it. Wisdom does involve discerning what to do in difficult cases not covered by a standard set of rules, but Proverbs indicates that this is not the essence of wisdom.

A better way to understand wisdom is as a perception or sense of how the world works and thus of what sort of conduct is likely to be effective or destructive in particular circumstances.[31] It grasps what behavior is fitting for a person in a concrete time and place, in light of its effects upon the person and those surrounding her.[32] Hence, Proverbs proceeds not by presenting lists of rules or showing how to apply rules to borderline moral problems, but by helping readers recognize recurring patterns—patterns of how certain kinds of character traits produce certain kinds of behavior, and of how certain kinds of behavior reap certain kinds of fruit.[33] Proverbs often uses analogies, which reveal the

---

29. Cf. Roland E. Murphy, *The Tree of Life: An Exploration of Biblical Wisdom Literature*, 3rd ed. (Grand Rapids: Eerdmans, 2002), 10–11.

30. For an example of this conventional opinion, see Jonathan Leeman, *Political Church: The Local Assembly as Embassy of Christ's Rule* (Downers Grove, IL: IVP Academic, 2016), 137. The International Theological Commission does not put it this way, but I wonder whether it is helpful to associate the need for wisdom so readily with making "concrete applications" of the natural law; see "In Search of a Universal Ethic," 60.

31. Aristotle's notion of *phronēsis*, or practical wisdom, points in the same direction; see *Nicomachean Ethics* 6. More recently, psychologist Elkhonon Goldberg refers to wisdom as "a deep insight into the nature of things, but also ... a keen understanding of what action needs to be taken to change them." See *The Wisdom Paradox: How Your Mind Can Grow Stronger as Your Brain Grows Older* (New York: Gotham, 2005), 79.

32. See James L. Crenshaw, *Old Testament Wisdom: An Introduction* (Louisville: Westminster John Knox, 1998), 11.

33. Similarly, Goldberg discusses how the human brain grows in abilities of "pattern recognition,"

true character of particular types of people and particular types of conduct by likening them to various phenomena in the world around. It instills a way of seeing the world. It conveys a connoisseur's taste for apt speech and behavior.[34] Even Proverbs' vocabulary reinforces this. Many of the words it uses to describe wisdom carry a range of overlapping meaning that communicates notions of discernment, adroitness, insight, competence, and resourcefulness.[35]

Perhaps implied in the preceding, but worth stating clearly, is that Proverbs presents wisdom not simply as perception of how the world works and thus of what sort of conduct is fitting within it. Proverbs also presents wisdom as the skillful action that puts this perception into practice. In the Old Testament, the most common Hebrew word for "wisdom" (*hokmah*) does not describe moral philosophers but God, craftsmen, and kings, all of whom display wisdom in action.[36] "By wisdom" God "founded the earth" and "established the heavens" (Prov 3:19). Elsewhere the Old Testament uses the same verbs to describe human construction of cities, houses, and temples (1 Kgs 6:37; 1 Chr 17:24; Ezra 3:12; Isa 14:32).[37] Throughout Proverbs the wise person is industrious and the fool lazy (e.g., Prov 10:5; 12:11, 24; 18:9; 19:24; 21:25; 26:13–16). As God brought order out of chaos in creating the world (8:27–29), so also wise farmers clear fields to produce a crop, wise parents discipline children to keep them on the straight path, and wise rulers bring justice to troubled societies (e.g., 20:8; 22:6; 27:23–27).[38] More than just an intellectual knowledge, therefore, wisdom also consists in skills that enable people to accomplish difficult but rewarding tasks.

A remarkable variety of scholars, without making reference to Proverbs, have grasped that effective action depends upon a perception that resembles

---

"the organism's ability to recognize a new object or a new problem as a member of an already familiar class of objects or problems"; see *The Wisdom Paradox*, 85. In their study of casuistry, Albert R. Jonsen and Stephen Toulmin argue for the importance of pattern recognition, analogical reasoning, and the like for ethics; see *The Abuse of Casuistry: A History of Moral Reasoning* (Berkeley: University of California Press, 1988), 40, 44, 252.

34. Cf. Stuart Weeks, *Early Israelite Wisdom* (Oxford: Oxford University Press, 1994), 74–75; R. N. Whybray, *Proverbs*, New Century Bible Commentary (Grand Rapids: Eerdmans, 1994), 32–33; and Michael V. Fox, *Proverbs 1–9*, The Anchor Bible (New York: Doubleday, 2000), 32–33. Another way to put it is that wisdom resides in certain sorts of people: people of virtuous character. See William P. Brown, *Character in Crisis: A Fresh Approach to the Wisdom Literature of the Old Testament* (Grand Rapids: Eerdmans, 1996).

35. See Fox, *Proverbs 1–9*, 29–38.

36. See E. W. Heaton, *Solomon's New Men: The Emergence of Ancient Israel as a National State* (New York: Pica, 1974), 18–19.

37. See Raymond C. Van Leeuwen, *Proverbs*, The New Interpreter's Bible (Nashville: Abingdon, 1997), 53–54.

38. See Fox, *Proverbs 1–9*, 279–80, 355–56; and Katharine J. Dell, *The Book of Proverbs in Social and Theological Context* (Cambridge: Cambridge University Press, 2006), 142.

the Proverbial wisdom just described. They propose different names to identify it. I think, for example, of Edmund Burke's "prejudice," John Henry
Newman's "illative sense," Michael Oakeshott's "practical knowledge,"
Michael Polanyi's "personal knowledge," Martha Nussbaum's "discernment
of perception," and James Scott's appeal to the ancient Greek *metis*.[39]

I cannot interact with all of these writers or the subtleties of their proposals, so I focus only on one. Polanyi's "personal knowledge," it seems to
me, gets rather close to how Proverbs describes wisdom. Polanyi argues that
maxims, or rules of art, govern certain activities and guide those who undertake them. But these maxims can never possibly substitute for skills. Polanyi
suggests that there are true maxims of golf and poetry, which give insight
into these activities, but "these maxims would instantly condemn themselves to absurdity if they tried to replace the golfer's skill or the poet's art."[40]
Elsewhere he notes the "well-known fact *that the aim of a skillful performance
is achieved by the observance of a set of rules which are not known as such to the
person following them.*"[41] This is clearly true. The real masters of golf are not
television commentators but accomplished players, whether or not they can
describe exactly what makes their game effective. The true masters of poetry
are not the literature professors who analyze beautiful poems but those who
write them, whether or not they can explain the delightfulness of their verse.
Expert golfers and poets have "personal knowledge" of their arts. The same
dynamic seems to be at work in Proverbs. The wise person is not so much
the soil scientist as the farmer who gathers a bountiful crop, not so much
the political theorist as the king who does justice, not so much the parenting
guru as a parent who raises children well. This is not to deny that the competent soil scientist, political theorist, and parenting guru also possess a genuine
wisdom—as Herbert Simon put it, "the boundary between knowledge and
skill is subtle"[42]—but Proverbs emphasizes the wisdom of practical skill more
than that of intellectual analysis.

---

39. See Edmund Burke, "Reflections on the Revolution in France," in *Edmund Burke and Thomas
Paine, Reflections on the Revolution in France and the Rights of Man* (New York: Anchor, 1973), especially
100–101; John Henry Newman, *A Grammar of Assent* (Notre Dame: University of Notre Dame Press, 1979),
ch. 9; Michael Oakeshott, *Rationalism in Politics and Other Essays*, new and exp. ed. (Indianapolis: Liberty,
1991), 6–16; Michael Polanyi, *Personal Knowledge: Towards a Post-Critical Philosophy* (Chicago: University of
Chicago Press, 1962); Martha Nussbaum, *Love's Knowledge: Essays on Philosophy and Literature* (New York:
Oxford University Press, 1990), especially 37, 41, 44; and James C. Scott, *Seeing like a State: How Certain
Schemes to Improve the Human Condition Have Failed* (New Haven: Yale University Press, 1998), ch. 9.
40. Polanyi, *Personal Knowledge*, 29–30.
41. Polanyi, *Personal Knowledge*, 49 (italics his).
42. Herbert A. Simon, *The Sciences of the Artificial*, 3rd ed. (Cambridge: MIT Press, 1996), 93.

While hardly a comprehensive account, the preceding discussion provides a sketch of wisdom: wisdom is not in essence a knowledge of rules or of how to apply them but a perception of how the world works and of what sort of conduct is therefore effective and fitting. This perception resides not only in the intellect but also in practical skills that enable execution of difficult but profitable activities. And with this we return to the main claim of this section: wisdom is the ability to understand and practice the natural law that directs us toward fulfillment of our proper purposes—in general, benevolent rule over the whole world, as the Noahic covenant points us to it. Several points of correspondence between the earlier discussion of natural law and the present study of wisdom support this conclusion.

First and most fundamentally, natural law, understood as a moral order rather than a series of rules, corresponds perfectly to wisdom, understood not as knowledge of rules or how to apply rules but as a perception of how the world works and of what sort of conduct is fitting within it. Wisdom is the appropriate *subjective* human faculty for apprehending the *objective* norm of natural law.[43] Different objects of knowledge call for different abilities in the knower. Knowing the European capitals requires powers of memorization; knowing arithmetic requires powers of computation. Knowing the natural law, a moral order directing humanity toward Noahic goals, requires powers of perception. Another way to put it is that understanding the natural law is more an art than an exact science. While people can write helpful books about diagnosing illnesses or navigating ships (or playing golf or writing poetry), accomplished physicians, captains, golfers, and poets possess skills that are never fully describable. They have a perception of or taste for what makes for excellence in their particular fields. Likewise, while people can (possibly!) write helpful books describing the natural law, true knowledge of something so complex demands the perception of a craftsman and the taste of a connoisseur. And such perception and taste are precisely what constitute wisdom.

Second, wisdom and natural law correspond not only because of *how* wisdom knows but also because of *what* wisdom seems particularly concerned to know. As argued in chapter 3, the ethic of the Noahic covenant implies the need for industriousness, creativity, and technological innovation, and hence the natural law presumably directs human beings in these directions. Corresponding to this, Proverbs exudes a spirit of enterprise—alongside many warnings against a greedy desire to become rich (e.g., 28:20, 22).

---

43. Cf. VanDrunen, *Divine Covenants*, 371–75.

Industriousness is one of the most prized features of wisdom, while Proverbs ridicules the lazy man as a paragon of folly (e.g., 10:5; 12:11, 24; 18:9; 19:24; 21:25; 26:13–16). The industry of the wise is not mere busyness. It is effective for turning little into much and scarcity into profit. Good people save up wealth little by little and make it grow (13:11), leaving an inheritance for their children's children (13:22). They work their land and have bread (12:11), bringing an abundant harvest out of fallow ground (13:23). The wise woman at the end of Proverbs is a person of industry *par excellence*. She not only cares for domestic chores such as preparing food and making clothes (31:15, 19–22, 27) but also plays the entrepreneur. She does research, purchases a field, and plants a vineyard (31:16). She buys raw materials from afar, turns them into valuable goods, and sells them to merchants (31:13–14, 18–19, 24). Thus the natural law's demand for industry and technological advance corresponds to the spirit of enterprise and entrepreneurial skill that wisdom instills.

As also considered above, the natural law directs human beings to be fruitful, multiply, fill the earth, and administer justice. Proverbs has a great deal to say about these as well. Wisdom resides in finding a good spouse (18:22), training children (22:6), and maintaining domestic joy (15:17). From the outset, Proverbs presents education in wisdom through the guise of a father instructing his son (1:8; 2:1; 3:1; 4:1; 5:1; 6:1; 7:1). Justice is also a pervasive theme in Proverbs. God is just (24:12), and an inscrutable justice seems to permeate the order of things, such that good tends to come to those who act well and destruction to those who do evil (e.g., 11:25; 21:5; 26:27). Wisdom guides the government of rulers (8:15–16), condemns bribery (17:23), supports the cause of the needy (31:9), and renders right judgment (17:15). Thus wisdom corresponds to natural law here as well. The foundational requirements of the natural law are matters in which wisdom has special interest.

A third and final point of correspondence is worth noting. My conclusions above suggest that nobody could have constructed from scratch, through abstract reasoning, the details of what the natural law prescribes. The human race has already made considerable progress toward the goals of the Noahic covenant, and this has required the development of complex networks of institutions and authority structures through an extended historical process. Corresponding to this, wise people do not gain their perception and skill as blank slates operating in a vacuum. They gain them in ways that depend upon the achievements of those who have gone before them. In youth, the wise learn from their parents and throughout life they seek counsel from others, accept correction, and honor the elderly. They gather knowledge through experience and evaluate new situations by comparison to old ones. As explored further below, the wise thoroughly depend upon the accumulation of insight that one generation passes down to the next and that often gets embodied in the fabric of the social order. Both wisdom and knowledge of the natural law depend upon the long flow of history.

Thus wisdom and natural law correspond: wisdom is the suitable way for human beings to apprehend subjectively what the natural law prescribes objectively. Wisdom is the ability to understand and practice the natural law that directs us toward the ends of the Noahic covenant.

Learning the Natural Law as Maturation in Wisdom

This last major section of the chapter began by asking how people come to understand what the natural law requires. If what I have argued thus far is true, and wisdom is indeed perception of the natural law, then the following must also be true: maturing in wisdom is essentially the same thing as coming to know and practice the natural law. Thus how do people come to understand what the natural law requires in the concrete particularities of life? By becoming wise. But how exactly do people mature in wisdom?

The end of the preceding discussion pointed toward an answer by describing growth in wisdom as a communal process.[44] Both the adjective and noun are important. Growth in wisdom is *communal* both in the sense that wisdom resides in communities and in the sense that individuals gain wisdom through participation in communities. And growth in wisdom is a *process* in that there are no short cuts to attaining wisdom. It is dearly acquired. On the individual level, wisdom is the achievement of a lifetime. On the societal level, it is the achievement of successive generations.

Proverbs makes clear that learning wisdom, on an individual level, is designed to begin from youth.[45] It counsels parents to train their children (e.g., 22:6) and exhorts children to heed their parents' instruction (e.g., 1:8–9). In adulthood, people should both accept and solicit instruction from a widening circle of teachers. The wise give heed when others correct or instruct them (e.g., 10:8; 12:15; 19:20). They do not merely wait for the outspoken neighbor to offer serendipitous advice but also actively seek the counsel of others as they contemplate their course of life (e.g., 15:20; 13:20). Thus learning wisdom is a

---

44. See also Russell Hittinger, "The Situation of Natural Law in Catholic Theology," in *Searching for a Universal Ethic*, 118; Porter, "Does the Natural Law Provide a Universally Valid Morality?," 91; and Polanyi, *Personal Knowledge*, 203, 249, 266.

45. Cf. Aristotle, *Nicomachean Ethics* 2.1.

communal process first of all because it entails the continual absorption and implementation of instruction from others.[46]

Maturing in wisdom is not limited to learning what others are able to pass down. Proverbs also describes the wise as gaining insight through a kind of self-education. This is perhaps most evident in how Proverbs guides readers through the experience of observation, reflection, and moral conclusion.[47] A passerby notices the dilapidated state of the sluggard's property (24:30–31), thinks about it (24:32), and concludes, "A little sleep, a little slumber, a little folding of the hands to rest, and poverty will come upon you like a robber, and want like an armed man" (24:33–34). A wise person who watches ants goes through a similar process and draws an identical conclusion (6:6–10). Someone else observes a young man seduced by a married woman, sees how it ruins his life, and recognizes the folly of adultery (7:6–23). These people had probably been taught to avoid laziness and adultery, but there was something powerful about seeing things for themselves. The process of observation, reflection, and conclusion brings insight into the true character of foolish behavior that mere warnings from others may not. Wise people, therefore, are constantly alert to the world around them and eager to gain new insight to incorporate into the beneficial knowledge they have learned by instruction—and to filter out foolish instruction they have also absorbed. But new insight is dependent upon knowledge already learned. The importance of analogical reasoning makes this clear.[48] Proverbs constantly compares certain kinds of people and certain kinds of behavior to a variety of well-known phenomena in the wider world (e.g., 25:11–14, 18–20, 25–26, 28). Through processes of pattern recognition the wise person learns about new things by comparing them to the old.[49]

The wise person, in short, participates in an ongoing, intergenerational process of gaining insight about the world and effective conduct within it. By receiving and soliciting instruction, the wise tap into a store of social capital they could never have created on their own, and by personal observation and reflection they not only refine their own understanding but may also be able

---

46. Polanyi would note that wisdom cannot be transmitted merely by "prescription" but also, and perhaps especially, "by example from master to apprentice"; see *Personal Knowledge*, 53–54, 62–63, 207.

47. See Leo Perdue, *Wisdom and Creation: The Theology of Wisdom Literature* (Nashville: Abingdon, 1994), 109–10; and R. E. Clements, *Wisdom in Theology* (Grand Rapids: Eerdmans, 1992), 21; cf. Aristotle *Nicomachean Ethics* 6.8.

48. See Crenshaw, *Old Testament Wisdom*, 55; Clements, *Wisdom in Theology*, 45–46; and Leo G. Perdue, *The Sword and the Stylus: An Introduction to Wisdom in the Age of Empires* (Grand Rapids: Eerdmans, 2008), 11.

49. Cf. Polanyi, *Personal Knowledge*, 103; Goldberg, *The Wisdom Paradox*, 20–21, 55, 76, 85, 149; and Simon, *The Sciences of the Artificial*, 88–89.

to add a small contribution to the store, which in turn can be transmitted to the next generation.[50] As wise people before them from time immemorial have received instruction, improved upon it, and passed it along, so do the wise today.[51] This individual experience is intertwined with communal experience. Human communities large and small exercise wisdom when they nurture the gains of the past alongside their attempts to gain insight in the present. The ethical method of casuistry and the judicial method of common law provide formal procedures for resolving moral problems and legal disputes in ways that reflect this perspective, insofar as they seek insight from past precedent, analogize to new situations, and forge resolutions that will serve in turn as precedent for the future.[52]

Thus people come to know and understand the natural law in the same way they mature in wisdom. Through a social process, beginning in youth and continuing throughout life, they receive and solicit instruction and combine the knowledge thus acquired with enriched and refined insights gained through their own observations, reflections, and conclusions. All of these instill a perception of how the world works and therefore what sort of conduct is fitting within it if we are to promote the goals of the Noahic covenant.

Perhaps this argument strikes readers as somewhat idealized, the description of a process that sounds nice in theory but is unlikely to transpire so smoothly in reality. But in fact, I do not claim that this process runs smoothly in real life. I claim that this is the path to gaining wisdom—that is, to learning the natural law—but folly continually interrupts and diverts human beings, individually and socially, from steady travel upon this path. On the one hand,

---

50. Along analogous lines, the International Theological Commission states that the world's wisdom traditions "constitute a type of 'cultural capital' available in the search for a common wisdom necessary for responding to contemporary challenges"; see "In Search of a Universal Ethic," 33. Language itself is part of this social capital; see Goldberg, *The Wisdom Paradox*, 89–94; Polanyi, *Personal Knowledge*, 112; and Simon, *The Sciences of the Artificial*, 45.

51. These considerations support the common notion that wisdom belongs to the aged. Proverbs associates wisdom with gray hair and often accords special honor to the elderly (e.g., 16:31; 20:29). Modern psychological research has suggested that the brain in middle age and beyond, although past its peak in terms of memorizing and computing, tends to become far more successful in powers associated with wisdom, thanks to its store of experience and web of well-filed and interconnected long-term memories; see generally Goldberg, *The Wisdom Paradox*; and Barbara Strauch, *The Secret Life of the Grown-Up Brain: The Surprising Talents of the Middle-Age Mind* (New York: Viking, 2010); see also Joshua K. Hartshorne and Laura T. Germine, "When Does Cognitive Functioning Peak? The Asynchronous Rise and Fall of Different Cognitive Abilities Across the Life Span," *Psychological Science* 26 (April 2015): 433–43.

52. On casuistry, see Jonsen and Toulmin, *The Abuse of Casuistry*. On the common law, see Anthony T. Kronman, *The Lost Lawyer: Failing Ideals of the Legal Profession* (Cambridge, MA: Belknap, 1993), 11–162; James R. Stoner Jr., *Common Law Liberty: Rethinking American Constitutionalism* (Lawrence: University Press of Kansas, 2003), 11–12, 23, 153; and Polanyi, *Personal Knowledge*, 53–54.

the tragedy of human sin may blind us to just how much the human race has accomplished toward the goals of the Noahic covenant. The growth of the human population and its diffusion throughout much of the globe, enabled by the development of languages, laws, and institutions, which in turn have enabled profound technological and economic advance, indicate that over time we have accumulated a treasury of wisdom and understanding of the natural law. Contemporary individuals who participate in the achievements of this project partake of this treasury in smaller or larger ways. Even the mildly competent person has amazing abilities to cope with the challenges of life. On the other hand, the wisest societies and individuals exhibit shocking lapses of folly. The seemingly most civilized communities have perpetrated barbaric atrocities. Highly accomplished people destroy their families and careers through sophomoric scandals. The human race pursues a bizarre course of knowing the natural law and simultaneously suppressing it—which Paul aptly describes as people turning into "fools" (Rom 1:18–22, 32; 2:14–15).

In certain respects, my argument is more pessimistic and gloomy than optimistically idealized. If the argument is accurate, then being born to foolish parents or into a corrupt political community severely impairs people's prospects for attaining wisdom and thus for learning the natural law due to factors out of their control.[53] Some people obviously overcome these hurdles in part, just as some people born into relatively wise cultural contexts squander their advantages. But our lifelong dependence upon the wisdom already attained in our social contexts is a sobering fact that can hardly be overestimated. Maturing in wisdom is inescapably a communal process, and thus our ability to learn the natural law is enabled and constrained in profound ways by the social structures in which we participate.[54]

We may now return to where we began this discussion about learning the natural law. Although natural law theorists produce a considerable body of literature presenting sophisticated rational arguments about contemporary moral controversies, they persuade very few people to change their minds. The people who actually live in some significant conformity to the natural law are rarely up to date on the philosophical literature. They simply live well in their homes, neighborhoods, and workplaces. And the people who resist the claims of the natural law are rarely persuaded to reform their ways by a sharp intellectual argument. The idea that people come to understand the

---

53. Aristotle made similar claims. E.g., see *Nicomachean Ethics* 1.4.
54. Cf. Polanyi, *Personal Knowledge*, 216–22.

natural law through maturing in wisdom explains these remarkable facts. The ordinary people who live well may not be philosophically sophisticated, but they are wise. They have gained their wisdom not through abstract reasoning but through the processes of listening, observing, and reflecting described above.

Furthermore, for natural law arguments to be sound, they must tap into the store of wisdom without which the natural law is incomprehensible. Yet that store of wisdom is attractive only to those who have been acculturated in its ways and have gained the perception of the world it provides. Those not duly acculturated, bereft of this perception, lack the wherewithal to appreciate the persuasiveness of such arguments. People who set themselves up against the norms of the natural law are not able to see the world in ways that make sense of them. They are foolish. And Proverbs emphasizes that it is very difficult to make headway arguing with foolish people, who ridicule and scoff (15:12; 21:24). It often may not be worth trying (23:9; 26:4).

CONCLUSION

The political theology developed in this book requires a conception of natural law. The origin of common political communities lies in the Noahic covenant, and God therefore governs and judges these communities by means of this covenant. Thus there must be some way to explain how members of these communities who lack access to Scripture nevertheless know the Noahic covenant's terms. The concept of natural law provides what we seek. This natural law, which God now communicates through the Noahic covenant, is a moral order directing human beings toward the proper purposes for which God made them. A person can attain a deep understanding of it only through maturing in wisdom.

These reflections on natural law are important background for part 2. Although the ethic of the Noahic covenant is modest, part 2 will attempt to identify the framework this covenant provides for Christians seeking to understand the purposes of political community and their responsibilities within it. This investigation in part 2, therefore, can be characterized as a reflection on natural law. Although the natural law is relatively indeterminate with respect to the specific moral contours of political community, it provides direction and boundaries that ought to guide Christians' reflection on legal and political life.

CHAPTER 6

RESPONSIBLE CITIZENS, PATIENT SOJOURNERS

Christians' Public Life under Two Covenants

Christians live under two divinely established covenants. With the whole human race, they claim the blessings and responsibilities of the Noahic covenant. God set this in place for as long as the present world exists (Gen 8:22) to sustain the natural moral order and human society within it. With their fellow Christians, they also enjoy the blessings and responsibilities of the new covenant in Christ's blood, by which God rescues them from the curse of sin and grants them citizenship in the everlasting kingdom of his Son. While living under one Lord who works out all things according to the counsel of his will (Eph 1:11), Christians thus have a dual identity in this present world. They continue to participate in the institutions and communities emerging out of the Noahic covenant and its natural law, even as the Spirit of Christ acclimates them to the life of the new creation through the word, sacraments, prayer, and fellowship of the church.

Understanding the distinctive moral life that anticipates the new creation is a major, though often overlooked, issue for Christian ethics.[1] But it is not our focus here. Instead, this chapter concludes part 1 by investigating Christians' identity and responsibilities in their political communities that exist under the authority of the Noahic covenant. Christians wonder about

---

1. I discuss this topic in David VanDrunen, *Divine Covenants and Moral Order: A Biblical Theology of Natural Law* (Grand Rapids: Eerdmans, 2014), 447–76, and I also revisit it briefly several times in part 2 of the present work.

their place in public life. What is their status? Toward what goals should they labor? With what attitude and strategy should they pursue these goals?

In answering such questions, this chapter aims to keep in view two fundamental theological ideas defended in previous chapters: Christians live under two covenants, and political institutions are legitimate but provisional, and common but accountable. Without asserting any comprehensive solutions to the challenges of faithful Christian life in a fallen world, I hope to round out this study of political theology by pointing believers in the direction of holy and loving service to their creator and fellow creatures.

THE CHRISTIAN'S CIVIL IDENTITY

Perhaps the most fundamental of the questions posed above concerns Christians' identity or status in their political communities. At the time I write this chapter, issues of identity and status are at the forefront of public interest. Immigration policy, for example, is one of the most controversial topics in American politics and also threatens the unity of Europe. Of course, these are only the latest forms of perennial conflicts. Social status and identity matter deeply.

Christians around the world find themselves in many different social stations in the midst of these perennial debates, and their experience as natural-born citizens, refugees, or persecuted minority inevitably shapes the way they conduct themselves in their own time and place. Yet the question before us is not Christians' present legal status but their *theological* identity, whatever their legal status happens to be. In other words, how should they understand their identity and status *as Christians* called to participate in political institutions under the Noahic covenant? Is there any identity that all Christians share, despite their deep differences in concrete experience?

Sojourners and Exiles

The New Testament is not chiefly concerned with Christians' status in their earthly communities. Central to the New Testament's message, instead, is Christians' status with respect to the new creation, their heavenly community. The New Testament draws upon rich imagery to describe believers' relationship to the new creation: it is their mother (Gal 4:26), homeland (Heb 11:14), city (Heb 13:14), and place of citizenship (Phil 3:20). Whatever we say about Christians' identity in earthly communities must be understood in light of their new-creation identity.

When the New Testament does identify Christians' status in earthly communities, two terms stand out: Christians are *sojourners* and *exiles*. These labels appear together in 1 Peter 2:11: "Beloved, I urge you as sojourners and exiles to abstain from the passions of the flesh, which wage war against your soul." On first reading, it seems possible that Peter speaks this way because his readers are Jewish, scattered in the Greco-Roman world as part of the Diaspora.[2] Or perhaps they are displaced persons living as "resident aliens" in four provinces of Asia Minor (1:1).[3] If this is what Peter has in mind, then he refers simply to their political status: they are "sojourners and exiles" because they are living away from the promised land (if Jewish) or some other place of origin (if gentile). But this is unlikely. Even if his original readers were primarily of Jewish ethnicity and not Roman citizens, Peter never exhorts them in a way that depends upon this social identity. In the immediate context of 2:11, everything Peter writes is equally true for a gentile or a Roman citizen. He tells them to abstain from fleshly passions because they are sojourners and exiles. But indulging fleshly passions would not have been acceptable if they were living in Jerusalem or were Roman citizens. He goes on to tell them to keep their conduct among the gentiles honorable (2:12) and to be properly submissive to every human institution (2:13). These are the same kind of instructions the New Testament gives to Palestinian Jews (Matt 22:21) and Roman Christians (Rom 13:1–7). In any case, it seems improbable that a Christian congregation in Asia Minor at this time would consist entirely of political aliens.[4]

The more common interpretation of 1 Peter 2:11 is much stronger: Peter identifies his readers as sojourners and exiles in a *theological* sense. As Christians (of whatever origin) they live in earthly societies (of whatever sort) as sojourners and exiles. In the preceding verses, Peter has described his readers as a distinctively new-covenant community. Being Jewish (or something else) is no longer their primary identity. They are a "holy priesthood" offering up "spiritual sacrifices" (2:5), a "chosen race, a royal priesthood, a holy nation" (2:9), those who once were not God's people but now are (2:10).

2. As claimed by Nicholas Wolterstorff, *The Mighty and the Almighty: An Essay in Political Theology* (Cambridge: Cambridge University Press, 2012), 43.

3. As argued in John H. Elliott, *A Home for the Homeless: A Sociological Exegesis of 1 Peter, Its Situation and Strategy* (Philadelphia: Fortress, 1981), ch. 1.

4. For critical interaction with Elliott's thesis, see also John W. Pryor, "First Peter and the New Covenant (II)," *The Reformed Theological Review* 45, no. 2 (1986): 45–46; and Paul J. Achtemeier, "Newborn Babes and Living Stones: Literal and Figurative in 1 Peter," in *To Touch the Text: Biblical and Related Studies in Honor of Joseph A. Fitzmyer, S.J.*, ed. Maurya P. Horgan and Paul J. Kobelski (New York: Crossroad, 1989), 216–18.

These are strange things to say if Peter were speaking to Jews as Jews, or to political aliens as political aliens.

This theological interpretation of "sojourners and exiles" is consistent with Hebrews 11:9–16, which describes Abraham as a model of Christian faith. Abraham went to live in a "foreign land" (11:9), but did so under heavenly auspices, "looking forward to the city that has foundations" (11:10). He and his family were "strangers and exiles"—not primarily as those lacking a permanent address in Gerar or Sodom but as strangers and exiles "on the earth" (11:13), as those "seeking a homeland" and desiring "a better country, that is, a heavenly one" (11:16). Abraham was literally a *political* sojourner, but more important, as a person of faith he was a sojourner *theologically.* Thus Christians rightly affirm that they are sojourners and exiles *wherever* they are and in *whatever* social or political circumstances, because the new creation is their true home.

When New Testament authors identified Christians as sojourners and exiles, they were not using brand new terms. The terms had rich Old Testament resonance. Abraham and his house were the paradigmatic sojourners (Gen 12:10; 15:13; 20:1; 21:34; 23:4) and the Israelites were exiles in Babylon. Texts such as 1 Peter 2 and Hebrews 11 thus send readers back to these Old Testament accounts, which evidently provide normative instruction for Christians today. Of course, we must be mindful of important differences between the experience of Old Testament sojourners and exiles and that of new-covenant Christians. The church's missionary mandate to make disciples of all nations (Matt 28:19) is one obvious difference with weighty consequences for how Christians relate to non-Christians. But if texts such as Hebrews 11:9–16 and 1 Peter 2:11 are to make much sense, there must also be crucial similarities between the experience of these saints of old and that of Christians today. Let us now consider what it meant to be a sojourner and exile in Old Testament perspective. We will then return to the New Testament.

Abraham's Sojourn

What does it mean to live as a sojourner? As far as Genesis indicates, God never provided Abraham with a blueprint for how to conduct himself in relation to his neighbors in Canaan. It is also clear that Abraham sometimes conducted himself poorly. These considerations suggest that we should have modest expectations as we look to the Abrahamic narratives as a source of moral insight. Nevertheless, two observations provide interesting material for reflection.

First, Abraham participated in the activities of ordinary life in conjunction with his neighbors, although they were strangers to the covenant God made with him (Gen 15; 17). Being a sojourner did not require isolation from the surrounding societies. For example, Abraham participated in a military conflict among a number of local kings (Gen 14) and engaged in property transactions (Gen 23). He was summoned to a legal trial by a local king whom he had wronged, and he defended himself, however ineptly (20:8–13). Later, Abraham entered into a covenant—an oath-bound political treaty— with the very same king who had indicted him (21:22–34; cf. 14:13; 26:26–31). Abraham had theological justification for engaging his neighbors in these ways: they were all equal participants in the Noahic covenant and thus shared many common interests in earthly affairs.

Second, however, Abraham interacted with different people and cities in different ways. On one end of the spectrum, Abraham rebuffed the king of Sodom's offer of fellowship that would have brought him considerable wealth (Gen 14:17–24). The account is cryptic, but Abraham appears determined to remain aloof from him. It is not difficult to guess why, given what Genesis discloses about the character of Sodom (13:13; 18:22–19:14). On the other end of the spectrum, Abraham accepted a more intimate proposal (an oath-bound treaty) from king Abimelech of Gerar (21:22–34). Since Abraham had discovered that Gerar had some fear of God (20:11), this decision is also understandable. But his relationships even with these two cities were complicated. His military venture in Genesis 14 was a *de facto* alliance with Sodom and Gomorrah, and he was initially so suspicious of Gerar that he said his wife was his sister to protect himself from jealous suitors (20:1–2; cf. 12:11–13). All in all, Abraham seems to have understood the need to exercise prudential judgment about how, when, and with whom to share common activity. One approach did not fit all cases.

Abraham conducted himself poorly at times. But sharing common activity with his neighbors, in a discrete and flexible manner, seems to be of the essence of a sojourning life. When the New Testament calls Christians sojourners, presumably it expects the same of them. We will keep this in mind when we return to the New Testament.

Israel's Exile

Compared to Abraham's sojourn, Israel's experience in exile is a more accessible source of normative guidance for contemporary Christians, for the prophet Jeremiah wrote a letter giving the exiles specific instructions for life in Babylon (Jer 29:4–14). Jeremiah's letter, supplemented by a number of narratives about exilic life, provides a useful picture of what godly behavior in exile looked like. Three things stand out.

First, despite the massive disruption they experienced when Nebuchadnezzar hauled them to Babylon, the exiled Israelites were to continue pursuing the ordinary affairs of life. Jeremiah 29, in fact, highlights the three explicit moral concerns of the Noahic covenant: the exiles were to get married, have children, and multiply in number (Jer 29:6; cf. Gen 9:1, 7), to work in support of their material needs, including housing and food (Jer 29:5; cf. Gen 9:3–4), and to promote the welfare of the city in which they now lived (Jer 29:7; cf. Gen 9:6). With respect to the last of these, since Daniel and his three friends served Babylon through holding political office, it is no stretch to associate seeking Babylon's welfare with the Noahic mandate to pursue justice.

Second, although Jeremiah's letter indicates that the exile was going to last for a while and thus that the Israelites should settle down and participate in Babylonian affairs, it also emphasizes that they were not to think of Babylon as their permanent home or try to turn it into a new Jerusalem. Instead, God promised to bring them back to the real Jerusalem after seventy years (29:10). *This* was to be their "future" and "hope" (29:11). Thus they had a kind of dual allegiance, although their ties with Jerusalem were profoundly greater than those with Babylon.

Third, the stories in Daniel provide vivid illustration of how the general charter of Jeremiah 29 was lived out by four godly and competent exiled Israelites. These stories are especially remarkable in light of the sobering fact that Babylon had a reputation for brutality and arrogance rather than civility (e.g., see Ezek 30:11; Hab 1:5–2:20). Daniel and his three colleagues were educated in a Babylonian school to great acclaim (Dan 1:3–7, 18–20), and they served in high office under Babylonian and later Persian administrations (1:2; 2:48–49; 5:29; 6:1–3, 28). There was no "ground for complaint" against Daniel "with regard to the [Persian] kingdom" (6:4). At the same time, they refused to eat food unclean according to the Mosaic law (1:8–16), to bow down to an idol (3:8–18), or to pray to the king (6:10). And despite his high position and probably luxurious life, Daniel longed for the promised return to Jerusalem after seventy years (9:1–19). In short, they were intimately involved in Babylon's civil life without trying to turn it into a new holy city, yet they strove to avoid complicity in its evil and kept their hearts fixed upon the city to which they truly belonged.

These instructions in Jeremiah 29 and their application in Daniel are consistent with the parameters of Christian political theology laid out in chapter 1. The exiles were to regard Babylonian political institutions as *legitimate* and thus worth their service, even while regarding them as *provisional* in view of their future return to Jerusalem. They were also to regard these institutions as *common*, finding their own welfare in Babylon's welfare (Jer 29:7), while recognizing their moral *accountability*. Whatever Christians' many differences with these saints of old, when the New Testament calls Christians "exiles" it must refer at least to these fundamental issues.

New Covenant Sojourners and Exiles

As observed earlier, the New Testament calls Christians sojourners and exiles, and we have now seen what the life of sojourning and exile looked like in the Old Testament. To be a sojourner is obviously not exactly the same thing as being an exile, but 1 Peter 2:11 indicates that Christians are both simultaneously. Thus there must be something that unites these ideas. What sojourning and exile have in common is the experience of not truly belonging to the place in which one resides. Both sojourners and exiles may have opportunity to participate in the life of their city of residence, but their ultimate attachments and sense of belonging lie elsewhere.

The New Testament makes clear why Christians are sojourners and exiles: their ultimate allegiance and affections do not belong to their earthly political communities. They have no enduring city here (Heb 13:14). Instead, they are citizens of heaven (Phil 3:20) and look to the Jerusalem above as their mother (Gal 4:26). Having any earthly address thus places them in a foreign land. From political perspective, most Christians today are not migrants, aliens, or refugees. They are simultaneously citizens of their nation and sojourners and exiles within it. Another way to put it is that they are *dual citizens* of their heavenly city and of their earthly city. But precisely because heavenly citizenship constitutes their ultimate allegiance, their earthly citizenship takes on the ambience of exile. Christians who do not feel homesick are spiritually ill.

But this is not meant to ignore Christians who are migrants, aliens, or refugees. They are not exactly dual citizens, but from a theological perspective their situation is not much different from Christians who are. They share heavenly citizenship with all of their Christian brothers and sisters, and they also claim membership in the Noahic covenant alongside all of their neighbors, no matter how unsettled their political status. Whether or not Christians are officially citizens of the political community in which they reside, they ought to participate in and promote the welfare of its institutions as far as possible. Theologically speaking, then, even Christians who are native-born citizens are sojourners, and even Christians who are refugees have a dual fealty.

Likewise, Christians who enjoy a broad degree of religious liberty and Christians who suffer severe persecution are in similar positions theologically, although their political experiences differ markedly. It is difficult to read the New Testament and not get the sense that suffering persecution is the norm for those who profess Christ—then, now, and until he returns. Those who wish to lead a godly life in Christ will be persecuted (2 Tim 3:12), and they are blessed (Matt 5:10–12). Severely persecuted Christians must remember to continue loving their neighbors and praying for their civil magistrates, trusting that God will keep his promises under the Noahic covenant and maintain some degree of commonness in this present age. Those who suffer few legal or cultural liabilities for their Christian profession must remember that their situation is the exception, not the expectation. While having much to be grateful for, they need to be vigilant about the spiritual dangers that accompany ease, wealth, and success. God does not promise these things to Christians. When he gives them, he may well take them away soon. Even the most free and prosperous political community should remain a foreign place to Christians in crucial respects.

What kind of moral life does identity as sojourner and exile entail? Several things emerge from our study of the Old Testament above. Sojourner-exiles pursue ordinary earthly affairs, and they do so in conjunction with their unbelieving neighbors, not in isolation. They seek the welfare of their political communities, yet do not think of them as permanent. They respect political authorities but disobey them when necessary to remain faithful to God. They are cautious and flexible with their earthly attachments.

Many pieces of evidence indicate that the same obligations remain binding for New Testament Christians. They too should pursue the ordinary earthly affairs of the Noahic covenant. The New Testament treats marriage and child-rearing as normal activities for Christians (e.g., Eph 5:22–6:4; Col 3:18–21). It generally urges Christians to marry (1 Cor 7:1–5; 1 Tim 5:14), although it highly honors the nonmarried life (1 Cor 7:6–8, 32–38). It also exhorts all Christians to work hard and to provide food and other material needs for themselves and others (e.g., 1 Thess 4:11–12; 2 Thess 3:7–12). The New Testament does not treat law enforcement as a task for all Christians, but the apostles evangelize civil officials and apparently permit them to keep their office when they become believers (e.g., Acts 10:34–48; 13:6–12). Furthermore, the New Testament does not call Christians to pursue these Noahic obligations in holy isolation from their unbelieving neighbors. Although Christians are only to marry in the Lord (1 Cor 7:39), they are not more married than unbelieving couples (e.g., Matt 27:19). Those who find themselves married to an unbeliever ought to remain in that relationship, if possible (1 Cor 7:12–16). When they work, they work in sight of those outside the church (1 Thess 4:12). If they govern, they govern political communities filled with unbelievers. The New Testament has no conception of a Christian ghetto into which believers ought to retreat.

But even as they take up these tasks, while living and working alongside unbelievers, Christians have to maintain a certain detachment. Paul puts it most poignantly: "The appointed time has grown very short. From now on, let those who have wives live as though they had none, and those who mourn as though they were not mourning, and those who rejoice as though they were not rejoicing, and those who buy as though they had no goods, and those who deal with the world as though they had no dealings with it. For the present form of this world is passing away" (1 Cor 7:29–31). Christians have to walk a fine line. The familial and economic activities Paul describes are good. Christians pursue them. But they pursue them as sojourners, knowing that they are precarious, mutable, and fleeting. Christians are engaged in them and hope to bless others through them, while striving not to love these activities too much. They ought to pursue Noahic affairs, but with a degree of reserve. They have a keen eye for the temporary. They know that they brought nothing into this world and can take nothing out of it (1 Tim 6:7). In other words, they should pursue Noahic affairs as sojourners.

New Testament teaching also suggests that Christians, like the Old Testament sojourners and exiles, should be cautious and flexible in their political attachments. As a theological matter, the New Testament teaches that civil magistrates are divinely appointed to promote justice (Rom 13:1–4; 1 Pet 2:14). But as a practical matter, things are complicated. The political officials that appear in the Gospels and Acts are a diverse lot. As considered in chapter 1, some of them act sensibly and express a mild concern to do what is just, while others grossly abuse their power. And Revelation portrays political power in decidedly negative—even Satanic—terms. But in no case is a political official the kind of person to whom Christians would really want to entrust themselves. Like Paul, Christians might appeal to them for help in a just cause (Acts 16:37; 25:10–11), but the New Testament supports the

Psalmist's sentiment: "Put not your trust in princes" (Ps 146:3). Christians pray for them, but with the modest goal of being able to live a peaceful and quiet life (1 Tim 2:1–2). They generally submit to their magistrates and pay their taxes (Rom 13:1–7; 1 Pet 2:13–17), but know they may have to disobey when loyalty to Christ requires (Acts 4:19–20). A sojourner's caution and flexibility is good practice.

SEEKING A JUST COMMONALITY

As sojourners and exiles, Christians are active participants in their political communities with a degree of reserve and detachment. Thoughtful Christians will inevitably wonder what goals they should seek as they participate in this manner. Part 2 will reflect on a number of perennial issues of legal and political theory in light of the political theology developed in part 1. Here we consider generally the proper end of political life for Christians when they approach it as sojourners and exiles. *Just commonality* is a good way to describe this end. (I remind readers that I use *political* not to refer strictly to civil government, but to life in those larger communities in which many smaller institutions and associations interact.)

Just Commonality

First, Christians are to seek *commonality*. God has ordained that political communities arising out of the Noahic covenant are common, rather than holy, as argued in chapters 2–4. Positively, Christians should promote arrangements that serve and unite all the individuals and associations in their political community rather than those that exclude some of them, as far as that is possible and as far as they have opportunity. Negatively, Christians should not seek to make their political communities holy by trying to unite the royal and priestly dimensions of the original human calling in a Christian sort of way. And when others seek to make these communities holy by trying to unite the royal and priestly dimensions through another religion, Christians should look for creative ways to resist. Of course, in many cases (like Daniel in Babylon or Paul in the Roman Empire), exigencies may force them merely to find ways to survive and maneuver around these illegitimate attempts to sanctify what should remain common. Given the fallen world in which we live, promoting commonality inevitably entails promoting a kind of pluralism. If the state does not compel people to pursue holiness in a single sort of way, they will pursue it (or not) in a variety of ways. Without forced conformity, there will be diversity. Chapter 7 considers the complex issues of pluralism in much more detail.

Second, however, this pursuit of commonality is not to come at any cost. Christian sojourners ought to promote a *just* commonality. The Noahic covenant ordains political communities that are common but also those that enforce justice, at the very least against the violent (Gen 9:6). Individuals and institutions that perpetrate violence relinquish their otherwise legitimate claim to be included in the political community. To speak of justice is to raise a host of perennially intractable debates. In chapter 9, we will consider how the Noahic covenant should guide Christians as they reflect on justice and pursue it in their political communities. For now, it suffices to say that Christians should pursue a modest and provisional justice, not a comprehensive or final one. In the Noahic covenant, the mandate to seek justice is grounded in the image of God (Gen 9:6).[5] While God promises to be the ultimate judge of the world (9:5), he also promises to sustain the world and hence to postpone the final judgment (8:21; 9:11, 15). That is, God restrains the full manifestation of his perfect justice as he governs the present age, showing forbearance to sinners while this earth endures. Thus the Noahic mandate for humans to pursue justice *in the image of God* suggests that they must temper this pursuit with forbearance and not engage in an all-consuming quest to right every wrong. Only at the final judgment will God bring perfect justice.

Opposition to Just Commonality

If Christians promote commonality and a modest, provisional justice, they will distinguish themselves from others. A great many peoples through history have tried to incorporate the holy into affairs of state or sought a more comprehensively just social arrangement. Among many possible examples, the importance of radical Islam on the recent world stage makes it worthy of brief reflection.[6] Sayyid Qutb's *Milestones* provides a useful theoretical explanation and defense of the radical Islamic vision. Qutb (1906–1966) was a prolific author and activist who played a leading role in the Muslim Brotherhood and was executed by the Egyptian government.

---

5. As noted earlier, I take the appeal to the image of God in Genesis 9:6 not as an explanation of why murder is so bad but as an explanation of why *human beings* are to enforce the penalty. See VanDrunen, *Divine Covenants*, 115–18.

6. Of course, many Muslims repudiate radical Islam. A few even advocate a conception of political community that bears a distant resemblance to the Christian conception I defend here; see especially Abdullahi Ahmed An-Na'im, *Islam and the Secular State: Negotiating the Future of Shari'a* (Cambridge, MA: Harvard University Press, 2008).

Qutb emphasizes that Islam is "a comprehensive concept of life and the universe," providing "the only principle on which the totality of human life is to be based."[7] "Our principles of government, politics, economics and all other aspects of life" derive from the Qur'an.[8] Islam, he claims, "cannot fulfill its role" unless it takes "concrete form" in a "nation" and thus produces a "Muslim society."[9] This entails that Muslims have a "God-given right" to seize political power in their communities in order to depose unbelievers from leadership, to "implement" and "establish the Divine system on earth," and to "enforce the particular way of life."[10] Islam thus properly advances by both persuasion and physical coercion.[11] Therefore, Qutb is unsatisfied with a system of justice developed in conjunction with non-Muslims or with a society that is anything other than "Islamic."[12] Muslims have no dual citizenship that involves nationality or membership in a country where sharia law is not established.[13] "It is not the function of Islam to compromise with the concepts of *Jahiliyyah* . . . or to coexist in the same land together with a *jahili* system."[14]

Christianity is obviously different from radical Islam. But it is not different, I contend, because it replaces "Islam" with "Christianity" while sympathizing with radical Islam's social-political vision. Rather, it is different because it rejects radical Islam's social-political vision in an altogether fundamental way. A political theology grounded in the Noahic covenant discourages Christians from seizing civil power for the purpose of enforcing a comprehensive way of life and establishing a Christian society. It does not prohibit living and working for justice alongside non-Christians or repudiate membership in religiously mixed communities. Christianity *can* "fulfill its role" without taking "concrete form" in a nation. Insofar as Christians seek the "concrete form" of Christianity, the place to find it is the *church*, the only institution Christ established through the new covenant. He commissioned it to fulfill its mission in a world governed under the Noahic covenant, whose citizenry is mixed, whose justice is provisional, and whose civil rulers have no authority to turn their societies into holy communities.

Even while forswearing radical Islam, many Christians today are still

---

7. Sayyid Qutb, *Milestones* (New Delhi: Islamic Book Service, 2002), 129, 84.
8. Qutb, *Milestones*, 21
9. Qutb, *Milestones*, 9–11.
10. Qutb, *Milestones*, 33, 76, 131.
11. Qutb, *Milestones*, 55–76.
12. Qutb, *Milestones*, 27, 83–84, 93–94, 111, 117.
13. Qutb, *Milestones*, 118–19, 123.
14. Qutb, *Milestones*, 129. The words in italic refer to non-Islamic ideas and community.

attracted to the idea of a thoroughly Christian society analogous to Qutb's thoroughly Islamic society. In a line of thought compelling to many conservative Christians, for example, political and broader cultural events are driven by an underlying philosophy and theology of life—an "institutionalized worldview." If Christianity does not provide this worldview, another religious belief system will. As Brad Gregory has argued, a nondivided church in the Middle Ages provided Europe with a fundamental theological and ethical unity, until nominalism, the Reformation, and the Enlightenment broke Christendom apart and put Western civilization on the road to the regnant secularism of the present day. This breakdown of the medieval Christian institutionalized worldview "would eventually make almost impossible the pursuit of the kingdom of God as preached by Jesus."[15] For all of their differences, this "Christian" vision and Qutb's radical Islamic vision seem to agree that their respective faiths *require* socio-political embodiment through an institutionalized worldview if its adherents are to live fully faithful lives.[16]

Seeking to establish a proper institutionalized worldview does have practical attractions. How else can the disparate members of a political community be united around shared purposes and live in peace? So often in history those who share a prevailing institutionalized worldview think it reasonable and morally compelling to suppress those who do not share it, while those who do not share it appeal for toleration. And so often when those previously out of the mainstream find their worldview becoming dominant, they think it reasonable and morally compelling to suppress those who had previously suppressed them, while those who formerly ignored others' pleas for toleration now demand toleration for themselves. This dynamic may seem inevitable. But the political theology defended in these pages urges Christians to seek to break this pattern rather than reinforce it. As difficult to achieve as a provisionally just commonality may be, this is the proper political end that Scripture sets before Christians.[17] Christians ought to believe that some mea-

---

15. Brad S. Gregory, *The Unintended Reformation: How a Religious Revolution Secularized Society* (Cambridge, MA: Belknap, 2012), 147. Among an earlier generation of conservatives promoting similar ideas, see, e.g., Christopher Dawson, *The Judgment of the Nations* (New York: Sheed & Ward, 1942), 27–28, 104; and T. S. Eliot, *The Idea of a Christian Society* (New York: Harcourt, Brace and Company, 1940), 10, 16, 33, 45–46. Rod Dreher has recently utilized this basic perspective to set the historical context for his constructive proposals in *The Benedict Option: A Strategy for Christians in a Post-Christian Nation* (New York: Sentinel, 2017), as considered below.

16. In additional to citations above, see Qutb's version of "institutionalized worldview" in, e.g., *Milestones*, 21, 32, 84, 107, 129.

17. Coming to a similar conclusion, but approaching it from an ecclesiological perspective, Nicholas Wolterstorff writes, "A persistent lament in the writings of traditionalists and conservatives in recent years,

sure of agreement on penultimate issues *is* possible, thanks to the preservative grace promised in the Noahic covenant.[18] Who knows how history might have turned out if medieval or early modern Christians, in the midst of their cultural predominance, had voluntarily and proactively refocused their political activity to embrace just commonality, as a matter of theological principle?

Articles of Peace

In the pursuit of just commonality, Christians will have to make compromises. The Noahic covenant presumes the innate sinfulness of all the people it aims to preserve (Gen 8:21), and it requires Christians to work for justice in collaboration with their neighbors, despite inevitably large differences in religious and moral conviction. It is not as though Christians will agree with each other on exactly what justice requires, and they will certainly not always agree with their non-Christian neighbors. No one has the right to demand justice solely on his own terms. Collaborative effort means each attains less than her own ideal dictates. And this entails that in political life Christians cannot let the better become the enemy of the good. A more pointed way to put it is that achieving some degree of justice is better than seeking the ideal and getting no justice at all.

The analysis in chapter 5 bolsters this claim. Human beings learn the natural law in essentially the same way they mature in wisdom. This process is not a solitary endeavor but requires immersion in communities that have come to embody an understanding, gained over time, of how the world works and how human beings can live productively within it. Individuals are responsible for their actions and thus ought to maintain a certain independence of thought and critical distance from their communities, but they always remain dependent upon them. Political communities are among those communities that embody hard-earned wisdom gained over time—though

both Christian and non-Christian, is that the polity of a liberal democratic state rejects in principle the project of giving political expression to a shared religio-moral vision and that, on that account, it lacks a moral basis for its structure and actions. Rather than being the political expression of a community with a shared religio-moral vision, it is at best an association of such communities, a way of getting along, a *modus vivendi.* . . . It cannot long endure. It's a strange lament for Christians to sound. The coming of the church into a society destroys whatever religious unity the society might previously have had and does not replace it with another." See *The Mighty and the Almighty*, 123. Christopher J. Insole also comes to some similar conclusions, from a still different perspective, in *The Politics of Human Frailty: A Theological Defense of Political Liberalism* (Notre Dame: University of Notre Dame Press, 2005), ch. 5.

18. Contra Richard M. Weaver, another conservative voice of a previous generation, in *Ideas Have Consequences* (Chicago: University of Chicago Press, 1948), 23: "How can men who disagree about what the world is for agree about any of the minutiae of daily conduct?"

always an imperfect wisdom. Christians rightly desire the excellence of their political communities, but if the wise ordering of society is only the achievement of a multi-generational process of communal discovery, then Christians properly contribute to their societies' well-being not by the sudden imposition of an ideal vision of justice but through collegial participation in the incremental development of wisdom over time. Sweeping changes may sometimes be appropriate, but they risk destroying important but barely perceived accomplishments along the way.[19]

Christians should not become apathetic about injustice or numb to the harm it wreaks upon real human lives. But to a great extent they have to channel their desire for justice into hope for the eschatological reckoning that will settle all accounts at Christ's return. "Blessed are those who hunger and thirst for righteousness [or, justice], for they shall be satisfied" (Matt 5:6). Hunger is a mark of sojourning. Satisfaction awaits the consummation of all things.

A number of social thinkers writing from intellectual perspectives different from my own have recognized that modesty and compromise are inevitable, or at least the best of available options. I mention three that propose potentially helpful terms for framing these issues. All three writers were reflecting on liberalism as a form of social ordering. I am not interested in any particular form of political polity at this point, only in the terms these writers use to assess their own contexts. For political scientist John Mueller, it is best to seek the "pretty good" in a social system rather than the ideal. The soundness of institutions, he argues, lies in their ability to function adequately when they account for human imperfections and thus do not require people to rise above their intractable flaws. This, he believes, is a great advantage of a liberal democratic system.[20] From another perspective, political philosopher John Rawls proposed the idea of an "overlapping consensus." Members of political societies inevitably subscribe to a range of comprehensive doctrines, or what others might call worldviews. To achieve a unified and stable political

---

19. As Michael Polanyi put it, "Unjust privileges prevailing in a free society can be reduced only by carefully graded stages; those who would demolish them overnight would erect greater injustices in their place. An absolute moral renewal of society can be attempted only by an absolute power which must inevitably destroy the moral life of man. . . . The attempt made in this book to stabilize knowledge against skepticism, by including its hazardous character in the conditions of knowledge, may find its equivalent, then, in an allegiance to a manifestly imperfect society, based on the acknowledgment that our duty lies in the service of ideals which we cannot possibly achieve." See *Personal Knowledge: Toward a Post-Critical Philosophy* (Chicago: University of Chicago Press, 1962), 245.

20. See John Mueller, *Capitalism, Democracy, and Ralph's Pretty Good Grocery* (Princeton: Princeton University Press, 1999).

order, he suggests, people must seek an overlapping consensus of reasonable comprehensive doctrines rather than try to impose their own comprehensive doctrine on all others. Individuals are then free to relate the political consensus to their comprehensive doctrines in ways they see fit.[21] Whatever critiques of Rawls's thought are necessary (a topic for part 2), some idea of an "overlapping consensus" seems to correspond to the modesty that is content to enjoy the "pretty good."

Perhaps an even better way to put it comes from Jesuit theologian John Courtney Murray, who claimed that there is much to appreciate in a constitutional order that provides "articles of peace." Writing at a time when the Roman Catholic Church was still officially opposed to liberal church-state arrangements, as exemplified in the United States, Murray argued approvingly that the American founders were not radical theorists trying to work out a doctrinaire blueprint but sensible artisans trying to find a way to preserve public peace and the common good "under a given set of conditions."[22] Whatever Murray's acuity as American historian, his praise of those who refused to destroy public peace for the sake of imposing an abstract justice has a pronounced Augustinian character collegial to my claims above.[23] Christians should seek justice—a modestly provisional justice, a justice attained not through a theoretically ideal constitution but through "articles of peace." From the perspective of world history, articles of peace are a rare and valuable achievement.

THE WAY TO GET THERE

Christians who know their political identity (sojourners and exiles) and their political end (a just commonality) will still wonder what this entails for the concrete problems and daily decisions of public life. Such problems and decisions are of practically infinite variety. It is difficult to discuss this topic without either becoming so tied to particular details that the analysis is inapplicable to most readers or remaining so vague and general that the analysis is of limited use, even if accurate. With these challenges in view, this section

---

21. See John Rawls, *Political Liberalism*, exp. ed. (New York: Columbia University Press, 2005), lecture 4.

22. See John Courtney Murray, SJ, *We Hold These Truths: Catholic Reflections on the American Proposition* (New York: Sheed and Ward, 1960), 56–63.

23. See, e.g., Augustine's discussion of how Christians make use of the "earthly peace" of their temporal societies and try to maintain common agreement as much as possible with unbelievers for the sake of life's necessities. See *The City of God* 19.17.

addresses questions about how Christians can advance their political goals in ways consistent with their God-given identity. We first contemplate the proper attitude of Christians as they participate in their political communities and then examine whether they ought to follow any specific strategy.

The Christian's Attitude

Some Christians feel profound agitation as they observe the vicissitudes of their favored political parties and agendas. Different Christians are moved by different things, of course. Many have greater emotional investment in the fortunes of a beloved athletic team than in the outcome of national elections. But political events do involve matters of wealth and poverty, liberty and constraint, and even life and death, and their *gravitas* weighs on many believers. How to maintain a godly attitude in the midst of the corruption and manipulation that so often clouds the political process deserves more than a little reflection.

My decision to focus upon the issues I do has surely been shaped by my perception of the special temptations and challenges facing Christians in my own time and place. In the United States and other Western nations today, many devout Christians are gripped by fear, melancholy, and resentment at the course of political life. Whatever the accuracy of my perception, whatever other characteristics of the present age would have been helpful to mention, and however different readers' circumstances are from my own, I trust that the three things discussed below are universally important and always timely.

A first feature that ought to characterize Christians' attitude as they participate in public affairs is *accepting the fleetingness of life*. This present life is important, and political events can promote great good or impose true misery. Yet Scripture warns believers not to lose heart by letting weighty temporal matters overwhelm them. They should recognize that their lives are short and thus keep proper perspective when the problems of the moment threaten to blind them to all other reality. Or, to put it in terms familiar to the present study, Christians must remember that some things are provisional. When the wicked surround the psalmist, and distress and anger build up in his heart (Ps 39:1–3), he cries:

> O LORD, make me know my end
> and what is the measure of my days;
> let me know how fleeting I am!
> Behold, you have made my days a few handbreaths,

and my lifetime is as nothing before you.
Surely all mankind stands as a mere breath!
Surely a man goes about as a shadow!
Surely for nothing they are in turmoil;
    man heaps up wealth and does not know who will gather!
    (39:4–6).

Another psalmist, wrestling with the sighs and afflictions of life (90:9, 15), asks God to "teach us to number our days that we may get a heart of wisdom" (90:12). God is "from everlasting to everlasting," older than the ancient mountains (90:2), but he "return[s] man to dust," for "a thousand years in your sight are but as yesterday when it is past, or as a watch in the night" (90:3–4). Human beings are swept away "like grass that is renewed in the morning: in the morning it flourishes and is renewed; in the evening it fades and withers" (90:5–6). The psalmist continues: "The years of our life are seventy, or even by reason of strength eighty; yet their span is but toil and trouble; they are soon gone, and we fly away" (90:10).

Both psalmists express something of the insight central to Ecclesiastes: all is temporary and passing in this life under the sun. "A generation goes, and a generation comes," "the sun rises, and the sun goes down," "around and around goes the wind," and "all streams run to the sea, but the sea is not full" (1:4–7). "There is nothing new under the sun" (1:9), nor will there "be any remembrance of later things yet to be among those who come after" (1:10). The New Testament reinforces this outlook. According to Paul, Christians' "outer self is wasting away" and their afflictions are "light" and "momentary." "The things that are seen are transient" (2 Cor 4:14–16). As quoted above, Paul elsewhere observes that "the appointed time has grown very short" and that "the present form of the world is passing away" (1 Cor 7:29–31).

Christians thus ought to view political affairs with due perspective. When I first drafted this chapter, an American presidential election drew near that some Christians declared the most consequential in the country's history. It could seem that way at the moment, but now the next election seems more important. Presidential elections have implications for ordinary lives, to be sure, but each one takes its place in the great stream of human events that have come and gone.

Gaining a heart of wisdom through numbering their days does not leave Christians in despair, for *confidence in the Lord* is a second characteristic that should shape their attitude. A sense of the fleetingness of life is hardly balm in itself. It becomes a consolation for beleaguered Christians only when they turn to God as the one who endures, as the Lord of history who gives history its meaning. After asking God to teach him the measure of his days and the fleetingness of his existence, the psalmist continues: "And now, O Lord, for what do I wait? My hope is in you" (Ps 39:7). Indeed, Scripture repeatedly points to God's sovereignty as encouragement for his people as they confront the precariousness of life. God brings princes to nothing, causing them to wither as soon as they take root (Isa 40:23–24). He "works all things according to the counsel of his will" (Eph 1:11). And God directs the course of human affairs for the welfare of his people, "for those who love God all things work together for good, for those who are called according to his purpose" (Rom 8:28). They cast all of their anxieties upon him, because he cares for them (1 Pet 5:7). They call upon God in the day of trouble, and he delivers them (Ps 50:15).

Another psalm captures this aspect of the Christian's attitude. In the face of evildoers, believers "fret not" (Ps 37:1). They trust in the Lord and delight themselves in him (37:3–4). They commit their way to God, being still and waiting for him patiently (37:5, 7). They refrain from anger and forsake wrath (37:8). Again, they fret not, and still a third time, they fret not (37:7, 8). Their calmness of spirit comes from confidence that the Lord will act for them (37:5). They also recognize how the fleetingness of life is their friend, since the very people who threaten to oppress them stand on tenuous ground. They will "fade like the grass and wither like the green herb" (37:2). They will be "cut off" and "no more" (37:9, 10). Political affairs are understandably a source of fear and anxiety. The stakes can be high, and the victors bear the sword. But even when nations rise and fall, Christians fret not. Their God is King of kings and Lord of lords (Rev 19:16). They do not know the outcome of world affairs, but he does.

Finally, the Christian's attitude should be charitable, compassionate, and cheerful. If Christians are truly confident in God, as just discussed, they must show charity to their neighbors, for faith works through love (Gal 5:6). They should overflow with the compassion of their Lord (e.g., Col 3:12; cf. Matt 9:36, e.g.). Christians are often quick to view people of different political opinion as their enemies. In some cases, they may indeed be enemies, yet love for enemy is a chief attribute of Christ's disciples (Matt 5:43–48). It is deeply unbecoming when Christians complain incessantly about the state of political affairs, especially Christians who enjoy levels of prosperity, freedom, and peace that are the envy of the world. It is easy to be angry about losing one's country—as if any country ever belonged to Christians. It is easy to demonize political opponents—as if Christians themselves are not sinners saved entirely by grace. It is easy to become bitter—as if "the lines" had not "fallen for [them] in pleasant places," as if they did not have "a beautiful inheritance" (Ps 16:6). Christians have become heirs of a kingdom that cannot be shaken, and thus they say, "My heart is glad, and my whole being rejoices" (Ps 16:9). Those who are heirs of new creation are truly the most blessed of people, and while they wait for their Lord's return they have opportunity to love and bless all of their neighbors, even those who do not respond in kind, and to do so with a joyful spirit.[24]

The Christian's Strategy

Is there a particular strategy for political engagement that corresponds to the kind of attitude described above or with the theological perspective of previous chapters? Devising a political strategy depends so much upon the particular exigencies of a social-cultural moment, and upon a person's ability to understand it properly, that it seems precarious to suggest an answer.

It is not just any present moment is so difficult to understand precisely but that the future effects of any action are impossible to predict. Honest people recognize that most of their opportunities and accomplishments have come about at least partially through serendipitous events they never could have planned or predicted. We can put ourselves in positions to do something useful, but plotting and scheming rarely gets us exactly where we intend. No individual's life is the product of a master strategy. And if this is true on an individual level, it is exponentially truer on a political level. As social institutions become increasingly more numerous and intertwined, and as economies grow more complex and globalized, any person's, party's, or movement's ambition to mold the future of a political community is bound to be stymied by a myriad of unpredictable events.[25] Scripture indicates as much: "The race is not to the swift, nor the battle to the strong, nor bread to the

---

24. Aristotle Papanikolaou helpfully remarks, "Against the urge to monsterize and project unto the other, the Christian will attempt to engage in practices exhibiting humility, patience, respect, temperance, courage, and discernment." See *The Mystical as Political: Democracy and Non-Radical Orthodoxy* (Notre Dame: University of Notre Dame Press, 2012), 155.

25. F. A. Hayek helpfully explored this issue, and I interact with his insights in chapter 10. It is interesting that the event that probably brought him his greatest fame, the wide popularity in the United States of his book, *The Road to Serfdom*, was entirely unforeseen to Hayek, who wrote it primarily for British intellectuals. See Alan Ebenstein, *Friedrich Hayek: A Biography* (New York: Palgrave, 2001), 114–15, 128–37; and Bruce Caldwell, *Hayek's Challenge: An Intellectual Biography of F. A. Hayek* (Chicago: University of Chicago Press, 2004), 257–58.

wise, nor riches to the intelligent, nor favor to those with knowledge, but time and chance happen to them all" (Eccl 9:11). Of course, human beings are volitional creatures and must make purposeful decisions. We cannot avoid devising strategies as we accept our moral responsibilities. But we ought to wear our strategies lightly.

I offer no perfect political strategy in this section. Instead, I simply introduce several recent proposals meant to guide, warn, or inspire American Christians in the early decades of the twenty-first century, and I offer some commentary on them.

Sociologist James Davison Hunter's *To Change the World* is an interesting place to begin.[26] In the first of the book's three essays, Hunter notes the long-standing desire of American Christians to change the world, but he argues that the world does not change in the way they have thought. Many have assumed that it changes through shaping individual hearts and minds, and thus they have emphasized education and worldview training. But in fact, Hunter contends, the world changes through networks of elites at high-profile centers of cultural production. Christians have not changed the world as hoped because they have been absent from elite centers of influence, not because they have failed to promote a worldview. In his second essay, Hunter observes that changing the world requires power, and many American Christians have understood power primarily in terms of political success. Accordingly, they have tended to equate changing culture with winning political battles and have often fallen subject to the anger and resentment that politics breeds. This has been true on both the Christian right and the Christian left. Hunter calls Christians to think about cultural engagement in less politically charged ways and to reconsider the idea of power in a more Christ-centered manner.

These opening essays are incisive, and many of their main contentions correspond to concerns of the present study. But Hunter's third essay is particularly relevant here, for he proposes his own model for Christian cultural engagement. Hunter calls his paradigm "faithful presence." As God has been faithfully present to his people in Christ, so also Christians should seek to be faithfully present to him and to other people, whether in the church, daily occupations, or their various spheres of influence. Such faithful presence creates wholesome relationships and institutions that promote the well-being of

---

26. James Davison Hunter, *To Change the World: The Irony, Tragedy, and Possibility of Christianity in the Late Modern World* (New York: Oxford University Press, 2010).

all people and bring forth the *shalom* of the new creation. If Christians follow this path they may make the world a little better, Hunter suggests. Yet they should not be obsessed with this goal, since the world cannot be controlled or managed, and Christians should make God and his worship their primary goal in any case.

In light of the political theology developed in previous chapters, Hunter's model of "faithful presence" has much to commend it as a strategy for Christian participation in politics and their many other cultural endeavors. Perhaps most noteworthy is its modesty in eschewing both a grand optimism and a paralyzing pessimism. It is modest in not burdening Christians with the responsibility to *redeem* culture or *build the kingdom* in their ordinary occupations,[27] while still upholding the importance of the Christian's call to be faithful in all areas of life. It is also modest in refusing to make world-changing a goal in and of itself and in not promising that certain results can be attained by following a master plan, while still affirming, in the words that end the book, that it is "possible, just possible" that faithfully present Christians will make the world "a little bit better."[28] In my judgment, Hunter's proposal could use considerably more theological precision, especially in affirming a distinction between the Noahic and new-creation moral orders and in recognizing how different institutions are grounded in each. Nevertheless, as a strategy for Christians seeking to live godly lives in the contemporary (American) world, "faithful presence" seems generally in accord with a sound political theology and well worth Christians' consideration.

Other recent contributions communicate a different mood from Hunter's and a more optimistic tone. One such work is Greg Forster's *Joy for the World*. The book's subtitle indicates both its premise and its goal: *How Christianity Lost Its Cultural Influence and Can Begin Rebuilding It*. For Forster, Christians ought to be seeking "influence" and "impact" upon their broader cultures.[29] Central to the biblical story is that human beings ought to "cultivate blessings" out of the creation order in service to one another, and the greatest failure of the American church is not affirming "the goodness of civilizational life."[30] Forster urges Christians to change course. His concrete strategic proposals are modest in their own way. For instance, he contends

---

27. See Hunter, *To Change the World*, 233–34, 253.

28. Hunter, *To Change the World*, 286.

29. E.g., Greg Forster, *Joy for the World: How Christianity Lost Its Cultural Influence and Can Begin Rebuilding It* (Wheaton, IL: Crossway, 2014), 78–79.

30. Forster, *Joy for the World*, 161, 89.

that Christians' influence and impact can come in small ways in ordinary activities as Christians seek to bless those around them. But he declares his optimism for America's future with regard to sex, economics, and politics.[31] Although unabashedly conservative in his views and believing that America's present cultural direction is morally destructive, he thinks positive change is coming. Another example from conservative provenance is William Edgar's *Created and Creating*. Edgar's main thesis is that "the cultural mandate, declared at the dawn of human history, and reiterated through the different episodes of redemptive history, culminating in Jesus' Great Commission, is the central calling for humanity."[32] Christians build Christ's kingdom in obedience to this call.[33] Edgar does not explicitly declare his optimism, but it is interesting that the shifts in moral ethos that have so agitated many conservative American Christians in recent years seem to have no effect upon Edgar's enthusiastic summons to be active in all sorts of cultural endeavors as the heart of the Christian life.[34]

The political theology of preceding chapters implicitly critiques several aspects of Edgar's theology of culture. But our focus at present is on Forster's and Edgar's versions of a relatively optimistic approach in calling Christians to fidelity in their political and broader cultural lives. This shared optimism is evident in their similar criticisms of Christians who neglect to be engaged in the entirety of human activity. Forster calls for "active participation in the whole fabric of society" and warns against "cultural withdrawal."[35] Edgar, appealing to the letter of Jeremiah 29, calls Christians to be fully engaged and rebukes Rod Dreher and his "Benedict Option" for failing to have the "outward-looking cultural engagement" that Jeremiah commends.[36]

Dreher's proposal, in fact, provides a useful pessimistic counterpart to consider alongside Forster's and Edgar's work. While the latter two are noticeably more optimistic than Hunter, Dreher is considerably more pessimistic. Dreher's Benedict Option draws from the final paragraph of Alasdair MacIntyre's *After Virtue*. MacIntyre posited an analogy between the West in

---

31. Forster, *Joy for the World*, 202–3, 245, 271.

32. William Edgar, *Created and Creating: A Biblical Theology of Culture* (Downers Grove, IL: IVP Academic, 2016), 233.

33. Edgar, *Created and Creating*, 231.

34. In an epilogue, Edgar acknowledges that he focuses upon developing a biblical theology of culture rather than addressing many concrete issues. His decision to write a biblical theology of culture in the present day, to a predominantly conservative audience, without lingering on themes of cultural decline, seems difficult to explain apart from some sense of optimism.

35. Forster, *Joy for the World*, 55.

36. Edgar, *Created and Creating*, 207–8.

his own time (the early 1980s) and the decline of the Roman Empire into the Dark Ages, and he called for a new St. Benedict to show the way forward.[37] According to Dreher, Christian churches in the West are going to face times of great crisis in the years to come. Rather than devoting energy to winning political battles or shaping law, Christians should follow Benedict's example. They ought to focus on constructing their own institutions and networks that can cultivate Christian virtues and practices and resist the evils of the broader culture. Churches need to wake up from their "moralistic therapeutic deism," embrace some version of Christian orthodoxy, and devote themselves to their own moral and spiritual renewal. Dreher insists that this is not a call to abandon the world, but he encourages Christians to remove their children from public schools immediately, to consider moving away from urban centers of wealth and power, and to embrace local community.[38]

I have no idea whether the Benedict Option will be a short-lived attraction for some or will take deep hold among Christians as the twenty-first century unfolds. Whatever the case, contemporary interest in this movement provides an occasion for some final reflections on matters of strategy.

One of the themes recurring in the present study is that Christians are participants in the Noahic covenant, and thus always retain obligations toward the common institutions that arise under it. Christians also have to exercise prudential judgment as to which of these institutions should receive their primary attention at any particular time and place. Abraham the sojourner had to exercise prudential judgment, and Christians in more complex societies today have even greater need for it. All of the writers discussed in the preceding paragraphs would probably agree in general with these two claims. If the Benedict Option encourages Christians to focus upon their local neighborhoods and to downplay politics at a national level, that is a matter of prudential strategy about which Christians may disagree. But if instead the Benedict Option encourages believers to focus upon building *Christian* communities and to give up on *common* institutions, it runs into theological problems.

This raises the question as to what extent debate about the Benedict Option is substantive and to what extent it is merely about strategic judgments. What are the real issues at stake? Two may be of particular importance.

---

37. See Alasdair MacIntyre, *After Virtue: A Study in Moral Theory*, 2nd ed. (Notre Dame: University of Notre Dame Press, 1984), 263.

38. Dreher, *The Benedict Option*. For another study with many claims and proposals similar to Dreher's, published at nearly the same time, see Charles J. Chaput, *Strangers in a Strange Land: Living the Catholic Faith in a Post-Christian World* (New York: Henry Holt, 2017).

One substantive issue is whether having strong churches devoted to formation and discipleship is more necessary now than before. Some contemporary debates seem to presuppose that the answer is affirmative due to cultural shifts hostile to Christianity. Yet building churches devoted to formation and discipleship surely must *always* be Christians' chief concern. If anything, perhaps it is more of a need when the ambient culture seems most friendly rather than when it seems most hostile, since a relatively friendly culture may lull the church into forgetting what truly makes it distinct. Even during times when Noahic institutions function relatively well, according to the natural law, Christians need to be trained in the way of life that anticipates the new creation through continual habituation and acculturation in the worship and life of the church. If ominous cultural developments call Christians back to the importance of faithful churches, that is good. But if Christians act as though this is a temporary measure to survive a coming Dark Age, they have missed an important theological and practical truth.

Thus the many concerns and proposals of Dreher with which I agree are concerns and proposals I would embrace under every conceivable cultural moment. But when he calls for the church "*to be the church*" or "to embrace 'exile in place' and form a vibrant counterculture,"[39] he seems to suggest that there is a unique need for Christians to do this now—especially when he takes pains to compare the present day with a premodern, medieval social order.[40] In contrast, the church, insofar as it uniquely anticipates the life of the new creation, will *always* be a distinctive body. It must be a countercultural body in exile from its eschatological home, even when the common institutions of this world, operating according to the natural law of the Noahic covenant, are at their best. To think that these common institutions could possibly embody the life of the new creation is a fundamental error, or so I have argued here and elsewhere.[41]

A second issue concerns the narrative of decline and entrance into a second Dark Ages. Dreher has closely linked the Benedict Option to MacIntyre's critique of modernity. The movement is for cultural pessimists. I do not know what the near-term or long-term future looks like, and neither does Dreher, despite his confident statements about the days to come.[42] But there are good

39. Dreher, *The Benedict Option*, 3, 18.
40. See Dreher, *The Benedict Option*, ch. 2.
41. See VanDrunen, *Divine Covenants*, especially ch. 9.
42. E.g., from the outset, Dreher declares that a "relentless occupation" of anti-Christian forces is "inevitable" and that "the hour is late." See *The Benedict Option*, 3–4.

reasons to be skeptical about any kind of one-sided narrative of decline rooted in the Enlightenment, and perhaps in the Reformation, Renaissance, and nominalism before that, all of which were preceded by an imperfect but profoundly insightful "medieval model."[43]

Life in medieval society, on the contrary, was in fact pretty horrible. Medieval communities were unattractive places to live in terms of violence, life expectancy, hygiene, diet, and occupational options, not to mention the relative unavailability of the Christian Scriptures and absence of churches that clearly preached the gospel of Jesus Christ.[44] In the past several centuries—that is, in the aftermath of the Enlightenment—the West has witnessed a decline in violence, the abolition of slavery, massive economic growth, great discoveries in science, medicine, and technology, expanded opportunities for women, and the wide availability of Scripture in vernacular languages, to name a few important developments. There is something perplexing about many Western Christians becoming so distraught about the state of Noahic institutions when, in many respects, they have never been in better shape. Of course, impressive progress can coexist with much that is rotten, and progress can be reversed. There are indeed many disturbing contemporary trends in familial, economic, and political life that may well bode ill for orthodox churches and committed Christians. Yet the fact that cultural life has positively advanced in a plethora of ways since the Enlightenment era indicates that something about MacIntyre's analysis, however insightful, does not quite work. And this also raises questions about the Benedict Option, built as it is upon conviction that MacIntyre's analysis was profoundly correct.

Committed Christians surely ought to adjust their strategy for political engagement in light of contemporary cultural shifts, but they need to be careful not to be driven by a misleading or incomplete—or at least highly debatable—historical narrative. The fact that Daniel and his friends were intimately involved in the civil affairs of Babylon for many years should give Christians pause about turning away precipitously from the political life of their nations and cities. Are contemporary American and other Western political institutions worse than those of brutal Babylon, which destroyed Jerusalem and threw worshipers of Yahweh into fiery furnaces? In any case,

---

43. Again, see Dreher, *The Benedict Option*, ch.2. This is a common narrative among some scholars, particularly Roman Catholics. Gregory's *The Unintended Reformation* expounds it in detail, as noted above.

44. Dreher acknowledges that medieval society was "no Christian utopia" and filled with corruption; see *The Benedict Option*, 25, 31. These are helpful acknowledgments, but in my judgment Dreher gives far too little attention to them, in light of the tenor of his broader argument.

Christians always need strong churches to which they are devoted above all else, no matter what the surrounding cultural ethos.

Ultimately, Christians should be neither optimists nor pessimists. Instead, Christians are people of faith and hope—faith that God will keep all of his promises, including the sustaining of common human communities under the Noahic covenant, and hope in the second coming of Christ, the resurrection of the body, and the new creation. The fortunes of the present world rise and fall, and its political communities remain strange combinations of good and evil, in ways difficult to untangle even in hindsight and always impossible to predict for the future.

CONCLUSION

As sojourners and exiles away from their heavenly homeland, Christians are called to be responsible participants in their societies, seeking a just commonality with a reserved, confident, cheerful, and charitable attitude.

On this note, part 1 concludes. I have argued that the Noahic covenant is foundational for Christian political theology. Building on this foundation, Christians recognize political institutions as legitimate but provisional, and common but accountable. They strive to live in accord with the natural law that provides the normative structure for these and other common institutions, and they promote excellence in these institutions according to their respective purposes. Yet they simultaneously cling to an unshakable hope in Christ for a new creation and thus also seek to conform their heart and conduct to the life of the new creation already made manifest in the church. Part 2 shifts slightly from a political theology to a political ethics. If common institutions are indeed grounded in the Noahic covenant, what framework does this provide for evaluating perennial questions of legal and political theory? Or, what are justice, commerce, and community supposed to look like under Noah's rainbow?

PART 2

POLITICAL ETHICS

Part 1 argued that public life and political community are grounded in the Noahic covenant and thus that this covenant provides the framework for developing an account of Christian political theology. Part 2 explores some of the implications. If the Noahic covenant is indeed foundational in the way argued in part 1, how should that shape the way Christians reflect on perennial issues of legal and political theory? What difference does it make as we confront matters of justice, authority, and religious freedom, for example?

It is important to clarify several things about my purpose and plan. First, I am not attempting to unfold a detailed Christian political and legal theory or a concrete Christian public policy agenda. I do not believe the Noahic covenant, or anywhere else in Scripture, provides such things. My claim, instead, is that the terms of the Noahic covenant provide a *framework* for sound thinking about political and legal theory. What the Noahic covenant offers is a perspective on life in this world, a perspective that orients one's mind for productive reflection. To develop mature views on political debates, Christians will have to exercise good judgment, putting to use the virtue of wisdom discussed in chapter 5. Therefore, while Christians are free to try to persuade others to agree with their political judgments, they should ordinarily not present them as *the* Christian view, that is, as necessary points of Christian dogma or biblical exegesis.

Second, in certain respects I am not providing a *Christian* analysis at all. This point requires plenty of nuance. What follows is not a *Christian* analysis, in the sense that I am exploring what public life and political community ought to look like for the human race in general, not for Christians in particular. As argued in part 1, God instituted the Noahic covenant for the human race universally, and the coming of Christ and the establishment of the New Testament church has not changed the norms that God ordained for political life. Nevertheless, I do write and reason explicitly as a Christian in the chapters to come. I reflect on legal and political issues in light of the covenant with Noah recorded in Genesis 8:21–9:17 and in light of other biblical evidence and relevant theological categories. Thus this is a Christian exercise and works from Christian premises, but I am exploring the structure and character of political communities that God has established for Christians and non-Christians alike.

Third, if Christians and non-Christians alike share in the life of the political community, this suggests that non-Christians are not ignorant of its normative structure and character. Of course, non-Christians lack the clarifying light Scripture brings to political and legal reflection, including the account of the Noahic covenant in Genesis 8–9. Yet I argued in part 1 that natural law is grounded in the Noahic covenant, and natural law thus reveals the moral order in which political communities emerge. This means that as I reflect upon the Noahic covenant in the following chapters, the conclusions I draw ought to correspond to the unwritten testimony of natural law. Because of this, I will reflect on occasion on how the natural law corroborates my conclusions and thus why Christians often find themselves able to collaborate and make alliances with non-Christians in the public square. These reflections, secondarily, may also suggest ways in which Christians might engage and persuade non-Christians on contentious political issues.

In these chapters, I try to capture a healthy balance of the theoretical and specific. On the one hand, I reflect on issues primarily at a general level, without getting lost in the special controversies of a particular time and place. Doing the latter would unduly limit the audience of this volume and also risk getting absorbed in the political crises of the moment. Perhaps the most useful thing my book can do is to help readers step back from present intrigues and personalities and to ponder the broader issues at stake. On the other hand, I can hardly be oblivious to my own context. Reflecting on inherently practical legal and political issues on a purely theoretical level would have many drawbacks of its own. While trying to fly a bit above the contemporary partisan fray, therefore, I also keep an eye on debates going on around me and make an occasional interjection—in a way that reflects my American standpoint, inevitably.

The chapters and topics in part 2 proceed with a logic that I hope will be evident. Each chapter builds on those that have come before, and I do not believe their order could well be reversed.

CHAPTER 7

PLURALISM AND
RELIGIOUS LIBERTY

Every human community and institution must reckon with the degree of diversity it will embrace, or at least tolerate. No institution can stand completely open. To accomplish the ends for which it was established, an institution must have meaningful criteria for what membership and participation require. Whether directly or indirectly, each one makes decisions about who is in and who is out, and on what terms. Such decisions shape the identity of an institution and are inseparable from other decisions about its internal rules and their enforcement. While every community has to wrestle with questions of diversity to some degree or another, contemporary American society seems especially exercised by the issue. Controversies about race, immigration, and terrorism present some obvious examples.

In this chapter, I explore the issue of pluralism under the Noahic covenant. Building on part 1, I argue that the Noahic covenant, as universal in scope, prescribes that the human community protect diversity among its members to a maximal degree. Through this covenant, God authorizes the establishment of familial, enterprise, and judicial institutions as well as the broader community in which these institutions interrelate. These many institutions necessarily develop different policies regulating their standards for membership and participation as required by the distinctive purposes each aims to serve. But God entered the Noahic covenant with the human race as a whole. Accordingly, this covenant sets a low bar for participation in the broader community and thus welcomes all people (with exceptions) to join in the activities and institution-creating work of the covenant.

To develop and unpack the themes of this chapter, I first defend and describe the pluralistic character of the Noahic covenant in general. The chapter then considers pluralism and race before turning at greater length to religious liberty. I argue that the Noahic covenant lays foundation for a robust culture of religious liberty, although one which inevitably has to acknowledge limits to the bounds of its tolerance.

THE PLURALISM OF THE NOAHIC COVENANT

The present investigation of diversity and pluralism draws upon a simple but consequential conclusion argued in chapter 2: the Noahic covenant is *universal* in character. God instituted the covenant for the entire world. He entered this relationship with all human beings, for all future generations (Gen 9:1, 8, 9, 12), as well as with "every living creature" in the animal kingdom (9:9–13, 15–17) and the broader cosmic order (8:21–22; 9:11, 13). Genesis 8:21–9:17 indicates that there is nothing in the world that stands outside the bonds of this covenant.

Universal Access to Noahic Institutions

Although this chapter argues for a strong conception of pluralism under the Noahic covenant, that does not mean we must live as generic cosmopolitans, whose only allegiance is to humanity as a whole. We are all "tribal,"[1] in need of membership in smaller or larger associations that shape our identity and affections. Accordingly, it is helpful to recall the argument in chapter 3 that the Noahic covenant implicitly authorizes human beings to form a variety of institutions. These provide us with the associational life we need and also enable us to carry out the three main moral requirements of the covenant: to procreate and fill the earth, to provide for material needs, and to enforce justice in the face of violence. I called the three kinds of institutions *familial, enterprise,* and *judicial.* How should we think about these institutions in light of the universal character of the Noahic covenant?

Familial institutions are, by definition, relatively small and exclusive. One of the purposes of families is to bring a limited number of people together into intimate relationships from which other people are necessarily excluded. A person's relationships with spouse, children, siblings, and parents

---

1. Among writers using this terminology, see Amy Chua, *Political Tribes: Group Instinct and the Fate of Nations* (New York: Penguin, 2018).

are unique. Thus the universality of the Noahic covenant obviously does not mean that membership in a particular family should be open-ended. What it does imply is that participation in family life is generally open to all. God issues the command to be fruitful, multiply, and fill the earth (Gen 9:1, 7) not to certain sorts of individuals but to the human race as a whole. This does not require every person to enter every sort of familial relationship—as a spouse, parent, or sibling—but it does mean that no kind or class of people is disqualified from entering such relationships.

A similar analysis applies to enterprise institutions. Such institutions come in various shapes, and some of these institutions will want to maximize their reach and draw as many people as possible into their orbit of activity— such as a business corporation seeking to expand its customer base. But to accomplish the purposes for which they exist, all enterprise institutions have to establish authority structures, internal rules of operation, credentials for employment, and the like. Such standards necessarily exclude some people from participation. The universality of the Noahic covenant, however, implies that participation in the life of enterprise associations should be open generally to all. The Noahic covenant does not require any particular person to participate in any particular enterprise association, but neither does it disqualify any kind or class of person from participating in the life of enterprise.

Judicial institutions require a somewhat different analysis. Although we ordinarily think of judicial institutions as organs of the state, they can also be private and voluntary. For example, parties to a contract may agree to utilize arbitration or mediation services in case of dispute. The Noahic covenant commissions the human community to enforce justice against wrongdoers (Gen 9:6) but does not indicate that only the state can do it. Thus there can be no a priori objection when parties agree to resolve their disputes privately. In such circumstances, judicial institutions, like enterprise associations, establish their own internal standards that necessarily exclude some people. An arbitration organization serving companies in a certain industry, for instance, understandably excludes those outside the industry. But here again, the universality of the Noahic covenant implies that no kind or class of people should be excluded generally from participating in private judicial institutions.

Nevertheless, in other circumstances judicial institutions must be universal in a way that enterprise institutions need not be. Disputes often arise between parties that have not agreed to be governed by a private judge, such as cases of physical violence that serve as the paradigmatic judicial case in the Noahic covenant (Gen 9:6: "Whoever sheds the blood of man . . .").

Every individual and institution can potentially become a victim of any other individual's or institution's wrongdoing. As discussed in chapters 9 and 11, government institutions are necessary for resolving (at least) these kinds of disputes. Such public judicial institutions, unlike familial and enterprise institutions, must be open to all people indiscriminately, for justice requires that parties to a dispute be treated fairly and equally. If everyone is liable to becoming a victim of another's wrong—and, conversely, able to inflict a wrong on others—then each person and institution ought to have equal access to these public courts and receive equal treatment when litigating disputes within them. To shut someone off from public courts of justice effectively excludes that person from the life of the Noahic covenant altogether. Thus public courts must be open equally to all people within their jurisdiction.

This last statement implies that the public courts of justice must be open even to people who are aliens rather than citizens of a given locale. This raises controversial questions about immigration policy that the terms of the Noahic covenant itself can hardly solve. Nevertheless, the preceding conclusions suggest that all who find themselves within a given political community ought to be able to appeal to its courts for protection against wrong—and by reciprocation ought to abide by that community's law. This theme emerges powerfully in the Genesis narratives describing life under the Noahic covenant. As Abraham and family sojourn from place to place, one of the chief things that morally distinguishes one community from another is how it treats the stranger within its gates. The archetypally wicked city, Sodom, treated its guests with shocking brutality (Gen 19:1–11). Other places that make a bad impression have a similar vice. In Haran, the resident Laban wronged his guest Jacob by enforcing a local custom of which Jacob was not (and presumably could not have been) aware (Gen 29:25–27). In Shechem, the heir to the throne violated Jacob's daughter Dinah when she visited the city (Gen 34:1–2), an "outrageous thing" (34:7). On the other hand, Gerar makes a relatively good impression on readers. It respected the marriage of a stranger such as Abraham and gave him a fair trial when accused of wrong (20:1–16). This city was civil enough that Abraham and Isaac later entered into covenants with its king (21:22–34; 26:26–31).[2] Political communities may have legitimate interest in regulating their borders, granting certain privileges to

---

2. For discussion of these texts and themes, see David VanDrunen, *Divine Covenants and Moral Order: A Biblical Theology of Natural Law* (Grand Rapids: Eerdmans, 2014), 134–57.

those it deems citizens, and demanding lawful conduct of its guests (20:8–10), but treatment of strangers is a key test of a community's rectitude under the Noahic covenant.

Are there any exceptions to this initial claim, namely, that under the Noahic covenant all people are eligible to participate in familial, enterprise, and judicial institutions, and that public courts of justice ought to stand equally open to all? Yes, there must be. Those who shed the blood of fellow human beings make themselves unwelcome in the human community and disqualify themselves from its activities. Whether or not the terms of Genesis 9:6—"Whoever sheds the blood of man, by man shall his blood be shed"— require capital punishment as recompense for murder or permit a lesser penalty, the perpetrator clearly forfeits his ordinary standing in the community. And perhaps the principle expressed in Genesis 9:6 should be extended, such that those who wrong others in lesser ways should also have their access to Noahic institutions curtailed proportionately. I will have to address exceptions to Noahic pluralism in more detail below. For the moment, one consequence of this broader discussion should be emphasized: Many of the reasons why political communities have in fact excluded people from full participation in their institutions and activities—such as racial identity or religious profession—are not justifiable reasons under the Noahic covenant.

Initial Implications of Noahic Pluralism

Before focusing on racial and religious pluralism, we might reflect on several initial implications of the preceding discussion. The first two put this discussion in broader theological perspective. The last two attempt to penetrate a bit deeper into the character of Noahic pluralism itself and are foundational for the rest of the chapter.

First, the pluralism of the Noahic covenant requires members of the human community, Christians included, to cultivate the virtue of tolerance. Tolerance is a proper feature of justice in our fallen but preserved world: acting justly may require us to tolerate people we do not like and modes of conduct we disapprove. The pluralistic character of the Noahic covenant makes clear why tolerance is so important. Everyone who participates in familial, enterprise, and broader political communities inevitably has to interact with people having a variety of personalities, opinions, and lifestyles, but we have to put up with them—as we expect them to put up with us. Cultivating and practicing tolerance, in and of itself, is difficult. Cultivating and practicing tolerance without simultaneously becoming indifferent to truth and moral rectitude is all the more difficult.[3] And it ought to be a special challenge for Christians, who do not refuse to associate with the sexually immoral, the greedy, swindlers, and idolaters (1 Cor 5:10), and yet "abhor what is evil" (Rom 12:9) and consider it "shameful even to speak of the things" the wicked do in secret (Eph 5:12). As "sojourners and exiles" (1 Pet 2:11), called by God "out of darkness and into his marvelous light" (1 Pet 2:9), Christians continue to live in a sinful world without feeling fully at home. They need to be tolerant of much they must never approve of.

Second, while Christians ought to support the pluralism of the Noahic covenant, and may hope to derive some benefits from it, they also partake of a different kind of pluralism in the church of Jesus Christ. In some respects, churches should be considerably less pluralistic than the Noahic communities in which they exist. For one thing, the church consists of those baptized into *Jesus Christ* and thus is not religiously pluralistic in the way political communities may be. In addition, while Paul acknowledges that Christians will associate with sexually immoral, greedy, and idolatrous people in their common affairs (1 Cor 5:10), he commands the church to "cleanse out the old leaven" and "purge the evil person" from its midst (1 Cor 5:7, 13). The Noahic covenant's bar for exclusion is exceedingly lower than the new covenant's.

In other respects, God grants the church a far richer pluralism than any political community can attain. In fact, this ecclesiastical pluralism creates such a unity among Christians that *pluralism* may no longer be the right word to describe it. Like the political community, the church should be open to people of every sort. Even more than being open to them, it seeks to make disciples of every nation (Matt 28:19)—people from Jerusalem, Judea, Samaria, and the end of the earth (Acts 1:8). But while the political community is to bring people who are different from one another into peaceful coexistence, Christ accomplishes something subtly but wonderfully different in his church. "There is *neither* Jew *nor* Greek, there is *neither* slave *nor* free, there is *no* male or female, for you are all one in Christ Jesus" (Gal 3:28; emphasis added). Similarly, among "God's chosen ones" (Col 3:12) there is "*not* Greek and Jew, circumcised and uncircumcised, barbarian, Scythian, slave, free; but Christ is all, and in all" (Col 3:11; emphasis added). This is not a peaceful coexistence among those who remain different but a unity in Christ that removes their differences. It is not that Christians cease to have an ethnic identity or to bear distinguishing marks on their bodies, but *in*

---

3. Cf. John R. Bowlin, *Tolerance among the Virtues* (Princeton: Princeton University Press, 2016), 20.

the church these differences fade in comparison to the shared glory in Christ that unites them. Of course, one can hardly speak of these things without feeling grieved at how often the church fails to reflect their truth. But the church's profound unity is a fact. Colossians 3 roots it in believers' privilege of being "raised with Christ" in heaven, where he is seated at God's right hand and where Christians' very life is now "hidden with Christ in God" (Col 3:1, 3). Their many differences are thus subsumed in an eschatological unity. Christians enjoy a foretaste of their new-creation unity in the church—and ought to repent when they act as though this were not true. The peaceful coexistence of a political community, in contrast, cannot anticipate this eschatological harmony.[4]

The third point raises an important consideration for subsequent discussion. Many opinions on political theory and public policy hinge on whether one believes that political communities have a *common good* and, if so, how to define it. Since the notion of a common good seems to imply the existence of a shared moral vision among members of the community, it is not immediately clear whether a genuinely pluralistic community can have a common good at all. How can a community that welcomes people from a broad range of backgrounds simultaneously have a shared moral vision substantive enough to be meaningful? Posing this question may challenge the very possibility of a stable and enduring political community that maintains a commitment to pluralism, for a functioning political community can hardly lack a shared moral vision altogether. It must have some lodestar by which it orders its life together through customs and laws.[5]

The Noahic covenant offers a plausible and realistic way of viewing the common good in light of these difficulties. This covenant indicates that political communities do in fact have a common good, but a modest one. A political community needs *some* shared moral vision, but this vision need not be substantively rich in order to sustain a peaceful coexistence. According to Noahic standards, a political community ought to share a commitment to the good of forming familial institutions for purposes of procreation and filling

---

4. Thus I believe John D. Inazu is correct: "Instead of the elusive goal of *E pluribus unum*, it suggests a more modest possibility—that we can live together in our 'many-ness.'" See *Confident Pluralism: Surviving and Thriving through Deep Difference* (Chicago: University of Chicago Press, 2016), 6. The American slogan of *E pluribus unum*, indeed, seems to describe the church in a way it can never describe the United States or any common political community.

5. As Brian Leiter notes, "Every state establishes a Vision of the Good—through its constitutions, its laws, and the public pronouncements of its leaders." See *Why Tolerate Religion?* (Princeton: Princeton University Press, 2013), 130.

the earth, the good of forming enterprise institutions to supply human needs, and the good of forming judicial institutions to promote justice in the face of violence. These commitments are substantive but relatively indeterminate. They leave wide berth to the judgment of the community's diverse people as to how these institutions will take shape, pursue their general purposes, and relate to one another. Political society under the Noahic covenant is thus to be broadly pluralistic without being infinitely so. By affirming a modest vision of the common good constituted by the advancement of family life, enterprise, and justice against the violent, a political community is to maintain both a peaceful coexistence and a broad pluralism in which individuals and institutions can pursue their own richer notions of the good.[6]

The fourth and final point concerns how Noahic pluralism corresponds to the natural law. If the argument in part 1 is correct, then the moral order upheld in the Noahic covenant is not obscure, for this moral order is a *natural* order and thus ought to resonate with human beings living in this world and make sense to them at some basic level, however much they may sinfully oppose it. How exactly is this true with respect to pluralism? There is probably much more to say, but I point to two interrelated ideas.

The first has to do with the equal worth and dignity of all human beings. Such equality is foundational for the pluralism I have defended, which asserts that no person should be disqualified from full participation in familial, enterprise, and judicial institutions and that everyone should have equal access and standing before public courts of justice. Many have denied that all people have equal worth and dignity, of course, but that denial is gratingly unnatural. All people who look into the eyes of another human person and are honest about what they see must acknowledge the presence of someone who shares their same basic bodily features and who experiences the same range of needs, emotions, and aspirations, a person with whom they can communicate, cooperate, and potentially procreate.

Reciprocity is a second idea that illuminates why the pluralism of the Noahic covenant is not obscure but resonates with every person at some level.[7]

---

6. Again, Inazu's conception of a viable pluralism is similar, in tamping down hopes of a grand common vision for something much more modest: it "does not give us the American Dream. But it might help us avoid the American Nightmare." See *Confident Pluralism*, 125. Yuval Levin's general call for decentralization and for empowering mediating institutions seems to be a similar response to diversity that rejects attempts to crush one side or to win a culture war but instead seeks to work with the diversity and try to bring the best possible outcome from it. See *The Fractured Republic: Renewing America's Social Contract in the Age of Individualism* (New York: Basic, 2016).

7. Many of the early modern proponents of religious liberty discussed below appealed to the idea of reciprocity at some point in their arguments. E.g., see Sebastian Castellio, *Advice to a Desolate France*

By reciprocity, I mean, first, that we should do to others the good we expect them to do to us, and, second, that we deserve to have the evil done to us that we do to others. Chapter 9 will explore these two notions, the so-called Golden Rule and the *lex talionis*, respectively. These ideas have had remarkable reach across diverse cultures through history. Reciprocity has a claim to lie at the heart of the natural law. The importance of reciprocity in the present context is clear: If I am in the ethnic, moral, or religious majority (or at least wield social power), I need to consider how I would want and expect to be treated were I in the ethnic, moral, or religious minority (or at least lacked social power), and I must strive to treat the minority in this way. Of course, people who are in the ethnic, moral, or religious majority have often spurned this maxim, and one might claim this is evidence that reciprocity is not part of the natural law. But there is a simple response. The very same people, when they cease to be the majority and become a minority, plead passionately for the kind of tolerance they failed to grant others.[8] Every person either has experience being a power-lacking minority or can appreciate the risk of becoming one, and thus every person, I suggest, should recognize the compelling character of Noahic pluralism.

RACIAL PLURALISM

Before turning to our primary focus, religious liberty, I take the perilous step of addressing race. The tense and seemingly intractable controversies about race in many societies—perhaps nowhere more than in my American context—make it a tempting topic to bypass. Yet to ignore it in a discussion of pluralism seems negligent. My general conclusion in this section is that under the Noahic covenant race is an altogether illegitimate basis for excluding people from participation in social institutions and for treating some differently from others in the administration of justice.

(Grand Rapids: Acton Institute, 2016), 7–17; Pierre Bayle, *A Philosophical Commentary on These Words of the Gospel, Luke 14.23, "Compel Them to Come In, That My House May Be Full,"* ed. John Kilcullen and Chandran Kukathas (Indianapolis: Liberty Fund, 2005), 191–93; John Milton, "Areopagitica," in *Great Books of the Western World*, vol. 32, ed. Robert Maynard Hutchins (Chicago: Encyclopaedia Britannica, 1952), 410; and John Locke, "A Letter Concerning Toleration," in *Great Books of the Western World*, vol. 35, ed. Robert Maynard Hutchins (Chicago: Encyclopaedia Britannica, 1952), 19. More recently, Inazu suggests that we might embrace tolerance, humility, and patience toward others because these same traits in others will protect our own idiosyncrasies; see *Confident Pluralism*, 85.

8. As also noted by Locke, "Letter," 7. Along similar lines, Steven D. Smith says that "secular egalitarianism" is like "a secular version of Christendom," in which government imposes a "favored orthodoxy." See *The Rise and Decline of American Religious Freedom* (Cambridge, MA: Harvard University Press, 2014), 153–54.

It seems reasonable to ask at the outset what "race" is. To speak of race implies that the peoples of the world can be categorized into a handful of distinct groups based primarily upon shared physical features associated with particular geographical regions—features such as skin color, hair texture, or the shape of eyes, nose, or mouth. Saying even this much provokes serious questions about the validity of "race." In American slavery and South African apartheid, perhaps the most famous examples of race-based injustice, race was understood in terms of skin color, specifically "black" and "white," and this remains the chief paradigm in much racial thinking today. Yet classifying people by color has numerous conceptual problems. Even when differences in pigmentation between two people are obvious—say, in comparing a random Norwegian with a random Nigerian—separating them by color picks out only one of a multitude of characteristics that distinguish humans from one another. Why is *this* one so important? Furthermore, in many instances differences in pigmentation are *not* obvious. Africans and Europeans bear lighter and darker shades of "black" and "white." Some people from India are darker skinned than many Africans, yet they are not deemed "black." In the United States, some groups widely considered "white" today (such as Jews or Italians) were not counted as "white" in earlier eras.[9] And billions of people are neither "white" nor "black." Americans have sometimes tried to classify these other people by color too, but calling Native Americans "red" and East Asians "yellow" is simply inaccurate, except for those who are sunburned or jaundiced. Perhaps more commonly now, nonwhite/black people are designated by the catch-all "brown," or in terms other than color, such as "Asians" or "Hispanics." While such designations helpfully expose problems with categorization by color, they create whole other sets of conceptual difficulties.

Biological research confirms these suspicions that "race" is a problematic idea. As one geneticist puts it, "There are no essential genetic elements for any particular group of people who might be identified as a 'race.' As far as genetics is concerned, race does not exist." Race "has no useful scientific value."[10] Human populations have simply migrated and interbred too frequently to permit any clear racial boundaries. Physical and genetic variations are not sharp but continuous. They lie not in distinct categories but along a spectrum.[11]

---

9. See Richard Delgado and Jean Stefancic, *Critical Race Theory: An Introduction*, 3rd ed. (New York: New York University Press, 2017), 88–89.

10. Adam Rutherford, *A Brief History of Everyone Who Ever Lived: The Human Story Retold through Our Genes* (New York: The Experiment, 2017), 218, 262.

11. For example, see Rutherford, *A Brief History*, 248–55.

The compelling conclusion is that "race" is a social construct,[12] or perhaps a "political economy, an *ordo* or a social arrangement."[13] To classify people by race has no objective justification and creates a deceptive picture of how human beings are similar and different from one another. Race, therefore, can hardly serve as a legitimate basis upon which to differentiate people's access to familial, enterprise, and judicial institutions under the Noahic covenant. The justice this covenant prescribes must be based upon truth and reality. Bolstering this conclusion is that construction of "race" was hardly a neutral or benevolent act but arose historically as powerful groups sought to advance their unjust domination over others.

But let us for a moment ignore all of the above and assume that race *is* a legitimate idea, a meaningful and genetically justified way to classify human beings. Would race then create a problem, exception, or qualification with respect to the discussion of pluralism under the Noahic covenant earlier in the chapter? The answer must be negative.

Even if people could be distinguished by race, both Scripture and mainstream science point to an even more fundamental biological unity of the human community. Contemporary biology holds that every person alive today descends from a very small group of humans. Scripture speaks of God making all people from one man (Acts 17:26) and calls one woman the mother of all the living (Gen 3:20). Despite this discrepancy between contemporary science and Scripture, both alike portray human beings as one family, derived from a common stock. Noteworthy for present purposes, Genesis also presents *Noah* as a new father of the human race. Biblical scholars may debate whether Scripture presents the flood as worldwide or as a catastrophic local event. But in any case, Genesis 9 calls readers to place themselves among the offspring of Noah (9:9, 12, 15, 17). Thus all humans have an equal claim to the covenant's promises and blessings. What ought to matter in human political communities is whether one is created in God's "image," a "man" (Gen 9:6)—whether male or female (Gen 1:27). Everyone who meets that criterion has the same claim as everyone else to participate in the covenant's institutions and to benefit from its administration of justice.

To view it from another angle, race is not a relevant criterion for making legal distinctions between one person and another because unjust *conduct* is what justifies penalizing people or excluding them from the political

---

12. For example, see Delgado and Stefancic, *Critical Race Theory*, 9, 51, 80, 85.
13. J. Kameron Carter, *Race: A Theological Account* (Oxford: Oxford University Press, 2008), 8.

community under the Noahic covenant. As considered above, perpetrators of violence are the ones who merit punishment (Gen 9:6). And even were race an objectively meaningful concept in terms of genetics, there is no inherent connection between race and behavior. Of course, there may be correlation between the race which a society has assigned someone and that person's cultural habits, since categorization by race encourages people to live and associate primarily with others in their category. But such correlation is not genetic causation. There is no genetic link between the color of one's skin, the shape of one's eyes, or the texture of one's hair, on the one hand, and that person's inclination to violence (or taste in music, athletic prowess, mathematical abilities, etc.), on the other.[14]

It may be important to note that *ethnicity* requires a different analysis. While ethnicity is often understood to include a biological component (descent from common ancestors), it is primarily about *culture*. People of a certain ethnicity—Russians, Egyptians, Japanese—share a distinctive history, language, literature, and land. This is not true of race, which lumps people together who have major differences in culture, as if these differences are unimportant. Insofar as a particular community consists primarily of people of a certain ethnicity—as in Russia, Egypt, and Japan—its ethnic culture will inevitably shape its laws and customs. As considered in part 1 and revisited in chapter 10, the Noahic covenant's moral vision is modest, and thus every political community has broad discretion in how it develops its laws and customs in accord with the relatively indeterminate natural law. Thus there is nothing objectionable when a community's law reflects its predominant ethnic identity, so long as it does not exclude those of different ethnic background from participation in familial, enterprise, and judicial institutions.

The conclusion to which these discussions point is that race is an illegitimate basis on which to exclude someone from participation in institutions or from equal justice under the Noahic covenant.[15] This is true whether race is a misleading construct or an objectively meaningful way to categorize human beings. But since race is in fact a misleading construct, and since the Noahic

---

14. See generally Rutherford, *A Brief History*, ch. 5.

15. The question of how to respond justly to injustices perpetrated on the basis of race is a pressing and difficult one in many communities. One route, represented by classical liberalism and the American civil rights movement, promotes policies that eliminate "race" or color as a way to classify people. Others criticize this approach as too shallow and incremental. Critical race theory, for example, calls for "color-conscious efforts to change the ways things are." See Delgado and Stefancic, *Critical Race Theory*, 27. This approach also guides the contemporary Black Lives Matter movement: "We see ourselves as part of the global Black family." https://blacklivesmatter.com/about/what-we-believe/. I leave it to readers to assess whether the Noahic covenant provides insight for this debate.

covenant focuses on conduct rather than biological differences, Martin Luther King Jr.'s vision of a society in which people are judged not "by the color of their skin but by the content of their character" seems to capture the Noahic vision.[16] The *Noahic* character of this vision is worth emphasizing in light of some racist theologians' appeal to the story of Noah's curse upon Canaan, son of Ham (Gen 9:18–28), as justifying the subjugation of African people.[17]

RELIGIOUS LIBERTY

Like race, religion also raises serious challenges to understanding pluralism under the Noahic covenant. Religious conviction is usually not a mere internal and private affair but a commitment that shapes external behavior and public conduct, often in ways that adherents regard as unsuitable for compromise. The goal of bringing people of different religious persuasions together into a peaceful political community with some shared vision of the common good presents seemingly intractable intellectual and practical problems. To step back and consider the depth of these problems makes one able, perhaps, to forgive the United States Supreme Court for its meandering First Amendment jurisprudence. Even in the United States, which continues its remarkably long-running experiment with a robust religious liberty, neither the official law nor public opinion is remotely settled. Perhaps most disconcerting about the contemporary American scene is the wide divergence in public perception. While some writers issue dire alarms about the imminent collapse of religious liberty at the hand of hostile secularists, others decry the unique legal privileges people can gain by asserting religious scruples.[18]

---

16. Martin Luther King Jr., "I Have a Dream," in *A Testament of Hope: The Essential Writings and Speeches of Martin Luther King Jr.*, ed. James M. Washington (New York: HarperCollins, 1986), 219. King went on, however, to portray his dream in terms of the realization of Scripture's eschatological promises, which no present political community is able to achieve.

17. For an example from a prominent Presbyterian theologian of the American South, see Robert L. Dabney, *A Defence of Virginia* (New York: Hale & Son, 1867), 101–4. Dabney did not believe this story was especially crucial to his defense of domestic slavery, but he did think it identifies slavery's origins: "It was appointed by God as the punishment of, and remedy for . . . the peculiar moral degradation of a part of the race." He adds that this was a verdict of God, and Noah's other sons, Shem and Japheth, had no need to feel guilty about "accepting that control over their guilty fellow-men." Toward the end of this discussion, he states, "It may be that we should find little difficulty in tracing the lineage of the present Africans to Ham." But he does not present any evidence.

18. For an example of the former, see Os Guinness, *The Global Public Square: Religious Freedom and the Making of a World Safe for Diversity* (Downers Grove, IL: InterVarsity Press, 2013); for an example of the latter, see Marci A. Hamilton, *God vs. the Gavel: Religion and the Rule of Law* (Cambridge: Cambridge University Press, 2005). One might conclude that the simultaneous existence of such starkly different perceptions is evidence that the American experiment continues to get many things right and has found

Is religious freedom in grave danger, or is it protected in unfairly generous ways? It is hard to believe these writers are talking about the same society.

In keeping with the purposes of this book, I will not offer detailed commentary on the state of religious liberty in the United States or anywhere else, although I will interact here and there with First Amendment scholars. Instead, I wish to contemplate the question of religious liberty in light of the Noahic covenant and, from this perspective, to propose a basic framework for Christians grappling with the issue. In this section, I offer some historical reflections and then make a general case for religious liberty. In the following section, I consider what sorts of exceptions to a broad-based religious liberty may be necessary.

Historical Reflections

The general framework I propose for religious liberty is so different from that of much of the Christian tradition, including many of its most prominent theologians, that it seems appropriate to acknowledge this clearly and to let a couple of these theologians have the floor for a moment. Christians ought to respect their forbears in the faith and not hastily condemn them for opinions different from their own, forged in very different cultural circumstances. The theologians I call forward are Augustine, a revered father of Western Christianity as a whole, and John Calvin, the most famous figure of my own Reformed tradition. I leave aside the whole Eastern Christian tradition, which has itself been no bastion of religious freedom.

I recognize Augustine and Calvin as truly great theologians, but I must admit that I find their writings on this subject to be embarrassing. I am grateful that my own Reformed tradition, with many other Christian traditions, has largely reversed course on issues of religious liberty.[19] Reading Augustine's letters against the Donatists may make a person wonder how such a profound theological mind could resort to such poor argumentation. With regret, I agree with a famous defender of religious liberty, Pierre Bayle, commenting on Augustine's defense of persecuting Donatists: "He had a

---

surprisingly effective and enduring ways to keep people with very different views together in a single, peaceful society. Cf. Andrew Koppelman, *Defending American Religious Neutrality* (Cambridge, MA: Harvard University Press, 2013), 166–67.

19. The change of judgment in the Reformed tradition spurred many ecclesiastical bodies to modify statements in confessional documents such as the *Belgic Confession* and the *Westminster Confession of Faith and Larger Catechism*. For example, whereas the original Answer 109 of the Westminster Larger Catechism listed "tolerating a false Religion" as one of the sins forbidden in the second commandment of the Decalogue, the American Presbyterians' revision in 1788 eliminated this phrase.

great share of Intelligence, but he had more Zeal; and so much as he indulged his Zeal . . . so much he fell away from solid Reasoning."[20] Nevertheless, I let Augustine and Calvin have their brief say.

These theologians made various biblical appeals to defend the state's special support of the (true) church and its use of coercion against those who oppose it. Augustine found evidence already in Genesis, where Sarah punished her servant Hagar for rebellion and restrained her pride, after Sarah had generously allowed her to become a mother.[21] Both Augustine and Calvin also cited the Israelite kings who defended true worship in accord with the law of Moses.[22] For Augustine, the lack of explicit New Testament authorization for such state action was no problem. We have no reason to expect such authorization, since Old Testament prophecies about righteous kings defending the church had not yet been fulfilled in the days of the apostles.[23] Even so, Romans 13 teaches that God appointed magistrates to punish evildoers—and resisting the claims of the true church is evil.[24] In addition, God compelled people to embrace the faith, as with Paul on the Damascus Road,[25] and one of Jesus's parables speaks of God's servants compelling unbelievers to take their place at the banquet (Luke 14:21–23).[26]

Augustine and Calvin made an assortment of other arguments for the same cause. Augustine often insisted that compelling those outside the church was a merciful and loving act performed for their own good. If we help people bodily, how much more should we help their souls?[27] It is like aiding a person delirious with fever who thinks he needs no assistance, or like a father who disciplines a wayward son.[28] For Calvin, fostering proper worship and restraining idolatry and blasphemy was a necessary aspect of the government's responsibility to maintain civil peace and order.[29] He also noted

---

20. Bayle, *A Philosophical Commentary*, 284. I also agree with Bayle that Augustine's defense of persecution was "scandalous to the last degree" (290), that his arguments regarding Sarah and Hagar expose Scripture "to the Raileries of the Profane" (307), and that he used "much fallacious reasoning" (411).

21. Saint Augustine, *Letters*, vol. 2, trans. Sister Wilfrid Parsons (New York: Fathers of the Church, 1953), 61; and Saint Augustine, *Letters*, vol. 4, trans. Sister Wilfrid Parsons (New York: Fathers of the Church, 1955), 149–51.

22. Augustine, *Letters*, 4.159–60; and John Calvin, *Institutes of the Christian Religion*, 4.20.9.

23. Augustine, *Letters*, 2:64–65; 4:80, 149, 159–61.

24. Augustine, *Letters*, 2:18–20, 56–57.

25. Augustine, *Letters*, 2:60–61; 4.75.

26. Augustine, *Letters*, 2:60–61; 4:80–81.

27. Augustine, *Letters*, 2:59–60, 62; 4:74–75, 161.

28. Augustine, *Letters*, 2:58; 4:75, 147–48, 162–63.

29. Calvin, *Institutes*, 4.20.23.

that even pagan writers recognized magistrates' responsibility to have religion and divine worship as their chief concern, making it especially shameful when Christian magistrates fail to make it theirs.[30] And as Augustine repeatedly claimed, compelling people into the true church works! Compulsion had already reclaimed many people who would not have returned to the faith by persuasion alone.[31]

In the pages to come, I intend to build a positive case for religious liberty by reflecting on the implications of the Noahic covenant, not to offer a point-by-point critique of such arguments. But I observe in passing how many of these arguments depend upon (undemonstrated) assumptions about the authority of civil magistrates. These theologians argue that magistrates have authority to punish unbelief and compel unbelievers because God himself does it, because Old Testament kings did it, because parents compel disobedient children, because Sarah compelled Hagar, and because kind people help delirious individuals who do not know they need help. In many of these cases, the actors indeed have rightful authority to do such things (although we may feel skeptical, for example, that Sarah had authority to make Hagar a sex slave and later punish her for pride). But none of these appeals prove that civil magistrates today have authority to use coercion against people who espouse heterodox religious views or refuse to join the (proper) Christian church. We will return shortly to the issue of civil authority.

Before doing so, I wish to mention some of the ways in which early modern proponents of religious liberty responded to these earlier arguments and blazed a new course. They offered many helpful retorts to the likes of Augustine and Calvin. Some of their points have problems of their own, I fear, but it may be useful to put some of their concerns on the table before I suggest a better approach. The figures from whose work I draw are Sebastian Castellio, Pierre Bayle, John Milton, John Locke, and Roger Williams.

One of their common arguments was that it is heinous to try to coerce a person's conscience, which brings no benefits for salvation but forces people to become hypocrites and to act with intent to disobey God.[32] These writers also asserted the distinctiveness of the Old Testament Israelite theocracy,[33]

---

30. Calvin, *Institutes*, 4.20.9.

31. Augustine, *Letters*, 2:58–59, 72–73; 4:154.

32. E.g., Castellio, *Advice*, 32; Bayle, *Philosophical Commentary*, 76–77, 220–24, 227; and Locke, "Letter," 10.

33. E.g., Bayle, *Philosophical Commentary*, 175–83; Locke, "Letter," 14; and Roger Williams, "The Bloody Tenent of Persecution for Cause of Conscience," in *On Religious Liberty: Selections from the Works of Roger Williams*, ed. James Calvin Davis (Cambridge, MA: Belknap, 2008), 136–37, 141–42.

appealed to the spirit and gentleness of Christ and his gospel,[34] and noted that for the first three centuries after Christ the church fathers repudiated compulsion.[35] Contemporary magistrates lack biblical authorization to compel people into the right church, they wrote, and their jurisdiction is limited to outward, civil matters, not matters of the soul.[36] These writers also claimed that the art of ruling does not require expertise in religion and that political commonwealths can flourish even where there is no church.[37] Finally, they warned about an assortment of practical dangers, such as turning heretics into martyrs,[38] the interminability of conflict when every side claims to be orthodox,[39] and the damage to human learning if free inquiry is curtailed.[40]

The Noahic Covenant and Religious Liberty

Some of the preceding arguments have strength, although several centuries of the Western experiment with religious liberty have revealed complexities that these writers did not anticipate. Thus I now begin a constructive case for religious liberty based upon the terms of the Noahic covenant. There may well be other good theological, philosophical, or pragmatic arguments for religious liberty. But if the Noahic covenant establishes the pluralistic character of political communities and also indirectly authorizes the work of civil government, as I have argued, this covenant is the proper starting point for our discussion. I first make a general case for religious liberty, both in terms of *establishment* and *free exercise* issues (to borrow First Amendment language). Then I wrestle with nuances and qualifications.[41]

A note of clarification before proceeding: Some readers may instinctively interpret my argument as a case that political community has no "religious" foundation. That is not a helpful or accurate way to put it. Since part 2 works from the idea that God's universal covenant with Noah is the foundation for political community, it would be strange to say that political community's foundation is not religious. What this section advances is not a nebulous

---

34. E.g., Castellio, *Advice*, 33; Bayle, *Philosophical Commentary*, 84; and Locke, "Letter," 2.

35. Bayle, *Philosophical Commentary*, 121.

36. E.g., Castellio, *Advice*, 42; Bayle, *Philosophical Commentary*, 112–13; Locke, "Letter," 3–5; and Williams, "Bloody Tenent," 87, 152–53.

37. E.g., Locke, "Letter," 9; and Williams, "Bloody Tenent," 98, 129–30.

38. Castellio, *Advice*, 52.

39. Bayle, *Philosophical Commentary*, 133; and Williams, "Bloody Tenent," 125.

40. Bayle, *Philosophical Commentary*, 197; and Milton, "Areopagitica," 383–84, 397, 402, 404, 406, 409. Contemporary advocates of free speech continue to make similar appeals; e.g., see Erwin Chemerinsky and Howard Gillman, *Free Speech on Campus* (New Haven: Yale University Press, 2017).

41. Cf. VanDrunen, *Divine Covenants*, 505–11.

claim that political community is religion free but that political communities ought to be maximally tolerant and open when it comes to the religious commitments and actions of their members.

A *NATURAL RIGHT* TO RELIGIOUS LIBERTY?

In chapter 9, we will consider the idea of *natural rights*, which refers to claims that all human beings may properly assert in every cultural and political context. Among the purported natural rights, religious liberty traditionally enjoys eminent standing. I believe there is an important place for speaking about natural rights and for including religious liberty among them. But it is not immediately obvious how to describe this natural right in a theologically helpful way.

One unhelpful route is to understand religious liberty as absolute or ultimate, in the sense of being a right to claim before God. In Paul's famous discussion of natural revelation in Romans 1, he speaks not of any *right* to think and worship according to one's own lights but rather of a *responsibility* to think properly of the true God and to worship him alone. Those who turn to idols are "futile" in thought and "foolish" in heart and stand without excuse before God, for God has made himself known plainly and clearly through the created order (1:19–23). No one can successfully claim a natural right to worship as she pleases. Instead, God will judge those who abandon their natural responsibility to worship him.

These considerations suggest Christians ought to be cautious about using arguments that defend the right to religious liberty by appealing to the goodness and worth of religion generally. Robert George, making one such argument, claims that religion in general "enriches, ennobles, and fulfils the human person in the spiritual dimension of his being," which leads to "a rational affirmation of the value of religion as embodied and made available to people in and through many traditions of faith." Honoring the right to religious freedom, he adds, permits people of many faiths to "engage in the sincere religious quest and live lives of authenticity reflecting their best judgments as to the truth of spiritual matters."[42] George is making a philosophical argument meant to appeal to all rational people, and his understanding of religion as a rationally intelligible basic good is arguably consistent with the

---

42. See Robert P. George, "Religious Liberty and the Human Good," *International Journal of Religious Freedom* 5, no. 1 (2012): 35–44. See also similar arguments in Kathleen A. Brady, *The Distinctiveness of Religion in American Law: Rethinking Religion Clause Jurisprudence* (Cambridge: Cambridge University Press, 2015), ch. 3.

theological concern expressed above.[43] But Romans 1 sounds rather different from George. It challenges the idea of religion in general as ennobling or of religious quest as sincere and authentic. Throughout Scripture, people are thoroughly religious: the main problem is not the occasional fool who says there is no God (Ps 14:1; 53:1) but the incessant idolatry that degrades the people who practice it (e.g., Ps 115:4–8; Isa 44:9–20). This is not to deny that belief in a transcendent being may curb excesses of injustice,[44] but George's argument seems in some tension with biblical testimony that most human religious practice insults the true God. From a Christian theological perspective, perhaps there is a better way to speak of a right to religious liberty.

THE NOAHIC COVENANT AND THE ESTABLISHMENT OF RELIGION

The Noahic covenant reframes the issue of religious liberty and places it on more solid theological (and natural-law) foundation. While Romans 1 rules out the notion of an absolute or ultimate right of religious liberty before God, the Noahic covenant indicates the importance of a qualified right of religious liberty *before fellow human beings* as a matter of civil justice.[45] I will avoid common terminology that speaks of the state being "secular" rather than "religious." Instead, I claim that the state, because it has no authority to act contrary to the Noahic covenant, ought not to establish a particular religion or religious body or to restrict the free exercise of religion within its jurisdiction.

The Noahic covenant is a divine blessing (Gen 9:1). In it, God grants many privileges to all human beings: protection from another judgment by flood (8:21; 9:11, 15), participation in the ordinary human affairs of familial and economic life (9:1–3, 7), and access to the protection of civil justice (9:6). As emphasized above, God bestows this blessing universally, without regard to a person's religious confession. And if God grants this blessing, then no human being has authority to strip it away from someone else. In terms of intrahuman justice, therefore, each person has a divinely bestowed natural right not to be disqualified from the political community because of the religion he or she professes.

---

43. George is a Roman Catholic, and he follows one of the lines of analysis of religious liberty in the Vatican II documents *Dignitatis Humanae* and *Nostra Aetate*.

44. The presence of a "fear of God" in the Old Testament among non-Israelites who have respect for justice suggests this point; see VanDrunen, *Divine Covenants*, 157–61.

45. For another work that seeks to ground religious liberty in the Noahic covenant, making similar arguments to mine, although without reliance on my previous work, see Jonathan Leeman, *Political Church: The Local Assembly as Embassy of Christ's Rule* (Downers Grove, IL: IVP Academic, 2016), 201.

The Noahic covenant also allows us to take the preceding argument a step further. Not only should a political community not disqualify a person from its activities and institutions because of her religious profession, but it should also not establish a particular religion or religious body.[46] That is, it should not recognize one religion as the true religion or one religious body as the true "church" or equivalent, nor should it grant special privileges to such a body or to its members.[47] At least three reasons support this claim.

First, as suggested in chapter 3 and elaborated in chapters 9 and 11, institutions of government properly emerge under the Noahic covenant to enforce the claims of justice. But I noted above that the Noahic covenant's mandate to pursue justice presupposes the general equality of all people before the law. Since the Noahic covenant does not distinguish among people based on religious profession, the requirement of equal justice stands at odds with granting some individuals and institutions a favored legal status on this basis. Second, civil governments that emerge out of the Noahic covenant have no basis for determining which specific religious institution or doctrine is the true, or truest, one. The terms of the Noahic covenant are too sparse for adjudicating details of theological doctrine or spiritual devotion. And natural revelation manifests the true God but not his Trinitarian nature, the incarnation of his Son, or the doctrine of salvation—essential matters of the Christian faith.[48] Determining the true religion or most pure religious body, on the basis of the Noahic covenant and its natural revelation, is perhaps analogous to performing brain surgery on the basis of a high school biology textbook. There is nothing wrong with the latter, but it lacks information necessary to guide the former.

Third, and from a deeper theological perspective, a biblical theology of the image of God shows the problematic nature of religious establishment. As discussed in part 1, the image of God at creation centered around royal

---

46. I believe this argument applies even with respect to an establishment scheme that grants "entrenched, constitutional encouragement to Christian mission not afforded to other religious beliefs" but does not "restrict the civil liberties of any non-Christian" or seek to defend itself against reform, as defended by Oliver O'Donovan in *The Desire of the Nations: Rediscovering the Roots of Political Theology* (Cambridge: Cambridge University Press, 1996), 224.

47. This need not mean that the state thereby denies a higher divine authority, which would itself run contrary to the Noahic covenant. Ira C. Lupu and Robert W. Tuttle fear that a state acknowledging that it acts under divine authority essentially claims "comprehensive jurisdiction" for itself; see *Secular Government, Religious People* (Grand Rapids: Eerdmans, 2014), 148, 155. But such acknowledgement could, on the contrary, be an act of considerable humility that recognizes important limits on its jurisdiction.

48. For a classic account of the limits of natural revelation from my own Reformed tradition, see, e.g., Francis Turretin, *Institutes of Elenctic Theology*, vol. 1, trans. George Musgrave Giger, ed. James T. Dennison Jr. (Phillipsburg, NJ: P&R, 1992), 9–16.

authority: God created human beings in his image and likeness so that they might exercise benevolent dominion in the world (Gen 1:26). To this royal authority, God added a priestly task, that of guarding the holiness of Eden from all that defiles (Gen 2:15).[49] When the Noahic covenant reaffirmed that human beings are the image of God, this also centered around royal authority: because God made humans in his image, they must enforce the claims of justice (Gen 9:6).[50] But in this context God added no priestly responsibility to promote the holiness of the human community.

In principle, there does seem to be something fitting about crowning royal rule on God's behalf with priestly consecration, yet God did not extend this privilege to fallen humanity. It is not difficult to imagine why so many human rulers have usurped authority over the worship of the people they rule. It may express a pining for the original integration of royal and priestly functions lost in the fall and also a longing for its restoration. But Scripture reserves this restoration for the redeemed communities he established through special covenant relationship. At Sinai, God said *Israel* would be "a kingdom of priests and a holy nation" if they obeyed his voice (Exod 19:5–6), and the New Testament declares that *the church* has already become "a royal priesthood, a holy nation" (1 Pet 2:9). Christ Jesus has become the heir of David's throne and a high priest according to the order of Melchizedek. Those united to him by faith share in his unified kingship and priesthood. Even now they enjoy a foretaste of the new creation, where the kings of the earth will offer glory to God in the everlasting city, which is a holy temple (Rev 21:22–27). When a political community grounded in the Noahic covenant weds itself to a particular religion or religious body, it adds a priestly dimension to its royal rule. This, I conclude, usurps a divine privilege granted only to the church.

THE NOAHIC COVENANT AND THE FREE EXERCISE OF RELIGION

The preceding argument advances the important claim that no political community ought to exclude people from participating in its activities and institutions because of their religious profession, nor should it create a religious establishment. But this leaves an important question outstanding: even if the political community may not exclude people from its activities and institutions on the basis of religious profession, may it perhaps prevent them

---

49. For discussion of this point, see, e.g., G. K. Beale, *The Temple and the Church's Mission: A Biblical Theology of the Dwelling Place of God* (Downers Grove, IL: InterVarsity Press, 2004), 66–69, 84–87.

50. On the appeal to the image of God in Genesis 9:6 as grounding the commission to do justice (rather than explaining why murder is so bad), see VanDrunen, *Divine Covenants*, 115–18.

from carrying out worship rituals or teaching doctrines it deems contrary to sound religion? To put it more concretely: even if a political community may not rightly exclude people from participating in familial, commercial, and judicial affairs because they affiliate with religion x, might it perhaps rightly prevent them from worshiping and teaching in ways religion x prescribes, because it considers such worship and teaching impious?

Genesis 9:6 suggests otherwise. The Noahic covenant concerns *intra-human* justice, not the punishment of wrongs *against God*: "Whoever *sheds the blood of man*, by man shall his blood be shed" (Gen 9:6; emphasis added). Of course, every wrong against a fellow human being is simultaneously and ultimately a wrong against God, the supreme judge to whom all must answer (9:5). But insofar as God delegates judicial authority to human judges, he commissions them to administer penalties proportionate to wrongs done to fellow humans, not penalties proportionate to wrongs done to him. Worshiping in an idolatrous way and teaching false religious doctrine are wrongs against God, and in this sense they stand outside the jurisdiction of human justice.

Yet one might object that they are also wrongs against fellow human beings, since they lead others astray and do them spiritual harm. In response, I note two reason to think that such spiritual harm is not the kind of intra-human wrong God commissions people to punish (again, I postpone fuller treatment of justice until chapter 9). First, as argued above, the Noahic covenant (and natural revelation) provides too small a body of truth to enable civil magistrates to determine exactly which modes of worship and which theological doctrines inflict exactly what spiritual harm. Second, there is no evident way by which human judges can determine a *proportionate* penalty for spiritual harm, even were they able to specify precisely what spiritual harm was done. Blood-for-blood is proportionate, but what would be the proportionate human penalty for persuading someone of a false view of, say, the Lord's Supper?

Supplementing these arguments is a third consideration, arising from a specifically Christian concern: according to the New Testament, how the church is to worship, teach, and be governed and disciplined is under the church's own jurisdiction, not that of the state. Bodies of qualified elders appointed by the church bear authority over such matters.[51] To put it in terms

---

51. See Acts 14:21–23; 1 Tim 3:1–7; Tit 1:5–9. I acknowledge the Presbyterian flavor of this claim. For a classic and a recent defense of Presbyterian church government, respectively, see, e.g., George Gillespie, *Aaron's Rod Blossoming* (London, 1646); and Guy Prentiss Waters, *How Jesus Runs the Church* (Phillipsburg, NJ: P&R, 2011).

familiar to this volume, Christian worship, doctrine, and discipline are affairs of the new covenant, not of the Noahic covenant. Christians therefore ought to resist state encroachment upon these affairs. And if Christians believe it is improper for the state to assume governing authority over the church, then they should also be alarmed if the state claims authority over other religious bodies. Once the state gets in the business of censoring religious worship, doctrine, and discipline, what stops it from usurping the church's authority? Thus, if for no other reason, the church's concern for the integrity of its own life and ministry ought to make Christians concerned about the integrity of other religious bodies in the face of an aggrandizing state.[52]

THE LIMITS OF RELIGIOUS LIBERTY

In the previous section, I made a general case for religious liberty in terms of establishment and free exercise. Yet such religious liberty cannot be absolute. No just society can tolerate every possible religious institution and practice. Discussion of religious liberty inevitably confronts questions about religious liberty's limits.

In this final section of the chapter, I attempt to discuss the limits of religious liberty in terms broad enough to be relevant for every common political community. Nevertheless, I recognize that every human society faces these questions in a unique way, and the distinctive terms of American debates have clearly shaped my own reflections on the issue. Accordingly, I will refer to several American judicial controversies in order to bring a concrete dimension to what could otherwise be too abstract a discussion. I will consider three classes of (possible) exceptions to the general protection of religious liberty promoted above, moving from the easier to more difficult.

Harm to Others

When considering possible exceptions to religious liberty, some scholars have proposed a *harm* criterion: people should be granted freedom to believe, worship, and practice their conscientious convictions, except when their conduct harms other people.[53] This claim is initially appealing, but it suffers from the chronic problem that afflicts the so-called "harm principle."

---

52. This argument bears some similarity to the claim of many defenders of religious liberty that government control corrupts religion. For discussion of this idea, see, e.g., Koppelman, *Defending American Religious Neutrality*, ch. 2.

53. E.g., see Hamilton, *God vs. the Gavel*, 3, 8, 205.

It is inherently vague.[54] Harm, or alleged harm, comes in a great many forms—physical, financial, emotional, spiritual. Without specification of what sorts of harm are in view, asserting that harm is the criterion for limiting religious liberty accomplishes next to nothing. Unfortunately, no shortcut or pithy formula can settle the question before us.

To work through the issue, I begin with the easiest kind of case: instances of force and fraud, or harm as violence against person or property. The Noahic covenant commissions human society to enforce justice by avenging bloodshed with a proportionate penalty (Gen 9:6). Therefore, it seems safe to say that the Noahic covenant *at least* commissions human society to punish acts of violence. No society can survive if it gives free rein to those who shed blood or commit analogous violent acts, that is, those who kill, rape, steal, and the like. Political communities thus rightly deny claims to religious liberty for conduct that involves violence against other people.[55] To mention a couple of extreme examples: while political communities ought to grant broad freedom to individuals and organizations to carry out religious rituals according to their own judgment, they should not permit them to carry out rituals that conscript people for human sacrifice or female circumcision.

Tolerance of the Intolerant

More difficult are situations in which a religion or religious body stands fundamentally opposed to the pluralism and religious freedom required under the Noahic covenant, as interpreted here. This is a perplexing issue. The Noahic covenant promotes the virtue of tolerance, but some people are convinced, as a matter of religious conscience, that political communities ought not to be broadly pluralistic. Such people may feel obligated to work for the legal establishment of their own religious body, for a confessional state, or for the suppression of other religions. How tolerant toward the intolerant should a political community be?

Tolerance, by definition, entails putting up with those who hold different views and follow different ways from one's own—even those that are offensive. Tolerance calls me, as an individual, to endure those who offend me, but it does not call me to stand by idly while others try to destroy me. By analogy,

---

54. The foremost defender of the harm principle in recent decades, Joel Feinberg, took four thick volumes to work it out; see *The Moral Limits of the Criminal Law*, 4 vols. (New York: Oxford University Press, 1984–1988). For critical discussion of the helpfulness of the harm principle in the context of religious freedom, see Smith, *Rise and Decline*, 42, 44; cf. 170.

55. Early modern defenders of religious liberty also made similar qualifications; e.g., see Castellio, *Advice*, 55; Bayle, *Philosophical Commentary*, 189–90; and Locke, "Letter," 12–13.

a tolerant political community puts up with a plethora of views and behavior, including much that is offensive to many members of the community. Those in the majority or with political power do not impose their own convictions on the minority and the powerless. But such tolerance does not imply that a political community must put up with those who seek its destruction. At some point, inevitably, even the tolerant cannot tolerate the intolerant.[56] If it is just for political communities to be broadly pluralist, to refuse to establish a particular religion or religious body, and to protect the free exercise of religion generally (as argued above), and if political communities exist to promote justice rather than impede it (per Gen 9:6), then they ought to resist the destruction of pluralism and religious liberty. To put it another way, since it is proper for pluralist political communities to emerge from the Noahic covenant, such communities justly defend their own existence.[57] The concept of reciprocity may again have purchase: Those who are intolerant of others' religious beliefs and practices cannot justly demand tolerance for their own religious beliefs and practices.[58]

What exactly does this imply in concrete circumstances? An antipluralist religious organization, making credible threats of terrorism, presents a simple case. A political community must take action against it and maintain justice for those threatened in accord with its responsibility to combat force and fraud. At the other end of the spectrum seems to be another simple case: a small and powerless religious organization that proclaims the wickedness of a pluralist and religiously tolerant social order but inflicts no force or fraud and poses no credible threat to the peace of the political community. The political community has no reason not to tolerate it, however intolerant that organization may declare itself to be.

But there are many potentially difficult cases in between. We might imagine an influential religious organization convinced that its mode of worship

---

56. Winnifred Fallers Sullivan reflects on similar issues when, commenting on the development of early modern ideas about religious freedom, she writes, "The precondition for political participation by religion increasingly became cooperation with liberal theories and forms of governance." "As a result, the modern religio-political arrangement has been largely, although not exclusively, indebted, theologically and phenomenologically, to protestant reflection and culture"—meaning "protestant" in the sense of "private, voluntary, individual, textual, and believed." See *The Impossibility of Religious Freedom* (Princeton: Princeton University Press, 2005), 7–8.

57. Cf. Brady, *Distinctiveness of Religion*, 235–39.

58. As noted above, many early modern proponents of religious liberty used reciprocity arguments, and sometimes did so in order to argue against full toleration for Roman Catholics, whom they regarded as intolerant. E.g., see Bayle, *Philosophical Commentary*, 191–93; Milton, "Areopolitica," 410; and Locke, "Letter," 17–18.

should be the only one legal. It forswears violence but is committed to using legal means to reshape the constitution for its own ends. Or we might think of another religious organization convinced that its worship alone should be legal, and its creeds praise violent rebellion as a means for attaining political goals. It does not foment such violence at the moment, but there is reason to suspect that it is merely waiting for an opportune time to wreak havoc. How should a just and pluralist political community address such situations? May it defend itself preemptively? I do not believe the framework provided by the Noahic covenant offers a definitive answer.

Exemptions to General Laws

We now come to the final and most difficult class of cases in our investigation of potential exceptions to the general protection of religious liberty. This class of cases arises in the context of laws or government policies that aim to accomplish more ambitious social goals than mere protection against the harms of force and fraud considered above. The problem emerges when individuals or organizations seek exemption from obeying these more ambitious laws because obeying them would violate their religious convictions or in some way hinder their religious devotion. (For purposes of this discussion I assume that such laws were not enacted with intent to suppress anyone's religious worship or practice.) Such cases have become particularly contentious in American law in recent decades. How should a political community deal with such requests for exemption, given the parameters of the Noahic covenant?

THE ATTRACTION AND THE HAZARDS OF EXEMPTION

To promote conceptual clarity, it may be helpful to distinguish cases of this kind into two main categories, although this distinction is not airtight. First, some laws or policies require people to act in ways contrary to their religious convictions as they pursue the common activities of the Noahic covenant. This is the sort of situation that prompted the famous *Hobby Lobby* (2014) and *Yoder* (1972) cases of the United States Supreme Court.[59] Second, other laws or policies hinder a religious body's ability to worship or govern

---

59. In *Burwell v. Hobby Lobby Stores, Inc.* 573 U.S. ___ (2014), the owners of a for-profit business sought (and received) exemption, based on religious objections, from government requirements to provide its female employees with health-insurance coverage for contraceptives that the owners believed could destroy embryos. In *Yoder v. Wisconsin* 406 U.S. 605 (1972), the Supreme Court exempted Amish families from mandatory school requirements for their children beyond eighth grade.

its internal affairs according to its own convictions. The Supreme Court has confronted such situations when considering the sacramental use of the illegal narcotic peyote, the practice of animal sacrifice in violation of local health codes, and the ability of churches to appoint their own "ministers."[60] For situations that fall in these categories, the United States has adopted various (sometimes conflicting) legislative and judicial standards, which often depend on balancing tests or judgment calls seeking to determine which is weightier, the burden that a law places upon a religious person or the state's interest in accomplishing its policy goals. As one writer has put it, "The task of accommodation is essentially that of balancing the good of religion against other goods."[61] The federal *Religious Freedom Restoration Act* (1993) and its many state-level versions are examples of one approach to the issue.

These cases can be perplexing. On the one hand, the conclusions drawn earlier in the chapter imply that political communities should try to avoid conflicts between laws and conscientious religious objections. With respect to the first category in the preceding paragraph, the universal and pluralistic character of the Noahic covenant directs political communities away from laws and policies that force people with minority religious convictions into a very unwelcome dilemma: either submit to the government's decree at the cost of violating their conscientious convictions, or follow their conscientious convictions at the cost of being fined, losing their businesses, or the like. With respect to the second category above, the Noahic covenant authorizes government to adjudicate *intrahuman* conflicts, and thus it directs political communities away from restraining religious organizations from worshiping and governing themselves in ways they believe proper.

On the other hand, such conflicts can hardly be avoided altogether. A person or organization might claim anything as a sincere religious conviction, and thus every law and policy potentially conflicts with someone's religious sensibilities. No political community can dispense with laws and policies, so how best to evaluate the inevitable conflicts between general legal requirements and conscientious religious objections?

One possible way forward is to accommodate religious objections generously by granting broad exemptions to general laws. In some situations, this is clearly a simple, decent, and sensible solution. In the United States,

---

60. *Employment Division v. Smith* 494 U.S. 872 (1990); *Church of the Lukumi Babalu Aye, Inc. v. City of Hialeah* 508 U.S. 520 (1993); and *Hosanna-Tabor Evangelical Lutheran Church and School v. EEOC* 565 U.S. ___ (2012).

61. Koppelman, *Defending American Religious Neutrality*, 107–8.

for example, laws prohibiting employment discrimination on the basis of religion regularly exempt religious institutions, thereby permitting churches (for instance) to hire only people who share its convictions. A policy aiming to protect a person's religious commitments would make little sense if it simultaneously prohibited his church from adhering to *its* commitments. Yet when a political community begins to open the exemption spigot wide, a number of serious problems emerge. One set of problems is practical. Granting exemptions to a small number of people or organizations in a narrowly defined area of law can work cleanly, but granting them to large numbers of people in many areas of law becomes chaotic and ultimately unworkable. A political community can hardly function well when its laws apply only to people who find them unobjectionable. Another set of problems is moral: can a legal system liberally dispense exemptions to religious objectors in an equitable way? This moral concern has several dimensions.

First, how are legislatures or courts to determine the sincerity of a particular person's religious objection or its importance to him? If a legal system grants exemptions to laws on the basis of religious conviction, it needs some assurance that those who plead for exemptions are not using religion as a pretext for avoiding laws they simply find inconvenient or expensive. Just taking a person at his word provides no assurance at all. Legal officials might instead seek proof of sincerity through investigation or soliciting evidence about a person's life. But any such proof of a person's subjective state of mind is tentative at best, and this would be a burdensome process in any case. Another possibility is that courts could test sincerity by looking to more objective measures, such as whether the official tenets of the objector's religion correspond with her claims of a tender conscience. But this too is tenuous. Not all religions have official doctrine that is clear and consistent, for one thing, and many adherents of a religion are poorly educated in its teachings and are less than fully orthodox. All of this should be irrelevant for legal purposes, since the Noahic covenant provides no basis for thinking that the only people who deserve religious freedom are well-educated, orthodox adherents of religions with clear and official doctrine. In short, the need to limit religious exemptions to those who are sincere presents a significant obstacle to applying exemptions equitably.

A second aspect of this moral concern involves the very category of "religion." If a political community is to grant exemptions to those with religious objections, it must be able to determine what sorts of convictions are actually religious. From a Christian perspective, it makes sense to think of religion in terms of devotion to God, whether that entails a true or mistaken notion of the divine. Yet not every tradition widely regarded as a religion even believes in a personal deity—Buddhism, for example. "Religion" is a vague concept, and this presents another challenge to the equitable application of religious exemptions.[62]

Third, even if we could define "religion" with sufficient legal clarity, it is not immediately clear why a political community should grant exemptions only to those with religious objections and not also to those with nonreligious moral objections. From a Christian perspective, it seems reasonable to conclude that a conscientious objection arising from a sense of obligation to God is of greater weight than a moral conviction arising from a nontranscendent source. Nevertheless, the Noahic covenant does not make anyone's participation in the political community contingent upon affiliation with a particular religion or religious body, and Scripture does not present religion in general as a wonderfully noble phenomenon but as usually degrading and God-dishonoring. Scripture regards as foolish both the person who makes an idol (Rom 1:22–23) and the person who says there is no God (Ps 14:1; 53:1). Hence, being able to label one's conscientious objection as "religious" rather than nonreligious is, arguably, a rather arbitrary basis for justifying exemptions to a general law. At least, it raises further doubts about a legal system's ability to apply exemptions equitably.[63]

Fourth and finally, the practice of granting exemptions from general laws raises serious questions about the protection of the (often vulnerable) people those laws were meant to serve in the first place. A useful example is mandatory schooling laws meant to ensure that every child receives at least a basic education. Granting parents an exemption due to religious scruple may be attractive because of the respect it shows for their conscientious convictions. But if receiving a basic education is so important for a child's well-being that a legislature has seen fit to make it mandatory, then does the law show careless disregard for the value of Amish children by allowing their parents

---

62. For an extended argument for the impossibility of giving "religion" a suitable legal definition, see generally Sullivan, *Impossibility of Religious Freedom*. Koppelman, however, notes that it is seldom a problem for courts to determine whether something is a religion (even though settling on a perfect definition of "religion" is elusive); see *Defending American Religious Neutrality*, 7.

63. Among rigorous attempts to defend the special place for religion in American law, see especially Brady, *Distinctiveness of Religion*, ch. 4. Among those arguing that religion should not receive special legal protection, but that rights of belief, worship, conscience, and the like should be protected in other ways, see Sullivan, *Impossibility of Religious Freedom*; and Leiter, *Why Tolerate Religion?* Perhaps Locke also disagreed with the idea that religion is legally special. He wrote that it should be lawful for every church to do what is lawful on other occasions in life. See "Letter," 20.

to keep them out of high school (as in *Yoder*)? The issue is much more acute in the case of parents who seek legal immunity for withholding medical care from their children on religious grounds.[64] To put the point concisely, granting exemptions to one person usually comes at the expense of someone else.

For these many reasons, exempting people from obligation to general laws because of religious objection raises serious practical and moral concerns, particularly if practiced in a widespread manner. We thus seem trapped in an unfortunate dilemma. On the one hand, political communities under the Noahic covenant should avoid impinging upon religious organizations' ability to worship and self-govern and should avoid obstructing people of minority religious beliefs from full participation in ordinary affairs. On the other hand, these same political communities ought to promote the orderliness and justice of society, in ways attentive to the equal worth of all its members, and thus should look warily upon expansive grants of exemption from general laws. Both concerns have deep roots in Noahic covenantal soil. Is there another way to approach these issues that relieves this tension and provides a more coherent perspective?

OVERCOMING THE DILEMMAS OF EXEMPTION

I believe there is a way, but it requires us to face some larger issues that will confront us again in subsequent chapters. To put it frankly, a robustly pluralist society and a legislatively aggressive government are an uncomfortable, and perhaps even impossible, combination. The more detailed and numerous the goals that government attempts to achieve, the more occasions for conflict arise with those whose convictions lie outside the mainstream.

The preceding course of discussion illustrates the point. We first considered the kinds of laws that the Noahic covenant seems to envision when commissioning humanity to pursue justice, that is, laws prohibiting violence against others—murder, rape, theft, and the like. Someone might assert a religious objection to such laws, of course, but these tend to be outlier cases. Most religions and most religious people affirm that such laws are good. Although people with different religious convictions may dispute the definitions of murder, rape, and theft around the margins, they will tend to concur about the chief things to be prohibited and punished. And whatever disagreements they have, they will almost always agree that their political communities must enforce laws against this kind of behavior if these communities are to

---

64. For discussion of such cases, see, e.g., Hamilton, *God vs. the Gavel*, ch. 2.

endure.[65] Developing such laws should serve to bind people together across moral and religious divides and promote their peaceful coexistence.

Subsequently, however, we considered laws that seek to do more than address violence against others. These include laws designed to protect people from harming themselves (such as narcotics laws at issue in *Smith*), to make them more virtuous or productive (such as laws regulating public education at issue in *Yoder*), and to provide them with various services to enhance their quality of life (such as health care laws at issue in *Hobby Lobby*). These sorts of issues tend to expose the differences in deeply held moral and religious conviction among people in a pluralistic society. While most people across the moral-religious spectrum agree about the necessity and basic content of laws against violence, their differences are inevitably more pronounced in areas of personal well-being, education, and healthcare. Such matters concern the most profound and most controversial areas of human existence. It is surely no coincidence that the major United States Supreme Court cases dealing with exemptions involve laws in these areas, rather than laws prohibiting violence. Relatively small and homogenous societies may be able to enact the former sort of laws without generating a large number of pleas for exemption, but in a large society such laws are practically designed to evoke crises of conscience from someone or another.[66] Such laws also inevitably trigger political battles over control of government-directed entitlements and services, battles which tend to exasperate social divisions rather than bridge them.

Is there a way to enact such laws without triggering these concerns? Some legal scholars assert that societies can give due respect to religious liberty while enacting such laws if the laws remain "neutral" and legislatures seek to serve the "public interest" or "public good."[67] But such a response does not even begin to solve the problem. No government can enact laws that are truly neutral. Every law reflects some commitment to what is good, valuable, and true, and this may be especially unavoidable with laws dealing with matters such as education and healthcare.[68] A law may appear neutral to the

---

65. Locke makes a similar point: if government sticks to the public good, that is, to secure each person's possession of the things of this life, conflicts of conscience will be rare. See "Letter," 16.

66. As Lupu and Tuttle note, courts rarely heard requests for exemptions (and rarely granted them) in nineteenth-century America, which was dominated by a Protestant ethos. Things are different now thanks to "the combination of wide-ranging pluralism . . . and the far-reaching expansion of government." See *Secular Government*, 181, 196–97.

67. This is illustrated on many occasions in Hamilton, *God vs. the Gavel*.

68. On the impossibility of state neutrality, in the context of religious liberty, see, e.g., Francois Venter, *Constitutionalism and Religion* (Northampton, MA: Edward Elgar, 2015), 230–33; Smith, *Rise and Decline*, 130–32; and Leiter, *Why Tolerate Religion?*, 13. Koppelman generally defends the idea of

people who share the assumptions of the mainstream powers that enacted it, but people who reject those assumptions will view it as anything but neutral. Assurances about the public interest or public good likewise offer little solace. The "public interest" and what serves it are in the eye of the beholder. Even tyrannical governments stamp out inconvenient dissent with appeal to the public good.[69]

In short, the more things a government tries to do and to regulate in a pluralistic society, the more intensely it will face an unpleasant dilemma between two options. One option is to try to uphold the pluralistic character of society and respect people's differences by liberally granting exemptions to its laws at the price of many attendant problems discussed above. The other option is to compel the political losers—ordinarily the less powerful and the moral and religious minorities—either to resist the laws that trouble them, to withdraw from aspects of public life, or to sacrifice their conscientious religious convictions, to the detriment of both these people themselves and the pluralistic nature of the community. The more areas of life in which government is active, the less room remains for people to express and live their differences. A number of First Amendment scholars do have a sense that expansive government threatens the robustly pluralistic character of society, but none of them seems to face the implications as directly as I have attempted to do here.[70]

If we begin with a premise supplied by the Noahic covenant—that political communities ought to be as open as possible to all human beings without regard for their religious identity—a case emerges for maintaining a limited government of tempered ambition. My earlier claim that the Noahic covenant provides political communities with a substantive but modest common good

<hr/>

religious neutrality in American law, but not in the sense that the law lacks all substantive commitment or conception of the human good; e.g., see *Defending American Religious Neutrality*, 17, 26.

69. In the second edition of her book, Hamilton refers to granting promiscuous religious exemptions to general laws, as exemplified in the federal and state Religious Freedom Restoration Acts, as "licentiousness," and she calls for all entities to be subject to "the rule of law." See Marci A. Hamilton, *God vs. the Gavel: The Perils of Extreme Religious Liberty*, 2nd rev. ed. (Cambridge: Cambridge University Press, 2014), 3, 239. It is indeed doubtful that a legal system can apply widespread exemptions in an equitable manner, as discussed above. But I also fear that giving legislatures broad power to seek the "public interest" by multiplying entitlements and regulating intimate areas of life may be an even greater threat to the rule of law, as I explore in chapter 10.

70. I see something of this dynamic at work in Brady, *Distinctiveness of Religion*, ch. 8; Lupu and Tuttle, *Secular Government*, 175–77; and Sullivan, *Impossibility of Religious Freedom*, 158–59. As described by Brady, the view of John Leland and Thomas Jefferson, who opposed religious exemptions from general laws but also thought governmental authority should be limited in scope, seems to concur with my suggestions here; see *Distinctiveness of Religion*, 116–17, 168–69.

also supports this case for limited government. A modest conception of the common good does not seem well-suited to ground the kind of substantively ambitious decisions necessary for a government to design an educational curriculum or establish a comprehensive health-care system. When the Noahic covenant commissions the defense of justice only in terms of intrahuman violence, perhaps this is more than coincidence or convenient illustration.

CONCLUSION

The covenant with Noah does not elaborate a detailed public policy, but the present chapter has offered some initial suggestions about how this covenant establishes important parameters for Christian reflection on perennial issues of legal and political theory. The Noahic covenant ordains that ordinary human activities and institutions be open to all people, and thus that the human community be broadly pluralistic, held together by a substantive but modest common good. This entails a pluralism that unambiguously rejects racial discrimination and promotes a broad and generous (if often not unambiguous) religious liberty. This in turn implies that governments should be limited in scope and modest in ambition. We will return to the scope and ambition of government in later chapters.

CHAPTER 8

FAMILY AND COMMERCE

Part 1 discussed the ethic of the Noahic covenant, rooted in three basic obligations: to be fruitful, multiply, and fill the earth, to provide for human material needs, and to promote rectifying justice. These three obligations implicitly commission the human race to do many other things as well, including the establishment of familial, enterprise, and judicial institutions. These three kinds of obligations and institutions, in turn, take us into three of the most important and controversial areas of public life: family, economics, and law. This chapter considers the first two of these. Later chapters explore the third.

Considering the complex matters of family and economics in the same chapter is a big task. Yet they are intertwined, both theoretically and practically, and it makes good sense to deal with them simultaneously. This should become clear as the chapter proceeds.

In the industrial revolution of the nineteenth century and the globalization of the twentieth and twenty-first centuries, the economies of Western societies and increasingly the rest of the world have changed drastically. These events have brought previously unimaginable wealth to billions of people but have also disrupted many traditional ways of life and provoked strong voices of protest. The sexual revolution beginning in the 1960s overturned numerous long-standing norms about sex, marriage, and gender roles in Western culture. Arguably, these latter shifts have been even more consequential and controversial than the economic changes. In keeping with the plan set out in the previous chapter, I will not focus on these events or comment on the latest controversies about them. Instead, I try to identify what framework the Noahic covenant provides for reflecting in a morally sound way on the nature and purpose of family and economic life in common political communities. The conclusions I draw cannot be neatly translated into a dogmatic public policy. Readers should not equate my claims about the Noahic norms for family and commerce with the claim that the state ought to enforce all of them. In what follows, the traditions and debates of my own Western context have obviously shaped the way I address these issues. Concrete contemporary problems occasionally emerge in the pages that follow and keep the discussion from becoming too abstract, I hope.

I begin this chapter with a general discussion of the issues before us, and then address matters of family and commerce, respectively. I conclude by reflecting on whether the conceptions of family and economics I defend here are mutually incompatible in the modern world.

THE NOAHIC COVENANTAL RELATIONSHIP OF FAMILY AND COMMERCE

As discussed in chapters 2–3, the Noahic covenant's set of moral exhortations (Gen 9:1–7) begins and ends with a call to be fruitful, multiply, and fill the earth, repeating part of the primordial creation mandate (Gen 1:28). The Noahic covenant thus views the increase of human population throughout the world favorably. This text also speaks about eating: God gives animals and plants to humans for consumption, but they should not eat meat with its blood (9:3–4). They should eat widely, but within humane limits. These two aspects of the text correspond. A human race expanding throughout the earth is going to have many material needs, food chief among them. But the necessary resources are not just there for the taking. As human communities pressed into new areas, they did not find grocery stores waiting to be shopped or homes looking for inhabitants. They had to find and develop their own resources, and this was no small task. In certain parts of the world, human communities could live for a time as hunter-gatherers. But as their numbers grew this became a decreasingly viable option. They had to develop settled agriculture, a laborious endeavor.[1] This involved developing land to farm, discovering which crops could grow there, and figuring out how to cultivate them. Meanwhile, they had to combat threats to their crops from droughts, floods, disease, fire, and covetous neighbors, and to construct suitable shelter and clothing. If all of

---

1. See, e.g., Colin Tudge, *Neanderthals, Bandits and Farmers* (New Haven: Yale University Press, 1999).

this went tolerably well, they might hope to survive a long, cold, dark winter without the benefit of electricity, running water, or modern medicine. Many women died in childbirth. Most children did not survive to adulthood.

I just have tried to describe the task of filling the earth as difficult and miserable, since that is precisely what it has been for most of humanity through most of history. But here it is important to consider the conclusion of Genesis 1 again. God created the human race not only to be fruitful, multiply, and fill the earth but also to "subdue" the earth and to "have dominion" over the other creatures (1:28). He equipped them for this task by making them in his own image and likeness (1:26–27). As noted in chapter 2, to be made in God's image constituted a commission: God made humans in his image *so that* they might rule. According to Genesis 1, God is fruitful and creative, and thus those who bear his image should be fruitful and creative. In Genesis 1, God orders the various spheres of life for productive purposes, and thus those who bear his image should bring further order, for the good of creation. To be sure, God made human beings part of this world—constituted by the same material stuff as the other creatures (2:7)—but he called them to be active rather than passive. They were not simply to receive the world as they found it and live as unobtrusively as possible but to make their mark on the world, bringing it to even greater order, productiveness, and beauty than it had apart from the human touch.

This point deserves emphasis. Despite the grandeur of creation in Genesis 1 and the bounty of Eden in Genesis 2, Adam had a lot of work to do. Genesis 1:28 implies that God did not create the animals domesticated and at Adam's beck and call. Adam had to figure out how to subdue them. God filled the world with natural resources, but it seems more a matter of potentiality than actuality. The Lord planted a garden in Eden (2:8), but the human community was to expand far beyond Eden, where they would have to plant their own gardens. In the fallen world of the Noahic covenant, human beings face three additional challenges: their sinful nature (Gen 6:5; 8:21), God's curse upon the ground (3:17–18), and their inevitable death (3:19). For Adam and his sinless progeny, presumably, the image-bearing task of dominion would have been challenging but continuously joyful, the process long but the progress quick. For Noah's sinful progeny, in contrast, filling the earth and developing provisions sufficient for doing so has been agonizingly hard and slow. It is interrupted with some joy and satisfaction but saturated with failure, pain, and sorrow.

And yet, Noah's sinful progeny continued to bear the image of God (Gen 9:6). They retained a penchant for reproducing, exploring, discovering, and inventing and thus found ways to preserve and advance their lives, utilizing and beautifying the world around them. As image-bearers of a wise and creative God, they have not been satisfied with providing for their bare material necessities but have also dabbled in sports, music, art, poetry, and mathematics. Once one person discovered a way to do something useful, someone else developed a better way. Progress was slow, and subject to sudden reversals thanks to war and natural disaster. But as image-bearers upheld by divine providence, they got up and pressed on.

In the course of filling the earth, providing for their material needs, and developing their image-bearing potentialities, human beings under Noah have collaborated with one another. They are social creatures who both desire others' company and find themselves able to achieve much more when they cooperate. Thus they have formed a variety of associations and institutions in order to collaborate in effective ways toward the accomplishment of different ends. In chapter 3, I identified three main types of institutions: familial, enterprise, and judicial. The first two are of special interest here. To procreate and raise their offspring, people have established family relationships. To fill the earth, develop the resources this requires, and advance broader image-bearing cultural pursuits, they have established various enterprise associations. Human life under the Noahic covenant should be neither individualist nor collectivist. Human success and contentment comes neither by going it alone nor by being absorbed into a single institution.[2]

Before unpacking the nature and purpose of familial and enterprise institutions, I pause to ponder the significance of the general perspective just outlined. The first moral commission in Scripture—to fill the earth and to rule and subdue the other creatures—encapsulates the original task of humans as image-bearers of God. However difficult and frustrating it has become in a fallen world, the task remains. To advance this work brings benefit for humanity and makes the world a better place. This claim is hardly uncontroversial. Lynn White famously accused the Judeo-Christian idea of dominion of wreaking harm in the world: whereas paganism had portrayed human beings as comfortably part of nature, the triumph of Christianity in the West turned humans into exploiters of nature. White thought Christianity might

---

2. See the work of Max L. Stackhouse, for example, who reflected on the importance and multiplicity of voluntary associations in a number of works. E.g., see *Public Theology and Political Economy* (Lanham, MD: University Press of America, 1991), 125–26; *Covenant and Commitments: Faith, Family, and Economic Life* (Louisville: Westminster John Knox, 1997), 64; and *God and Globalization*, vol. 4, *Globalization and Grace* (New York: Continuum, 2007), 48–50.

be salvaged, but only through a kind of Franciscan spirituality much different from the attitude commended at the end of Genesis 1.[3] White's attack has provoked Christian counteroffensives. Many writers have defended the benevolence of the dominion mandated in Genesis 1 (as I did in chapter 2). But others have accepted White's background story: human population growth and economic and technological development have brought the world to a precarious place, and Western culture (including Christianity) bears much of the blame.[4] Timothy Gorringe has appealed to the story of Noah to propose a solution. For Gorringe, there are too many people, too much human activity, and not enough planet, and thus "the Noah model/option" calls Christians to retreat into metaphorical ark-building. Their "arks" can become havens for other people as the world economy and ecosystem collapse in the years to come.[5] One also thinks of Wendell Berry, whose praise of what is small, local, and primitive has given many Christians pause about global economic growth.[6]

Concerns about ecological damage and globalization's effects on local communities are important. But Scripture does not instruct Christians or anyone else to retreat from the world back into arks. It commissions them to go out from Noah's ark so they can fill the world. If filling the earth and its corresponding technological advance and economic growth are fundamentally harmful, then some foundational biblical texts are misguided. With traditional Christian confidence in Scripture, I affirm that these activities are fundamentally beneficial (while always subject to corruption). But we know this not simply by an act of faith. The moral commission of the Noahic covenant is consistent with the world as we experience it. As explored below, there is good reason to think this commission corresponds to the natural law.

FAMILY

According to Scripture, God instituted family relationships at creation (Gen 1:28; 2:22–24) and, in our fallen world, continues to do so through the Noahic covenant (9:1, 7). Familial institutions thus exist for the human

---

3. Lynn White Jr., "The Historical Roots of Our Ecologic Crisis," *Science* 155, no. 3767 (March 10, 1967): 1203–7.

4. E.g., see Steven Bouma-Prediger, *For the Beauty of the Earth*, 2nd ed. (Grand Rapids: Baker Academic, 2010), 80.

5. Timothy J. Gorringe, "On Building an Ark: The Global Emergency and the Limits of Moral Exhortation," *Studies in Christian Ethics* 24, no. 1 (2011): 26–33.

6. E.g., see Wendell Berry, "The Total Economy," in *Wealth, Poverty, and Human Destiny*, ed. Doug Bandow and David L. Schindler (Wilmington: ISI, 2003), appendix A.

race universally and serve God's temporal and provisional purposes for this present world. Our sole interest here is in these temporal and provisional purposes, but I first make very brief comments on the relationship of family and the new covenant, since Christians live under this covenant too.

First, the new covenant grants Christians hope of everlasting life in the new creation, where marriage and family as we know it will no longer exist. Marriage relationships end with one spouse's death (Rom 7:2–3) and no one gets married again in heaven (Luke 20:35). The purposes of marriage and childrearing are fulfilled in this present age. In anticipation of the age to come, Christians now regard their fellow saints in the church, the household of faith, as most dear to them (e.g., Mark 3:31–35; 10:29–30), and they may honorably remain unmarried and childless for better service to the Lord (1 Cor 7:6–8, 32–35). Accordingly, the New Testament never issues the oft-repeated Old Testament command to be fruitful and multiply. What now bears fruit and multiplies is "the word of truth, the gospel" (Col 1:5–6).[7] Second, however, the New Testament treats marriage and childrearing as the course most Christians will and should follow (1 Cor 7:2; 1 Tim 5:14). And when they marry, Christians participate in the same institution their non-Christian neighbors do.[8] In his earthly ministry, Christ did not establish marriage and family for his people (as he did the church—Matt 16:18) but simply affirmed the already-existing institution of marriage originating in creation (Matt 19:4–9). Third, although they participate in the same marriage institution as do non-Christians, Christians experience some unique privileges in it. For example, Christ's redemptive grace sanctifies believers for carrying out more diligently the family duties they already have, and adds a depth of responsibility to them.[9] Furthermore, membership in Christ's church extends to the young children of believers, such that the church properly baptizes households rather than simply individuals (Acts 10:22; 11:12, 14; 16:14–15; 16:30–34; 18:8; 1 Cor 1:16; 7:14).[10]

---

7. See also David VanDrunen, *Divine Covenants and Moral Order: A Biblical Theology of Natural Law* (Grand Rapids: Eerdmans, 2014), 470–73. I hope to explore these issues in much more detail in a future volume.

8. This view differs from the Roman Catholic view of a sacramental marriage that imparts grace, distinct to baptized Catholics who marry in the church. E.g., see *Catechism of the Catholic Church* (New York: Doubleday, 1995), §§1601, 1617, 1638–42. I find no evidence in Scripture that marriage is a means of redemptive grace for two Christians who marry.

9. For example, all parents are obligated under the Noahic covenant and natural law to train their children, but Christians are to raise their children "in the discipline and instruction of the Lord" (Eph 6:4). All husbands ought to love their wives, but Christian men should love their wives "as Christ loved the church and gave himself up for her" (Eph 5:25).

10. I write as an adherent of the classical Reformed view of baptism, as expressed, for example, in the *Westminster Confession of Faith*, 28.

These issues are obviously important for Christian ethics but are not our concern here. This section now focuses upon familial institutions as God ordains them for the entire human race, Christians and non-Christians alike, through the Noahic covenant.

"Families" can obviously take a multitude of forms. The question before us is what sort of family structure is consistent with the Noahic covenant and promotes its moral commission. The text of the Noahic covenant is tantalizingly vague. Thus let us reflect upon its implications and see what conclusions we can properly draw.

Families Are for Children

The Noahic covenant does not directly command people to get married and establish families. It implicitly calls them to do so by commanding them to be fruitful, multiply, and fill the earth. Thus, as far as the text of the Noahic covenant is concerned, families serve one purpose: not to satisfy a need for intimacy or companionship among adults but to facilitate the procreation of children so that humans might fill the globe. Of course, this does not mean family relationships can serve no other purposes, such as intimacy and companionship. Elsewhere Scripture affirms such worthy causes (e.g., Song of Songs; 1 Cor 7:1–5). But the Noahic covenant points to what is essential and nonnegotiable for attaining God's preservative purposes in this world. Humans must procreate and raise children if human society is to survive. *This* is the bedrock purpose of families for the human race in common under the Noahic covenant. My first conclusion, therefore, is that our exploration of how familial institutions ought to be organized should begin by considering what conduces to effective childbearing and childrearing, and not what serves purposes of romance, pleasure, or camaraderie.

Children Need Nurture

The second point builds on the first. Every child born into the world requires a great deal of nurture. Unlike children of many animal species that are able to fend for themselves shortly after birth, newborn humans are absolutely helpless in their early months and remain incapable of independent living for many years thereafter. The goal of the Noahic covenant is not the raw number of babies produced but an expanding community of competent and productive children who become adults and are able in turn to raise up another generation. Thus, if the human race is not only to be fruitful but also to *multiply* and *fill the earth*, families must procreate children and also provide for their needs and train them in the ways of the world. These inter-related tasks are the core rationale for organizing families, according to the Noahic covenant.

Monogamous, Heterosexual, and Permanent

This raises a further question: what specific sort of family structures advance the goals of childbearing and childrearing? Since the command of Genesis 9:1, 7 to be fruitful, multiply, and fill the earth repeats part of the original creation mandate (1:28), the former should be interpreted against the background of the latter. This background helps to answer our question.

In Genesis 2, Adam successfully performed some aspects of the creation mandate by naming the animals (2:20), in obedience both to God's direct command (2:19) and to his indirect commission to further God's work of ordering the world (see 1:5, 8, 10, 26–28). But Adam had no partner suitable for him (2:20)—certainly not one with whom he could procreate. God therefore created the requisite partner and joined the two in marriage (2:21–24). This account indicates the basic pattern for organizing families. Marriages should be *monogamous*: the need to procreate and raise children evokes the union of *one* man and *one* woman. They should be *heterosexual*: to procreate and raise children evokes the union of one *man* and one *woman*. And they should be *permanent*: a man leaves his prior relationship with his parents, "holds fast" to his wife, and they become "one flesh" (2:24). Genesis 1–2 itself does not say whether monogamous, heterosexual, and permanent marriages should be regarded as the only morally sound or legally permissible family structure, but it communicates that they constitute the foundational family structure undergirding the call to be fruitful, multiply, and fill the earth. With no evidence to the contrary, this must continue to be true when the Noahic covenant issues the same call.

Confirmed Elsewhere in Scripture

The rest of Scripture confirms these conclusions about family drawn from the Noahic covenant, as read against the background of Genesis 1–2, although there is ambiguity on one point.

First, Scripture broadly confirms that marriage and family relationships are for the human race in general. In the course of the biblical story, both participants and nonparticipants in the covenants with Abraham, Israel, and the church get married, have children, and engage in family life. Although both Old and New Testaments exhort participants in these covenants to marry within the faith, Scripture nowhere treats other people's marriages and families as invalid or even second-class. Second, Scripture consistently presents children as a blessing (e.g., Ps 127:3), although one that carries weighty responsibilities (e.g., Prov 22:6; Eph 6:4). Third, while Scripture speaks of divorce and remarriage as permissible under some circumstances (e.g., Matt 19:9), it presents marriage relationships as designed to be permanent (Mal 2:16; Matt 19:6; 1 Cor 7:10–13). It grounds this permanence in the created order (Matt 19:4–8). Fourth, Scripture uniformly describes marriage as heterosexual. It does not speak often about homosexual conduct, but the evaluation is negative every time it does. And most of these texts communicate the normativity of heterosexual relations for humanity in general, not just for worshipers of the God of Israel (Gen 19:1–29; Lev 18:22 [cf. 18:24–28]; 20:13 [cf. 20:22–23]; Rom 1:26–27 [cf. 1:18–20]).

Things are more complicated with monogamy. While Scripture nowhere prescribes polygamy, it nowhere forbids it either. It appears many times in the Old Testament, and several famous Old Testament figures practiced it. Still, the Old Testament never makes polygamy look attractive. Polygamy brought tension and grief to all of the prominent polygamous families—of Abraham, Jacob, David, and Solomon. And the New Testament points back to the monogamous marriage of Adam and Eve as paradigmatic (Matt 19:4–8) and prohibits polygamists from holding church office (1 Tim 3:2). It seems safe, if not sophisticated, to say that Scripture frowns upon polygamy even while never forbidding it.

Corresponding to the Natural Law

If prior discussion of the Noahic covenant and natural law is accurate, the present claims about family ought to be in accord with the world as God made it and we experience it. That is, these claims should not be obscure to ordinary people but should resonate with what they already know at some basic level. Thus we now consider how that is true, first in a more theoretical way and then in a more empirical way. As elsewhere in this book, these natural-law reflections are not intended to prove a moral point in a technically rigorous or mathematically certain way but to contemplate how the moral order of the Noahic covenant corresponds to the natural order in which all people live.

First, I concluded that bearing and training children should be the primary concern when considering how to order familial institutions. Does this conclusion make sense of the world as we know it? Yes, that seems to be the case. For one thing, it makes sense in light of the absolute necessity of raising up future generations if the human race is to survive. It also makes sense since newborn humans are helpless and remain deeply dependent upon others for years to come—both in terms of basic necessities and training in life skills.[11] It is not inconceivable that stable adults, thinking only of their own needs, could enter into boutique contracts with other consenting adults and satisfy their basic desires for intimacy, pleasure, and companionship. But the initial helplessness and long-continuing dependence of children indicates the need for family structures designed to care for them.[12] Every person benefited from caregivers when he or she was young, and thus no one can dismiss their importance without hypocrisy.

As we begin our contemplation with the needs of children, we also recognize that children are procreated through the sexual union of one man and one woman. Someone must care for these children, and it makes a good deal of sense that the two people who procreate a child ought to provide this care. It makes sense because of the natural affection most people feel toward their biological offspring, an affection far greater than what they feel toward other people's children. It also makes sense given the widespread human conviction that people ought to bear responsibility for their actions, and the realization that society will crumble if such responsibility ceases on a broad scale. Accordingly, if two people have acted so as to bring a child into the world, those people have primary responsibility for the child's care. Assigning responsibility to *both* parents makes sense, furthermore, because under normal circumstances it takes *two* parties to care for a child. For many years, a child needs a caregiver on hand almost continuously, and thus the caregiver usually needs another adult to provide materially for him or her as well as for the child.[13] Thus (ordinarily) the parents are the two parties best suited to care for a child (which does not imply that each parent must play only one role—caregiver or provider—all the time).[14]

---

11. Jennifer Roback Morse makes this case at length. See her summary of the case in *Love and Economics: It Takes a Family to Raise a Village* (2001; reprint, San Marcos, CA: Ruth Institute, 2008), 5–7. Cf. Stackhouse, *Covenant and Commitments*, 44.

12. John Witte Jr. comments, "Other forms of civil union and intimate association might work for consenting adults, but marriage is the best institution for children." See *The Sins of the Fathers: The Law and Theology of Illegitimacy Reconsidered* (Cambridge: Cambridge University Press, 2009), 182. Elsewhere he notes that we appropriately build the law of marriage around the typical case, not the exceptional case; see John Witte Jr., *The Western Case for Monogamy over Polygamy* (Cambridge: Cambridge University Press, 2015), 461.

13. Cf. Morse, *Love and Economics*, 34–36.

14. On the general superiority of parental care to paid child care, see Morse, *Love and Economics*, 171–74. Cf. Stackhouse, *Covenant and Commitments*, 74.

What, then, about monogamy? Given how most people feel about sexual relations, envy and competition are a major threat to familial peace in polygamous or polyandrous homes. And given most people's natural affections, a household in which different children belong to different sets of parents is a breeding ground for complex divisions among overlapping subfamilies within the broader household. Polyandry has suffered the additional drawback of leaving paternity uncertain (although genetic testing can now answer that question). Polygamy also has an additional drawback, at least if practiced on any wide scale: a relatively small number of rich and powerful men, who can attract multiple wives and afford to support a large household, will marry a disproportionate number of women and leave less-well-off men with a smaller pool of potential wives. This is not only unjust in principle toward less-well-off men but also creates social instability by relegating large numbers of men to being unmarried and even unmarriable. These considerations confirm that monogamy too is in accord with the moral order of the world as we know it.[15]

Thus far, I have suggested that the ideas of heterosexual and monogamous marriage as the foundational pattern for the family resonate with our knowledge of the world. What about marriage as *permanent*? The preceding considerations indicate that marriage should have at least some enduring character: children need not only to be conceived but also to be nurtured and trained for a lengthy period of time, and the two biological parents are generally the best people to do so. As their children mature and learn to provide for themselves, however, this rationale for keeping marriages together dissipates. Yet other good reasons remain. Natural affection continues to bind parents and children together after the latter reach adulthood. Husband and wife remain linked through their children, the product of their union, and children remain linked to their parents as a unit, not simply to their mother and father as independent individuals. Grandparents have strong natural affection for their grandchildren, and grandparents can often provide parents with wise help in nurturing their children. These considerations suggest the wisdom of viewing marriage and family relations as lifelong and not simply as short-term arrangements. Thus all three aspects of the foundational pattern for family indicated by the Noahic covenant—heterosexual, monogamous, and permanent marriage—make sense of the world as we know it and correspond to its moral order.

---

15. Witte, *The Western Case*, 453–64, summarizes the traditional argument against polygamy, which includes many of these points.

As noted in chapter 5, Proverbs engages in a type of natural-law exercise insofar as it instructs readers about the way of wisdom by reflecting on human nature and human relations in the world we inhabit. Thus it is relevant to note that Proverbs confirms the prior conclusions. First, it teaches that getting married is a good thing (18:22), although it is important to marry well, since an unhappy marriage is miserable (21:9, 19). Those who have children, second, should raise them diligently so they become wise (e.g., 22:6). Proverbs begins with a father and mother instructing their son (1:8 and following) and ends with the son finding an excellent wife (31:10–31). That is, parents train children so they too can marry and continue the process for the next generation. Third, despite its Solomonic origins (see 10:1; 25:1), Proverbs invariably contemplates marriage in monogamous terms. A child has a father and a mother (1:8), a man finds a wife (18:22; 31:10), and a man is to be faithful to and satisfied with the wife of his youth (5:18–19). Fourth, Proverbs implies the permanence of the marriage relationship by characterizing adultery as destructive of families and the epitome of folly (2:16–19; 5:1–23; 6:20–7:27). The exhortation to be faithful to the wife of one's *youth* (5:18) implies that marriages are to endure into older age. Fifth, successful training of children is good for society. When it fails, children collaborate with those who harm others (1:8–19) and destroy their own and others' lives (6:33–35). Finally, a happy marriage and successful child-rearing is also good for the parents themselves, bringing them joy and satisfaction (10:1; 15:17; 31:10–11, 23, 27–29).

Corresponding to Empirical Evidence

While the preceding discussion was somewhat theoretical, concrete evidence from recent social science also suggests that the Noahic covenant's foundational family pattern is not obscure but should make sense to honest observers of the world. The significantly higher rates of divorce, nonmarital births, single parenthood, and extramarital cohabitation in recent decades have provided plenty of opportunity to study different family patterns. The scholars I cite below span the political spectrum. As far as I can tell, there is no serious debate about the following phenomena.

Many studies have found that children raised in mother-only homes and in stepfamilies have lower rates of education, lower earnings, earlier ages of marriage and child-bearing, higher divorce rates, higher criminal rates, and higher rates of substance abuse.[16] Children of cohabiting but nonmarried

---

16. See Charles Murray, *Coming Apart: The State of White America 1960–2010* (New York: Crown

parents do not do appreciably better than those of single, non-cohabiting mothers.[17] Cohabiting boyfriends abuse children living in the home at far higher rates than do husband-fathers, even if they are the children's biological fathers.[18] In general, distant or absent fathers deprive children of many benefits that those with close relationships with their fathers enjoy.[19] (None of this, I should emphasize, is meant to underestimate the importance of mothers.)[20] Having stable families also greatly aids children's development of a sense of social trust and reciprocity, which are crucial for their future productive participation in society.[21] Recent neuroscience has discovered how much children's early life experiences—such as having parents who talk with them frequently, or being surrounded by stressful home lives—shapes the very architecture of their brains and thus promotes or inhibits their development of executive functions and other crucial capabilities.[22]

The social (and even hard) scientific evidence is overwhelming. As Max Stackhouse puts it, "The idea that all family forms do an equally effective job in raising children, given enough money, is simply wrong."[23] The Noahic foundational pattern for family organization makes sense of human beings and the world as they actually exist. And this pattern not only establishes the best setting for nurturing children. A good marriage is also about the best predictor available for whether a person considers himself or herself generally happy.[24] Marriage also seems to foster improvement in people's (and especially

Forum, 2012), 158; Robert D. Putnam, *Our Kids: The American Dream in Crisis* (New York: Simon & Schuster, 2015), 78–79; Morse, *Love and Economics*, 106–7; Don S. Browning, *Marriage and Modernization: How Globalization Threatens Marriage and What to Do about It* (Grand Rapids: Eerdmans, 2003), 18; and Witte, *Sins of the Fathers*, 8.

17. See Murray, *Coming Apart*, 163–64.

18. See Morse, *Love and Economics*, 109; cf. Browning, *Marriage and Modernization*, 112–13.

19. See Browning, *Marriage and Modernization*, 18; ch. 4. On the greater degree of sexually risky behavior among girls without quality fathers, see Danielle J. DelPriore, Gabriel L. Schlomer, and Bruce J. Ellis, "Impact of Fathers on Parental Monitoring of Daughters and Their Affiliation with Sexually Promiscuous Peers: A Genetically and Environmentally Controlled Sibling Study," *Developmental Psychology* 53, no. 7 (July 2017): 1330–43. Cf. J. D. Vance, *Hillbilly Elegy: A Memoir of a Family and Culture in Crisis* (New York: Harper, 2016), 88: "Of all the things I hated about my childhood, nothing compared to the revolving door of father figures."

20. See, e.g., Erica Komisar, *Being There: Why Prioritizing Motherhood in the First Three Years Matters* (New York: TarcherPerigee, 2017).

21. See Murray, *Coming Apart*, ch. 14; Putnam, *Our Kids*, 219–20; and Morse, *Love and Economics*, 44–56.

22. See Putnam, *Our Kids*, 109–17.

23. Stackhouse, *Covenant and Commitments*, 130. Cf. June Carbone and Naomi Cahn, *Marriage Markets: How Inequality Is Remaking the American Family* (New York: Oxford University Press, 2014), 19–20; and Vance, *Hillbilly Elegy*, 245.

24. See Murray, *Coming Apart*, 256.

men's) moral character. For example, married men commit fewer crimes and are more industrious workers.[25]

Consistent with Limited Government

To conclude this discussion about family under the Noahic covenant, we return for a moment to the end of chapter 7. After arguing that political communities should be generally open to all people and should generously protect religious liberty, I suggested that this implies a *prima facie* case for limited government. The more areas of life into which government intrudes, the more crises of conscience—and thus religious-liberty dilemmas—it is likely to provoke in a diverse society. Does the foundational family pattern emerging from the Noahic covenant also indicate that government should be limited? Yes, it does—though without establishing just how limited. (In the discussion that follows, I assume that government is at least responsible for enforcing justice against those who wrong others, even those who wrong others under the guise of familial authority. Restraining violent men who abuse their wives and children is an obvious example.)

One consideration is that the very legitimacy of familial institutions sets limits on government. Were the government's jurisdiction all-encompassing, other institutions could not claim their own spheres of authoritative jurisdiction, or could do so only with the government's permission. The mere fact that there are multiple kinds of legitimate authority necessarily constrains government authority. Second, the relative effectiveness of married couples raising their biological children exposes the relative incompetence of government trying to do so. The natural affection and intimate knowledge that parents have toward their own children is something no government agency can replicate.[26] Furthermore, when government does take over functions in family life, even in response to genuine needs, it tends to weaken family structures further. The prospect of government assistance diminishes parental responsibility and serves as disincentive for parents to pursue the disciplines of work and marriage—what their children desperately need from them and what makes their own lives satisfying.[27] This feeds a vicious

---

25. See Robert J. Sampson, John H. Laub, and Christopher Wimer, "Does Marriage Reduce Crime: A Counterfactual Approach to Within-Individual Causal Effects," *Criminology* 44, no. 3 (2006): 465–508; and Murray, *Coming Apart*, 182–83. Cf. Vance, *Hillbilly Elegy*, 5–7, 57–58.

26. See Stackhouse, *Covenant and Commitments*, 108; and Morse, *Love and Economics*, 171–72.

27. See Stackhouse, *Covenant and Commitments*, 120–21; Murray, *Coming Apart*, 282; and John F. Cogan, *The High Cost of Good Intentions: A History of U.S. Federal Entitlement Programs* (Stanford: Stanford University Press, 2017), 2.

cycle: the breakdown of familial institutions provokes calls for government assistance, and government assistance tends to weaken familial institutions further.[28] Whatever safety-net provisions may be just or merciful, the need for strong families is itself an argument for limited government.

Finally, when government expands its reach into child-rearing, it draws this area of life into political debate. And since child-rearing is perennially controversial, government intrusion tends not only to divide and heighten tensions within a society but also to diminish its pluralistic character, which government ought to protect. This illustrates the observation in the previous chapter: the more activities the government assumes beyond protecting against violent harm, especially in intimate and personal areas of human life, the more it will marginalize people with views at odds with those of the majority or politically powerful.

COMMERCE

We will revisit some issues related to family and the Noahic covenant, but now we turn to enterprise institutions and the life of commerce. The question before us is this: What is a fitting economic system for the human community *under the Noahic covenant*?[29] That is, what kind of economy provides for humanity's needs as it spreads through the earth? What sort of economy advances humanity's benevolent dominion over the rest of creation? What sort of economy enables image-bearers to develop their creative potentialities? From another angle, we are asking what kind of economy is in accord with the natural law and thus corresponds to the reality of the world as ordinary people experience it. Insofar as Proverbs shows the way of life that fits the natural moral order, what sort of economic practices does it commend?[30]

I begin by defending this approach that focuses upon *penultimate* and *natural* things of the present world, since many Christian writers take a very different approach to economic issues. Then I suggest a number of features that ought to characterize an economy under the Noahic covenant.

---

28. See Morse, *Love and Economics*, xi, 4, 55.

29. Biblical studies of economics generally give little, if any, attention to the Noahic covenant. For two exceptions, see Donald A. Hay, *Economics Today: A Christian Critique* (Grand Rapids: Eerdmans, 1989), ch. 1; and Jean Lee, *The Two Pillars of the Market: A Paradigm for Dialogue between Theology and Economics* (New York: Peter Lang, 2011), ch. 3.

30. According to Harold C. Washington, Proverbs discusses themes of work, idleness, wealth, and poverty more frequently than any other Old Testament book; see *Wealth and Poverty in the Instruction of Amenemope and the Hebrew Proverbs* (Atlanta: Scholars, 1994), 1.

The section concludes by considering whether a market economy displays these features.

Provisional and Eschatological Perspectives on Economics

In recent decades, many writers have offered extensive Christian analyses of economic issues, often with drastically different conclusions. While several factors contribute to these differences, an important one is the basic moral-theological vision a person adopts when evaluating modern economic systems. A number of writers critique modern economies by the benchmark of Christ's eschatological kingdom and invariably conclude that they fall far short.[31] Other writers hold modern economies to a more modest standard, asking whether they advance certain limited goods for the present world. These writers tend to be more appreciative of what contemporary developed economies provide, however imperfectly.[32] Yet most contributors to this literature do not seem aware of how much effect this fundamental difference in approach can have. I thus wish to clarify and defend my own approach.[33]

Many of the most trenchant Christian critics of modern economies (implicitly) follow the first approach described above: they prosecute a deep and holistic critique of modern economies because these economies fail to meet the standards of the kingdom of God that Jesus preached. Methodist Daniel Bell and Roman Catholic David Schindler exemplify this sort of

---

31. E.g., see Daniel M. Bell Jr., *The Economy of Desire: Christianity and Capitalism in a Postmodern World* (Grand Rapids: Baker Academic, 2012); Daniel M. Bell Jr., *Liberation Theology after the End of History: The Refusal to Cease Suffering* (New York: Routledge, 2001); David L. Schindler, "'Homelessness' and Market Liberalism: Toward an Economic Culture of Gift and Gratitude," in *Wealth, Poverty, and Human Destiny*, 347–413; Kathryn Tanner, *Economy of Grace* (Minneapolis: Fortress, 2005); D. Stephen Long, *Divine Economy: Theology and the Market* (New York: Routledge, 2000); Bob Goudzwaard, *Capitalism and Progress: A Diagnosis of Western Society*, trans. Josina Van Nuis Zylstra (Grand Rapids: Eerdmans, 1979); Andrew Kirk, *The Good News of the Kingdom Coming: The Marriage of Evangelism and Social Responsibility* (Downers Grove, IL: InterVarsity Press, 1983); and M. Douglas Meeks, *God the Economist: The Doctrine of God and Political Economy* (Minneapolis: Fortress, 1989).

32. E.g., see John Bolt, *Economic Shalom: A Reformed Primer on Faith, Work, and Human Flourishing* (Grand Rapids: Christian's Library Press, 2013); Robert Sirico, *Defending the Free Market: The Moral Case for a Free Economy* (Washington, DC: Regnery, 2012); Jay W. Richards, *Money, Greed, and God: Why Capitalism Is the Solution and Not the Problem* (New York: HarperOne, 2009); Samuel Gregg, *Economic Thinking for the Theologically Minded* (Lanham, MD: University Press of America, 2001); Ronald H. Nash, *Poverty and Wealth: The Christian Debate over Capitalism* (Westchester, IL: Crossway, 1986); Brian Griffiths, *The Creation of Wealth: A Christian's Case for Capitalism* (Downers Grove, IL: InterVarsity Press, 1985); and Michael Novak, *The Spirit of Democratic Capitalism* (New York: Simon & Schuster, 1982).

33. For more detailed discussion, see David VanDrunen, "The Market Economy and Christian Ethics: Refocusing Debate through the Two-Kingdoms Doctrine," *Journal of Markets and Morality* 17, no. 1 (Spring 2014): 11–45.

critique. Bell contrasts "capitalism" with "the divine economy made present by Christ and witnessed to by the church."[34] He rejects any compatibility between Christianity and capitalism, since the latter marketizes all of life, corrupts human desire, and distorts communion with God.[35] Bell dismisses capitalism's enormous ability to produce wealth as inadmissible evidence and argues that capitalism is inherently wrong because it actively works against humanity's renewal of communion with God and against its "chief end" of glorifying and enjoying God forever, that is, humanity's "ascent to God."[36] He notes that Christian proponents of capitalism praise it on theological grounds as being realistic about the presence of sin in the world and as nurturing God-given abilities to choose and create.[37] Bell finds this move seriously problematic, a denial of God's present redemption of economic life.[38] For Bell, the divine economy that heals human desire from its corruption under capitalism is at work now, in the church and in all of creation.[39]

Schindler reasons similarly.[40] He identifies the "inner logic" of a market economy as rendering people "homeless," that is, fragmented from their original ontological community with God, and hence also with each other.[41] Wishing to look at wealth and poverty in terms of their "deepest and most proper meaning," he proposes an ontology of gift and gratitude.[42] The very character of things depends on whether they are integrated into a grateful sense of reality as gift. Thus an "economy of love deepens the reality" and thereby enhances the worth of everyone and everything involved in producing and exchanging goods.[43] Schindler acknowledges that one might object that his analysis reflects the "ultimate" or "ideal" yet is practically unworkable in the real world, but he dismisses the objection on various grounds.[44] Though he accepts in part the concern that a market economy be evaluated in comparison with other historical economic systems, he insists that all systems must ultimately be compared to the human destiny that Christianity calls us to embody "here and now on earth, however much that call will be

---

34. Bell, *The Economy of Desire*, 20.
35. Bell, *The Economy of Desire*, 24, 88.
36. See Bell, *The Economy of Desire*, 83–89.
37. Bell, *The Economy of Desire*, 91.
38. See, e.g., Bell, *The Economy of Desire*, 112–14, 124–27.
39. See, e.g., Bell, *The Economy of Desire*, 146–47.
40. Schindler, "Homelessness," 347–413.
41. Schindler, "Homelessness," 351–53.
42. Schindler, "Homelessness," 356.
43. Schindler, "Homelessness," 358–59, 363.
44. See Schindler, "Homelessness," 366–69.

fully realized only eschatologically."[45] For Schindler, this embodiment occurs both in the church and in all of life, for Christians are called to "transform whatever culture" in which they live.[46]

As these summaries illustrate, such thinkers critique modern economies by ultimate, redemptive, and eschatological standards: such economies do not realize the kingdom of Christ or embody humanity's eschatological destiny, and thus Christians must seek a radical alternative. In one sense, these writers are profoundly correct. Today's globalized economy indeed does not embody or realize Christ's kingdom. Christians who do not long for more have missed something deeply important. But in another sense, writers such as Bell and Schindler err because they look for the embodiment of Christ's eschatological economy in the wrong place. As defended in part 1, God grants the redemptive blessing of Christ's kingdom through the new covenant, and he has established the church as the community designed to manifest this kingdom here and now. Thus, if we presently wish to find the embodiment of the eschatological economy, we ought to look to the church, not to the commercial life of common political communities, which arise under the nonredemptive and noneschatological Noahic covenant. In short, the writers considered above correctly conclude that the globalized economy does not embody Christ's kingdom, but they are wrong to think it should.

The church's eschatological economy is not the subject of this book, but a brief comment about it may help clarify the present chapter's approach.[47] The new creation is a place of overflowing abundance (e.g., Joel 3:18; Rev 22:1–2), not subject to the scarcity that constrains earthly economic life. The church exists in the present world and is subject to its constraints in many respects. For instance, preachers need to get paid like other workers (1 Cor 9:4–14). Yet Christ also grants the church a mysterious grace, reflecting new-creation abundance, to engage in a kind of crazy defiance of earthly economic reality. As if oblivious to scarcity and the virtues of thrift and frugality, the church can practice a lavish generosity. Its members are able to give beyond their means (2 Cor 8:3). They begin with "extreme poverty," give more than they have, and somehow produce a "wealth of generosity" (2 Cor 8:2–3). It is as if they tap into the limitless abundance of the new creation (cf. Phil 4:19). This abundance comes from Christ, who, although rich, became poor for their sake so that they might be rich in him (2 Cor 8:9).

---

45. Schindler, "Homelessness," 400.
46. Schindler, "Homelessness," 396.
47. For more discussion, see VanDrunen, *Divine Covenants*, 473–76.

This eschatological economic dynamic is inaccessible to the Noahic covenant and the political communities it governs. That covenant promises and imparts no redemptive grace or eschatological bounty. Whatever relevance the Noahic covenant has for economic life concerns human beings in general, in their common life, not Christians in their distinctive heavenly citizenship. Insofar as the Noahic covenant implicitly commissions human beings to pursue commercial activity, its ends are natural and provisional, not eschatological. Since our concern is economic life within common political communities, our task is to identify these provisional ends and the sort of commercial activity that corresponds to them. Christians ought to promote this sort of commercial activity among the common institutions in which they participate, even as they also delight in their opportunities to embody inchoately the abundance of new creation.

One of the tragedies of sin is that even humanity's successful fulfillment of the economic dimension of the Noahic covenant tends to turn into another idol to seduce sinners. Tyre, the economic powerhouse of Ezekiel's day, facilitated much commerce that was good in itself but viewed its economic empire as a kind of holy temple (Ezek 27:3–11) and was filled with a god-like arrogance (Ezek 28:10–10). One of its chief problems, it seems, was eschatologizing its commerce rather than recognizing its limited, provisional purpose. With an idolatrous materialism no less a temptation in the present day of Tyresque globalized commerce, Christian theologians may do the church and world a great service by reminding their listeners that common economic activity is a good, but a *provisional* good.

The Proper Features of Commercial Life under the Noahic Covenant

The text of the Noahic covenant says nothing specific about the nature of enterprise institutions or the structure of an economic system. But what the text does say has many implications for commercial life. There are probably more, but here I suggest that economic systems under the Noahic covenant ought to promote at least the following seven features.

First, it ought to encourage and reward industriousness. The Noahic covenant treats people as image-bearers of God, which recalls Genesis 1. As argued earlier, Genesis 1 presents God as industrious, exercising a grand benevolent dominion over the world as he constructs and orders its various parts. God then creates human beings in his image and likeness, to rule as he did and to carry on his work as his representatives (1:26, 28). An economic system fit for the Noahic covenant, therefore, ought to facilitate the hard work required for pursuing this commission. Accordingly, as Proverbs reflects on the natural moral order, it frequently praises the industrious person as a paragon of wisdom and mocks the lazy person as a fool. Hard work ordinarily brings profit and wealth (6:9–11; 8:18, 21; 10:4–5; 12:11, 14, 24, 27; 19:10, 15; 20:4; 21:5, 21, 25; 22:4; 23:21; 24:33–34; 27:18, 23–27; 28:19; 31:13–31), although there are exceptions (10:16; 11:18; 17:1; 23:6–7; 28:6, 11), especially due to injustice (1:19; 17:8; 28:16).[48] Proverbs treats wealth as a blessing, not as a problem, so long as one gains it honestly, is generous to the needy, and maintains a certain detachment from material possessions.

Second, an economic system fitting for the Noahic covenant ought to encourage technological development. This follows from the discussion above. For the human race to grow and expand throughout the earth, it required a great deal of resourcefulness and innovation. People needed to establish and expand agriculture, which entailed identifying useful crops, developing good farm land, fighting off pests, inventing methods of irrigation, and domesticating animals. They needed to build vehicles, roads, and bridges to transport their produce. They needed to develop medicine to stave off early deaths and heal work-ending injuries. They needed to develop mathematics and the natural sciences to advance the study of engineering. And this was really just getting started. As noted, God's commission to rule, to fill the earth, and to subdue the other creatures did not exhort human beings to hide unobtrusively in the world but to go out into it and to do something with it, figuring it out and making it useful. God began from nothing and fashioned a beautiful world; human beings were to fill that beautiful world and make it even better.[49] This required creativity according to the image of God.

Third, an economic system under the Noahic covenant ought to be of benefit to the human community generally. This point follows from the conclusions of chapter 7. Since God made the Noahic covenant with the entire human race, and since political communities should thus welcome people of various backgrounds as full participants, such a community's economic system ought to incorporate and benefit all sorts of people—at least those who are willing to work. This includes minorities of various sorts, but in economic

---

48. See VanDrunen, *Divine Covenants*, 407–9.

49. Among helpful discussions of this point, see Bolt, *Economic Shalom*, ch. 1; Novak, *The Spirit of Democratic Capitalism*, 39–40; Sirico, *Defending the Free Market*, 21; and Griffiths, *The Creation of Wealth*, 34. Cf. Allessandro Roncaglia, *The Wealth of Ideas: A History of Economic Thought* (Cambridge: Cambridge University Press, 2005), 23–24.

context it especially includes the poor. Confirming this, Proverbs not only praises those who work hard and gain wealth but also frequently urges them to be generous to the needy. It often does so for good Noahic reasons: the rich and poor alike share a common Creator and a common humanity (Prov 14:31; 17:5; 22:2; 29:13). An economic system ought to benefit the poor rather than make their condition worse.

Fourth, an economic system under the Noahic covenant ought to be just. As considered at length in the next chapter, Genesis 9:6 ("Whoever sheds the blood of man, by man shall his blood be shed") is a version of the *lex talionis*, a classic expression of reciprocal justice: give to each his due. Negatively speaking, commercial activity under the Noahic covenant ought to be protected by laws that prohibit and punish assaults on property. In Proverbs, theft ought to be punished (6:30–31), and dishonesty in commerce is abominable to God (20:10, 23). But justice not only demands penalizing the person who steals bread off the store shelf (rectifying justice) but also requires sellers to put a good product on the shelf and buyers to pay for it as a fair exchange (primary justice). Such acts, when performed, make judicial punishment unnecessary. Thus an economic system under the Noahic covenant ought to encourage collegial and productive exchange and discourage its opposite.

Fifth, such an economic system ought to respect and promote the good of the broader natural order. God entered the Noahic covenant not only with the entire human race but also with all living creatures (Gen 9:10, 12, 15–17). Its concern extends to the earth itself (8:21; 9:11, 13) and even the cosmic forces (8:22). All of creation is party to the covenant. Thus, if economic life should exist for the good of all human beings generally, it follows that it also ought to promote the good of these nonhuman participants. What exactly this means is not so obvious. It seems odd to say that eating an apple or a chicken is good for the apple or chicken itself, yet the Noahic covenant gives plants and animals to humans for food (9:4). Chopping down a tree to build a home is destructive of the natural world in a sense, yet a covenant that commissions human beings to fill the earth can hardly deny them shelter. Promoting the good of the broader world cannot mean leaving it just as it lies. It thus seems safe to say, in general, that part of the good of the nonhuman world is to serve useful purposes for human beings. An apple or chicken eaten to nourish human beings or a tree felled to build a home has served a good end; humanity has not wronged them. At the same time, human beings are obligated to honor the natural world, to respect its diversity, and to promote its beauty. Even when using other creatures for their own ends, human beings should surely esteem them as covenant participants rather than dispose of them as worthless instruments.

Sixth, an economic system under the Noahic covenant should at least leave room for, and preferably enable, development of the finer attainments of human culture, such as music, art, and literature. Since the Noahic covenant speaks of human beings filling the earth and eating, it seems proper to conclude that material needs are its chief economic interest. Yet the Noahic covenant treats human beings as the image of God, who is beautiful and creative. Thus this covenant cannot be indifferent to aesthetic achievements. That this covenant of preservation would be concerned first of all with satisfaction of material needs makes good sense. But if an economic system can succeed in this basic task and also facilitate the pursuit of higher culture, it would be all the better fit for the Noahic covenant.

Seventh and finally, an economic system under the Noahic covenant ought to be consistent with a limited government. As argued previously, extensive government reach into human life hampers a political community's ability to honor the kind of pluralism and family structures the Noahic covenant requires. An economic system that does not entail such reach, therefore, seems best suited for the communities God governs under the Noahic covenant.

The Noahic Covenant and Market Economies

Evaluating a particular economic system according to the standard of these seven features is much more difficult than identifying the features themselves. A national economy is a complex thing, and the global economy exponentially more so. The scope of the present project does not permit any kind of detailed critical analysis of, say, the American economy or global capitalism. But it might be helpful to think a little further about commercial life under the Noahic covenant in somewhat more concrete terms than the preceding paragraphs did.

I will do so by asking whether a *market* economy realizes the seven features just identified—and thus this is a *moral* question rather than one of economic efficiency or the like.[50] By a market economy, I refer to economic

---

50. To put it another way, although economic efficiency is hardly unimportant, there is no such thing as the purely rational *homo economicus*. Most of the Christian writers whom I cite below helpfully refuse to examine issues in this way. In addition to these writers, it is also worth mentioning the (primarily mid-twentieth-century German) *ordoliberal* school of economic thought, which offered often insightful moral analysis of modern Western economies. On this movement, see Lawrence H. White, *The Clash of Economic Ideas: The Great Policy Debates and Experiments of the Last Hundred Years* (Cambridge: Cambridge University Press, 2012), ch. 9; cf. Angus Burgin, *The Great Persuasion: Reinventing Free Markets*

life in which goods and services are produced, offered, priced, and sold primarily on the basis of voluntary exchange rather than by order of government. I do not use "market economy" as a synonym for "capitalism."[51] The primary alternative to a market economy is a command economy, in which the production, offer, and pricing of goods and services are based primarily on government orders and plans. Of course, no existing market economy is free of government involvement, and command economies leave some room for consumer choice and tend to spawn black markets.[52] There is no such thing as a pure market or pure command economy. But since so much of the world's present commercial activity is driven by voluntary initiative and exchange, it seems worth asking whether a primarily market-based economic life is generally consistent with the moral order of the Noahic covenant. In the following pages, I argue that it is, although a great many details must be left open for debate. We briefly consider each of the seven features in turn.

INDUSTRIOUSNESS

The first feature was that an economic system ought to encourage and reward industriousness. A market economy seems to do this. Insofar as a person's degree of economic well-being in a market economy depends to a great extent upon finding work, performing it well, discovering new ways to do things, and investing resources wisely, such an economy presents many incentives to work hard and opportunities to profit. Furthermore, the moral culture of a market economy tends to honor those who work for a living and

---

since the Depression (Cambridge, MA: Harvard University Press, 2012), 82. Representative works include Wilhelm Röpke, *A Humane Economy: The Social Framework of the Free Market* (Chicago: Regnery, 1960); Ludwig Erhard, *Prosperity through Competition* (New York: Frederick A. Praeger, 1958); Walter Eucken *This Unsuccessful Age or the Pains of Economic Progress* (New York: Oxford University Press, 1952); and Alexander Rüstow, *Freedom and Domination: A Historical Critique of Civilization*, trans. Salvator Attansio, ed. Dankwart A. Rustow (Princeton: Princeton University Press, 1980).

51. While it seems accurate to regard "capitalism" as one form of a market economy, it is hardly the only one. A market economy does not necessarily involve the legal and political structures that reference to "capitalism" usually presumes. People have established markets and voluntarily exchanged goods and services since time immemorial. As Adam Smith noted, human beings have "propensity to truck, barter, and exchange"; see *An Inquiry into the Nature and Causes of the Wealth of Nations* (1776; Indianapolis: LibertyClassics, 1981), 25 (I.ii.1). In any case, writers mean a variety of things by "capitalism," and clearly what goes by this term takes different forms in different places. And accumulation of capital is not really what is most distinctive about modern developed economies anyway, as helpfully explained in Deirdre Nansen McCloskey, *Bourgeois Equality: How Ideas, Not Capital or Institutions, Enriched the World* (Chicago: University of Chicago Press, 2016), especially ch. 12.

52. On how black markets prolonged the existence of twentieth-century communist systems by masking the deficiencies of the latter, see James C. Scott, *Seeing like a State: How Certain Schemes to Improve the Human Condition Have Failed* (New Haven: Yale University Press, 1998), ch. 6.

tends to disdain those who will not and do not.[53] So far, so good. Yet one of the common complaints about a market economy is that it tends to encourage and reward hard work too much, creating a cadre of imbalanced workaholics. While probably exaggerated, this complaint does identify a moral temptation to which participants in a market economy may be especially subject.

TECHNOLOGICAL DEVELOPMENT

Second, a Noahic economic system should encourage and advance technological development, both to help meet the burgeoning needs of the human race filling the earth and to express the creative potentialities of those made in God's image. A market economy seems well-designed for this. By permitting people freedom to try new things, to interact with whom they wish, and to reap benefits from successful ideas, market economies tend to be, as one book title vividly puts it, an "innovation machine."[54] Its ethos includes "betterment, novelty, risk-taking, creativity" and "the spirit of development, risk, experiment, adventure."[55] "Entrepreneurial boldness and imagination" are its driving force.[56] Yet here again the market economy's strength also creates moral concerns. While its "perennial gale of creative destruction"[57] helpfully stimulates ingenuity and brings many improvements to the human condition, it often simultaneously destabilizes older institutions and practices important to a meaningful and balanced human life. We will revisit this issue below. The rapid introduction of new technologies can also cause real harm to individuals and societies alongside their benefits.[58] Human beings should

---

53. See especially Deirdre N. McCloskey's comparison of "bourgeois" and aristocratic attitudes toward work, in *The Bourgeois Virtues: Ethics for an Age of Commerce* (Chicago: University of Chicago Press, 2006), 74–75; and in *Bourgeois Equality*, 452. Cf. Murray, *Coming Apart*, 131–33.

54. William J. Baumol, *The Free-Market Innovation Machine: Analyzing the Growth Miracle of Capitalism* (Princeton: Princeton University Press, 2002). Among other recent books exploring the rapid technological advances and economic growth of market economies, see Joel Mokyr, *A Culture of Growth: The Origins of the Modern Economy* (Princeton: Princeton University Press, 2016); Joyce Appleby, *The Relentless Revolution: A History of Capitalism* (New York: W. W. Norton, 2010); and Gregory Clark, *A Farewell to Alms: A Brief Economic History of the World* (Princeton: Princeton University Press, 2007).

55. Respectively, McCloskey, *Bourgeois Equality*, 279; and Novak, *The Spirit of Democratic Capitalism*, 48. Cf. John Mueller, *Capitalism, Democracy, and Ralph's Pretty Good Grocery* (Princeton: Princeton University Press, 1999), 5, 37.

56. Israel M. Kirzner, *The Driving Force of the Market: Essays in Austrian Economics* (New York: Routledge, 2000), 19.

57. Joseph A. Schumpeter, *Capitalism, Socialism and Democracy*, 3rd ed. (1950; New York: Harper, 2008), 81–86.

58. An obvious example at the time I write is the effect of the new media on the human brain and human interaction, as explored, e.g., in Nicholas Carr, *The Shallows: What the Internet Is Doing to Our Brains* (New York: Norton, 2010); and Maggie Jackson, *Distracted: The Erosion of Attention and the Coming Dark Age* (Amherst, NY: Prometheus, 2008).

not embrace technological innovation without also maintaining respect for old institutions and being wise about the new.

OF GENERAL BENEFIT

I suggested, third, that an economic system consistent with the Noahic covenant should be widely beneficial, extending participation to the human community as a whole. In part, this prompts us to ask how market economies do with respect to minority groups. On the one hand, there is nothing about open markets, in and of themselves, that promote or hinder the extension of commercial life to such minority groups. It permits people to do business with whom they wish, and thus could be a means of greater or lesser inclusion, depending upon the attitude of market participants. But on the other hand, key features of a market economy encourage inclusion. Most important, it provides incentive for economic actors to focus upon the quality and price of a potential exchange, not upon the creed or color of the trading partner. People who insist upon doing business only with their own kind of folks will end up paying more money for worse products and services. Over time, their economic standing will decline while the standing of people open to commercial relations with all will increase. Other things being equal, a market economy rewards the tolerant.[59]

Another issue is important. If an economic system ought to benefit all people generally and incorporate all people into its life, that should include the neediest. Many people regard market economies as beneficial to the rich over the poor,[60] but that judgment seems misguided from any big-picture perspective. Prior to the rise of modern market economies, every nation on earth was very poor. Even the wealthiest in these poor societies lived without modern medicine and dentistry, running water, electricity, and a host of other contemporary conveniences. By today's standards, everyone was poor, most dreadfully so. For millennia, economic growth was little better than stagnant. Then economic growth accelerated at an unprecedented rate. In little more than two hundred years the gain in goods and services in market societies has grown by a factor of somewhere between thirty and one hundred—which is

---

59. See similar arguments, e.g., in McCloskey, *Bourgeois Equality*, 354–55, 558; Novak, *The Spirit of Democratic Capitalism*, 119; Milton Friedman, *Capitalism and Freedom*, 40th anniv. ed. (Chicago: University of Chicago Press, 2002), ch. 7; and Ludwig von Mises, *Human Action: A Treatise on Economics* (New Haven: Yale University Press, 1949; reprint, Auburn, AL: Ludwig von Mises Institute, 1998), 689.

60. Some theologians repeat this idea. For example, Tanner says the market economy leaves the masses "wallow[ing] in poverty and despair"; see *Economy of Grace*, 32.

to say, by somewhere between 3,000 percent and 10,000 percent.[61] The masses of the poor have become the masses of the rich in communities that have embraced open markets. In such communities, most people are not poor, and even the relatively poor enjoy innumerable benefits that would have been unimaginable luxuries for the relatively rich a few centuries ago. As market economies extend their reach globally, the number of the poor continues to decline, both as a percentage of the population and in absolute terms.[62]

Open markets are the only thing known to the human race that has lifted the masses out of poverty. Such economies have always benefited the relatively rich, but they have "saved their best gifts for the poorest."[63] Keeping those who remain desperately poor away from access to market economies seems to be an immoral betrayal of fellow human beings.[64] This leaves many questions open as to how individuals and communities should help the needy *in addition to* incorporating them into market economies, but markets are proven poverty fighters.

JUST

The fourth feature is that an economic system should be just. In terms of assaults upon property, a market economy looks to courts to administer appropriate punishments and remedies. The more interesting question, I suggested above, is how well an economic system itself promotes collegial and productive exchange, which bolsters right relations within the community. On this count, market economies again have many points in their favor.

In and of itself, a market economy encourages independence and responsibility rather than reliance upon government or a patron.[65] If all people remain God's image-bearers under the Noahic covenant, widespread independence and responsibility is fitting. But this independence is not social autonomy,

---

61. McCloskey discusses this at length in *Bourgeois Equality* and in Deirdre N. McCloskey, *Bourgeois Dignity: Why Economics Can't Explain the Modern World* (Chicago: University of Chicago Press, 2010). For a summary, see *Bourgeois Dignity*, ch. 7. Cf. Baumol, *The Free-Market Innovation Machine*, 3; and Bjørn Lomborg, *The Skeptical Environmentalist: Measuring the Real State of the World* (Cambridge: Cambridge University Press, 2001), 328.

62. McCloskey notes that less than half a century ago the world had five billion people, and four billion were desperately poor, while now the world has seven billion people, and one billion are desperately poor. See *Bourgeois Equality*, 74.

63. Clark, *A Farewell to Alms*, 3. See McCloskey's extensive discussion of this point in *Bourgeois Dignity*, ch. 44; and *Bourgeois Equality*, chs. 5, 61.

64. See, e.g., McCloskey, *Bourgeois Equality*, 8; and Lomborg, *The Skeptical Environmentalist*, 328–29; cf. Victor V. Claar and Robin J. Klay, *Economics in Christian Perspective: Theory, Policy and Life Choices* (Downers Grove, IL: IVP Academic, 2007), 144.

65. E.g., see Röpke, *A Humane Economy*, 98.

for market economies depend upon collaboration and exchange. And in an open market, collaboration and exchange transpire voluntarily, by consent rather than compulsion. People are free to seek better deals elsewhere, and others are free to offer them. When people make a deal, one or both parties may think it less than perfect, but each enters it because she believes it more beneficial than not making the deal at all. Thus market exchanges produce mutually beneficial results. They are win-win, not zero-sum. They reward people for meeting other people's wants and needs.[66]

Because they rely upon voluntary exchange, market economies both depend upon and encourage honesty, trust, courtesy, and deference. People prefer to avoid deals with people they cannot trust. Customers choose sellers they think are honest about their products. Sellers are friendly to the customer and treat her as if she is always right—or else she will shop elsewhere.[67] This reliance on voluntary exchange also seems to correspond to a general decline in violence and warmongering in societies with market economies. Montesquieu's famous maxim—"It is almost a general rule that . . . wherever there is commerce, there we meet with agreeable manners" (or, "gentle mores")[68]—has a ring of truth. People who are trading in a marketplace are not fighting. Historically, societies with open markets have tended to grow less violent over time,[69] and today the least violent nations have relatively open markets and the most violent do not.[70] Market societies have ceased to honor the heroic and chivalrous (which tend to glorify violence) and come to see trade rather than conquest as the route to wealth.[71] Furthermore, markets themselves serve an important, if mysterious, coordinating function that fosters cooperation. They are a clearinghouse for information, linking people together who do not know each other and coordinating their plans

---

66. See, e.g., Claar and Klay, *Economics in Christian Perspective*, 47–50; Sirico, *Defending the Free Market*, 72, 82; Novak, *The Spirit of Democratic Capitalism*, 129; and McCloskey, *Bourgeois Equality*, xx, 21, 141, 572.

67. See, e.g., McCloskey, *Bourgeois Equality*, xxiv–xxvi; Mueller, *Capitalism*, 23, 95–98; and Morse, *Love and Economics*, 51–53. As Mueller puts it, "Nice guys . . . tend to finish first"; see *Capitalism*, 7; cf. 21, 42–43.

68. Montesquieu, *The Spirit of Laws*, trans. Thomas Nugent (Chicago: University of Chicago Press, 1952), 20.1.

69. See, e.g., Steven Pinker, *The Better Angels of Our Nature: Why Violence Has Declined* (New York: Viking, 2011), 75–78, 284–88, 682–84; McCloskey, *Bourgeois Equality*, 27; and Claar and Klay, *Economics in Christian Perspective*, 43.

70. See Matt Ridley, *The Evolution of Everything: How New Ideas Emerge* (New York: Harper, 2015), 32.

71. E.g., see Schumpeter, *Capitalism*, 127–29; McCloskey, *The Bourgeois Virtues*, part 3; and Mueller, *Capitalism*, 66, 112–13.

and purposes in ways otherwise impossible. Markets bring together a mass of decisions and actions into an otherwise unattainable whole.[72]

THE GOOD OF THE NATURAL WORLD

Ecological issues present some of the most challenging questions for market economies. Since the Noahic covenant demands that human beings treat the nonhuman world with honor and respect, these are questions to take seriously. A number of Christian writers publish alarming diagnoses of the current state of nature.[73] They believe, in part, that human population growth is overwhelming the earth and that the world simply does not have enough resources to feed or fuel so many people, at least by current first-world standards.[74] They blame the "Western culture" of recent centuries, with its "materialism" and "corruption of desire."[75] Market economies are clearly in the crosshairs.

It is obviously true that people have done serious damage to the natural environment through market exchanges. At the same time, many command economies (such as twentieth-century Eastern European communist societies) have had much worse environmental records than their more market-based counterparts. It seems accurate to say that no economic system *per se* guarantees ecologically responsible behavior. Many factors contribute to how the broader world fares in any particular place.

Yet no compelling reason exists to set a market economy and its corresponding culture in opposition to concern for the natural world. For one thing, although market-driven innovation, especially in earlier stages of development, can create new sorts of ecological damage by doing things to the world previously unimagined, evidence indicates that as societies with open markets grow truly wealthy, ecological problems tend to decrease, and their environments tend to grow cleaner. The advance of technology provides

72. See especially Kirzner, *The Driving Force of the Market*, 79, 81, 143. Cf. McCloskey, *The Bourgeois Virtues*, 242; Novak, *The Spirit of Democratic Capitalism*, 117, 134; and Kathryn D. Blanchard, *The Protestant Ethic or the Spirit of Capitalism: Christians, Freedom, and Free Markets* (Eugene: Cascade, 2010), 176.

73. Bouma-Prediger, for example, speaks of a "crisis," for the earth is "groaning," "being degraded," and "out of kilter." *For the Beauty of the Earth*, xii, 5, 24. At one point he admits that the state of the planet is actually "mixed," yet the "overarching conclusion is not pretty"; *For the Beauty of the Earth*, 54. Gorringe warns of imminent "resource-based wars," "mass destitution," "economic collapse," and "global emergency"—"the seriousness of the issues that face us cannot be overestimated." See "On Building an Ark," 24–25.

74. E.g., see Bouma-Prediger, *For the Beauty of the Earth*, 24–28, 38–39, 43–46; and Gorringe, "On Building an Ark," 26.

75. See Bouma-Prediger, *For the Beauty of the Earth*, 80; and Gorringe, "On Building an Ark," 25–26.

formerly unavailable resources both for environmental cleanup and for cleaner alternatives to whatever caused the damage in the first place. And as people's basic needs are increasingly satisfied, they gain the luxury of being able to do something about their ecological surroundings without having to go cold and hungry.[76] Thus, although open markets themselves do not guarantee greater ecological responsibility, they do provide important resources and opportunities for it.

Another issue mentioned above is overpopulation and consequent resource depletion. Dire predictions about these matters have perennially accompanied modern market economies, from Thomas Malthus to Paul Ehrlich.[77] The Noahic covenant commissions humanity to fill the earth, and I have argued that this implies the need for technological innovation, which market economies encourage. Thus the concern about overpopulation and scarce resources offers challenges close to the heart of the Noahic moral order, as I have presented it.

The prophecies of Malthus, Ehrlich, and the like, however, have turned out to be not just somewhat untrue but fantastically erroneous.[78] The economic growth and technological innovation accompanying market economies have not caused overpopulation or resource crises, and several interrelated factors seem to explain why. For one thing, birth rates tend to drop dramatically with economic development and the urbanization, improvement in health, and increase in education that accompany it.[79] Contemporary demographic trends in first-world societies actually indicate that, if the entire human community were to embrace open markets, a steep decline in population would be a far greater danger than overpopulation.[80] And insofar as populations do continue to grow rapidly for a time after open markets take root in a society (due to spikes in life expectancy), there seems to be little danger of exhausting

---

76. See McCloskey, *Bourgeois Equality*, 66–70; and Claar and Klay, *Economics in Christian Perspective*, 92, 113–14.

77. See Thomas Malthus, *An Essay on the Principle of Population* (London, 1798); and Paul R. Ehrlich, *The Population Bomb* (New York: Ballantine, 1968).

78. For large-scale studies of these predictions and why they failed to materialize, see especially Julian L. Simon, *The Ultimate Resource* (Princeton: Princeton University Press, 1981); and Lomborg, *The Skeptical Environmentalist*. For a similar analysis from a Christian perspective, see E. Calvin Beisner, *Prospects for Growth: A Biblical View of Population, Resources, and the Future* (Westchester, IL: Crossway, 1990).

79. This is the "demographic transition." See, e.g., Simon, *The Ultimate Resource*, 184; Lomborg, *The Skeptical Environmentalist*, 46; Alistair Young, *Environment, Economy, and Christian Ethics: Alternative Views on Christians and Markets* (Minneapolis: Fortress, 2015), 100–104; and Clark, *A Farewell to Alms*, 8.

80. On the deep problems looming for China due to its decades of one-child policy, see Mei Fong, *One Child: The Story of China's Most Radical Experiment* (Boston: Houghton Mifflin Harcourt, 2016). Of course, the one-child policy itself was not the result of voluntary choices of the Chinese people.

the world's resources. Whether the concern is farmland, precious metals, or fossil fuels, where human beings have had need and motivation, they have exerted the effort and ingenuity necessary to discover more, to increase productivity, and to find alternatives. For nearly every valuable resource, supplies have increased, and their relative prices have decreased.[81] Julian Simon attributed this to "the ultimate resource": inquisitive, creative, and resourceful human beings. That is, the human mind is a far more valuable economic resource than oil or soil, and increase in population tends to make human society wealthier, not poorer.[82] This makes good theological sense if humans are indeed created and sustained in the image of God. God surely equips human beings with the ingenuity necessary to carry out their required tasks without destroying the world in which they live.

FINER CULTURE

The sixth feature of an economic system under the Noahic covenant suggested above is that it should at least leave room for, and preferably foster, the finer attainments of human culture, such as music, art, and literature. A common complaint about market economies is that they stimulate a kind of mass low culture, exemplified in fast-food restaurants and big-box stores, along with greed and materialism, all of which tend to dumb down human life and kill appreciation for the finer things.

Open markets do indeed provide many opportunities for low culture to flourish. But is this so bad? People who have the education, taste, and wealth to enjoy aspects of higher culture need to beware of despising those who do not, and things such as big-box stores provide ready access to affordable goods that are of great help to many people with limited resources. Furthermore, open markets do not force people with finer tastes to settle for low culture. On the contrary, those who favor the more exquisite things of life—fine wine, good coffee, opera, golf—will tend to find them in abundance in market economies and with difficulty elsewhere. The wealth created through open markets both permits popular culture and enables obscure niche cultures to find their devotees, and this allows many artists to support themselves through their work and thus to enjoy independence rather than rely on the

---

81. For extensive discussion of this initially puzzling reality, see, e.g., Simon, *The Ultimate Resource*, part 1; and Lomborg, *The Skeptical Environmentalist*, part 3. For shorter treatments, see also Claar and Klay, *Economics in Christian Perspective*, 95–98; and Sirico, *Defending the Free Market*, ch. 9.

82. For helpful distillations of this point, see, e.g., Simon, *The Ultimate Resource*, 196–97, 216, 345–48; and McCloskey, *Bourgeois Dignity*, 433–38 and *Bourgeois Equality*, 627–30.

whims of a patron.[83] And while open markets themselves do not guarantee a general rise in the quality of culture, such a rise has occurred in modern market economies, which have literacy rates previously unimaginable, schools of every sort, libraries in every small town, books published by the hundreds of thousands, and philanthropic foundations whose resources are greater than those of some small nonmarket countries.[84] The masses in a desperately poor society have precious little opportunity to develop as musicians, artists, or writers, or to enjoy other people's music, art, and literature, while these opportunities abound for the masses in modern market economies.[85]

LIMITED GOVERNMENT

The final feature of an economic system discussed above is that it be consistent with a limited government. Since market economies, by definition, are driven primarily by voluntary exchange rather than government command, the maintenance of open markets implies very important limits on government action. Yet in other respects, market economies encourage, or at least enable, the expansion of government. The basic work of law enforcement, for example, requires increased resources as an economy becomes more complex and its technology more sophisticated. The wealth that people create in open markets also provides a much larger pool of potential tax revenue that governments seem inevitably eager to tap. And what we know as modern capitalism has involved entanglements between private and public actors that welcome state action into areas of life it ordinarily did not enter under more primitive economies. In short, markets themselves imply limitations on government, but how much government does and grows in actual market economies can differ widely. And how much it should do and grow will undoubtedly remain a source of contention.

THE UNEASY RELATIONSHIP OF FAMILY AND COMMERCE IN THE MODERN WORLD

This chapter has argued that the Noahic covenant implicitly calls human beings to establish families characterized by child-bearing and child-rearing

---

83. Tyler Cowen explores these themes in *In Praise of Commercial Culture* (Cambridge, MA: Harvard University Press, 1998).

84. Cf. Novak, *The Spirit of Democratic Capitalism*, 174–75; and Lomborg, *The Skeptical Environmentalist*, 81–82.

85. Cf. McCloskey, *Bourgeois Dignity*, xiii, 69, and *Bourgeois Equality*, 631.

within monogamous, heterosexual, and permanent marriages, and that it calls them to pursue commerce characterized by several features, which include innovation and technological development. But are these visions of family and commerce actually compatible? Does the modern world provide evidence against it? This chapter concludes by reflecting on such questions.

The Alleged Incompatibility

In the mid-twentieth century, eminent economist Joseph Schumpeter propounded a now-famous thesis. Although in many ways an admirer and advocate of "capitalism," Schumpeter believed that innovative modern economies contained the seeds of their own demise within them. Their very success would be their undoing. Schumpeter recounted how their emergence broke down the structures of medieval feudalism—with many benefits but also some drawbacks. Their ongoing process of "creative destruction" instills a critical frame of mind among those who experience them, and they end up undermining the moral authority of the institutions upon which they rely for support. Innovative economies provoke hostility to their own order, especially from "the intellectual." They will destroy themselves from within.[86]

For Schumpeter, the family is among the undermined institutions. When people begin applying economic calculation to the home, they sense the costs of family ties and especially parenthood. Their innovative economies provide alternatives to the traditional family home and make the latter less desirable. According to Schumpeter, family life is a great asset to a vibrant economy, because it promotes physical and moral health and ingrains a long-term horizon for planning and investing. In weakening the family, innovative economies weaken themselves.[87]

Three-quarters of a century later, many of Schumpeter's predictions have not come to pass, but his analysis of innovative economies and their supporting institutions remains relevant. Probably the most important development in many Western societies has been the sharp change in sexual mores and especially the breakdown of the family over the past half-century or so, particularly in lower-class communities. I consider the United States as an example. Beginning in the 1960s, American society experienced rapidly increasing rates of divorce, extramarital cohabitation, out-of-wedlock births,

86. See especially Schumpeter, *Capitalism*, 61, 135–62. Daniel Bell (not the theologian discussed above) presented another case for capitalism sowing the seeds of its own destruction; see *The Cultural Contradictions of Capitalism* (New York: Basic, 1976).

87. Schumpeter, *Capitalism*, 157–62.

and single parenthood. These changes transpired during a time of relatively rapid economic growth, explosive technological development, and increased trade with nations newly joining international markets. After an extended period of time in which these family trends were manifest among all socio-economic groups, however, they leveled off (or even somewhat reversed) among more affluent groups while they continued among poorer groups. As a result, people in the socio-economic underclass (across ethnic lines) live increasingly apart from traditional family structures, while those in upper-middle class and elite circles still retain much of traditional family life—at least, they marry at much higher rates than the underclass, divorce less frequently, and usually marry before having children. Among the underclasses, economic struggle and family instability reinforce each other. Among the upper classes, economic prosperity and family stability reinforce each other.

The scholars who chronicle these developments tend to agree on the basic facts and on the tragedy of the American lower-class plight, but they do not agree on the remedy. Charles Murray, for example, does not want to abandon the innovations and economic development that a market economy has produced over past decades and sees many governmental attempts to help the less fortunate (such as growth of the welfare state) as harmful and counterproductive. He observes that the upper classes remain fairly industrious and responsible in family affairs but insist on being nonjudgmental about work, sex, and marriage. Murray thus calls them to start preaching what they practice and stop communicating that out-of-wedlock births and single parenthood are just alternative lifestyles.[88] June Carbone and Naomi Cahn, on the other hand, accept Murray's facts and statistics but belittle his prescription. They believe the situation is primarily an economic rather than a cultural problem, caused by the growing inequality brought about by the modern economy. They propose a host of government programs they believe will bring greater economic equality.[89] Robert Putnam concludes that both economic and cultural factors have created the new two-tier class system, and that causes and effects are entangled. He calls for both a reversal of private norms and a strong economic revival among the lower classes as necessary for restoring strong families among them.[90]

Christian thinkers have also reached diverse conclusions as they reflect on contemporary trends and dynamics. Stanley Hauerwas claims that

---

88. See especially Murray, *Coming Apart*, 289–94.
89. See especially Carbone and Cahn, *Marriage Markets*, 1–5, 29–32, and part 4.
90. See especially Putnam, *Our Kids*, 74–77, 244–45.

"marriage as lifelong monogamous fidelity in which children are desired" is incompatible with "capitalism." He approves of this conception of marriage, and thus capitalism is the "enemy."[91] Jennifer Roback Morse, in a different key, strongly affirms "laissez-faire" economics and argues that the economic and political freedom it entails requires stable, committed, and loving families. Thus she seeks both a robust market economy and broad commitment to traditional family structures.[92] Finally, Don Browning wants both marriage and "modernization" but says the traditional Western family needs to be partially reconceived and modernization partially curtailed. He thinks that a view like Morse's is rational but believes it may be unrealistic, unfair, and too optimistic about the ability of families to survive market forces.[93]

Keeping Noahic Family and Commerce Together

Untangling these issues is difficult. Hauerwas, Morse, and Browning are not even referring to exactly the same things by "capitalism," "laissez-faire," and "modernization." But perhaps we can bring the issues into workable focus by asking whether Noahic families (as described above) and Noahic commerce (as described above, but especially with respect to innovation and technological development) are truly compatible or ultimately at odds.

Important evidence suggests that the Noahic covenant's moral order is coherent. People obviously can establish faithful family relationships in all sorts of economic contexts, but a context that exhibits the features of Noahic commerce makes family life better in all sorts of ways. Such families will be better fed, be healthier, have far lower rates of infant mortality and maternal death in childbirth, and have greater opportunities to educate their children. In the other direction, Noahic families provide many benefits to commercial life. Children who grow up in stable homes with their married biological parents tend to develop better habits of industriousness, honesty, prudence, and peacefulness than those who do not, and married men tend to be better workers than those who do not marry. Without people who manifest these traits, Noahic commerce cannot thrive, if even survive.[94] Noahic families and Noahic commerce have many mutually beneficial features.

---

91. See Stanley Hauerwas, *A Better Hope: Resources for a Church Confronting Capitalism, Democracy, and Postmodernity* (Grand Rapids: Brazos, 2000), 50–51.

92. See Morse, *Love and Economics*, 4, 69, 189–91. Novak advances a similar perspective in *The Spirit of Democratic Capitalism*, ch. 8.

93. See Browning, *Marriage and Modernization*, 5, 25–27, 37–38. Browning does not mention Morse specifically.

94. Cf. Claar and Klay, *Economics in Christian Perspective*, 26; Murray, *Coming Apart*, 128–29; Morse,

Yet the potential tensions between them are not difficult to notice, especially in the present world in which innovation has become so rapid. The pressures to work long hours, to move, or to keep one's skills up to date can put real strain on a person's family. It is understandable that the person who loves the stability of the Noahic family could find the constant innovation and creative destruction of Noahic commerce distasteful, and that the person who becomes absorbed in the innovation of Noahic commerce could grow impatient with the constraints of Noahic families. Yet adopting one of these attitudes is ultimately self-defeating. Flourishing families need a vibrant economy; a flourishing economy needs strong families. From one perspective, the contemporary American cultural situation actually illustrates this point. Familial and economic thriving tend to go together, in a virtuous circle, while familial and economic floundering tend to go together, in a vicious circle.[95]

I conclude with no master policy prescription but simply with the observation that individuals and communities ought to honor both Noahic families and Noahic commerce, and beware of absolutizing one of them. To the extent that individuals and communities honor both, these aspects of life should tend to be mutually reinforcing. To the extent they absolutize one, they will tend to lose not only the other but the one they absolutize as well. Yet since God established the Noahic covenant for sinners (Gen 8:21), self-destructive temptations to absolutize will probably never abate.

Love and Economics, 5–9, 189–91; Röpke, *A Humane Economy*, 126; and Novak, *The Spirit of Democratic Capitalism*, 163, 168.

95. This point is well illustrated in Murray, *Coming Apart*, chs.8–9.

CHAPTER 9

JUSTICE AND RIGHTS

Thus far, part 2 has considered the pluralistic character of political communities under the Noahic covenant (chapter 7) and the first two aspects of this covenant's basic ethic: family and commerce (chapter 8). We now come to the third aspect, the pursuit of justice: "Whoever sheds the blood of man, by man shall his blood be shed, for God made man in his own image" (Gen 9:6). This does not prescribe the eschatological justice God will accomplish on the last day but a provisional, intrahuman justice fit for fallen human beings in common political communities.

Justice is a central, controversial, and complex topic of political and legal theory. At least there is no need to argue whether justice is worthy of pursuit. Everyone agrees it is. Yet under the canopy of "justice" lie a host of different and often contradictory ideas about human relationships and institutions. We all profess to love justice, but we mean different things by it.

A study of justice gets us into a constellation of issues difficult to untangle from one another. When we think about *justice*, we inevitably have to consider our communities' *law*, which ought to reflect and uphold justice. When we think about law, in turn, our minds inevitably turn to *government authority* and its responsibilities to obey, make, and/or enforce the law. Given the close relationship of these topics, they provide the main subjects for the following three chapters.

What exactly is their relationship? Justice should be the foundation of law and government authority, for law and government ought to be just. But what is just? In any real-life human community, what is just is determined in part by what its laws are. No one can claim, in the abstract, that driving on one particular side of the road is just, but if a community's law stipulates driving on the right, it becomes just to drive on the right and unjust to drive on the left. Likewise, law should be the foundation for government authority, for we laud the idea of the "rule of law, not of men." But what is the law? Human communities not only claim that their government authorities should be under the law but also grant these authorities power to make laws. Thus the law determines in part what is just, and government authorities determine in part what is law. Yet the basic hierarchy of justice (first), law (second), and government authority (third) seems sound, and we will focus upon them in that order.

To put things another way, this chapter will focus upon *natural* justice, that is, a justice universal to human beings to which all human legal systems and government authorities ought to adhere. But this natural justice is under-determinative. It is only general and does not specify a detailed public policy or comprehensive rules for conduct. Human laws and government authorities ought to operate within the bounds of natural justice, but natural justice itself cannot dictate exactly what these laws should say and exactly what these authorities should do. These laws and authorities are thus necessarily *conventional*: they should be rooted in the natural but are not exhaustively determined by it. And these conventional laws and authorities in turn provide necessary details for understanding what is just and unjust in a particular community.[1]

The chapter begins with reflections on the significance of using the *Noahic covenant* as the lens through which to examine justice. Then I introduce some of the main lines of debate about justice in recent philosophy and theology and suggest what perspective the Noahic covenant offers. I identify the basic contours of Noahic justice and then propose a corresponding understanding of natural human rights. The chapter concludes by considering judicial institutions and making an initial argument for what they are called to do.

CHRISTIANS AND NOAHIC-COVENANT JUSTICE

Before we focus on justice under the Noahic covenant, it is important to say that there is much more for Christians to know about justice than what the Noahic covenant and natural law communicate. As considered in the previous two chapters, although Christians remain members of the Noahic

---

1. On the relationship of the natural and conventional with respect to justice, picking up on her previous work on the indeterminacy of natural law, cf. Jean Porter, *Justice as a Virtue: A Thomistic Perspective* (Grand Rapids: Eerdmans, 2016), 272.

covenant and share a common human obligation to promote its purposes, their membership in the new covenant changes their relationship to these purposes in important respects. They are already citizens of a new creation in which present-day pluralism, family, and commerce do not exist, and they have the privilege of anticipating the life of the age to come now, especially corporately in the church. The same is true with justice.[2]

The Noahic covenant speaks of *rectifying* justice: the justice that seeks to right wrongs. This sort of justice is for *the present world* (cf. Gen 8:22) and has no place in the new creation. The final judgment will right every wrong once and for all, those who enter the new creation will be pure, and "everyone who loves and practices falsehood" will be excluded (see Rev 22:12–14). There will be nothing left to rectify.

Even while living in the present world, Christians enjoy an anticipation of this new-creation reality. Through faith in Christ, Christians are justified. God reckons them fully righteous before his law on the basis of Christ's life, death, and resurrection, not their own achievements (Rom 3:21–5:21).[3] Christians thereby already enjoy the judicial status of new-creation citizens: there is "now no condemnation for those who are in Christ Jesus" (Rom 8:1). Through Christ's atonement, God found a way simultaneously to forgive wrong and to satisfy the demands of justice against wrong (e.g., Rom 3:25–26). Thus, united to Christ by faith, Christians show the same forgiving love God first showed them in Christ (e.g., Luke 7:41–48; Rom 15:1–3, 7; Eph 4:32–5:2; 1 John 4:7–12). The Noahic and Mosaic covenants required eye for an eye, but because Christ has fulfilled the law, Christians now turn the other cheek instead (Matt 5:17, 38–42; cf. Rom 12:17; 1 Pet 3:9).

The New Testament indicates that this marvelous ethic finds institutional embodiment in the church. As is all too obvious, Christians do not yet experience the perfect personal holiness of the new creation, and thus they continue to sin and have disputes among themselves. But as appropriate for the community of the justified, the church does not seek rectifying justice to resolve its disputes. It does not treat its members as people under condemnation. In response to sin and conflict, the church follows a disciplinary procedure that inflicts no retribution but appeals for repentance and freely forgives, reconciles, and restores (Matt 18:15–20). Its purpose is salvific,

2. See the more detailed discussion in David VanDrunen, *Divine Covenants and Moral Order: A Biblical Theology of Natural Law* (Grand Rapids: Eerdmans, 2014), 448–69.
3. I state the traditional Reformed understanding of justification; e.g., see *Westminster Confession of Faith*, 11.

not punitive (1 Cor 5:4–5). In the image of its Lord, its members bear any burden to reclaim the wandering (Gal 6:1–2; cf. Matt 18:10–14). Even when wrongdoers do not repent, the church still does not inflict retribution but simply excommunicates them in recognition that it can no longer consider them members (Matt 18:17).

How Christians are to live out this anticipation of the new creation even while pursuing their obligations under the Noahic covenant is a key, if often not-quite-recognized, question of Christian ethics. One thing the New Testament makes clear is that Christians are to honor and support *both* the church that arises from the new covenant *and* the common political communities emerging from the Noahic covenant. Our concern in this chapter is not the mysterious anticipation of new creation in the former but the nature of justice under the latter.

CONTEMPORARY DEBATES ABOUT JUSTICE

It is not easy to know how to sort through recent philosophical and theological debates about justice in a concise and useful way. For present purposes, perhaps it is most helpful to classify theorists not in terms of whether they fall on the left or right of the political spectrum but in terms of what role justice is supposed to play in their broader social vision. As we will see, the Noahic covenant presents a distinct perspective on this important matter that will shape the argument of the chapter.

Constitutive Justice and Foundational Justice

To understand some of the important intellectual issues at stake, I suggest seeing recent philosophical debates about justice as an ongoing struggle between two basic approaches, what I call *foundational justice* and *constitutive justice*. The first approach focuses upon general rules and principles, on the basis of which individuals and communities with diverse convictions can agree to coexist and collaborate in a single civil society. Within such a society, people can pursue their own visions of the good. A society is considered just, therefore, because people honor the general rules and principles, not because the society itself attains some ideal form. From this perspective, justice is *foundational*: it aims to establish a legal framework within which people of diverse convictions can order their lives together in mutual peace, the end result of which remains open-ended. For the second approach, in contrast, justice is what reflects and protects the virtuous society. To specify what constitutes just relations among human beings, therefore, one needs to know what the good society looks like. From this perspective, justice is a *constitutive* aspect of a rich moral vision of the common good.

From a broader historical perspective, this distinction largely tracks the perennial political-philosophical debate about which is primary, the *right* or the *good*. Furthermore, foundational justice (as I described it) roughly corresponds to the approach of predominant strains of modern political liberalism, and constitutive justice roughly corresponds to classical approaches represented by Plato, Aristotle, and their followers.[4]

The most famous work on justice in the past half-century, John Rawls's *A Theory of Justice*, offers a good example of foundational justice. Rawls offers an intricate defense of the "maximal individual liberty principle" accompanied by the "difference principle." The former is largely self-explanatory. The latter proposes that social and economic inequalities, which inevitably result from the liberty principle, are justified when they work to the benefit of the least well-off. The application of these two principles results in a procedural view of justice. Rawls does not present a rich vision of what the good society looks like. Instead, he asserts that as long as the basic laws and institutions of a society honor his two principles of justice, that society is just, whatever exactly it looks like and however its resources are distributed.[5] Shortly after the publication of Rawls's work, F. A. Hayek presented another version of foundational justice. For Hayek, justice requires following general rules of conduct applicable to all people. He dismisses the idea of "social justice" as an incoherent superstition—a "mirage." Justice can pertain only to human conduct and not to a state of affairs. Therefore, as with Rawls, Hayek's just society operates according to general rules, and it is impossible to predict ahead of time what that society will look like.[6] A number of other influential

---

4. Cf. generally Alasdair Macintyre, *Whose Justice? Which Rationality?* (Notre Dame: University of Notre Dame Press, 1988); and John Rawls, *Political Liberalism*, exp. ed. (New York: Columbia University Press, 2005), 134–35.

5. See John Rawls, *A Theory of Justice* (Cambridge, MA: Belknap, 1971), §14. But also see Rawls' discussion of conceptions of the good and their relation to his liberal notion of the priority of the right, in *Political Liberalism*, lecture 5.

6. See Friedrich A. Hayek, *Law, Legislation and Liberty*, vol. 2, *The Mirage of Social Justice* (Chicago: University of Chicago Press, 1976). This association of Rawls and Hayek may be surprising, in light of Rawls' reputation as a champion of the socialist left and Hayek's as a champion of the libertarian right. They did indeed use very different conceptual tools in developing their ideas about justice—the "veil of ignorance" and "spontaneous order," respectively. But Hayek himself professed basic agreement with Rawls's theory, although he disliked his use of "social justice" terminology. See *The Mirage of Social Justice*, 100. Furthermore, despite their reputations, Rawls was not a doctrinaire socialist and Hayek not a doctrinaire libertarian. E.g., see Rawls, *A Theory of Justice*, 270–74; Rawls, *Political Liberalism*, 338–39;

theorists pursue a foundational-justice approach, although they assess Rawls in different ways.[7]

Many of Rawls's most prominent critics, in contrast, have objected to his theory from a constitutive-justice perspective. Michael Sandel, for example, criticized Rawls for making justice primary in his political philosophy, thereby elevating the right over the good and making justice independent of any particular substantive goal. For Sandel, justice cannot be primary because it depends upon a rich conception of the good.[8] Similarly, Michael Walzer subordinates justice (and rights) to a theory of the good—specifically, to a theory of the various goods properly differentiated through his notion of "complex equality."[9] John Finnis presented a natural-law version of constitutive justice. Grounding his conception of justice in a rich account of the common good, Finnis thinks justice concerns distributive and commutative requirements of practical reasonableness.[10] More recently, influential thinkers such as Amartya Sen and Ronald Dworkin (and perhaps Thomas Piketty) develop their ideas along constitutive-justice lines.[11]

Justice as Rights and Justice as Right Order

Nicholas Wolterstorff has suggested another way to frame debates about justice, proposing a distinction between justice as *rights* and justice as *right order*. This has garnered interest especially among Christian intellectuals.

---

and Friedrich A. Hayek, *Law, Legislation and Liberty*, vol. 3, *The Political Order of a Free People* (Chicago: University of Chicago Press, 1979), 41.

7. E.g., see Robert Nozick, *Anarchy, State, and Utopia* (New York: Basic, 1974); and Brian Barry, *A Treatise on Social Justice*, vol. 2, *Justice as Impartiality* (Oxford: Clarendon, 1995), especially 76–77, 80–83.

8. See Michael J. Sandel, *Liberalism and the Limits of Justice* (Cambridge: Cambridge University Press, 1982).

9. See Michael Walzer, *Spheres of Justice: A Defense of Pluralism and Equality* (New York: Basic, 1983).

10. See John Finnis, *Natural Law and Natural Rights* (Oxford: Clarendon, 1980), especially chs. 7–8.

11. Amartya Sen works out his "idea of justice" not with a neat definition of justice but with a theory of the good society with flourishing people—or, better, a theory of identifying *better* societies by comparison of real-world alternatives. See *The Idea of Justice* (Cambridge, MA: Belknap, 2009). Ronald Dworkin's work arguably resembles a foundational-justice approach, due to his emphasis upon the right to equal concern and equal respect, and to his devotion to rights as "trumps." Yet his notion of equal concern and respect is vague, and he gives it content only by "interpreting" the notion through development of a full-orbed political morality. For Dworkin, the idea of justice is "integrated" with a host of other ideas (such as equality, liberty, democracy, and law), and his theory of rights as trumps is ultimately a mode of inquiry about the full-orbed implications of equal concern and respect. See *Justice for Hedgehogs* (Cambridge, MA: Belknap, 2011). On rights as trumps, see also Ronald Dworkin, *Taking Rights Seriously* (Cambridge, MA: Harvard University Press, 1977), xi. Thomas Piketty never defines what he means by social justice in his surprise bestseller, but his general moral perspective is clearly utilitarian; e.g., see *Capital in the Twenty-First Century* (Cambridge, MA: Belknap, 2014), 31, 471, 480. He envisions social justice in terms of an "optimal" level of in/equality in an "ideal" society, although what exactly these mean is vague; e.g., see *Capital*, 505.

Wolterstorff embraces the former. He sees justice as "grounded ultimately on inherent rights," for some rights are inherent and not conferred.[12] God and humans both have inherent rights; humans have them because of their status of being loved by God.[13] For Wolterstorff, then, a social order is just "insofar as its members enjoy the goods to which they have rights."[14] For justice as right order, in contrast, "justice is present in society . . . insofar as the society measures up to whatever is the standard for the rightly ordered society."[15] Without speaking of rights, Plato's *Republic* exemplifies this view. According to Wolterstorff, contemporary right-order thinkers do not believe there are natural rights, but only those conferred by legislation, social practices, or the like.[16] He identifies Oliver O'Donovan, Joan Lockwood O'Donovan, and Alasdair MacIntyre with this view.[17]

Wolterstorff's distinction is similar to the one suggested above. His own approach resembles what I called foundational justice, for he believes that honoring inherent rights provides a standard for determining whether a community is just. It is no surprise, then, that Wolterstorff defends the general tenets of the liberal society.[18] On the other hand, the right-order approach requires a vision of a well-ordered society by which justice may be measured, similar to a constitutive-justice approach. Again, it is no surprise that many proponents of this view are critics of modern liberalism.[19]

JUSTICE AND RIGHTS UNDER THE NOAHIC COVENANT

What insight does a political theology centered on the Noahic covenant bring to this discussion? Of course, no detailed public policy emerges directly from Genesis 8:21–9:17, but I will ponder the implications of Genesis 9:6 and see how far this can take us. As in previous chapters, I will also reflect on

12. Nicholas Wolterstorff, *Justice: Rights and Wrongs* (Princeton: Princeton University Press, 2008), 21, 36.

13. See Wolterstorff, *Justice*, 317, 352–53, 360.

14. Wolterstorff, *Justice*, 10.

15. Wolterstorff, *Justice*, 30.

16. See Wolterstorff, *Justice*, 26–28, 31.

17. Wolterstorff, *Justice*, 31–33.

18. E.g., see Nicholas Wolterstorff, *The Mighty and the Almighty: An Essay in Political Theology* (Cambridge: Cambridge University Press, 2012); and *Understanding Liberal Democracy: Essays in Political Philosophy*, ed. Terrence Cuneo (Oxford: Oxford University Press, 2012).

19. See chapter 12 for discussion of the liberal tradition and its relation to the political theology developed in this book.

the natural-law basis of justice under the Noahic covenant, not by trying to establish a theory of justice from scratch but by contemplating how Noahic justice corresponds to human experience of the world.

Genesis 9:6 treats justice as something to be manifest within human relations. Therefore, as in most modern discussions, I deal with justice as embodied in social institutions rather than with justice as an individual virtue. But I do regard the virtue of justice, which disposes a person to act justly in relationship with other humans, as a necessary complement to the justice that ought to be embodied in social institutions.[20]

The Noahic Covenant and Contemporary Debates about Justice

What perspective does the Noahic covenant offer on the competing approaches I called foundational justice and constitutive justice? In my judgment, both approaches have attractive aspects from Noahic perspective, but neither is entirely satisfactory.

One of the attractive things about the foundational-justice approach is its fit for life in a pluralistic society, whose members do not share the same ultimate commitments. Proponents of the approach seek basic, foundational rules of justice geared for neighbors wishing to live in peace despite deep philosophical or theological disagreements. Since the Noahic covenant ordains *common* political communities, open to all people regardless of religious profession or philosophical conviction, a theory of justice does well to account for this. Furthermore, the Noahic covenant arguably provides a basic, foundational rule of justice—the *lex talionis*, or principle of reciprocity (Gen 9:6)—that offers a way to unite people of diverse ultimate commitments in a peaceful society while permitting them broad scope to organize their lives as they think proper.

Yet one of the powerful objections to a foundational-justice approach is that a conception of the right inevitably draws upon some conception of the good, implicitly if not explicitly. And this is undoubtedly true with respect to the reciprocity principle of the Noahic covenant. In Genesis 9:6, the *lex talionis* is grounded in the image of God and appears within a broader covenantal context through which God upholds a normative moral order for human society. Thus it surely presupposes a conception of the good. We might also consider Rawls's attempt to establish rules of justice by imagining people in an original state behind a "veil of ignorance." Some writers charge that this

---

20. For discussion of these two ways of thinking about justice, see Porter, *Justice as a Virtue*, 1–5, 269–73.

envisions people as disembodied individuals stripped of any interests, passions, and other concrete attributes that make them the people they actually are.[21] The Noahic covenant would agree that this is a problem: the *lex talionis* clearly does not envision people without interests and passions!

In short, a conception of justice arising out of the Noahic covenant will not fit solely within either the foundational-justice or the constitutive-justice approach. On the one hand, a Noahic conception must be fit for a pluralistic society that lacks a common commitment to the ultimate good, but on the other hand, it should not pretend that its principle(s) of justice is altogether independent of a conception of the good. What the Noahic covenant seems to provide, as argued in part 1, is a modest conception of the common good, aimed to join diverse people in real (although not substantively rich) moral bonds.[22]

Wolterstorff's rights/right-order distinction demands similar evaluation. From Noahic perspective, there is something attractive about Wolterstorff's strong affirmation of natural rights as key for understanding justice. As argued below, Genesis 9:6 implies certain universal human rights that a just society must protect. Yet Genesis 9:6 is inseparable from the context of God's creating and covenantal preservation of the world. That is, God's creation and covenant with Noah provide the substantive context for understanding natural rights. And once we say this, it begins to look suspiciously like a "right order" approach that Wolterstorff rejects.[23]

But right-order approaches have some difficulties of their own, from a Noahic perspective. It is useful to consider Oliver O'Donovan's response to Wolterstorff's critique of the right-order perspective. Several of O'Donovan's criticisms of Wolterstorff seem somewhat exaggerated to me,[24] but most pertinent for now is his claim that the language of rights rises out of despair—

---

21. E.g., Sandel presses this critique in *Liberalism and the Limits of Justice*.

22. Although I work out my proposal in many ways different from hers, Grace Y. Kao seems to express a similar desire to avoid extreme views that oversimplify our options. She seeks a kind of middle way between "maximalists," who think human-rights claims can be intelligibly grounded only in a rich set of religious convictions, and "minimalists," who think they can defend human rights without recourse to any controversial philosophical or theological premises. See *Grounding Human Rights in a Pluralist World* (Washington, DC: Georgetown University Press, 2011), 4–9.

23. Cf. similar comments in John D. Carlson, "Rights versus Right Order: Two Theological Traditions of Justice and Their Implications for Christian Ethics and Pluralistic Polities," *Journal of the Society of Christian Ethics* 36, no. 2 (2016): 86–88, 92.

24. E.g., O'Donovan says that a "multiple-rights" view such as Wolterstorff's rests on a moral ontology that assumes the fundamental difference (rather than similarity) between individual people; see "The Language of Rights and Conceptual History," *Journal of Religious Ethics* 37, no. 2 (2009): 202–3. A theory of natural rights *could* be individualistic, but it is hard to see how affirming that all human beings have exactly the same natural rights makes each of them "irreducibly *one*, not interchangeable with any other" and not "brothers and sisters, under the skin."

despair about the ability to identify "the intellectual and moral coherence to found a civilization free of brutality."[25] When we consider the historical contexts in which modern emphasis upon rights emerged, O'Donovan's claim has a ring of truth. But perhaps this "despair" was not so much an anti-Christian hopelessness as a simple realism, a true-to-life recognition that landing upon a shared, rich moral ontology is impossible in large political communities. Contra O'Donovan, one might argue that building a conception of justice around natural rights is not substantively vacuous but simply requires a more modest conception of the common good than right-order theorists seek, and is thus more likely to gain broad consent.

In short, I conclude that all four approaches to justice described above capture elements of truth, but none of them express exactly what the Noahic covenant communicates. We need to work through the implications of justice as expressed in Genesis 9:6 without being constrained ahead of time by exclusive devotion to any one of these approaches.

Rectifying Justice

The obligation to pursue justice takes both positive and negative form. *Primary* justice requires treating people justly by giving them their due proactively—for example, paying the store for one's loaf of bread rather than sneaking away with it. In comparison, *rectifying* justice imposes a just remedy in response to violations of primary justice—for example, fining or imprisoning the person who steals.[26] The Noahic covenant speaks of justice in rectifying terms, specifying the proper response when someone sheds another's blood (Gen 9:6). This does not nullify the reality of primary justice, since rectifying justice is only necessary when primary justice is violated. But since the Noahic covenant speaks as it does, I will focus first on what it communicates about rectifying justice and consider later what it implies about primary justice.

Retributive

The first and most obvious thing to observe about the rectifying justice prescribed in Genesis 9:6 is that it is *retributive* in nature. As explained below, there is more to Noahic justice than retribution, but retribution is clearly present in the *lex talionis* of Genesis 9:6. Commonly known by the formula "eye for an eye, tooth for a tooth," here it appears as blood for blood.

---

25. O'Donovan, "The Language of Rights," 204.
26. This is Wolterstorff's terminology; see *Justice*, ix–x.

Retributive justice communicates that those who harm others *deserve* a penalty in response. Even apart from other legitimate concerns—such as compensation, deterrence, or restoration of relationships—it is fitting to impose some corresponding loss upon the morally blameworthy person who inflicts loss upon another. People often associate retributive justice with vengeance and its negative connotations. Vengeance is indeed retributive, but vengeance and retribution are not identical. For example, while vengeance focuses upon satisfaction of personal outrage and thus can easily involve excessive and disproportionate response to injury, retributive justice by definition aims at a *proportional* response: wrongdoers should get only what they deserve, a penalty that matches the harm they perpetrated.[27]

The idea of justice-as-proportionality is familiar. For example, the figure of a woman with scales in her hand portrays justice in terms of a balance or equilibrium. When someone tips the balance by unjustly adding weight to one side, only an equivalent weight on the other side can put things back in order.[28] This is perhaps what the *lex talionis* captures most poignantly. What could be a more fitting penalty for destroying an eye than losing an eye? As William Ian Miller puts it, "Let's just say that the eye/tooth statement perfectly captures the rule of equivalence, balance, and precision in a stunning way. It holds before us the possibility of getting the measure of value right."[29] As considered below, the core idea of the *lex talionis* is not bodily mutilation, but the ideal of finding a penalty that is fit, even, and proportionate. Far from promoting unbridled vengeance, the *lex talionis* prohibits excessive retaliation.[30]

A couple of initial objections to retributive justice can be easily answered, I believe, at least if we take the Noahic covenant as benchmark. Some writers critique retributive justice because the idea of justice-as-balance is abstract and even imaginary.[31] But thinking of retributive justice in terms of the *lex*

---

27. As Peter French puts it, "Retributivism, in all of its forms, requires that wrongdoing be proportionately punished." See *The Virtues of Vengeance* (Lawrence: University Press of Kansas, 2001), 222.

28. For various discussions of retribution in terms of balance and the like, see, e.g., William Ian Miller, *Eye for an Eye* (Cambridge: Cambridge University Press, 2006), 1–7; Adonis Vidu, *Atonement, Law, and Justice: The Cross in Historical and Cultural Contexts* (Grand Rapids: Baker Academic, 2014), 138; Timothy Gorringe, *God's Just Vengeance: Crime, Violence and the Rhetoric of Salvation* (Cambridge: Cambridge University Press, 1996), 97, 232; Susan Jacoby, *Wild Justice: The Evolution of Revenge* (New York: Harper & Row, 1983), 333; and French, *The Virtues of Vengeance*, 3, 225–26.

29. Miller, *Eye for an Eye*, 30.

30. Many authors make this point; e.g., see French, *The Virtues of Vengeance*, 9. But Miller points out that the *lex talionis* puts not only an upper limit on penalty but also a lower limit; see *Eye for an Eye*, 20–21.

31. E.g., see Gorringe, *God's Just Vengeance*, 233.

talionis quiets this charge. The *lex talionis* is anything but abstract. It envisions real people with very practical and material concerns, showing a way to address injuries and soothe passions. Other writers critique retributive justice because ranking the badness of various wrongs and determining proportionality is often very difficult, if not impossible.[32] This is true at times. For instance, identifying a proportionate penalty for sexual assault seems particularly difficult. Nevertheless, people facing difficult real-life conflicts have been remarkably adept at discovering fair ways to settle accounts.[33] And although human ingenuity meets its limits, the Noahic covenant does not promise perfect, eschatological justice, which awaits the final judgment. If some human wrongs seem impervious to fully satisfactory proportionate penalty in this life, that does not make proportionality an improper goal of rectifying justice. As things go under Noah's rainbow, human beings can attain justice only proximately, not perfectly.

Since retributive justice is so objectionable even to some Christians, I now widen our scope beyond Genesis 9:6 and consider why, in light of broader biblical teaching, it is compelling to recognize retributive justice in the Noahic covenant. I first widen the scope only slightly. In the previous verse, God states, "And for your lifeblood I will require a reckoning: from every beast I will require it and from man. From his fellow man I will require a reckoning for the life of man" (Gen 9:5). Here God asserts his rights as judge of all the world. He will call all the violent to account. But as Genesis 9:6 then makes clear, God presently wills to do this, in part, through human instruments. God delegates responsibility to human beings to bring rectifying justice on earth. Genesis 9:6 refers to these humans as the image of God because image-bearing entails a commission to exercise benevolent rule as God's representative (Gen 1:26–28).[34]

Elsewhere, Scripture also speaks of human justice as a mirror of divine justice. For example, the Mosaic law prescribes, "You shall not pervert the justice due to your poor in his lawsuit. Keep far from a false charge, and do not kill the innocent and righteous, *for I will not acquit the wicked*" (Exod 23:6–7, emphasis added). That is, the standard for judgment in human courts ought to reflect the divine standard. In Romans 13, furthermore, the civil magistrate is God's "servant" and "minister," particularly in giving "approval" to the one

32. E.g., see Christopher D. Marshall, *Beyond Retribution: A New Testament Vision for Justice, Crime, and Punishment* (Grand Rapids: Eerdmans, 2001), 113–14.

33. See Miller, *Eye for an Eye*, 20.

34. See chapter 2 above; and VanDrunen, *Divine Covenants*, 41–67, 116–18.

doing right and in carrying out "God's wrath on the wrongdoer" (13:3–6). In their judicial task, therefore, magistrates do God's work on God's behalf.

In light of this, we would expect that any sort of justice God commissions humans to perform would find its origin in God himself. Finite human justice cannot be identical to God's infinitely perfect justice, but these biblical texts suggest an analogy between justice human and divine. If Genesis 9:6 really does prescribe retributive justice for human society, which its talionic formula indicates, then God's justice must be (at least in part) retributive. If God abhors retribution, on the contrary, we need to reconsider the interpretation of Genesis 9:6 above.

Scripture does, in fact, speak of God's justice in retributive terms, often portraying God as avenging wrong and visiting the wicked with a due and proportionate punishment.[35] God states, "Vengeance is mine, and recompense, for the time when their foot shall slip" (Deut 32:35). The psalmist writes, "O LORD, God of vengeance, O God of vengeance, shine forth! . . . He will bring back on them their iniquity" (Ps 94:1, 23). Likewise, the prophet says, "the LORD is a God of recompense; he will surely repay" (Jer 51:56). Descriptions of God avenging wrong can leave readers uneasy. Given the often excessive and imbalanced nature of human vengeance, this is understandable. But Scripture also emphasizes that God's retributive judgment is proportionate to the wrong perpetrated. Immediately after one of the texts just quoted, the psalmist adds, "Rise up, O judge of the earth; repay to the proud *what they deserve*" (Ps 94:2; emphasis added). Another psalmist adds: "You [God] will render to a man *according to his work*" (Ps 62:12; emphasis added). Scripture also uses the irony of poetic justice to depict the perfect fittingness and proportionality of God's retribution. Isaiah's oracle against the king of Babylon is a good example: "How you are cut down to the ground, you who laid the nations low" (Isa 14:12)—that is, the king suffers the same fate he imposed upon others. The king has boasted, "I will sit on the mount of assembly in the *far reaches* of the north" (14:13; emphasis added), but the prophet responds, "You are brought down to Sheol, to the *far reaches* of the pit" (14:15; emphasis added)—that is, instead of rising to the extremes of glory to which he proudly

---

35. For an argument against the retributive character of divine justice, see, e.g., Thomas Talbott, "Punishment, Forgiveness, and Divine Justice," *Religious Studies* 29, no. 2 (June 1993): 151–68. Although Talbott argues against divine retributive justice in Christian terms, his argument completely ignores biblical texts that seem to say what he denies, including the texts I discuss below. For a response to Talbott mainly along the philosophical lines Talbott follows, see Oliver D. Crisp, "Divine Retribution: A Defence," *Sophia* 42, no. 2 (Oct 2003): 35–50.

aspired, he sinks to the extremes of dishonor.[36] God gives the wicked precisely what their deeds deserve. His judgments are exactly fitting.

The New Testament speaks similarly. For example, Paul describes God by quoting one of the Old Testament texts cited above: "It is written, 'Vengeance is mine, I will repay, says the Lord'" (Rom 12:19). Perhaps most explicitly and intensely, in Revelation a voice from heaven calls out for God to judge "Babylon the Great," requesting judgment that is retributive, talionic, and poetic: "*Pay her back* as she herself has *paid back others*, and *repay her double* for her deeds; mix a *double portion* for her *in the cup she mixed*.[37] As she glorified herself and lived in luxury, so give her *a like measure* of torment and mourning, since in her heart she says, 'I sit as a queen, I am no widow, and mourning I shall never see.' For this reason her plagues will come in a single day; death and mourning and famine" (Rev 18:6–8; emphasis added; cf. 16:6).[38]

Biblical authors, far from being embarrassed by God's retributive justice, often ask for it (e.g., Ps 79:12; Rev 6:10), rejoice in it (e.g., Ps 58:10), and find it proof that there really is a God who judges the world (e.g., Ps 58:11).

Theological debates about retributive justice often focus on the atonement. Writers from different perspectives recognize that a person's view of the atonement and view of justice tend to cohere.[39] Some scholars argue that retributive justice became an important part of atonement theology only with Anselm's satisfaction theory in the eleventh century and came into its own with the Protestant reformers' penal substitutionary doctrine.[40] Without entering into detailed debates about the atonement, I simply appeal to the arguments above. If Scripture does indeed portray God as coming to judge sinners with retribution proportionate to their sins, then a Christian theology of the atonement wishing to be biblically grounded should account for retribution. It needs to interpret the cross, at least in part, as God's way of rescuing sinners from their condemnation under God's retributive justice. A sound theology of the atonement should reckon with themes such as Jesus's standing in sinners' place (e.g., Rom 5:8; 2 Cor 5:14), enduring God's wrath (e.g., Mark 10:38; 14:36; cf. Ps 75:8; Rev 16:19), and bearing his people's sins

---

36. Cf. VanDrunen, *Divine Covenants and Moral Order*, 183–84.

37. For an argument that "double" is probably better translated "equivalent," see Meredith G. Kline, "Double Trouble," *Journal of the Evangelical Theological Society* 32 (June 1989): 177.

38. In Revelation 11:18, the final judgment will also be a day "for *destroying* the *destroyers* of the earth."

39. E.g., see generally Vidu, *Atonement, Law, and Justice*; and Gorringe, *God's Just Vengeance*.

40. E.g., see Marshall, *Beyond Retribution*, 43–45; Gorringe, *God's Just Vengeance*, 6–7, 11–12; and Daniel Philpott, *Just and Unjust Peace: An Ethic of Political Reconciliation* (New York: Oxford University Press, 2012), 144–46.

(e.g., 1 Pet 2:24), so that they may be justified (e.g., Rom 5:16, 18) and their sins not be counted against them (e.g., 2 Cor 5:19). Retributive justice fits comfortably among these themes.

In short, retributive justice is a prevalent theme in Scripture. Several texts ground human pursuit of justice in the justice of God, the ultimate judge of all the world. Human beings are to uphold retributive justice as representatives of God delegated to bring a measure of his justice to the world now. The broader witness of Scripture confirms the conclusion that justice under the Noahic covenant is to be, in part, retributive.

Compensatory

Nevertheless, the Noahic covenant commissions the human community to do justice not only by giving wrongdoers what they deserve but also by compensating victims of wrong. Noahic justice is about paying back as well as payback. This claim may be surprising, since writers often describe compensatory justice as an alternative to retribution.[41] But we should not impose this dichotomy on the Noahic covenant.

Since the Noahic covenant issues its call to justice through a version of the *lex talionis*, we need to consider what the legal principle of *lex talionis* communicates. There is considerable evidence that it promotes compensation as well as retribution.

The Mosaic law promulgates the *lex talionis* on three separate occasions (Exod 21:23–25; Lev 24:19–20; Deut 19:21). But did the Mosaic law intend the *lex talionis* to be applied literally, that is, by imposing reciprocal physical harm, or was substitution possible? Numbers 35:30–32 warns the people against accepting compensation for murderers and requires their execution. In other words, those entrusted with avenging a murder victim were not to accept a monetary payment in lieu of shedding blood for blood. But the very need for this warning raises interesting questions. Would the law have bothered to discourage them from accepting compensation for murder if they were not tempted and even inclined to do so? And if the people were willing to consider compensation in case of murder, would they not have more readily accepted compensation for lesser physical assault? Yet in no case other than murder does the Mosaic Law prohibit substitution of monetary payment. For good reason, many ancient and more recent interpreters believe

---

41. E.g., see Randy E. Barnett, *The Structure of Liberty: Justice and the Rule of Law*, 2nd ed. (New York: Oxford University Press, 2014), 185–86; and Gorringe, *God's Just Vengeance*, 128.

that substituting monetary compensation in most cases is consistent with the intent of Mosaic jurisprudence.[42] In fact, the Mosaic law often explicitly prescribes compensation in cases of property damage, using talionic-type language to do so.[43] Thus extending use of compensation to cases of bodily injury utilizes an already prevalent idea in the Mosaic legal material.

Evidence for this sort of substitution appears in many other contexts as well. In Israel's own ancient Near Eastern world, the Code of Hammurabi prescribed literal application of the *lex talionis* in some circumstances and monetary compensation in others.[44] The Twelve Tables of early Roman law also permitted substitution: "If anyone has broken another's limb there shall be retaliation in kind unless he compounds for compensation with him."[45] Miller discusses how this worked on the ground in medieval Iceland.[46]

But why substitute compensation for literal application of the *lex talionis*? The initial answers are obvious. An injured victim can use cash to pay doctors and feed himself and his family while unable to work. This is more practically useful than becoming destitute while happily knowing that his assailant will suffer the same injury he did. In addition, most assailants will find it more attractive to suffer a monetary loss than to lose a body part that will never grow back. But these obvious answers are almost a little too easy. If monetary compensation is so superior, why bother starting with the *lex talionis* at all and not just establish fines for different sorts of injuries?

My first response addresses a practical problem. Monetary compensation benefits victims and their families and is also a humane way to penalize assailants. But how exactly to value a body part? What is someone's eye really worth in dollars or yen? The *lex talionis*, when standing behind monetary compensation, provides a brilliant solution. If a victim has a right to demand literal application of the *lex talionis* for the loss of her eye, we might imagine her asking her assailant, "How much are you willing to pay me to keep your eye?" We might also imagine the assailant taking the initiative and asking

42. E.g., see Marshall, *Beyond Retribution*, 80–83; Roland de Vaux, OP, *Ancient Israel: Its Life and Institutions*, trans. John McHugh (New York: McGraw-Hill, 1961), 149–50; and Miller, *Eye for an Eye*, 24–27. For a different perspective, see James F. Davis, *Lex Talionis in Early Judaism and the Exhortation of Jesus in Matthew 5.38–42* (New York: T&T Clark, 2005), ch. 3.
43. E.g., "Whoever takes an animal's life shall make it good, life for life" (Lev 24:18). See Jonathan Burnside, "Retribution and Restoration in Biblical Texts," in *Handbook of Restorative Justice*, ed. Gerry Jonstone and Daniel W. Van Ness (Cullompton, UK: Willan, 2007), 139.
44. See §§196–204, in G. R. Driver and John C. Miles, *The Babylonian Laws*, 2 vols. (Oxford: Clarendon, 1952), 2:76–79.
45. Table 8.3. This translation is taken from the Avalon Project at Yale Law School, avalon.law.yale.edu/ancient//twelve_tables.asp.
46. E.g., see Miller, *Eye for an Eye*, 51–52.

his victim, "How much money would it take for you to forego your right to my eye?" As the preceding paragraph suggests, both sides have incentive to reach a deal, and the deal is likely to land somewhere between the answers to these two questions. If we really want to know what a body part is worth, the background threat of the *lex talionis* provides an excellent calculator. When a real-life eye is at stake, we will find out how valuable it is. Without the *lex talionis* in the background, we can only guess.

My second response is this: the point of substituting monetary payment is not to replace retribution with compensation, as if rectifying justice can embrace only one or the other. Instead, promulgating the *lex talionis* but permitting substitution of monetary compensation enables rectifying justice to provide *both* retribution *and* restitution. Monetary compensation can be retributive, and retribution can be a form of compensation. Retribution and compensation are not independent but (at least potentially) two aspects of a single goal of rectifying justice: to penalize the wrongdoer with what he deserves and to compensate the victim for the harm she endured. In the image of justice as a woman with scales, an imbalance is corrected through both gain on the one side (the victim's) and loss on the other side (the assailant's). There is no justice if either the assailant walks away without suffering any consequences or the victim receives nothing back to restore the loss. To regain equilibrium, both sides of the balance must move.

And this can happen through both literal application of the *lex talionis* and figurative application by monetary payment. In each case, the assailant is penalized and suffers loss—the purposes of retribution are served. In each case, the victim also receives something back to restore her loss—the purposes of compensation are served. With respect to the victim, a monetary payment restores her loss by reimbursing financial costs of the injury and offsetting her pain and suffering. In comparison, literal application of the *lex talionis* restores her loss and serves as a kind of payment insofar as it redresses the assailant's assault upon her dignity and honor.[47] The victim, we might say, is *vindicated* when her assailant gets what he deserves.[48]

---

47. As Miller observes, "Revenge always coexisted with a compensation option. The conceptual underpinning was exactly the same in either case: both revenge and compensation were articulated solely in idioms of repayment of debts and of settling scores and accounts. Revenge was compensation using blood, not instead of money, but as a kind of money." See *Eye for an Eye*, 25. It seems to me that critiques of retribution fail precisely at this point when they emphasize that imposing harm on someone in response to a harm brings no benefit to the original victim. For such a critique, see, e.g., Gary Chartier, *Anarchy and Legal Order: Law and Politics for a Stateless Society* (Cambridge: Cambridge University Press, 2013), 289–94. My whole discussion of compensation is greatly indebted to Miller's work, especially *Eye for an Eye*, ch. 4.

48. Christians, at least, should appreciate the desire for vindication after being wronged. The

In short, the *lex talionis* concerns the rights and debts of both victim and wrongdoer, and thus requires attention to retribution and compensation alike, not as competing but as corresponding principles. Thus, by promulgating the *lex talionis*, the Noahic covenant ordains that justice in common political communities should be both retributive and compensatory.

Forbearing

While retribution and compensation seem to be the two main principles communicated by the *lex talionis* in Genesis 9:6, the idea of *forbearance* also lurks in the background. Through its imagery of balance and proportion, the *lex talionis* communicates the ideal of getting retribution and compensation exactly right, but in a fallen world we will not be able to get them exactly right in many circumstances. And sometimes when we might be able to get it right, we have a sense that we should hold back. These circumstances do not expose a flaw in the conception of Noahic justice sketched thus far. Rather, the Noahic covenant itself indicates that in some cases the best course is to forbear imposing the full brunt of rectifying justice, even if it leaves the scales of justice out of perfect balance.

In Genesis 9:6, God appoints humans, as his image-bearing representatives, to impart a measure of his justice here and now. Thus I argued that the retributive character of divine justice underlies the retributive character of human justice in Genesis 9:6. Yet God himself does not bring perfect retributive justice to the world at the present time but is longsuffering and forbearing. This is an aspect of the preservative mercy God bestows on all creation, as discussed in chapter 2. A world full of sinners could hardly survive the imposition of God's perfect justice. In the great flood, the world suffered a taste of what happens when God withdraws his preservative mercy, and the point of the Noahic covenant was to reestablish that preservation for the generations to come. It is best to call this preservation *forbearance* and not *forgiveness*. God does not pardon sins once and for all in the Noahic covenant but promises to maintain his preservative mercy "while the earth remains" (Gen 8:22). God holds back his just wrath. But there is a day coming when the Noahic covenant reaches its expiration date and God institutes the final judgment—akin to the great flood, but truly final this time (see 2 Pet 3:5–7).

In sum, justice under the Noahic covenant means doing justice in the

---

Revelation of John, for example, often portrays the righteous as desiring and rejoicing in God's vengeance upon their persecutors at the final judgment (e.g., Rev 6:9–11; 16:5–7; 18:20).

image of this God revealed in the Noahic covenant. If the human race pursues justice in the likeness of God, its justice will be tempered by forbearance. If even God, who is capable of bringing perfect justice, holds it back in order to accomplish his covenantal purposes, then human judges should hardly be surprised when they are unable to accomplish perfect justice or confront situations that make its accomplishment undesirable.

When is it proper to be forbearing and refrain from imposing a perfectly proportionate penalty upon the wrongdoer (which also means, regrettably, not providing the victim with proportionate compensation)? When to leave the scales unbalanced? In some obvious cases, a person's wrongdoing is so massive that no conceivable penalty would be proportionate. If we could bring Hitler or Stalin to trial, what recompense for their crimes against humanity could possibly bring the scales of justice into balance?[49] But the Noahic covenant gives no clear instruction about how to make judgments of forbearance in less drastic and thus more difficult cases. What it does give, I suggest, is a general orientation: Noahic justice is meant to advance the broader end of the Noahic covenant, which is preservation of the human race, particularly in its familial and enterprise callings discussed in chapter 8. Thus, when circumstances indicate that proportionate penalty would harm or even destroy a community, forbearance is surely in order. On a small scale, there are a dozen little harms that each of us inflicts and endures every day— verbal sleights, failure to use turn signals, bumps in the hallway. A society that tried to litigate every one, for the sake of doing perfect justice, would have no time or resources for anything else. On a larger scale, a society searching for reconciliation after a major upheaval—such as a civil war or revolt against a tyrant—may find that any attempt to call all perpetrators to account would make peaceful reconciliation impossible. The best hope for a peaceful future may lie with widespread agreement to let many wrongs go unpunished and uncompensated, under certain conditions. The route of South Africa under its Truth and Reconciliation Committee may be a good example.

Several other cases come to mind beyond these likely compelling cases. What to do about the guilty wrongdoer whose terrible childhood makes her plight sympathetic? What to do when a victim insists that he does not wish to press charges against someone who has done him great harm?

---

49. Andrew Nagorski comments that those who dedicated their lives to calling lesser Nazi officials to account found it simply too large of a task to settle all claims of justice or to prosecute all war criminals; see *The Nazi Hunters* (New York: Simon & Schuster, 2016), 2–3.

While providing no definite answers, the Noahic covenant's ethos of forbearance means that seeking perfectly proportionate justice is not always the
best option.

An Interlude on the Restorative-Justice Movement

In recent years, a movement committed to "restorative justice" has
gained considerable attention in Christian circles and elsewhere. Its advocates
seek reconsideration of criminal justice in Western societies. As they see it,
Western criminal justice proceeds as if the state and the alleged wrongdoer
are the two interested parties. The state presses charges, and it often punishes
by imprisoning convicts, which does little good for either the convict or the
victim. Proponents of restorative justice urge that wrongdoing be reconceived
as a dispute among a perpetrator, a victim, and their local community. They
argue that the wrong should ordinarily be addressed not through retributive
imprisonment but through programs of reconciliation that bring perpetrator,
victim, and the broader community together to work through the conflict,
build mutual understanding, and find ways for the perpetrator to provide
restitution for the victim. Wrongdoers should be punished, but in ways that
encourage their reincorporation into the community. The goal is to restore
broken relationships, insofar as perpetrators acknowledge their wrong and
work to make things right, and victims in turn forgive them.[50]

The concerns of the restorative-justice movement partially resemble
my description of Noahic justice to this point. For one thing, some of the
chief features of restorative justice mirror key aspects of Noahic justice, such
as assigning guilt, punishing perpetrators, and providing restitution for
victims.[51] Second, the call to make criminal justice less state-centered and
more focused on the relationship between victim and perpetrator is intriguing from a Noahic perspective. Although the Noahic covenant indirectly
authorizes human communities to establish civil governments under certain
conditions, as argued in this book, Genesis 9:6 directly speaks of a dispute
between "man" and "man," with no mention of a state. The interpersonal
relationship is more fundamental than the interests of civil government. To
the extent that state intervention in such disputes is justified, it ought to serve
the interpersonal, not replace it. Third, the critique of imprisonment as the

---

50. For a useful summary of these concerns, see, e.g., Philpott, *Just and Unjust Peace*, 64–67.

51. Philpott essentially communicates this point when he comments that most aspects of justice
as reconciliation (his version of restorative justice) can be conceived as giving to each what is due (which
I think also encapsulates the principle of the *lex talionis*). See *Just and Unjust Peace*, 68.

chief form of criminal punishment arguably resonates with the Noahic covenant. Under literal application of the *lex talionis*, imprisonment is not the proportionate response to wrong (except for the wrong of imprisoning someone else). If monetary compensation is substituted, the wrongdoer must repay the victim—in such cases, the wrongdoer needs to be gainfully employed rather than imprisoned. From Noahic perspective, therefore, the complaint that imprisonment often does little to help wrongdoer or victim is worth consideration.

Despite these important points of appreciation, my analysis of justice under the Noahic covenant also prompts some serious criticisms, two in particular. First, many proponents of this movement advocate restorative justice as a stark alternative to retributive justice.[52] But the latter is crucial to justice under the Noahic covenant, as important as other concerns may be. Second, Christian proponents of the movement often portray restorative justice as in some way redemptive, in the sense of participating in Christ's work and anticipating the blessing of new creation. The restoration in restorative justice, in other words, can be a share in Christ's redemptive restoration and eschatological renewal of all things.[53] Here I appeal back to the political theology of part 1. The Noahic covenant is the proper theological framework for interpreting and norming our lives in common political community. Since the Noahic covenant is preservative and provisional, and holds out no redemptive or eschatological hope, it is a category mistake to seek a civil justice loaded with redemptive and eschatological overtones.

To conclude these brief remarks on the restorative-justice movement: The justice we seek in our common political communities is always temporal and imperfect. Although Christian advocates of the movement also acknowledge this at times, their redemptive rhetoric, I fear, often infuses the quest for justice with an unhelpful utopian flavor. Often the best we can hope for amid conflicts in our earthly societies is merely protecting the safety of a (potential) victim. Just keeping violence at bay is more than a significant accomplishment in this fallen world (see Gen 6:11–13). Retributive and compensatory justice may often restore the peace and sometimes even enable victim and perpetrator to live cordially in the future. But to expect victim and

---

52. E.g., see Marshall, *Beyond Retribution*, 2.

53. For concise evidence that redemptive and eschatological themes animate both the substance and the motivation of many Christian theological cases for restorative justice, see Gorringe, *God's Just Vengeance*, 249, 253, 258; Marshall, *Beyond Retribution*, 21–23, 145, 284; and Philpott, *Just and Unjust Peace*, 147–49; ch. 12.

perpetrator to sit down together and work toward a wonderful new relationship may be too grand an ambition for a modest system of justice under the Noahic covenant.[54]

Natural Human Rights (1)

After this extended analysis of rectifying justice, it seems appropriate to turn to *rights*, one of the chief rubrics by which many scholars and activists have considered justice in recent centuries. Here we explore whether rectifying justice under the Noahic covenant implies any conception of rights and, if so, what these rights might be. To clarify, we inquire not about the *political* or *legal rights* that particular governments may grant or acknowledge but about *natural human rights*—that is, just claims that all individuals properly assert in every cultural context, simply by virtue of being human, and that laws and governments ought to respect as a matter of justice.[55] At least two compelling reasons indicate that the Noahic covenant implicitly recognizes natural human rights.

The first is that the human community should render justice because "God made man in his own image" (Gen 9:6). As noted, this reference to the image calls readers back to Genesis 1:26–27. Through the unique ways it describes human creation, this text emphasizes the special worth and dignity that image bearing entails. In earlier creating acts in Genesis 1, God's speech is impersonal and indirect: "let the waters swarm," "let the earth bring forth," and the like (1:20, 24; cf. 1:3, 6, 9, 11, 14). But when God creates human beings his speech turns personal and direct: "let us make man" (1:26). Earlier in Genesis 1, God makes the various creatures "according to their kinds" (1:11, 12, 21, 24, 25), that is, with reference to themselves. But he makes human beings "in our image, after our likeness" (1:26), that is, with reference to himself. Both human beings and other animals are "living creatures" (1:20, 21, 24; 2:7), but the text calls only humans "male and female"

---

54. For a critique of the restorative-justice movement that shares some of my conclusions, although from a different theological angle, see Maria Mayo, *The Limits of Forgiveness: Case Studies in the Distortion of a Biblical Ideal* (Minneapolis: Fortress, 2015), ch. 2, and especially 91–92.

55. I refrain from speaking of human rights as something distinct from natural rights. Some writers do distinguish them. For example, Kao sees natural rights as universal to all times and places, while human rights are universal in scope (that is, for all people) but not in time, since they depend upon political context and technological advance; see *Grounding Human Rights*, 122, 133–34, 203. It is difficult to see how human rights so understood are consistent with the way she says she will use the term *human rights* at the outset of her book: as "the set of entitlements and justified claims that every human being has simply by virtue of being human." See *Grounding Human Rights*, 9. If I have a right simply by virtue of being human, it should not depend on the time and place I happen to occupy.

(1:27; cf. 2:18–25). Finally, while God calls some of the other creatures to be fruitful and multiply and to fill their respective habitations (1:22), God calls humans alone to be fruitful, multiply, and fill the earth as part of a broader commission to subdue and have dominion over the rest of creation (1:26, 28).

This unique dignity evident in Genesis 1, furthermore, is not simply a corporate blessing or something only select persons possess. Rather, human beings as individuals bear God's image. Immediately after describing creation in God's image in corporate terms—"Let us make *man*" (1:26, emphasis added)—the text calls this image-bearing "man" "male and female" (1:27). Humans bear the image in their individuality and not merely in their unity. In addition, bearing the image was not only for the first generation. God originally created the male and female in his image (Gen 5:1–2), and they in turn bore children in their own image and likeness (5:3). A person shares human nature and dignity merely by being born of fellow human beings. Despite their moral turpitude and the judgment of the great flood, all individuals retain this status. Both the "man" who sheds blood and the "man" whose blood is shed belong to the "man" made in God's image (Gen 9:6).

Therefore, we have an initial reason to see a notion of natural human rights implicit in the Noahic covenant. The covenant recognizes all human beings as made in the image of God, and thus they possess a unique status and dignity and bear moral responsibility as participants in the commission to fill and rule the world.[56]

A second consideration from Genesis 9:6 confirms this initial conclusion: the talionic formula itself entails natural human rights. If the blood of a person (A) is shed, the person (B) who sheds it must be punished. This makes sense only if B *wronged* A, or in other words, if B treated A in a way that A should not have been treated. A has a just claim against B, and having such a just claim is precisely what we mean by a right. Furthermore, this right is universal, equal, and reciprocal. It is universal because all it takes to claim such a right is to be a "man"—a human being. It is equal and reciprocal because every person's blood has the same value. If A sheds B's blood, A's blood is an

---

56. In *Justice*, Wolterstorff grounds natural human rights in the worth that humans enjoy as image-bearers of God, a conclusion obviously similar to what I just argued. Yet I find unpersuasive his claim that these rights are inherent but not conferred. I agree with Wolterstorff that humans have natural rights that are not conferred by other humans, but any natural rights we enjoy are due to God's creating us and entering into covenant with us in a particular way. Surely such rights are conferred and not inherent, even if the conferral is natural and not simply by positive decree. To say, as Wolterstorff does, that we have natural rights that are inherent but not conferred, as God has natural rights that are inherent but not conferred, fails to account for crucial differences between the divine and human, in my judgment. For related comments on Wolterstorff's claims, cf. Carlson, "Rights versus Right Order," 85.

equivalent exchange. Thus, if a king sheds a pauper's blood, the shedding of the king's blood puts the scales of justice back into balance, and vice versa. No social status or other feature incidental to human identity distinguishes the natural rights of one person from those of another. Whatever distinctive roles or offices one may assume in a particular social context, in terms of the natural rights entailed in the Noahic covenant, each person claims the same thing and owes the same thing to everyone else.

What sorts of rights are these, more specifically? First, the natural rights just described are *negative* (or *liberty*) rights rather than *positive* (or *welfare*) rights. The former refers to rights to protection from harm inflicted by others, while the latter refer to rights to enjoy certain goods provided by others. I discuss later whether we should also infer the reality of positive natural rights from the Noahic covenant, but for now I focus on the negative natural rights that emerge directly from Genesis 9:6. Genesis 9:6 speaks not of A failing to provide certain goods or services to B but inflicting an injury upon B. B has a natural human right not to be harmed in such a way by another human being. "Harm" is a slippery concept.[57] What kinds of harm does Genesis 9:6 refer to? It mentions the shedding of blood explicitly, so it must include murders and other acts of violence that involve bloodshed. But since there is no morally or legally relevant difference between killing a person in a bloody way and doing so in a bloodless way, the harm of Genesis 9:6 must encompass all acts of murder. Likewise, injuries short of death can be painful and debilitating whether bloody or bloodless, and thus the harm also presumably encompasses all sorts of physical injuries.[58]

This much, I believe, we can say with full confidence about the harm in view in Genesis 9:6. But what about nonbodily harms, such as attacks upon property or reputation—that is, theft and slander? There are plausible, if not certain, reasons to think Genesis 9:6 encompasses these too. For one thing, like assaults on the body, theft and slander involve *immoral* harms (in distinction from "harms" people suffer to their interests when more skillful people best them in the classroom, athletic field, or business venture). Theft and slander can also be just as damaging to victims, if not more, than many sorts of bodily assault. Furthermore, theft and slander, like bodily injury, can be prohibited equally and reciprocally, as implied in Genesis 9:6. That is,

---

57. Cf. John Horton, "Toleration, Morality and Harm," in *Aspects of Toleration: Philosophical Studies*, ed. John Horton and Susan Mendus (London: Methuen, 1985), 113–35.

58. The *lex talionis* takes various forms in Scripture, including bloodless forms such as "burn for burn" (Exod 21:25).

any person can claim a right not to be robbed or slandered even while recognizing the same right of all other people not to be robbed or slandered by her. The Noahic covenant, it must be granted, provides no precise definition of what constitutes theft and slander—but that is also true for murder and battery. As we have seen repeatedly, the Noahic covenant never provides comprehensive solutions for public policy, only a general framework.

Thus I conclude that the Noahic covenant entails the existence of natural human rights that are negative in nature: undoubtedly, rights not to be injured bodily by fellow human beings and, plausibly, rights not to be robbed and slandered by them. To this we could also add a natural right to religious liberty, in the sense defended in chapter 7. We will consider again shortly whether the Noahic covenant also justifies appeal to positive (welfare) rights.

Primary Justice

To this point, we have considered justice under the Noahic covenant in terms of *rectifying* justice, for the basic reason that Genesis 9:6 speaks of justice in this way. But rectifying justice implies a conception of *primary* justice, because without the violation of primary justice there is nothing to rectify. Now that we have examined rectifying justice at some length, what can we say about primary justice under the Noahic covenant?

One thing seems clear. Since the Noahic covenant prescribes retributive and compensatory penalty for violations of natural human rights not to be injured bodily (and likely not to be robbed or slandered), Noahic primary justice requires all people to refrain from violating these natural human rights.

Can we say more than this? Yes, I think so. In considering rectifying justice, I often noted that Genesis 9:6 promulgates a form of the *lex talionis*, and then I stepped back to consider the implications, given what the *lex talionis* means. Following this route again here, I observe that the *lex talionis* expresses an ethic of *reciprocity*. The *lex talionis* is the negative form of a reciprocity ethic: a person who inflicts harm deserves a proportionate harm in return. But a reciprocity ethic also takes positive form: a person who does good deserves good in return. The Golden Rule provides another way to state it positively: do to others what you would have them do to you. As we seek good from others, so we give good to them.[59] Since Genesis 9:6 speaks

---

59. In Robert Axelrod's fascinating study of reciprocity, to be considered again below, he says that the Golden Rule implies always returning good for evil, since this is what we would want from others; see *The Evolution of Cooperation*, rev. ed. (New York: Basic, 2006), 136–37. If he is correct, the Golden Rule contradicts the *lex talionis*, and my suggestion that the Golden Rule is one way to think about

of justice in terms of reciprocity, the Golden Rule is a way to think about primary justice in this text.

This begs the further question: what positive good does the Golden Rule require us to do to each other, as a matter of primary justice? Unfortunately, it seems much more difficult to specify the positive good we should do than to specify the harms we should not do. The harms discussed above are clearly reciprocal in nature: I do not want to be murdered, and neither does anyone else; I do not want to be robbed, and neither does anyone else; I do not want to be slandered, and neither does anyone else. I am capable of not murdering, robbing, and slandering all others, and all others are capable of not murdering, robbing, and slandering me. But when I begin thinking about the good I would like others to do to me (so that I may know what to do to others), things get complicated quickly. I would like others to buy me rounds of golf at very nice courses, but this would be meaningless for most other people. I would like others to buy me lunch at White Castle, but many other people find White Castle hamburgers disgusting. From the other direction, many people would like others to send them on long fishing trips or buy them lunch at Taco Bell; these are of no interest to me. What's more, I am simply not capable of giving everyone any particular good she might want, and neither is everyone else capable of giving me any particular good I might want. If we think of the Golden Rule along these lines, it is not a helpful standard for determining the requirements of primary justice.

Given that the whole point of the Golden Rule is reciprocity, we have to understand the "good" it prescribes at a level of generality that both giver and receiver can appreciate and return. I would like to be treated with respect, and so does everyone else. I would like others to be cordial to me, and others want me to be cordial to them. Perhaps we could say that Noahic primary justice requires generally peaceful and cooperative interaction among

primary justice under the Noahic covenant must be false. I understand Axelrod's logic, but I believe he is wrong. For me to conclude from the Golden Rule that I should never seek retributive justice against the one who wrongs me because I would not want him to seek retributive justice against me if I wrong him is to defy the very spirit of the Golden Rule. Of course, there is a part of me that wishes I could harm other people without having to suffer any consequences, but that is completely selfish, whereas the Golden Rule, through the principle of reciprocity, requires me to consider all people as of equal worth to me. Ultimately, it makes no sense to interpret the Golden Rule by means of a selfish desire not to have to suffer consequences for wrongdoing. A fuller study of the Golden Rule would also have to consider Jesus's statement of it in the Sermon on the Mount, which also rejects the *lex talionis*. Jesus states the rule, in context, as a consequence of his conclusion that Christians should imitate God in giving good things to those who seek good things from them (Matt 7:7–12), so even here the rule does not imply a selfish desire to escape retributive justice.

human beings. These do not depend upon each individual's unique tastes and abilities. They can be reciprocated. Of course, in my concrete interaction with specific people, I should seek to do good to them in ways that respect their unique tastes and needs, but what this means in each time and place is impossible to specify through rules of justice enforceable in human courts.

Natural Human Rights (2)

Having considered primary justice, we may now take up the postponed inquiry about positive or welfare rights. I argued above that the Noahic covenant entails the existence of negative natural human rights, specifically rights not to be harmed by others in the ways identified. Welfare rights are rights to certain goods that other people or institutions are obligated to provide. Many rights specified in the Universal Declaration of Human Rights are of this character, such as rights to medical care and to periodic holidays with pay. Despite the popularity of claims to positive rights among so many contemporary and older writers, I conclude that no conception of positive rights that is *both coherent and useful* can be implied from the Noahic covenant.

A few clarifications are important at the outset. First, it is probably true and coherent to say that all human beings have a positive right to be treated well by any other person with whom they interact. That seems consistent with the preceding discussion of primary justice. But this is so vague that it yields no clear and enforceable rules and is thus not useful. To be useful, a conception of positive rights needs to have at least some degree of specificity.[60] The possibility of a more specific conception of positive rights is what we consider below. Second, there is an important natural-law obligation for people to be generous with their resources, as noted in the previous chapter. That is not the question here. And third, even if my conclusion is correct that the Noahic covenant does not imply positive natural rights, it does not end discussion about whether political communities should provide a safety net

---

60. A possible example of a specific positive natural right is a right of children to be provided for by their parents. Such a right cannot be reciprocated, narrowly considered, and hence cannot be simplistically implied from the *lex talionis* of Genesis 9:6. Yet there are reasons to recognize it. The parent-child relationship is unique. Unlike other lawful relationships, this relationship is established unilaterally: the parents decide to engage in behavior liable to producing a new human being, and that new human being has nothing to say about it. By engaging in this behavior, the parents have implicitly undertaken responsibility for whatever children they produce, who will have no way to care for themselves for many years. Were the parent-child relationship contractual or covenantal in nature, like a business or marriage relationship, we could regard the child's right to her parents' support as merely a legal right rather than a natural right. But since it is not contractual but unilaterally established by the action of the more powerful party, it seems proper to me to regard the child's right as a natural human right instead.

for the poor or supply services such as education and health care. We will return to such issues in chapter 11. For now, I simply address whether the Noahic covenant implies that there are natural human rights to such things.

I argued above that rights against being injured bodily are the only natural human rights we can specify with certainty from the Noahic covenant, although it probably also implies natural rights against being robbed and slandered. These latter rights, like rights against murder, battery, and rape, can be claimed universally and reciprocally. Everyone in the world can claim these negative rights against every other person without creating a conflict with another's claim to the same rights. When one claims such a right there is no need to ask "how much," "by whom," or "toward whom." The answer is always: *no one* should ever commit *any* murder, rape, theft, or slander against *any* other person. As universal and reciprocal, these rights are unambiguously *natural* and *human*. All people possess them by virtue of being human and can thus claim them against all other people and honor them in all other people. This is how the talionic formula in Genesis 9:6 works.

But welfare rights lack these elements of universality and reciprocity that would justify implying such rights from the talionic formula. Claims to welfare rights inevitably and inherently create conflicts and raise questions such as "how much" and "by whom" for which no clear answer is possible.[61] Consider the "how much" question. Does an alleged right to food involve a right to enough crumbs of bread to prevent starvation or a right to a well-balanced diet with plenty of fruits and vegetables? Does an alleged right to health care involve a right to bandages and aspirin or to the best treatment the Mayo Clinic can offer? There is no ready answer to such questions. And even to ask them is to talk in a distinctively early twenty-first century Western way. A discussion about rights to food or health care among people engaged in subsistence farming in a remote village several centuries ago, for instance, would have had to proceed on very different terms, and the idea of a right to

---

61. I make this point over against claims such as those by John Gray, *Beyond the New Right: Markets, Government and the Common Environment* (New York: Routledge, 1993), 100–103. Gray seeks to dismiss both negative and positive rights as indeterminate. Gray is probably correct with respect to some overblown claims to negative natural rights. But it is quite misleading when he argues that even the supposed right against rape, like supposed positive rights, is indeterminate and nonuniversal. There is an enormous difference between claiming a right not to be raped by anyone at any time (although each human legal system will have to make decisions about how exactly to define rape in order to clarify borderline cases) and inherently indeterminate claims of positive rights to things such as food and health care, which provoke clarifying questions far beyond matters of definition in borderline cases (i.e., far beyond questions such as "Is beef jerky food" or "Is acupuncture medical care?").

periodic holidays with pay would likely have made no sense to them at all.[62] In contrast, a mutually binding right not to be murdered or raped can make sense to anyone who has ever lived.

Similar difficulties emerge when asking "by whom." If someone claims a right to food or health care, who has the obligation to provide it? Person A might claim a right to health care from person B, but what if B does not have the skills or resources to deliver? Or what if B has the skills or resources to meet A's claims, but a million other people also claim a similar right from her?[63] One might appeal to the idea of *imperfect rights*: people have rights to things from *someone* even if we cannot specify whom in particular. But this idea is useful only if a person can actually claim such imperfect rights from the community as a whole. But this simply shifts the point at which analysis begins and does not really solve the conceptual problem. Claims against a community may meet the same difficulties that a claim against person A does.

Since welfare rights lack the universality and reciprocity of negative natural rights, we cannot imply their existence from the talionic formula of the Noahic covenant. Perhaps there is some other coherent intellectual basis for understanding welfare rights as natural human rights. Even so, a couple of related issues confirm the conclusions thus far.

First, while negative rights do not presume any particular stage of cultural achievement, welfare rights generally do. People do not need any special resources to honor negative rights, but they do need special resources to honor welfare rights, and in particular they need resources created or achieved by

---

62. Onora O'Neill summarizes this point in *Towards Justice and Virtue: A Constructive Account of Practical Reasoning* (Cambridge: Cambridge University Press, 1996), 133: "Even in the best case . . . , universal rights to goods and services and the corresponding obligations to provide them cannot be antecedently identifiable in the same way that liberty [negative] rights and their corresponding obligations are antecedently identifiable." Or as Maurice Cranston puts it, "The concept of rights . . . contained in the Universal Declaration is ruinously ambiguous." See "Are There Any Human Rights?," *Daedalus* (Fall 1983): 8.

63. As O'Neill says, "Unfortunately much writing and rhetoric on rights heedlessly proclaims universal rights to goods or services . . . without showing what connects each presumed right-holder to some specified obligation-bearer(s), which leaves the content of these supposed rights wholly obscure." See *Towards Justice and Virtue*, 131–32. Even some writers commonly cited as proponents of welfare rights seem to recognize the need to consider such situations in terms of an unspecifiable obligation of B rather than in terms of a specifiable right of A. E.g., see Thomas Aquinas, *Summa Theologiae* 2a2ae 66.7: "Whatever certain people have in superabundance is due, by natural law, to the purpose of succoring the poor. . . . Since, however, there are many who are in need, while it is impossible for all to be succored by means of the same thing, each one is entrusted with the stewardship of his own things, so that out of them he may come to the aid of those who are in need." The English translation is from *Summa Theologica*, 5 vols., trans. Fathers of the English Dominican Province (Allen, TX: Christian Classics, 1948).

innovative human effort. Houses, medical care, education, and jobs are not just there for the taking. Even food, in anything like the quantity and quality we have it today, is the result of human ingenuity. This point exposes a problem with the initially attractive claim that welfare rights must actually precede negative rights because people cannot enjoy the latter if they lack the basic means of life.[64] On the contrary, if people's person and property are not secure, they will not be able to generate these basic means for themselves or others.[65] Individuals and groups must expend energy, invest resources, and take risks in order to produce houses, food, and other goods of life before anyone else could conceive of a right to possess them. Since such rights claims depend upon a particular stage of cultural achievement, they do not apply to all people everywhere by virtue of their human identity, as do negative rights.

Second, claims to positive natural rights cannot exist in harmony with each other. Unlike negative natural rights, which all people can claim against everyone else without running into contradiction, positive rights claims make demands for limited, scarce resources. One person's claim inevitably encounters competition from somebody else's. Claims to positive natural rights also seem to conflict with negative natural rights, although I will not even press that claim now.

Many thoughtful skeptics about the pervasive appeal to "rights" in modern political discourse point to how these alleged rights have a competing and unreconciled character, which causes confusion and makes it necessary to balance one against another. They also note that the absolute character of rights claims tends to choke off debate and compromise.[66] These are fair complaints, but some of their proposed solutions are unsatisfactory. Some writers, for example, propose abandoning talk of natural rights altogether.[67]

---

64. E.g., see Jürgen Moltmann, *On Human Dignity: Political Theology and Ethics*, trans. M. Douglas Meeks (Minneapolis: Fortress, 2007), 6.

65. I believe this point is confirmed in the argument of Gary A. Haugen and Victor Boutros in *The Locust Effect: Why the End of Poverty Requires the End of Violence* (New York: Oxford University Press, 2014). Their main contention is that vulnerability to violence is a terrible plague for the global poor. While people in wealthy societies tend to think of the global poor's problems in terms of insufficient food, clean water, housing, medical care, hygiene, and education (that is, violation of welfare rights), Haugen and Boutros argue that violence (that is, violation of negative rights) is in fact their most serious problem and the chief reason great numbers of people cannot escape poverty. In effect, Haugen and Boutros show on a very practical level that negative rights are foundational.

66. These concerns are a major burden of Mary Ann Glendon in *Rights Talk: The Impoverishment of Political Discourse* (New York: The Free Press, 1991). From somewhat different perspectives, see also Oliver O'Donovan, *The Desire of the Nations* (Cambridge: Cambridge University Press, 1996), 248; and Gray, *Beyond the New Right*, 5–6, 78, 82, 100–103.

67. This is Gray's conclusion in *Beyond the New Right*.

Others think we should keep talking about a broad spectrum of rights (both negative and positive) but understand them in a more modest and non-absolute way.[68] Let us briefly consider each in turn.

With respect to the former proposal, I fear that we lose something important and useful (as well as theologically compelling) if we give up on the idea of natural rights altogether. Do we really want to abandon the claim that there are some ways in which we as human beings simply should not be treated? The latter proposal is more attractive: perhaps we can salvage the idea of welfare rights if we think of welfare rights as *prima facie* rights (that is, "rights" that may have to be set aside for some compelling reason). But it is puzzling why we would want to speak about *prima facie* claims as natural human *rights* at all. We all have *interests*, even highly desirable and beneficial interests, and they are constantly subject to balancing and compromise in political life. But these sorts of claims are not the same as claims to negative natural rights that should not be balanced or compromised.[69] The right not to be raped is not *prima facie* and should never be compromised or balanced against some other claim. Claiming a "right" loses its power when uncompromisable rights are confused with compromisable interests.

In accord with the general account of Noahic justice developed thus far, I suggest we should acknowledge as natural rights only what is truly foundational. Natural rights are not tools to provide detailed contours of the comprehensively good society, but this hardly makes them worthless.[70] On the contrary, they identify the preconditions for advancing toward a good society—preconditions which countless people have tried to subvert throughout human history, to the grave detriment of their communities.[71] Increasingly sufficient

---

68. This is Glendon's route in *Rights Talk*.

69. Although I have many disagreements with Dworkin about justice, I believe he is generally correct to say, "If someone has a right to something, then it is wrong for government to deny it to him even though it would be in the general interest to do so." See *Taking Rights Seriously*, 269. My remarks above concerning forbearance provide some qualification to my conclusion.

70. As Wolterstorff puts it, "Rights are boundary-markers for our pursuit of life-goods." See *Justice*, 5. In Kao's words, "We all should regard human rights much more modestly . . . , as setting a decent social minimum benchmark." See *Grounding Human Rights*, 136.

71. It may be worth trying to clarify one point briefly. As Kao (*Grounding Human Rights*, 171) notes, for example, the "human rights project" has a certain cosmopolitan flavor, envisioning humanity as ultimately constituting one moral community. She thinks this is a good thing. A critic of this human rights project such as Gray would agree that it has a cosmopolitan flavor, but he thinks it harmfully snuffs out the local, the particular, and the traditional in favor of abstract rules that can be specified once and for all; see, e.g., *Beyond the New Right*, viii–ix. It seems to me that Gray creates a false dilemma. If negative natural rights are understood not expansively but as constituting the minimal foundation of a just society, as argued here, there is still wide latitude for the distinctive development of particular communities according to their own traditions. But these foundational negative natural rights have the

and nutritious food, safe housing, and ever-improving medical care for all people are good and proper goals for human society. But they are just that: goals to be achieved through a long process of creative human effort, not rights to be claimed.[72] The Noahic covenant envisions human beings as creatures with work to accomplish (and with an obligation to be generous with their accomplishments!) but who also need protection from harm so they can pursue this work.

Noahic Justice and the Natural Law

Chapter 5 argued that God reestablished the natural moral order through the Noahic covenant. The moral obligations of the covenant are thus not arbitrary but make sense of the world and resonate with our experience of it. Accordingly, we now inquire how the preceding account of justice corresponds to the natural law.

One thing suggesting correspondence is the cross-cultural appeal of the *lex talionis* and the analogous ethics of reciprocity. The fact that people embrace these ideas across many times and cultures does not prove they are morally sound, of course. But their widespread appeal at least suggests the plausibility that they fit the world as we know it and resonate with human experience. The *lex talionis* was an important jurisprudential principle of the famous Code of Hammurabi, dating from the eighteenth century before Christ,[73] and later the Mosaic law stated it explicitly on three occasions (Exod 21:23–25; Lev 24:19–20; Deut 19:21). In the West, the talionic principle appears at the origins of the Roman law tradition, in the Twelve Tables (fifth century BC),[74] and was crucial for other Western legal cultures.[75] The English language itself continues to bear eerie testimony to the *lex talionis* through the overlap in meaning of

---

important function of affirming that there ought to be limits to how particular communities develop. Things such as murder and rape can never be justified by an appeal to one's local customs. This is a healthy cosmopolitanism.

72. For a similar analysis, see also Philip Turner, *Christian Ethics and the Church: Ecclesial Foundations for Moral Thought and Practice* (Grand Rapids: Baker Academic, 2015), 241–42. And see Cranston, "Are There Any Human Rights?," 12–14: "Such things ['amenities like social security and holidays with pay" that the United Nations postulated as human rights] are admirable as ideals, but an ideal belongs to a wholly different logical category." "Thus the effect of a universal declaration that is overloaded with affirmations of economic and social rights is to push the political and civil rights out of the realm of the morally compelling into the twilight world of utopian aspirations." "Nothing is more important to an understanding of a right than to acknowledge that a right is *not* an ideal." "An ideal is something to be aimed at, but which, by definition, cannot be immediately realized. A right, on the contrary, is something that can and, from a moral point of view, *should* be respected here and now. If it is violated, justice itself is abused."

73. See §§196–197, 200, in *The Babylonian Laws*, 2:76–79.

74. See section 8.2 of the Twelve Tables.

75. E.g., see Miller's extensive discussion in *Eye for an Eye* of the *lex talionis* in the early law of medieval Iceland.

"just" and "even," and the fact that "pay," "pacify," and "peace" all derive from the same Latin word.[76] The positive side of the reciprocity ethic is widespread as well. Confucius identified the Golden Rule as the core of his teaching.[77] Five centuries later, Jesus also commended the Golden Rule (Matt 7:12).

One might object that these examples are all very old, and contemporary legal systems have expunged the *lex talionis* from view. Yet the desire for retributive justice still has an instinctive hold on the human heart. While a widespread human instinct toward retribution does not prove its moral soundness, it adds further weight to the idea that Noahic justice makes sense of the world as we know it and accords with the natural law.

Scholars studying the ideas of vengeance, justice, and forgiveness often speak of a retributive instinct. Miller notes that the basic ideas underlying the *lex talionis* remain familiar to us today, whether in the schoolyard, workplace, pub, street, highway, conversation, or bedroom.[78] Jeffrie Murphy concludes that the appropriateness of revenge is "among our common-sense beliefs."[79] Susan Jacoby opines that institutionalized justice does not eradicate "the impulse toward revenge" and that "vindictive needs are strong."[80] Peter French claims that "the need for a hostile response is embedded in the very idea that an action or a person is bad or evil or wicked," and thus "retributivism still seems to appeal to our basic, or gut, intuitions." "This is what it is to be the sort of creatures we are."[81] Paul Bloom observes an "appetite for revenge" and an "inclination toward payback."[82] It is interesting that some of the strong critics of retributivism cited earlier in the chapter make similar remarks. Timothy Gorringe admits that the need to make satisfaction for wrongdoing "seems to be one of the most powerful human impulses," and Randy Barnett confesses to having retributivist feelings when he was a prosecutor.[83] Many biblical scholars comment on how Jesus's antitalionic teaching in the Sermon on the Mount (Matt 5:38–42) runs against the grain of human nature.[84]

---

76. See Miller, *Eye for an Eye*, 11–12, 15.

77. "Tsze-kung asked, saying, 'Is there one word which may serve as a rule of practice for all one's life?' The Master said, 'Is not RECIPROCITY such a word? What you do not want done to yourself, do not do to others.'" Translation taken from Confucius, *Confucian Analects, The Great Learning and The Doctrine of the Mean*, trans. James Legge (New York: Dover, 1971), 301 (*Analects* 15.23).

78. Miller, *Eye for an Eye*, 7–8.

79. Murphy, *Getting Even*, 21–22.

80. Jacoby, *Wild Justice*, 12, 351.

81. French, *The Virtues of Vengeance*, 207, 223–24.

82. Paul Bloom, *Just Babies: The Origins of Good and Evil* (New York: Crown, 2013), 85.

83. See Gorringe, *God's Just Vengeance*, 11; and Barnett, *The Structure of Liberty*, 321.

84. E.g., see Michael Winger, "Hard Sayings," *The Expository Times* 115, no. 8 (2004): 266; Walter Wink, "Jesus and the Nonviolent Struggle of Our Time, *Louvain Studies* 18, no. 1 (1993): 5; Jan Lambrecht,

Bloom's work on morality in babies and very young children provides intriguing evidence for the instinctiveness of retributive justice and reciprocity. Studies show that three-year-olds and twenty-month-olds tend to help those who help them or others but tend not to help the unhelpful.[85] Bloom also describes how children love to tattle on each other and usually do so accurately and for nontrivial things, wishing "to see justice done," out of "an appetite for payback, a pleasure in seeing wrongdoers . . . being punished."[86] His research concludes that among our "natural endowments" is "a rudimentary sense of justice—a desire to see good actions rewarded and bad actions punished."[87]

Can we dismiss this pervasive impulse for retribution as irrelevant for morality in the same way we dismiss the pervasive impulse to eat too much as irrelevant for the ethics of eating? Probably not. The instinct to eat too much reflects the vice of gluttony but does not make eating itself morally objectionable. Eating too much is a perversion of the good desire to eat in a way appropriate to hunger and health. Similarly, the common impulse toward *disproportionate* vengeance is arguably a corruption of an appropriate desire for retributive justice. An instinct toward retributive justice can hardly be dismissed as merely selfish, since we desire proportionate penalty not only for those who wrong us but also for those who wrong others—sometimes even those we do not know. We worry about the moral maturity of someone who reads a book or watches a film and does not find satisfaction when the evil character gets his comeuppance.

Still, we wonder whether the prevalent instinct toward retribution, reciprocity, and the like have anything to do with their success as a pattern of moral behavior. They may make us feel better subjectively, but do they make us better off objectively? "One should behave like a gentleman when dealing with gentlemen and like a bastard when dealing with bastards"[88]—what sort of common political community would we get if people practiced this ethic?

Likely a pretty good one. This says something important, since pretty good is an accomplishment under the Noahic covenant. Robert Axelrod's

SJ, "The Sayings of Jesus on Nonviolence," *Louvain Studies* 12, no. 4 (1987): 304; and Dorothy Jean Weaver, "Transforming Nonresistance: From *Lex Talionis* to 'Do Not Resist the Evil One'," in *The Love of Enemy and Nonretaliation in the New Testament*, ed. William M. Swartley (Louisville: Westminster John Knox, 1992), 54–55.

85. Bloom, *Just Babies*, 52.
86. Bloom, *Just Babies*, 95–96.
87. Bloom, *Just Babies*, 5.
88. The words of Pedro Camacho in Mario Vargas Llosa, *Aunt Julia and the Scriptwriter* (New York: Picador, 2007), 159.

computerized round-robin tournaments simulating the iterated Prisoner's Dilemma is instructive. Axelrod discovered that of all the many strategies his participants attempted, the simplest one of all, called Tit-for-Tat, was clearly the most successful over the long run. Tit-for-Tat is a reciprocity strategy in which the player always begins by cooperating with the other player, always responds to an act of cooperation by cooperating on the next turn, and always responds to an act of defection by defecting on the next turn. According to Axelrod, this strategy is simultaneously nice (in never being the first to defect) and retaliatory (in always defecting once in response to a defection). Axelrod observes that Tit-for-Tat won his tournaments not by beating others but by eliciting behavior from others that allowed both of them to do well. That is, it succeeded by fostering conditions that enable mutual success rather than one player's dominance and promote others' interests rather than exploit their weaknesses. Axelrod also discovered that cooperation can emerge and survive in real-life social settings involving antagonistic parties if even small clusters of people practice a Tit-for-Tat strategy, as illustrated by the experience of soldiers on opposite sides of the line during the trench warfare of World War I.[89]

As Axelrod himself notes, his work obviously does not demonstrate that Tit-for-Tat is the highest imaginable moral ideal. But it does indicate that the practice of reciprocity promotes social cooperation effectively, even in contexts when parties are antagonistic toward each other. Tit-for-Tat strategy does not presume widespread benevolence, good will, or bonds of affection among participants in society, nor does its success require conversion of heart. Rather, it fosters cooperation for mutual benefit even among those suspicious of each other. This adds further evidence that the reciprocal justice of the Noahic covenant corresponds to the world as we know it. The common political communities arising under the Noahic covenant are populated by sinners (Gen 8:21). The covenant promises them no conversion of heart but indicates that conflicts among them will continue (9:6), even while they engage in some measure of productive social interaction for mutual benefit (9:1–4, 7). In light of this, Axelrod's study seems to confirm that the Noahic covenant adopts neither an idealistic standard of justice unrealistic for sinners nor a nihilistic standard presuming a never-ending war of all against all. Rather, the *lex talionis* seems well suited for the fallen-but-preserved world of the Noahic covenant, and thus I think we can say, it is in accord with the natural law.

---

89. See generally Axelrod, *The Evolution of Cooperation*.

THE NOAHIC COVENANT AND
JUDICIAL INSTITUTIONS

Following this lengthy study of justice under the Noahic covenant, it is appropriate to consider *judicial institutions*. As argued in chapter 3, the Noahic covenant implicitly authorizes human beings to form institutions and associations, because the explicit commands of the covenant require joint, cooperative action. By calling human beings to pursue justice, therefore, the Noahic covenant authorizes them to form judicial institutions so they may do the job well. In this final section of the chapter, I first consider the necessity of judicial institutions and what form these institutions take. Then I address how civil government ought to function as a judicial institution and comment on what its obligation to promote *justice* has to do with *love*.

Why Judicial Institutions?

Among the reasons indicating that the Noahic covenant implicitly authorizes judicial institutions, two stand out. First, it is often hazardous and even impossible to secure justice by one's own efforts. An individual seeking to punish or obtain restitution from her oppressor has to use or at least threaten coercion. When the victim is much stronger than the wrongdoer, this may not be difficult. But in the many cases when the wrongdoer is stronger than his victim, the victim faces long and dangerous odds if she has to act on her own. Enforcing justice through institutions addresses this serious problem.

Second, even in cases when a wronged party is *capable* of securing justice by her own individual effort, we have good reason to doubt she is *trustworthy* to do so. Commission of wrong and accusation of wrong usually involve competing claims about what really happened and about who owes what to whom. The Noahic covenant oversees communities of sinners (Gen 8:21) with limited knowledge and selfish motives. We rightly do not trust others to be just judges in their own cause—nor should we trust ourselves in ours. Thus we have a better chance at achieving justice under the Noahic covenant if we establish judicial institutions that provide objective third parties to judge between conflicting claims.

What Kind of Judicial Institutions?

We need judicial institutions, but what kind of judicial institutions will do the job? The Noahic covenant provides no explicit answer. But that itself is worth pondering. Many people may hear "judicial institutions" and instinctively think of a branch of civil government. There is good reason to conclude that the call to do justice in Genesis 9:6 indirectly authorizes civil governments, but there are also reasons to think that the Noahic covenant authorizes nongovernmental judicial institutions as well.

As noted, judicial institutions are necessary because many victims are unable to secure justice by their own efforts. Privately formed judicial institutions can address this problem. For example, people employ security services to install and monitor home alarms, and businesses and universities hire security guards to forestall trouble on their premises. Judicial institutions are also necessary to provide objective third-party judges to resolve disputes. Here again, private and voluntary judicial institutions can be effective. In many business contracts, for instance, the parties agree to submit disputes to a mediation or arbitration organization rather than to government courts. In the case of both private security and third-party judges, people spend substantial amounts of money to protect their just interests even though their governments already provide such services through their police and courts. Not only is it possible for nongovernmental organizations to serve as judicial institutions under the Noahic covenant, but it also appears that many people prefer such organizations to their governments, or at least do not wish to entrust the maintenance of justice to their governments alone.

Civil Government and Noahic Justice

The preceding comments raise important but difficult issues regarding the relationship of civil government to other institutions in the pursuit of justice under the Noahic covenant, a topic central to the following two chapters as well. To close the present chapter, I briefly defend one basic proposition: whatever other authority civil government may have, its core responsibility is to enforce the Noahic justice contemplated in previous pages.

The *prima facie* case is simple. In the most direct and informative biblical text about civil government, Paul calls the magistrate "the servant of God, an avenger who carries out God's wrath on the wrongdoer" (Rom 13:4). First Peter 2:13 is similar, stating that "governors" are "sent by him [God] to punish those who do evil." In chapter 4, I argued that the Noahic covenant is very important background for interpreting Romans 13: what the Noahic covenant says generally about the human commission to pursue justice, Romans 13 attributes specifically to civil government. That is, God has delegated his own government of the world in part to human beings and has thus authorized them to enforce retributive and compensatory justice (Gen 9:5–6).

Therefore, the governments that human communities establish to carry out this task are divinely "instituted" and "appointed" (Rom 13:1–2). Legitimate civil governments carry out Noahic justice. I wish to point out one important implication of this and then respond to one important objection.

The implication is that governments ought to be *limited* in important respects. To say that a government enforces Noahic justice is to say that Noahic justice stands over that government and provides a standard which it must honor. In Paul's words, civil magistrates ought to approve people who do good and punish those who do wrong (Rom 13:3–4). Any government doing this would find its powers severely constrained. Such a government would not wrong anyone or be a respecter of persons. Nor would such a government wink at evildoers who happen to be in its good graces or ignore the wrongs done to those who are easily ignored. Although these brief comments leave many questions open about the extent of legitimate government authority, the requirements of Noahic justice ought to restrain many actions commonly perpetrated in the name of the state. Thus the conclusions about justice in this chapter point to important limits upon the authority of civil government, as did discussions in earlier chapters about pluralism, family, and commerce.

I also need to address a potentially serious objection. Some Christian scholars have argued from the New Testament that civil government should not enforce retributive justice. If true, there is something fundamentally erroneous about my argument in this chapter. But I believe these scholars' claim is simply not true. To explain why, I focus upon Nicholas Wolterstorff's recent analysis.

Wolterstorff argues that Jesus and the New Testament epistles reject the "reciprocity code," of which the *lex talionis* was a key aspect.[90] And rejection of the *lex talionis* "implies the rejection of retribution."[91] Wolterstorff also claims that Jesus did not mean to command Christians alone to reject the reciprocity code, for the Sermon on the Mount was "an ethic for everybody."[92] If correct, Wolterstorff has understandable reason to suspect, even before reading it, that Romans 13:1–7 will not promote retributive justice. Otherwise Paul would be in direct conflict with Jesus, and also in conflict with his own rejection of retribution a few verses earlier in Romans 12:17–19.

Concerning Romans 13:1–7, Wolterstorff writes, "Nothing is said about

---

90. Nicholas Wolterstorff, *Justice in Love* (Grand Rapids: Eerdmans, 2011), 120–26.
91. Wolterstorff, *Justice in Love*, 128.
92. Wolterstorff, *Justice in Love*, 127.

retribution, about getting even, about reciprocating evil with evil, about redress, about vengeance." Elsewhere he adds, "Nowhere does he [Paul] suggest that retributive punishment is a legitimate function of government." Paul does teach that government is to punish wrongdoers, Wolterstorff states, but this punishment is reprobative, not retributive, and it functions to deter wrongdoing.[93]

Some New Testament texts do indeed reject the *lex talionis*. But Wolterstorff's conclusion about Romans 13 and retribution is incorrect. Paul describes the magistrate in this way: "he is the servant of God, an avenger who carries out God's wrath on the wrongdoer" (Rom 13:4). An initial clue that Paul thinks a magistrate should enforce retributive justice is that he calls him an *avenger [ekdikos]*. If Paul meant to avoid any suggestion of retributive justice, he would surely not have used this title. An avenger seeks vengeance, and vengeance is at the heart of retributive justice. Blind or disproportionate vengeance is unjust, but the *lex talionis* aims to prescribe a proportionate penalty as a valid expression of just outrage. The New Testament and Septuagint (the Greek Old Testament of Paul's day) do not use the word *avenger* frequently, but the Septuagint often uses cognate words to describe vengeance,[94] sometimes in explicitly retributive ways. For example, God "avenges the blood of his children, and takes vengeance on his adversaries. He repays those who hate him" (Deut 32:43). God commands Jehu to "strike down the house of Ahab your master, so that I may avenge on Jezebel the blood of my servants the prophets, and the blood of all the servants of the LORD" (2 Kgs 9:7). This is precisely the kind of thing Wolterstorff claims the New Testament prohibits all people from doing. Yet Paul names the civil magistrate an avenger.

That Paul thinks of the avenging magistrate as pursuing retributive justice is all the more evident when we compare 13:4 with Paul's teaching a few verses earlier. I quote 13:4 again, this time using italics to highlight several key words: "he is the servant of God, an *avenger* who carries out God's *wrath* on the *wrong*doer." In comparison, Paul wrote in earlier verses: "Repay no one evil for evil [i.e., *wrong* for *wrong*]. . . . Beloved, never *avenge* yourselves, but leave it to the *wrath* of God, for it is written, '*Vengeance* is mine, I will repay, says the Lord'" (12:17, 19, emphasis added). The matching vocabulary is easy to see in English, and is even more evident in the original Greek.[95] It cannot

---

93. Wolterstorff, *Justice in Love*, 128–29, 198.

94. These cognate words include *ekdikesis* and *ekdikeo*.

95. Christians are not to return *kakon* for *kakou* (Rom 12:17), while magistrates are to punish those who do *to kakon* (13:4). Christians are not to avenge (*ekdikountes*) themselves, for vengeance (*ekdikesis*) is

have been coincidental. Paul's point in Romans 13:4 is that God commissions the civil magistrate to do the very things he prohibits his Christian readers from doing a few verses earlier. In Romans 12, Paul instructs Christians not to follow the *lex talionis*, repaying evil for evil. They are not to avenge themselves but leave it to the wrath of God. This task is God's, but he has also appointed civil authorities to do such work on his behalf. Thus Wolterstorff's claim about Paul, civil government, and retributive justice is factually incorrect. Paul believed that God has appointed civil magistrates to enforce retributive justice.

Justice and Love

The relationship of justice and love is a question that sometimes occupies Christian legal and political thinkers. Having just considered the basic responsibility of government to promote Noahic *justice*, and anticipating our study of law and authority in the next two chapters, I conclude this chapter by inquiring whether civil law ought to be organized and evaluated according to the standard of Christian *love*, or to put it similarly, whether *agape* "is the foundational norm that ought to structure political principles and policies."[96] I argue that law and government do promote a certain sort of love when they promote Noahic justice, but I also argue that a distinctively *Christian* love is not to be their standard or foundational norm.

Law and government promote love by promoting Noahic justice in at least three ways. First, through its work of rectifying justice, law and government encourage members of the community to observe the norms of primary justice, and these norms of primary justice include honoring others' life, bodily integrity, property, and reputation. To live in such a way toward one's fellows is to exercise a benevolence that constitutes a kind of love. Second, the work of rectifying justice is itself an act of love for individuals and the community. It expresses love toward victims by recognizing the serious nature of the harm done to them as dignified divine image-bearers and by accounting

---

the Lord's (12:19), while the magistrate, as servant of God, is to be an avenger (*ekdikos*) (13:4). Christians are to leave place for God's wrath (*orge*) (12:19), while the magistrate, again as God's servant, is to be an avenger unto wrath (*orgen*) (13:4).

96. Jeffrie G. Murphy puts it in the former way in "Law Like Love," *Syracuse Law Review* 55, no. 1 (2004): 18. Timothy P. Jackson puts it in the latter way in *Political* Agape: *Christian Love and Liberal Democracy* (Grand Rapids: Eerdmans, 2015), 2. For a recent exploration of this question by a number of authors, see *Agape, Justice, and Law: How Might Christian Love Shape Law?*, ed. Robert F. Cochran Jr. and Zachary R. Calo (Cambridge: Cambridge University Press, 2017). My essay in that volume, "Justice Tempered by Forbearance: Why Christian Love Is an Improper Category to Apply to Civil Law," 125–47, provides a somewhat contrarian contribution.

for their justified outrage through punishment of their assailants. If the assailant is punished through exacting compensation, rectifying justice also loves victims by providing restitution. Furthermore, rectifying justice exhibits love in protecting order and safety for the community as a whole, enabling people to collaborate peacefully and to pursue their vocations unmolested. Rectifying justice may even serve as an act of love to wrongdoers, insofar as their punishment—unpleasant as it may be—impresses the gravity of their action upon them and motivates them to reform. Third, the forbearing nature of rectifying justice under the Noahic covenant is an expression of love. As God manifests his common love to the human community by postponing the full manifestation of his rectifying justice, so also human law and government ought to reflect the image of God by administering justice tempered by forbearance.

But a distinctively *Christian* love is not to be the foundational norm of law and government. As argued above, the former is a love of *forgiveness* uniquely grounded in Christ's atonement (e.g., see Luke 7:41–48; Rom 15:1–3, 7; Eph 4:32–5:2; 1 John 4:7–12). The Noahic covenant does not reveal God's plan of redemption in Christ or promise forgiveness of sins, and thus it does not command this sort of love. Insofar as human law and government emerge out of the Noahic covenant, there is no ground for trying to make them instruments of Christian *agape*.

CONCLUSION

The Noahic covenant does not provide a comprehensive theory of justice, but it does offer a substantive framework for Christians wishing to think properly about justice in their political communities. The Noahic covenant treats all human beings as image-bearers of God who possess natural human rights not to be injured physically by others and probably also not to be robbed or slandered by them. Noahic justice requires rectification of such harms through penalties that are retributive and compensatory and at times forbearing. Furthermore, the Noahic covenant authorizes the establishment of judicial institutions to pursue this task well, and such institutions may or may not be arms of the civil government. Whatever else state-based judicial institutions may properly do—as the next two chapters continue to explore— they ought to enforce Noahic justice as the core of their responsibility.

CHAPTER 10

CUSTOMS AND LAWS

Chapters 8 and 9 considered the three basic moral obligations of the Noahic covenant: to be fruitful, multiply, and fill the earth, to provide for human material needs, and to promote justice. Chapter 9 noted that a study of justice inevitably raises questions about several related issues, especially the development of *law* and the nature of *government authority*. This chapter takes up the former and largely reserves discussion of the latter for chapter 11.

As explained below, by *law* I refer to norms of conduct considered obligatory in a community. Violating laws triggers penalties and remedies. The preceding chapter argued for a conception of *natural* justice rooted in the Noahic covenant and its natural law. That justice is natural in the sense of binding all people and all legal and political systems, in every time and place. There are some basic ways human beings should treat each other, and societies are unjust to the extent they fall short of these standards. But this natural justice is underdeterminative. It provides a framework for human relations without specifying in detail how it works out in the complicated circumstances of everyday affairs. No human community of any sort can function peacefully and productively on broad notions of natural justice alone. Communities need law in order to specify the details and thus to order human life in its complex interrelations. Many things entirely unspecified by natural justice (such as driving on the right side of the road) become just in a particular community when its law so determines.

In keeping with the plan of part 2, I now ask how the Noahic covenant helps us to think fruitfully about law. The Noahic covenant says nothing directly about law and provides no way to derive an ideal legal code. Human communities might develop their law within the bounds of natural justice in a variety of ways, depending on circumstances, the character of the community, and the prudential judgment of its members.[1] Human legal systems will always be conventional, not natural. The task of the present chapter is therefore not to suggest the substance of a Noahic body of law. Instead it reflects on the nature and purpose of law, on the development of law, and on how this development relates to the unfolding of the moral commission found in the Noahic covenant, as outlined in previous chapters. As the Noahic covenant affirms, all human beings are deeply sinful (Gen 8:21), and thus their institutions will be flawed and their laws imperfect. But a number of considerations drawn from this covenant point toward fruitful conceptions of law that promote productive and just human life.

I begin with some broad reflections on the development of law in the context of the Noahic covenant and suggest why they point to a conception of law that is *polycentric* rather than *monocentric*. That is to say, law properly emerges from a multiplicity of sources rather than from civil government as its single source. I then devote the rest of the chapter to unpacking and defending that claim.

THE DEVELOPMENT OF LAW UNDER THE NOAHIC COVENANT: PRELIMINARY CONSIDERATIONS

Chapter 3 reflected on how human activity properly unfolds under the Noahic covenant through the establishment of various institutions and associations. In this section, I recap that discussion and explain what this has to do with the development of law.

Human Activities, Institutions, and Norms

The Noahic covenant describes human beings as made in the image of God (Gen 9:6). This echoes the opening chapter of Scripture, which is thus necessary background for interpreting the Noahic covenant. Two features of the account in Genesis 1 are especially important at present. First, creation in the image of God entails a commission to engage in creative activity. God made human beings in his image *so that* they might "have dominion over the fish of the sea and over the birds of the heavens and over the livestock and

---

1. The idea that human law might take a variety of forms is common in the Christian tradition. For two prominent examples, see Thomas Aquinas, *Summa Theologiae* 1a2ae 95.3; 96.2; 97.1; and John Calvin, *Institutes of the Christian Religion*, 4.20.16.

over all the earth and over every creeping thing" (Gen 1:26). Genesis 1:28 elaborates: "Be fruitful and multiply and fill the earth and subdue it and have dominion over the fish of the sea and over the birds of the heavens and over every living thing that moves on the earth" (Gen 1:28)—a call to benevolent rule over the rest of creation. Second, Scripture ascribes the image of God to all people indiscriminately. The image of God entails ruling authority shared by all alike, without elevating anyone inherently over another. By treating humans as the image of God, the Noahic covenant confirms that they all continue to share a divine commission to rule, although it presents the commission in modified form, refracted for a fallen world.

This commission is terse, calling human beings to fill the earth, to provide for their material needs, and to administer justice. The Noahic covenant sets forth a general commission but provides no concrete plan for achieving it and no governing body to create such a plan. How then was the human race to pursue its commission? Apparently through an experimental, collaborative effort in which each person honors every other as of equal worth and dignity. Accomplishing the three general tasks of the commission obviously requires people to establish associations. To multiply and fill the earth calls for familial institutions that produce and train children; to provide materially for a growing population requires enterprise associations that promote hard work and technological development; and to administer justice demands judicial institutions for resolving disputes. These institutions also need to develop authority structures if they are to operate effectively. But since all people are of equal worth and dignity, these authority structures ought to develop organically and consensually rather than by some people coercively imposing their will upon others.

As human beings pursue their various image-bearing activities and establish institutions to support them, they inevitably develop two other things: *norms* to regulate their conduct and *remedies* by which to respond to violations of the norms. Each institution, presumably, will create and enforce its own internal norms by spontaneous and/or formal processes. As these institutions develop their own norms, the broader political community will also need norms that coordinate the interrelations among institutions and individuals. These norms of the political community (and their remedies) can develop in various ways: *spontaneously* through the formation of custom, *voluntarily* through agreements among institutions, and/or *legislatively* through institutions established to serve this coordinating function. These latter institutions could also help the other institutions settle the internal disputes they are unable to resolve peacefully by themselves.

The Customary and the Legal

I have just described the development of norms within institutions and between institutions. What is the nature of these norms? Is it accurate to call them *laws*? It may be helpful to begin by distinguishing the *customary* from the *legal*. By *customs*, I refer to those norms of conduct to which people in fact ordinarily adhere. By *laws*, I refer to those norms of conduct to which people are obligated to adhere, in the sense that penalties and remedies become due when the norms are violated.[2] The norms described above are either customs or laws, or both. This requires two points of clarification.

First, customs and laws, understood in these terms, emerge in all sorts of institutions—large and small, public and private. It seems obvious to say that customs pervade institutions of all kinds. In colloquial speech, however, people usually associate *law* with norms that the state approves and enforces. But this need not be its exclusive meaning. Both familial and enterprise institutions develop norms whose violations trigger penalties. Parents may enforce family norms by withholding dessert or access to the car, for example, and employers may enforce corporate norms by suspending or firing an employee. Employers and parents might not wield the physically coercive power of enforcement that the state usually claims, but the state is often willing to stand behind the enforcement decisions of other institutions in cases of conflict or necessity. It may send in the police, for instance, to escort a fired employee from business premises if he refuses to stop working there. For these reasons, it seems proper to recognize the presence of law in all sorts of institutions. Nevertheless, I will ordinarily use "law" to refer to laws recognized at the level of the political community, that is, civil laws, rather than to laws of private, voluntary associations per se. Nevertheless, even many of these private laws may become part of the civil law when recognized and enforced by the political community.

Second, custom and law are distinct but overlapping realities. On the one hand, many customs are not laws. In some settings, for example, people ordinarily shake hands when greeting each other, but refusing to do so carries no formal penalty (although it might bring informal disadvantages). On the other hand, many customs are laws. Driving on the right side of the road in the United States or on the left side in Australia provides obvious examples— these are customarily practiced *and* legally enforced. Furthermore, not all

---

2. Cf. Jean Porter, *Ministers of the Law: A Natural Law Theory of Legal Authority* (Grand Rapids: Eerdmans, 2010), 11.

laws are customs. We can easily think of "laws" that people widely violate and authorities inconsistently enforce. In my present American context, these include norms that prohibit using phones while driving, using certain narcotics, or crossing national borders without authorization. It is not immediately evident how to describe and evaluate these commonly flouted norms, and even whether they deserve to be called *laws* at all. We will return to this issue below.

MONOCENTRIC AND POLYCENTRIC CONCEPTIONS OF LAW

These preliminary considerations about the emergence of law under the Noahic covenant suggest that law is *polycentric* rather than *monocentric* in character. That is to say, law emerges from and is enforced by a multiplicity of sources rather than from the state as the single source.[3] This immerses us in interesting but complex debates in legal theory. I will first introduce these debates and then try to develop a more detailed defense of legal polycentrism by implication from the Noahic covenant. Although most contemporary Westerners instinctively think of law simply as norms imposed and enforced by the state, the political theology unfolded in this book provides many reasons for taking a richer and more complex view of law.

Monocentric Conceptions of Law

People today predominantly think of law as monocentric: "The very idea that the law might not be identical with legislation seems odd both to students of law and to laymen."[4] The school of legal *positivism* has provided some of the most popular and influential definitions of law in recent centuries, and it provides an excellent example of a monocentric legal perspective.

Positivists envision law as a set of commands imposed by political authorities upon members of society. The authorities that issue law may be morally obligated to decree what is just, but their decrees are "law" regardless of

---

3. Some readers may wonder why I speak of legal *polycentrism* rather than legal *pluralism*. "Legal pluralism" probably could be an appropriate way to describe what I mean by "polycentrism," although the former is used in a variety of ways, some of which would give a wrong impression of what I am arguing for here. For example, some use "legal pluralism" to describe multiple legal *systems* or competing legal *authorities* in a particular community. Careful readers of this chapter will see that neither of these exactly captures my concerns.

4. Bruno Leoni, *Freedom and the Law*, 3rd ed. (Indianapolis: Liberty Fund, 1991), 6; see also David J. Bederman, *Custom as a Source of Law* (New York: Cambridge University Press, 2010), ix–x.

the good or evil they accomplish. As the nineteenth-century positivist John Austin put it, law is "set by political superiors to political inferiors." It is a "rule laid down for the guidance of an intelligent being by an intelligent being having power over him."[5] Every law is a command.[6] Broadly speaking, therefore, "law" is simply and strictly the "aggregate of the rules thus established."[7] For Austin, the sovereign power is legally free to abridge subjects' political liberty at its own pleasure, although doing so may be contrary to positive morality and the law of God.[8] Similarly, twentieth-century positivist Hans Kelsen emphasized that his "pure theory of law" identifies what the law *is*, not what it *ought* to be.[9] Law represents *"coercive orders,"*[10] and such orders command "specific acts or omission of acts."[11] This classic positivist vision is thus monocentric because law emanates only from the state.[12]

Polycentric Conceptions of Law

In contrast, polycentrism holds that there are multiple sources of law, of which the state is only one, and perhaps not even the most important.[13] Polycentrists do not share a common definition of law, but they all reject conceptions of law as the sum of commands from political superiors to inferiors. Instead, polycentrists speak of law as a complex normative order—that is, law is a system, an ordering principle, or patterns of conduct.[14] Polycentrism has

---

5. John Austin, *The Province of Jurisprudence Determined*, ed. Wilfrid E. Rumble, 5th ed. (Cambridge: Cambridge University Press, 1995), 18.

6. Austin, *The Province of Jurisprudence*, 21.

7. Austin, *The Province of Jurisprudence*, 19. Cf. Jeremy Bentham, *An Introduction to the Principles of Morals and Legislation* (1789; New York: Hafner, 1948), 324: "Now *law*, or *the law*, taken indefinitely, is an abstract and collective term; which, when it means any thing, can mean neither more nor less than the sum total of a number of individual laws taken together."

8. Austin, *The Province of Jurisprudence*, 223.

9. Hans Kelsen, *Pure Theory of Law*, 2nd ed., trans. Max Knight (Berkeley: University of California Press, 1967), 1, 48.

10. Kelsen, *Pure Theory*, 33 (italics his).

11. Kelsen, *Pure Theory*, 43.

12. Another important jurisprudential school, legal realism, identifies law as what courts say it is, and thus is also monocentric. E.g., see Jerome Frank, *Law and the Modern Mind* (New York: Brentano's, 1930), 46: "We may now venture a rough definition of law from the point of view of the average man: For any particular lay person, the law, with respect to any particular set of facts, is a decision of a court with respect to those facts so far as that decision affects that particular person. Until a court has passed on those facts no law on that subject is yet in existence. Prior to such a decision, the only law available is the opinion of lawyers as to the law relating to that person and to those facts. Such opinion is not actually law but only a guess as to what a court will decide."

13. For an overview of some of the relevant literature, see Tom W. Bell, "Polycentric Law," *Humane Studies Review* 7, no. 1 (Winter 1991/92): 166–91.

14. Captured, for example, in Harold R. Berman, *Law and Revolution: The Formation of the Western Legal Tradition* (Cambridge, MA: Harvard University Press, 1983): "Law in action involves

some affinities with classical natural law theory, which is often considered the great alternative to positivism. But none of the recent prominent proponents of polycentrism are natural lawyers in a classical sense, and some natural lawyers are monocentric in outlook.[15] Polycentrists do not all share the same political ideology. Proponents include classical liberals,[16] radical leftists,[17] and anarchists (or something close),[18] as well as other scholars who do not clearly align themselves with any particular political philosophy when writing on this issue.[19]

---

legal institutions and procedures, legal values, and legal concepts and ways of thought, as well as legal rules. It involves what is sometimes called 'the legal process'" (4). Law "is a living process of allocating rights and duties and thereby resolving conflicts and creating channels of cooperation" (5). "To speak of the Western legal tradition is to postulate a concept of law, not as a body of rules, but as a process, an enterprise, in which rules have meaning only in the context of institutions and procedures, values, and ways of thought. From this broader perspective the sources of law include not only the will of the lawmaker but also the reason and conscience of the community and its customs and usages" (11). Cf. Eugen Ehrlich, *Fundamental Principles of the Sociology of Law* (1936; New Brunswick, NJ: Transaction, 2002), 24; Lon L. Fuller, *The Morality of Law*, rev. ed. (New Haven: Yale University Press, 1964), 74, 145; Bruce L. Benson, *The Enterprise of Law: Justice without the State* (San Francisco: Pacific Research Institute for Public Policy, 1990), 11; and Friedrich A. Hayek, *Law, Legislation and Liberty*, vol. 1, *Rules and Order* (Chicago: University of Chicago Press, 1973), 36. Although I do not treat him as a polycentrist for purposes of this chapter, Neil MacCormick's notion of law as "institutional normative order" seems to express an idea many polycentrists would share. He writes that law has an "aspiration to order" by prescribing "an elaborate set of patterns for human conduct," and the orderliness depends upon "the set of patterns amounting to a rationally intelligible totality." See *Institutions of Law: An Essay in Legal Theory* (Oxford: Oxford University Press, 2007), 1, 11.

15. For a good example of how two famous natural lawyers can go in different directions, see the comparison of Thomas Aquinas and Francisco Suárez in James Bernard Murphy, *The Philosophy of Customary Law* (Oxford: Oxford University Press, 2014), ch. 2. Among contemporary polycentrists, Gary Chartier has given most attention to natural law, rooting his conception of law in a version of the "new natural law theory" associated with the work of John Finnis and Germain Grisez; see *Anarchy and Legal Order: Law and Politics for a Stateless Society* (Cambridge: Cambridge University Press, 2013).

16. E.g., Hayek, *Law, Rules and Order*; Leoni, *Freedom and the Law*; and Randy E. Barnett, *The Structure of Liberty: Justice and the Rule of Law*, 2nd ed. (New York: Oxford University Press, 2014).

17. E.g., Chartier, *Anarchy and Social Order*, chs. 4, 7; and Robert M. Cover, "The Supreme Court, 1982 Term—Foreword: *Nomos* and Narrative," *Harvard Law Review* 97, no. 4 (1983): 4–68. On Cover's politics, see Franklin G. Snyder, "Nomos, Narrative, and Adjudication: Toward a Jurisgenetic Theory of Law," *William & Mary Law Review* 40, no. 5 (1999): 1627.

18. E.g., David Friedman, *The Machinery of Freedom: Guide to a Radical Capitalism*, 2nd ed. (La Salle, IL: Open Court, 1989); Michael van Notten, *The Law of the Somalis: A Stable Foundation for Economic Development in the Horn of Africa*, ed. Spencer Heath MacCallum (Trenton, NJ: Red Sea, 2005); John Hasnas, "The Obviousness of Anarchy," in *Anarchism/Minarchism: Is a Government Part of a Free Country?*, ed. Rodney T. Long and Tibor R. Machan (New York: Routledge, 2008), 111–31; Benson, *The Enterprise of Law*; Chartier, *Anarchy and Legal Order*, ch. 4; and Jonathan Crowe, "Anarchy and Law," in *The Routledge Handbook of Anarchy and Anarchist Thought*, ed. Gary Chartier and Chad Van Schoelandt (Abingdon, UK: Routledge, forthcoming).

19. E.g., Robert C. Ellickson, *Order without Law: How Neighbors Settle Disputes* (Cambridge, MA: Harvard University Press, 1991); James C. Scott, *Seeing like a State: How Certain Schemes to Improve the Human Condition Have Failed* (New Haven: Yale University Press, 1998); Fuller, *The Morality of Law*; Berman, *Law and Revolution*; and Bederman, *Custom as a Source of Law*.

Polycentrism also has precedent in the history of Christian thought. Thomas Aquinas defended polycentric views in the midst of his most comprehensive theological work,[20] and later Thomistic scholars such as Francisco Suárez followed suit.[21] Johannes Althusius (1557–1638) and Abraham Kuyper (1837–1920), important social thinkers in my own Reformed tradition, also espoused polycentric ideas.[22]

What are the nonstate sources of law, according to contemporary polycentrists? Among the most important sources are voluntary associations—"labor unions, professional associations, clubs, churches, and universities"— insofar as they create many norms guiding daily behavior.[23] A second example are contracts that private parties enter voluntarily in the course of ordinary relationships, which create enforceable rights and duties.[24] Furthermore, participants in various fields of commercial enterprise develop customary practices that define how they do business.[25] In general, polycentrists see all nonstate norms that shape the understanding and interpretation of law as genuine sources of legal obligation.[26]

Polycentrists identify not only multiple sources of law but also multiple means for enforcing law. They point especially to the widespread use of mediation and arbitration to resolve disputes outside of civil courts.[27] They also

---

20. As discussed below, see especially Thomas Aquinas, *Summa Theologiae* 1a2ae 95.3; 97.3.

21. See book 7 of Suárez's *Tractatus de legibus, ac Deo legislatore in decem libros distributes* (Lugdunum: Sumptibus Horatij Cardon, 1613).

22. For Althusius, the political commonwealth is composed of smaller associations. Each association has its own particular purpose, arising out of the various needs of human life. Their existence and structure depend upon the voluntary, covenantal consent of their members. See *Politica*, ed. and trans. Frederick S. Carney (Indianapolis: Liberty Fund, 1995). Kuyper contrasted the "mechanical" power of the state with the "organic" and "spontaneous" character of the various nongovernmental spheres of life, such as family, business, and science. For Kuyper, the latter do not owe their existence to the state, and the state ought not to impose its own laws upon them but respect the innate laws of each. See especially *Lectures on Calvinism* (Grand Rapids: Eerdmans, 1931), lecture 3.

23. The quotation is from Lon L. Fuller, *The Principles of Social Order: Selected Essays of Lon L. Fuller*, rev. ed., ed. Kenneth I. Winston (1981; Oxford: Hart, 2001), 232; cf. Fuller, *The Morality of Law*, 123–25. See also generally Cover, "*Nomos* and Narrative."

24. See Fuller, *Principles of Social Order*, 188–205, 244–48; and Benson, *The Enterprise of Law*, 227.

25. See Benson, *The Enterprise of Law*, 230.

26. According to Bederman, *Custom as a Source of Law*: "Customary regimes flourish . . . in pluralistic legal environments" (177) and in legal cultures "accepting of multiple sources of legal obligation" (180). This again stands in contrast to positivism. Fuller claimed that positivists have never been comfortable with customary law; see *The Morality of Law*, 232–33. This is evident in both Austin and Kelsen, who believed that customary "law" really becomes law only when authorized by courts or the legislature, thereby making it the command of the sovereign; see Austin, *The Province of Jurisprudence*, 34–36; and Kelsen, *Pure Theory*, 9.

27. See, e.g., Benson, *The Enterprise of Law*, 213–15, 228; Hasnas, "The Obviousness of Anarchy," 120–22; and Leoni, *Freedom and the Law*, 175.

observe how certain communities develop cooperative, self-help measures that bypass state-controlled judicial procedures.[28] As Robert Ellickson puts it, the idea that "governments monopolize the control of misconduct" is "utterly false," a "blunder that dates back at least to Thomas Hobbes."[29]

As these examples demonstrate, polycentrists do not simply assert that there ought to be multiple sources of law but claim that there are in fact multiple sources. As Harold Berman says about the Western legal tradition, "The conventional concept of law as a body of rules derived from statutes and court decisions—reflecting a theory of the ultimate source of law in the will of the lawmaker ('the state')—is wholly inadequate to support a study of a transnational legal culture."[30] Some polycentrists point to old Roman law and English common law notions that government institutions exist more to discover and recognize the law than to make it.[31] Others admire the ability of various medieval societies to make and enforce law effectively with little or no centralized political authority.[32] For example, several polycentrists highlight the medieval development of the *lex mercatoria*, a transnational body of norms and courts that merchants developed and administered across European borders.[33] Looking ahead many centuries, polycentrists also observe that

---

28. A central concern of Ellickson, *Order without Law.*

29. Ellickson, *Order without Law,* 4.

30. Berman also writes in the same context: "Perhaps the most distinctive characteristic of the Western legal tradition is the coexistence and competition within the same community of diverse jurisdictions and diverse legal systems." "From this broader perspective the sources of law include not only the will of the lawmaker but also the reason and conscience of the community and its customs and usages. . . . In the formative era of the Western legal tradition there was not nearly so much legislation or so much precedent as there came to be in later centuries. The bulk of law was derived from custom, which was viewed in the light of equity (defined as reason and conscience). It is necessary to recognize that custom and equity are as much law as statutes and decisions, if the story of the Western legal tradition is to be followed and accepted." See *Law and Revolution,* 10–11.

31. E.g., see Hayek, *Rules and Order,* 82–83; and Leoni, *Freedom and the Law,* 140–41. As Sir Edward Coke (1552–1634) described it, "The Lawes of England consist of three parts, The Common Law, Customes, & acts of parliament." See *The Selected Writings of Sir Edward Coke,* vol. 1, ed. Steve Sheppard (Indianapolis: Liberty Fund, 2003), 95.

32. E.g., the Anglo-Saxon law prior to the Norman invasion (see Benson, *The Enterprise of Law,* 21–30) or early Icelandic law (see Friedman, *The Machinery of Freedom,* 201–8). On the military implications of the polycentric medieval environment, see Sean McFate, *The Modern Mercenary: Private Armies and What They Mean for World Order* (New York: Oxford University Press, 2014), 5–6, 63, 72. Jean Bethke Elshtain notes the common mistake of associating the medieval era with absolutism, when in fact medieval societies had multiple sources of authority and held that rulers were bound to the law; see *Sovereignty: God, State, and Self* (New York: Basic, 2008), 43, 55, 65–66, 113.

33. E.g., see Leon E. Trakman, *The Law Merchant: The Evolution of Commercial Law* (Littleton, CO: Fred B. Rothman, 1983), 7–21; Berman, *Law and Revolution,* ch. 11; and Benson, *The Enterprise of Law,* 30–35. Some recent scholars have critiqued various aspects of these writers' claims. Emily Kadens, for example, argues that the merchant rules that were universal across borders usually came from contract or statute and that the existing commercial customs were primarily local; see "The Myth

high-seas whalers, working far outside the bounds of any formal political community, formed detailed but unwritten rules regulating how competing ships could hunt and claim whales.[34] In the case of both the Law Merchant and the whalers, many civil courts came to recognize these privately developed rules.[35]

Several more recent examples are also worth mentioning, although "once you learn to look for it [polycentric law], you see it everywhere."[36] First, a number of polycentrist writers discuss how the Uniform Commercial Code, widely adopted by the American states, explicitly grants binding force to customary commercial practice.[37] Second, Ellickson provides a detailed case study of ranching communities in Shasta County, California, in the 1980s, which largely governed themselves through unwritten norms and dispute-resolution procedures often at variance with statutory provisions.[38] Third, James C. Scott describes how an unplanned Brasilia grew up spontaneously around the carefully planned official city, and how the latter needed and was sustained by the former in a symbiotic relationship.[39] Based on this and several other cases, Scott concludes that every formal organization depends upon "implicit understandings, tacit coordinations, and practical mutualities that could never be successfully captured in a written code." "All socially engineered systems of formal order are in fact subsystems of a larger system on which they are ultimately dependent, not to say parasitic."[40] According to David Bederman, custom "continues to permeate almost all realms of contemporary law" and remains a mechanism for "bottom-up" lawmaking.[41]

In summary, advocates of polycentrism believe that law originates from a multiplicity of sources and not simply from the state. A host of human

---

of the Customary Law Merchant," *Texas Law Review* 90 (2012): 1153–1206. Kadens, however, does not challenge the importance of custom for the Law Merchant generally.

34. See Ellickson, *Order without Law*, 191–205.

35. Regarding the Law Merchant, see William Blackstone, *Commentaries on the Laws of England*, 4 vols. (1765–1769; Chicago: University of Chicago Press, 1979), 1:264; Trakman, *The Law Merchant*, 23–37; and Benson, *The Enterprise of Law*, 60–61. Regarding the whalers, see Ellickson, *Order without Law*, 192.

36. Tom W. Bell, *Your Next Government? From the Nation State to Stateless Nations* (Cambridge: Cambridge University Press, 2018), 72. In this work, however, Bell defends what he calls "autocentric" law (73).

37. Bederman, *Custom as a Source of Law*, 84–88; Fuller, *The Morality of Law*, 234; Ellickson, *Order without Law*, 254; and Benson, *The Enterprise of Law*, 227.

38. See generally Ellickson, *Order without Law*, part 1.

39. Scott, *Seeing Like a State*, 118–30.

40. Scott, *Seeing Like a State*, 255–56, 351.

41. Bederman, *Custom as a Source of Law*, 57, 112, 176.

communities are *jurisgenerative*, to borrow Robert Cover's terminology.[42] Furthermore, polycentrists believe that many laws arise spontaneously, as the product of human action but not of deliberate decision or conscious intent: it is a "fiction that all law is the product of somebody's will."[43] Polycentrists thus find it untenable when positivism insists that law represents coercive orders that instruct people to perform or refrain from specific acts.[44] Polycentrists lament that "the rule of the intermediate group . . . has been systematically marginalized in legal theory for the past few centuries."[45]

Polycentrism and the Identity of the Law

Implicit in the previous section, but worth stating clearly, is that legal polycentrism involves more than just affirming that law emerges from a multiplicity of sources. Even positivists may affirm that much (while claiming that judges enforce norms derived from nonstate sources because the higher law of the political sovereign requires them to do so).[46] Polycentrists also conceive of the very nature of law in a way different from monocentrists. On a polycentric conception, law cannot be identified with rules or commands. Law is something else. For most polycentrists, law is a normative order or patterns of conduct.

To explain this more carefully, I introduce two terms I will use through the rest of the chapter. First, *customary order* refers to the patterns of conduct to which members of a political community ordinarily adhere. This customary order emerges from the complex interaction among the community members in their many activities and institutions of everyday life. Second, by *customary legal order* I refer to those aspects of the customary order that members of the community regard as legally binding (not in terms of momentary public opinion, but of established patterns of thought and practice). In other words, the customary legal order is what they deem obligatory, such that a person who violates it deserves a formal sanction.

---

42. See generally Cover, "*Nomos* and Narrative."

43. Hayek, *Rules and Order*, 28. Cf. Ellickson, *Order without Law*, 184; and Snyder, "Nomos, Narrative, and Adjudication," 1630–31 (commenting on Cover).

44. See Kelsen, *Pure Theory*, 33, 43.

45. Snyder, "Nomos, Narrative, and Adjudication," 1636–37. Cf. Berman, *Law and Revolution*, 38–39.

46. Cf. Austin, *The Province of Jurisprudence*, 34–36. H. L. A. Hart's treatment of the issue is arguably more nuanced than Austin's; see *The Concept of Law*, 2nd ed. (Oxford: Clarendon, 1994), ch. 3. But he still thinks monocentrically, in terms of laws that "confer" legal powers on others to do things (such as make contracts and enter marriages) that can become legally enforceable if they follow certain procedures; see *The Concept of Law*, 27–28.

Although not all polycentrists may wish to put it this way, I suggest that from a polycentric perspective it is most coherent to understand the law as identical to the customary legal order. What is the law? While monocentrists answer, "The commands of the state," polycentrists respond, "The customary legal order." That is to say, law is what is understood, practiced, and enforced among the members of the community, not what is officially declared by the government.

Before I defend this understanding of law as most consonant with a political theology grounded in the Noahic covenant, several points of clarification may be helpful. For one thing, identifying the law with the customary legal order does not, in itself, imply any definite answer as to whether members of the community may ever disobey or resist the law, and under what conditions. Chapter 11 will consider that important question. For another thing, identifying the law with the customary legal order does not imply that the state is irrelevant or unnecessary. The state does not define what the law is under such a view, but state action can certainly play an influential role in shaping the content of the customary legal order. Although some polycentrists are anarchists, most are not.[47] In this chapter, I assume that civil government is legitimate and plays an important role in the life of a political community. Defense of that idea also awaits chapter 11.

Another point of clarification is that my defense of legal polycentrism should not be confused with a defense of democratic forms of government. When I refer to *jurisgenerative* activity as being widely dispersed or consensual, careful readers will see that I am not talking about making law by popular vote. I do not discuss which form of government is best, here or elsewhere. The Noahic covenant does not offer much insight on that issue, in my judgment.

A broader point of clarification is historical in nature. Since monocentric conceptions of law are so prevalent today, identifying law with the customary

---

47. Some writers have critiqued anarchic polycentric theories of law by arguing that state action is necessary for a peaceful and prosperous society and thus that law cannot develop solely through activities and institutions independent of government. For example, see William M. Landes and Richard A. Posner, "Adjudication as a Private Good," *Journal of Legal Studies* 8, no. 2 (March 1979): 235–84; and John K. Palchak and Stanley T. Leung, "No State Required? A Critical Review of the Polycentric Legal Order," *Gonzaga Law Review* 38, no. 2 (2002/03): 315–16. Since I am not defending anarchism, I do not believe it necessary to interact with these critiques. Among polycentrists who have tried to counter them, see Benson, *The Enterprise of Law*, chs. 11–12; Barnett, *The Structure of Liberty*, chs. 13–14; and Friedman, *The Machinery of Freedom*, 156–59. For critical comments on the polycentric theories of Hayek, Barnett, and Cover (respectively) on moral grounds, see A. I. Ogus, "Law and Spontaneous Order: Hayek's Contribution to Legal Theory," *Journal of Law and Society* 16, no. 4 (Winter 1989): 403–5; Palchak and Leung, "No State Required?," 309; and Synder, "Nomos, Narrative, and Adjudication," 1726.

legal order may strike readers as innovative and eccentric. This it is not. My
proposal not only resembles the views of several contemporary polycentrists
discussed above but also reflects prominent currents within the older Western
legal tradition.[48] In the Roman law, *Justinian's Digest* prescribes that where
there is "no applicable written law . . . the practice established by customs and
usage" ought to be followed. It also states, "Statutes themselves are binding
upon us for no other reason than that they have been accepted by the judgment of the populace." That is, enacted statutes become legally obligatory
only after they receive popular confirmation. This implies that the customary
legal order exercises veto power over official legislation. The *Digest* also asserts
this explicitly: "It is absolutely right to accept the point that statutes may be
repealed not only by the vote of the legislature but also by the silent agreement
of everyone expressed through desuetude."[49] Justinian's *Institutes* adds, "The
laws of nature, which are observed by all nations alike, are established . . . by
divine providence, and remain ever fixed and immutable: but the municipal
laws of each individual state are subject to frequent change, either by the tacit
consent of the people, or by the subsequent enactment of another statute."[50]

Thomas Aquinas and other medieval figures embraced this perspective.[51]
Writing in the wake of a revival of Roman law in Western Europe,[52] Thomas
followed Isidore of Seville's opinion that human law should be "according to
the customs of the country."[53] Aquinas elsewhere claimed that human law,
which proceeds "from the will of man, regulated by reason," can be manifest
by both speech and action. Thus, not only by legislation but "by actions also,
especially if they be repeated, so as to make a custom, law can be changed and
expounded." He concludes, "Accordingly, custom has the force of a law, abol-
ishes law, and is the interpreter of law."[54] When exercising this veto power
over official legislation, custom "shows that the law is no longer useful."[55]

48. For summary comments on the varied but important place of custom in the Western legal
tradition, see, e.g., J. M. Kelly, *A Short History of Western Legal Theory* (Oxford: Clarendon, 1992), 67–68,
100–102, 137–41, 184–86.

49. *The Digest of Justinian*, ed. Theodor Mommsen and Paul Krueger, trans. Alan Watson, vol. 1
(Philadelphia: University of Pennsylvania Press, 1985), 1.3.32.

50. *The Institutes of Justinian*, trans. J. B. Moyle, 5th ed. (Oxford: Clarendon, 1913), 1.2.11.

51. In addition to Aquinas, see, e.g., Gratian, *Decretum*, D.4, c.3. For English translation, see
Gratian, *The Treatise on Laws with the Ordinary Gloss*, trans. Augustine Thompson, OP, and James
Gordley (Washington, DC: Catholic University of America Press, 1993), 13.

52. For a brief history of the rediscovery of the *Digest*, see, e.g., Peter Stein, *Roman Law in European
History* (Cambridge: Cambridge University Press, 1999), 43–45.

53. Thomas Aquinas, *Summa Theologiae* 1a2ae 95.3.

54. Thomas Aquinas, *Summa Theologiae* 1a2ae 97.3.

55. Thomas Aquinas, *Summa Theologiae* 1a2ae 97.3, ad. 2. See generally David VanDrunen, *Law*

The Anglo-American legal tradition may not seem amenable to such a perspective, given the English idea of parliamentary sovereignty.[56] Yet this tradition has always left much of the work of legal ordering to the common law, a body of law developed independently of legislative institutions. The relationship of the customary order and the common law is complicated, but the former did play a significant role in shaping the latter, although in changing ways over time.[57] In the famous Dr. Bonham's Case (1610), Chief Justice Coke and the Court of Common Pleas ruled, "It appeareth in our Books, that in many Cases, the Common Law doth control Acts of Parliament, and sometimes shall adjudge them to be void: for when an Act of Parliament is against Common right and reason, or repugnant, or impossible to be performed, the Common Law will control it, and adjudge such Act to be void."[58] This suggests that common law trumps parliamentary acts when justice and reason are on the former's side,[59] which is similar to Aquinas's view.[60] According to Bederman, "Even today there may be situations where the conditions of statutory desuetude may be occasionally accepted by courts," although he admits it is difficult to find true examples.[61]

One final point of clarification seeks to answer the following question briefly: what does my proposal entail for situations in which the customary legal order is at odds with a governmental statute or regulation? Faced with such a dilemma, how is an ordinary person to steer his action, or how is a judge to render her verdict? My discussion above suggests that the customary

and Custom: The Thought of Thomas Aquinas and the Future of the Common Law (New York: Peter Lang, 2003).

56. While it does not touch upon the precise issue discussed in this section, the ancient independent governing authority of the City of London (the City of London Corporation) provides another interesting case study in legal polycentrism in the English tradition. For a brief (though critical) description, see Luke Bretherton, *Resurrecting Democracy: Faith, Citizenship, and the Politics of a Common Life* (Cambridge: Cambridge University Press, 2015), 63–67.

57. See especially Bederman, *Custom as a Source of Law*, ch. 3. Cf. Hasnas, "The Obviousness of Anarchy," 113–14, 116; and R. H. Helmholz, *Natural Law in Court: A History of Legal Practice in Theory* (Cambridge, MA: Harvard University Press, 2015), 99.

58. Coke, *Selected Writings*, 1:275.

59. The discretionary power this seems to leave to judges is undoubtedly why many positivists find Dr. Bonham's case disturbing and even illegitimate. Antonin Scalia, for example, calls Dr. Bonham's case "not orthodox at all," "an extravagant assertion of judicial power," and "eccentric." See *A Matter of Interpretation: Federal Courts and the Law*, ed. Amy Gutmann (Princeton: Princeton University Press, 1997), 129–30. For a polycentrist's interpretation of this case, see Fuller, *The Morality of Law*, 99–101.

60. In addition to the material quoted above, Aquinas explains in *Summa Theologiae* 1a2ae 97.3, ad. 2 that if the reason for a legislated law's usefulness remains, "it is not the custom that prevails against the law, but the law that overcomes the custom." The English translation is from *Summa Theologica*, 5 vols., trans. Fathers of the English Dominican Province (Allen, TX: Christian Classics, 1948).

61. Bederman, *Custom as a Source of Law*, 113, 178. Jury nullification may represent a contemporary way by which a groundswell of popular sentiment can effectively veto official legislation.

legal order rather than the statute is the law, and thus ought to be followed, but a somewhat more nuanced answer may be appropriate. Where the customary legal order itself—that is, the law—has authorized state legislative processes as valid means for making and changing the law, it seems proper for judges and ordinary people to acknowledge the results of those legislative processes as legally binding. Under such circumstances, legislation serves as a sort of default indicator of what the law is. But if a piece of legislation is not able to gain popular consent over time, and the customary legal order thus resists the legislators' desired result, my proposal implies that the customary legal order has effectively vetoed the legislative material and, all else being equal, ought to trump it in a court of law and the court of conscience.[62] Chapter 11 will revisit issues related to this as well.

LEGAL POLYCENTRISM AND THE NOAHIC COVENANT

With this detailed description of polycentrism before us, I now wish to argue that a vision of public life and political community shaped by the Noahic covenant offers many reasons to favor a polycentric conception of law. As in previous chapters, I seek to fly a bit above contentious debates of the moment. But recognizing that people can never escape their contexts, I offer some reflections from my own setting. I first address an objection to legal polycentrism that may arise from what I have said thus far and then offer six additional considerations in support of polycentrism from a Noahic perspective.

An Initial Objection

Earlier in the chapter, I recapped my argument from part 1 that the human race, to fulfill its moral commission in the Noahic covenant, must engage in a variety of creative activities and establish many institutions in support of these activities. I suggested that as people do so, they inevitably develop a multitude of norms—customs and laws—that order their life together. This envisions law as emerging from a variety of sources and thus provides a *prima facie* case for a polycentric conception of law.

Someone might argue, however, that this could well be the case for

---

62. For many discussions of situations in which statutes fall into desuetude due to customary practice, see Bederman, *Custom as a Source of Law*; and Murphy, *The Philosophy of Customary Law*. For important discussion of the foundation of law in consent, see also Alexander M. Bickel, *The Morality of Consent* (New Haven: Yale University Press, 1975), 106–11.

societies at early stages of development but need not and even should not be the case for more advanced societies like those of the modern West. The latter, after all, have well-established state institutions designed to make, interpret, and enforce the law. Therefore, the objection might go, my preliminary argument is irrelevant for contemporary developed societies.

This objection is unpersuasive. The Noahic covenant itself does not establish civil government but entrusts the formation of law and administration of justice to an experimental, collaborative, organic, and consensual process of developing institutions and authority structures. In the course of history, this process has produced civil governments. But this means civil governments are inevitably linked to the process. Government may even come to assert an important influence on the process of developing institutions and authority structures, but the process itself is more fundamental.[63] From the perspective of the foundational Noahic covenant, government properly develops as human beings pursue a creative and collaborative commission in accord with their nature as divine image-bearers—as unpacked further in chapter 11. If so, the establishment of government cannot be taken to annul the pursuit itself, any more than completion of a house makes its foundation unnecessary or the blossoming of a plant makes its roots superfluous. To put it another way, civil government properly emerges from the Noahic covenant, not to eliminate the activity and authority of other institutions but in dependence upon them and for their good. Thus, if a developed society maintains its respect for the organic process that produced its government, many nonstate institutions will continue to create and enforce law.

Sin and Power

The first additional consideration in support of polycentrism is short and simple. The Noahic covenant indicates that the people who populate civil communities are intractably sinful: "the intention of man's heart is evil from his youth" (Gen 8:21). No one who makes, interprets, and enforces the law is morally pure. Every legal and political system needs to reckon with this sobering reality and seek to mitigate its potential dangers. One conceivable option is to establish mechanisms to select the most virtuous and least corrupt people to be legislators, judges, police, and other state officials. But what those mechanisms might be is anyone's guess. Even if a community discovered a

---

63. Consistent with these claims is the fact that the modern state in fact emerged rather late in history. Cf. Scott, *Seeing like a State*, 183–84; and Hasnas, "The Obviousness of Anarchy," 122.

way to select the best and brightest to make and enforce law, it would still face the danger described in Lord Acton's dictum: "Power tends to corrupt, and absolute power corrupts absolutely." Holding great power is seldom good for one's moral character.[64]

If it is unsafe to entrust a great deal of power to particular people, dispersing power broadly seems to be the most promising way to mitigate the problem of sin in the formation of law. A monocentric legal system might disperse legislative and judicial power in various ways, but these would still, by definition, concentrate power in branches of the state. By contrast, legal power is truly dispersed in a polycentric system, in which a multiplicity of people interacting in a multitude of institutions engage in *jurisgenerative* activity. Not only state officials but every person active in institutions small and large can make at least some small contribution to the evolving shape of the law. Thus, insofar as the Noahic covenant suggests the danger of concentrating legal power in any single person or small group of people, it points to advantages of a polycentric system. No human legal system can be perfectly just, but a polycentric system seems to guard against certain evils by preventing massive accumulation of legal power.

Interpreting the Law

A second consideration appeals to the fact that law, if it is to be effective, must be coherent. That is, the law must have an integrated systemic consistency.[65] Law cannot effectively order individual and community life if it consists of a jumble of unrelated or even contradictory rules. But for law to be coherent, judicial interpretation of law must be as uniform as possible. When judges interpret applicable provisions in different ways, the law becomes inconsistent and unpredictable. And when ordinary people do not know how to interpret these provisions in ways that match the interpretation of judges, they will not know how to live under those rules. This suggests that judges and ordinary people need to share common ways of interpreting the law.

The Noahic covenant provides theological foundation for this conclusion. According to Genesis 1, I have argued, human beings have a divine commission to pursue creative activity and to exercise a benevolent rule in this world.

---

64. If one needs a biblical proof-text for this idea, Mark 10:42 may suffice.

65. On the ideal of coherence within the Western legal tradition, see Berman, *Law and Revolution*, 9, 11, 38. For related comments regarding the common law, see Coke, *Selected Writings*, 741; James R. Stoner Jr., *Common-Law Liberty: Rethinking American Constitutionalism* (Lawrence: University Press of Kansas, 2003), 11; and Gordon S. Wood, "Comment," in *A Matter of Interpretation*, 59.

Furthermore, God has endowed all human beings with his image indiscriminately and equally. When God reaffirmed humanity's image-bearing status in the Noahic covenant, he neither provided a master plan for putting the commission into concrete practice nor installed certain individuals with a special privilege of creating and imposing such a plan. Instead, the Noahic covenant appears to leave the human race to pursue its task through an experimental and collaborative process in which all should have a share. If judges interpret the law in ways out of touch with popular understanding, a legal system will fall far short of this ideal.

We must give attention to *interpretation* because no legal rule, even the most perfectly worded statute, is an island to itself whose meaning can be entirely determined from within. Statutes use words borrowed from an already existing language, and the ability to read and understand that language requires immersion in a universe of meaning. Languages emerge within specific cultural contexts and constantly develop in response to that culture's communication needs. Thus reading a statute well inevitably depends upon understanding the culture in which it exists, with its convictions, biases, and assumptions.[66] But language changes, cultures evolve, and judges often do not share the same convictions, biases, and assumptions, either with each other or with the drafters of the statute. To be useful, legal rules must be interpreted, and in a thousand ways this can be a daunting and controversial endeavor.

A central question for jurisprudence, therefore, is how to achieve relative uniformity, and thus coherence, in interpreting legal rules. Can a monocentric conception provide this? We might ask first whether legislative action can produce a background context by which judges and ordinary people can interpret the law. This is surely impossible. A background context involves perspectives, biases, and assumptions. A context is a holistic universe that shapes the meaning of things within it. A legislature can promulgate rules but it can hardly generate a context.[67]

What then about government courts? Can they do what legislatures cannot? Ronald Dworkin's influential theory of legal interpretation—"law as integrity"—offers an idea worth considering. Dworkin believes judges must be guided by a "political morality." Although he attempts to keep

---

66. Cf. Cover, "*Nomos* and Narrative," 4–5.

67. Cf. Murphy, *The Philosophy of Customary Law*, x, 113–16; Hayek, *Rules and Order*, 65, 78; Cover, "*Nomos* and Narrative," 11–12; MacCormick, *Institutions of Law*, 5, 31, 42–44; and Roscoe Pound, *The Ideal Element in Law* (1958; Indianapolis: Liberty Fund, 2002), 74, 82–87, 117–19, 139.

judges rooted in a broader tradition by making them participants in a narrative chain of judicial decisions, the political morality that guides Dworkin's judges is ultimately each judge's own philosophy. His ideal judge—tellingly dubbed "Hercules"—is able to perceive the purest form of the law through his own political judgment.[68] This is not a recipe for achieving relative *uniformity* of interpretation, for judges inevitably disagree about political morality. Thus Dworkin's "law as integrity" does not provide a background context that judges share in common.

A more promising option is to find a common background context in a wisdom internal to the judiciary. Many jurists have found such a wisdom in the common-law tradition. Sir Edward Coke wrote of the "artificial reason" of the common law, distinct from pure natural reason. Jurists gain it through long experience, by which they make the law's reason their own.[69] In Coke's vision, the experienced judge gains learning and judgment and attains mastery in an art.[70] Similarly, Karl Llewellyn described common law appellate judging as a kind of craftsmanship, an inexact science requiring "horse sense."[71] Over against legal realists' skeptical challenges to this tradition,[72] Roscoe Pound defended the ability of common law wisdom to build objectivity and impartiality in the judges who embraced it.[73]

If it exists, such a shared judicial wisdom approaches what we seek, a common background context for legal interpretation. But it is still inadequate. As internal to the judiciary, this wisdom risks becoming esoteric, self-referential, and isolated from the real world whose disputes it adjudicates. It acculturates judges into a craft and art that is, by definition, inaccessible to the nonjudge.[74] Thus, if law is to be accessible to all people, internal judicial wisdom in Coke's sense is not a sufficient common background context for interpretation.

What seems necessary is that the internal judicial wisdom correspond as much as possible to the wisdom internal to the customary order. This is because the customary order is surely the main grid through which ordinary

---

68. See generally Ronald Dworkin, *Law's Empire* (Cambridge, MA: Belknap, 1986).

69. See, e.g., Coke, *Selected Writings*, 481, 701, 742–43. Stoner gets at a similar point in writing that common-law judges were trained in Aristotelian practical wisdom; see *Common-Law Liberty*, 11–12.

70. See Stoner, *Common-Law Liberty*, 11–12.

71. See Karl N. Llewellyn, *The Common Law Tradition: Deciding Appeals* (Boston: Little, Brown and Co., 1960), 213–16 (on craftsmanship); 190, 213–16, 382 (on inexactitude); and 5, 19, 21, 53, 60–61, 202–3, 264, 268–70 (on horse sense).

72. For a classic example, see Frank, *Law and the Modern Mind*.

73. See, e.g., Pound, *The Ideal Element*, 268–69, 286, 291, 297–98, 305.

74. See related comments in Bederman, *Custom as a Source of Law*, 28–30.

people interpret the law. Different people have their own biases, but the customary order is something they hold in common and which they reasonably expect each other to know. The development of an *artificial reason* and distinctive *horse sense* within the legal profession through uniform practices of acculturation can undoubtedly promote relative uniformity of legal interpretation, but there needs to be a reciprocity between them and the *common reason* and *common sense* of the broader society.[75] The legal profession, and judges in particular, ought to keep their lawyer-like thinking tethered to the way they think as ordinary participants in their communities and open to testimony about the assumptions and practices of the customary order.

One might reason that since this is only a matter of *interpreting* law rather than generating law, a monocentric legal system could still be sound as long as its judges utilize the customary order in their legal interpretation. But this seems doubtful in light of how important interpretation is. If the customary order is always relevant background context for legal interpretation, then the customary order inevitably shapes the very substance of the law. And if this is true, a government's claim to have sole power to determine what "the law" is seems rather hollow. A polycentric conception of law more adequately explains how the law can be coherent, through relative uniformity of interpretation among *all* those participating in it. Polycentrism thereby promotes the Noahic ideal that law should develop through a collaborative and inclusive process.

Ordinary Expectations of the Law

The next consideration in support of legal polycentrism takes the preceding argument a bit further. In short, polycentrism generally protects people's ordinary expectations about the law. A legal system is surely more effective and just the more that common people in their daily lives actually understand its demands and can plan their lives around it. And widespread ignorance of the law is hardly consistent with the Noahic ideal that law should develop through an experimental and collaborative process in which all image-bearers have a share.

There is a simple reason to suspect that a monocentric system of law fails at this point: if the law is merely what the state says it is, most people will not know what the law prescribes because they are largely unaware of the content

---

75. Cf. Murphy, *The Philosophy of Customary Law*, 115–16; and Gerald J. Postema, "Coordination and Convention at the Foundations of Law," *Journal of Legal Studies* 11 (Jan 1982): 189–93.

of legislation, administrative regulations, and judicial decisions[76]—and it
is tedious, complicated, and expensive for them to try to find out. People's
ignorance of what state sources of law actually demand is both comical and
frightening. According to Harvey Silverglate, the average American professional unwittingly commits several federal crimes in the course of a typical
day. For the most part, no harm follows, but it poses a lingering threat and
makes the ordinary person vulnerable to unexpected, arbitrary, or vindictive
action on the part of law enforcement.[77]

What norms in fact structure the lives of ordinary people and guide their
expectations, if rules prescribed by the state do not? Many polycentrists have
offered a persuasive answer. They emphasize that people should understand
the law that rules them, for the sake of both the stability of a legal system[78] and
the dignity of the people.[79] They argue that what I have called the customary
legal order is what ordinary people know and what structures their lives.[80]
Polycentrists helpfully recognize that people do not come to know their communal obligations as a collection of rules they can name but as patterns of
expected and appropriate behavior.[81] Their knowledge of the customary legal

---

76. Cf. MacCormick, *Institutions of Law*, 71.

77. Harvey A. Silverglate, *Three Felonies a Day: How the Feds Target the Innocent* (New York:
Encounter, 2011). How has this happened? "The answer lies in the very nature of modern federal
criminal laws, which have become not only exceedingly numerous . . . and broad, but also . . . impossibly
vague" (xxxvi). The recent federal action against the Gibson Guitar Corporation arguably provides a
well-publicized case in point. For general background and analysis of this matter, see C. Jarrett Dieterle,
"The Lacy Act: A Case Study in the Mechanics of Overcriminalization," *Georgetown Law Journal* 102
(2014): 1279–1306. The US Fish and Wildlife Service sent armed federal agents to raid two Gibson Guitar
buildings to gather evidence that Gibson had violated an old and obscure US statute, which, to be true,
required Gibson to violate laws of India.

78. E.g., Fuller argued that legal systems miscarry when they fail to publicize rules and to make them
understandable, and that a virtue of the common law was how it worked out widely held conceptions;
see Fuller, *The Morality of Law*, 39, 49–51, 63–65. Cf. Charles Murray, *By the People: Rebuilding Liberty
without Permission* (New York: Crown Forum, 2015), 32–33.

79. E.g., Thomas Aquinas explained that the reason behind a law resides both in the lawgiver and,
by participation, in the one who receives the law to be ruled by it; see *Summa Theologiae* 1a2ae 90.1 ad.
1; 90.3 ad. 1; cf. 90.4.

80. For similar argument, see Hasnas, "The Obviousness of Anarchy," 118–19. Cf. Scott, *Seeing like
a State*, 49: "We must never assume that local practice conforms with state theory." Cf. George Klosko,
Political Obligations (Oxford: Oxford University Press, 2005), ch. 9, where Klosko presents data from focus
groups exploring popular opinion on obligation to the law. I do not suggest that Klosko is a polycentrist,
and I recognize that he presents his data for purposes different from mine here, but his evidence seems
to show that people think they are generally obligated to obey the law. But the "law" they obey is not the
official state rules per se but some kind of modification of them based on moral convictions, practical
consequences, and what other people are doing.

81. As Cover comments in *"Nomos and Narrative,"* 6, the varied and complex legal materials of
contemporary societies "present not only bodies of rules or doctrine to be understood, but also worlds to
be inhabited. To inhabit a *nomos* is to know how to *live* in it." Cf. Friedrich A. Hayek, *Law Legislation
and Liberty*, vol. 2, *The Mirage of Social Justice* (Chicago: University of Chicago Press, 1976), 11: "What we

order develops largely by perception and intuition, gained not by the study of books but by actually living in concrete communities, observing others' patterns of conduct, and making those patterns their own as a kind of habit.[82]

Since the customary legal order is what people actually know and expect others to follow, acknowledging its norms as the law protects ordinary expectations much better than does mere application of legislation and other state sources.[83] In this way too, therefore, polycentrism captures the collaborative and inclusive character of law—and hence the spirit of the Noahic covenant—in ways that even a democratically accountable monocentric legal system cannot.

The Information Problem

In chapter 3, I argued that fulfilling the Noahic moral commission requires the creative pursuit of many activities and the establishment of various institutions. Chapter 5 added that pursuing this process well requires wisdom and that individuals and communities grow in wisdom through a communal and cumulative process in which one generation imparts an inheritance of understanding to the next generation, which must imbibe, cultivate, and refine this inheritance. If forming and enforcing law is part of the process of fulfilling the Noahic moral commission, as argued above, then wisdom is a prerequisite for forming and enforcing law well. This insight suggests another consideration in support of legal polycentrism.

One of the marks of wisdom is that it takes all relevant facts and circumstances into account. Thus we may ask: What facts and circumstances are relevant for a legal system? An enormous number. Modern societies are incredibly complex, involving interaction among hundreds of millions of individuals in hundreds of thousands of associations undertaking a bewildering array of activities. The wisdom required to make just law for such societies must account for a vast amount of information. Polycentrism seems able to account for this predicament in ways that monocentrism is not.

The difficulty for monocentrism is that the information required for

---

have in common with our fellows is not so much a knowledge of the same particulars as a knowledge of some general and often very abstract features of a kind of environment."

82. Cf. Fuller, *The Morality of Law*, 51; and MacCormick *Institutions of Law*, 66–67. Cf. Michael Polanyi, *Personal Knowledge* (Chicago: University of Chicago Press, 1962).

83. Hayek comments in *Rules and Order*, 87, "The task of the [common law] judge will be to tell them what ought to have guided their expectations, not because anyone had told them before that this was the rule, but because this was the established custom which they ought to have known." Cf. *Rules and Order*, 97. See also Bederman, *Custom as a Source of Law*, 181.

the smooth operation of complex modern societies is scattered among a host of individuals and associations, such that each agent knows only a miniscule fraction of the whole.[84] Furthermore, the content of this aggregated knowledge and the relation of its pieces to one another is constantly in flux. This means that while state legislative activity can influence the shape of a complex modern society, legislators seeking to control it or even to achieve some particular change are bound to be disappointed. Legislators and other state officials have such a small degree of the pertinent information at hand that the complexity of society makes it impossible to predict all the results of legislation with any kind of precision.[85] Legislative attempts to achieve some particular social vision are at best an educated guess and often a shot in the dark. Even totalitarian regimes, while capable of wreaking much harm through their legislation, inevitably confront much that is out of their control.[86] Likewise, Western liberal democratic governments, with more modest goals, constantly find that unknown circumstances and unforeseen events stymie their seemingly reasonable aspirations.[87]

The development of the customary order does not face this same information problem. The customary order is constituted by the patterns of conduct resident in the overlapping real-life relationships among millions of individuals and associations. It is the product of the spontaneous coordination of the tiny bits of relevant knowledge possessed by all the participants of complex modern societies.[88] Thus, while state legislation is promulgated by those ignorant of most of the relevant information, the customary order emerges precisely through the spontaneous process that incorporates dispersed information into an integrated social system.

---

84. See especially the work of Hayek; e.g., *Rules and Order*, 12–13, 32. See also Barnett, *The Structure of Liberty*, ch. 2.

85. According to Scott (*Seeing like a State*, 92–93, 256), "Trying to jell a social world . . . seems rather like trying to manage a whirlwind"; societies are an "ineffably complex web of activity," and trying to replace this web with formal rules is "certain to disrupt the web in ways that they cannot possibly foresee." See also Hayek, *The Mirage of Social Justice*, ch. 7. Cf. Leoni, *Freedom and the Law*, 7; Benson, *The Enterprise of Law*, 131; and van Notten, *The Law of the Somalis*, 46.

86. Scott (*Seeing like a State*, 202, 203) comments that the Soviet experiment in agricultural collectivization, whose planners were "flying blind," endured as long as it did because of "the improvisations, gray markets, bartering, and ingenuity that partly compensated for its failures."

87. E.g., see Matt Ridley, *The Evolution of Everything: How New Ideas Emerge* (New York: Harper, 2015), particularly chapters 5–6, 13, 15. Central bankers' repeated failed attempts to bring about desired economic outcomes provide good contemporary examples. See, e.g., Sebastian Mallaby, *The Man Who Knew: The Life and Times of Alan Greenspan* (New York: Penguin, 2016).

88. See Hayek, *Rules and Order*, 38, 41, 44, 50–51, 63; and Barnett, *The Structure of Liberty*, ch. 3. On Hayek's contribution to explaining the "knowledge problem," see Bruce Caldwell, *Hayek's Challenge: An Intellectual Biography of F. A. Hayek* (Chicago: University of Chicago Press, 2004), 338.

These considerations suggest that a polycentric legal system better reflects the way of wisdom than a monocentric system. Law that derives from a multiplicity of sources is able to harness the vast information necessary to do justice in ways that a law deriving from a single source cannot. This does not mean that legislation and other state action cannot play an important role in shaping the customary legal order, but it does provide another reason to recognize the latter as *the law*.[89]

Change in the Law

Inherent in the preceding discussion, but worth brief comment in its own right, is that law is not established once and for all but constantly changes. On the one hand, law must change if it is to be, as Aquinas echoed Isidore, "suitable to place and time."[90] On the other hand, legal change has potentially undesirable consequences. People need to plan for the future. Developing skills, investing resources, and many other activities necessary for individual and social flourishing require predicting, with some degree of confidence, what coming months and years will bring. But the future, and thus predictions about it, are always uncertain. One helpful service law can provide is a degree of stability as people anticipate an uncertain future. Although much remains unpredictable, it is advantageous to know that one will be playing by the same basic set of rules—just as an athletic team, unable to plan for the exact circumstances in the fourth quarter of tomorrow's game, can still train intelligently knowing that the rules of the game will be the same as today. The prospect of legal change exacerbates uncertainty and detracts from ordinary people's ability to plan for the future rationally.[91] Here I suggest that in a polycentric legal system law can change in a manner that mitigates some of these concerns.

As discussed above, useful knowledge is acquired through a generation-spanning process that inherits a treasury of wisdom from the past and incorporates new insights into it. For law to reflect this process, it must retain the hard-earned gains of the past while refining them for the future. This indicates that beneficial legal change will generally be *gradual* and *incremental*. If law changes in this way, it should mitigate problems that arise when the

---

89. And it should therefore instill civil officials with a sense of often-missing modesty. Cf. Ellickson, *Order without Law*, 281–83; Scott, *Seeing like a State*, 345; and Hayek, *Rules and Order*, 33, 59.

90. Thomas Aquinas, *Summa Theologiae* 1a2a 95.3.

91. Thus, according to Fuller, a legal system can miscarry through frequent change; see *The Morality of Law*, 79–81.

future of law seems uncertain and people cannot plan for days to come or rely on legitimate expectations.

In a monocentric legal system, however, in which law can only be modified through legislation or other mechanisms of the state, law tends to change not gradually and incrementally but *abruptly* and *drastically*. Legislation is by nature abrupt since it is a punctiliar act. The law at one moment prescribes one thing, and then at the moment of legislative enactment the law becomes something else. Legislation is also at least potentially drastic. Legislators can attempt to tweak the law through small modifications, but faced with responsibilities to supervise the whole complex body of law and the pressures of competing factions and special interests, bold proposals are most likely to garner attention and seem worth the time. In these respects, at least, state legislation has serious drawbacks as a mechanism for changing the law.[92]

The customary order, in contrast, tends to change gradually, incrementally, and "fluidly."[93] The inertia of known and expected patterns of behavior creates barriers to changes in custom other than those that occur by small steps over periods of time, perhaps even imperceptibly to most people as they happen. Yet it is inevitable that such gradual and incremental change will occur, for patterns of expected conduct necessarily shift as people are born and die, associations rise and fall, and industry and technology develop. Customary development of law is thus a "living process," and the "plasticity" of customary systems can be a source of "microadjustments."[94] A customary legal order can change in ways analogous to change in language, markets, and science.[95] Thus the way law changes in a polycentric legal system has advantages in two directions over the way it changes in a monocentric system. In the latter, laws either do not change at all or they change abruptly and often drastically, while in the former, law inevitably changes but tends to do so gradually and incrementally.[96]

---

92. Cf. Leoni, *Freedom and the Law*, 9–10, 70–75, 78–79, 80–81, 90, 110.

93. For the latter term, see Bederman, *Custom as a Source of Law*, 177–78.

94. See Scott, *Seeing like a State*, 34–35. In comparison, Scott says that changing codes to reflect evolving social practice is "a jerky and mechanical adaptation."

95. On the analogy to language, see Ellickson, *Order without Law*, 5; Fuller, *Principles of Social Order*, 240; Scott, *Seeing like a State*, 143, 256, 357; van Notten, *The Law of the Somalis*, 36; and Leoni, *Freedom and the Law*, 9, 86, 130, 132, 135–36, 143, 146. On the analogy to markets, see Ellickson, *Order without Law*, 5; Benson, *The Enterprise of Law*, 15; and Leoni, *Freedom and the Law*, 22, 86–87, 108–9, 130, 132, 146, 150. On the analogy to science, see Leoni, *Freedom and the Law*, 147–49.

96. For comments on how the traditional common law system captured some of the concerns expressed here, see Barnett, *The Structure of Liberty*, 117; Leoni, *Freedom and the Law*, 179; and Ruben Alvarado, *Common Law and Natural Rights: The Question of Conservative Foundations* (Aalten, Netherlands: WordBridge, 2009), 40.

There may be circumstances, of course, when changing the law abruptly and drastically is desirable. At such times, legislation or other state action can shape the law in helpful ways. But as a general rule, the spontaneous, gradual, and incremental change of the customary legal order is the wise way for law to change, and this provides further reason to prefer a polycentric to a moncentric conception of law.

The Rule of Law

This penultimate consideration in support of polycentrism is perhaps the most important, and it prepares the ground for our reflections on authority in the next chapter. At the end of the previous chapter, I argued that whatever the proper extent of the state's authority, its core responsibility is to promote the justice required under the Noahic covenant. The state has no authority to define justice autonomously but ought to enforce a justice whose reality transcends the state and serves the good of the people. This is similar to saying that we seek the rule of law, not "the rule of man." Of course, this maxim cannot mean that law exists apart from human action, for law is always a human product. What the maxim envisions is that no individual or group of people are sovereign but that everyone is accountable to a legal authority independent of his or her own will. State officials are to be ministers of the law rather than lords of the law. Understanding the state along these lines, I now argue, reveals additional virtues of polycentrism and problems with monocentrism.

By making state officials the sole source of law, monocentrism permits a relatively small number of people to define what the law is—which looks rather like the "rule of man." Western societies have tried to mitigate this difficulty through several devices, such as holding legislatures accountable through regular democratic elections, written constitutions, and the separation of legislative, judicial, and executive powers. These initiatives have yielded some obvious benefits, at least in comparison with autocratic alternatives, but they primarily just shift around law-defining power among state officials, rather than make the law more fundamental than the state.[97]

Recognizing the customary legal order as the law seems to address this

97. In the English legal tradition, the tension between commitment to the rule of law and commitment to parliamentary sovereignty illustrates the problem. E.g., see Daniel Hannan, *Inventing Freedom: How the English-Speaking Peoples Made the Modern World* (New York: Broadside, 2013). Already on page 4 he speaks of these two ideas as if they are fully compatible. First, "the rule of law. The government of the day doesn't get to set the rules." Then less than half a page later, "Representative government. Laws should not be passed, nor taxes levied, except by elected legislators." Does government set the rules or

problem more satisfactorily.[98] The customary legal order, while still a human
product, is not ultimately the product of human will.[99] Generally speaking,
the customary order did not emerge through one person or group imposing
its will upon the rest of society. While legislation creates law by an act of will
under threat of force, the customary order creates law spontaneously, through
the reciprocal and collaborative interaction of innumerable individuals and
associations over the broad range of human endeavor.[100] Some people have
more influence than others upon development of the customary order, to be
sure, but no individual or association has the power to control it. The habits, sentiments, language, technologies, and innovative ideas that shape the
customary order do so because they have won assent (perhaps imperceptibly)
among people broadly, not because an individual or a particular group of
people has decreed them. Polycentrists often emphasize that while legislation
makes law by imposing the will of one upon the many, that is, by coercion,
the customary order makes law by consent.[101]

It must be admitted that this contrast between legislative coercion and
customary consent needs considerable nuance, since customs can be disad-
vantageous or even downright unjust for minority groups, who may adhere
to customary practices less out of consent than out of fear.[102] Yet there is a
real distinction between law decreed through legislation and law emerging
through customary development. The former requires only some kind of
majority vote, often as one slightly larger faction gains adversarial victory

---

not? Hayek confronts the problem directly when he declares that constitutional separation of powers
has failed in its objective; see *Rules and Order*, 1.

98. I mention a few pertinent comments from polycentrists. Berman (*Law and Revolution*, 38):
"The view that law transcends politics—the view that at any given moment, or at least in its historical
development, law is distinct from the state—seems to have yielded increasingly to the view that law is at
all times basically an instrument of the state, that is, a means of effectuating the will of those who exercise
political authority"; Pound (*The Ideal Element*, 352): "Law is the real foe of absolutism"; and Bertrand
de Jouvenal (*On Power: The Natural History of Its Growth*, trans. J. F. Huntington [1948; Indianapolis:
Liberty Fund, 1993], 334): "Beyond all question, the supremacy of law should be the great and central
theme of all political science. But, make no mistake about it, the necessary condition of this supremacy
is the existence of a law older than the state, to which it is mentor. For if law is anything which Power
elaborates, how can it ever be to it a hindrance, a guide, or a judge?"

99. See Hayek, *Rules and Order*, 28; and Murphy, *The Philosophy of Customary Law*, ix, 10, 23, 27,
36, 40.

100. On the importance of reciprocity for customary law, see Benson, *The Enterprise of Law*, 12–13;
and Fuller, *Principles of Social Order*, 194.

101. E.g., see Benson, *The Enterprise of Law*, 12, 45, 322; Hasnas, "The Obviousness of Anarchy,"
116; and Leoni, *Freedom and the Law*, 13, 100–110, 131, 146; cf. Stoner, *Common-Law Liberty*, 5.

102. For helpful discussion, see Murphy, *The Philosophy of Customary Law*, 51–52, 98–101. On the
related debate whether customary law promotes or hinders human freedom, see Murphy, *The Philosophy
of Customary Law*, xii; and Bederman, *Custom as a Source of Law*, 176.

over another slightly smaller faction. The latter, in contrast, requires people of different background and opinion to discover common ways of doing things through reciprocal collaboration.[103]

These considerations do not imply that political communities never need to make collective decisions by majority legislative vote. But if we aspire to the rule of law as an ideal, it seems wise to recognize the customary legal order as the law, and to hold government accountable to it. And this provides additional reason to appreciate polycentrism.

Polycentrism and Justice

The final consideration is brief but nevertheless important—if nothing else, at least again to prepare ground for the next chapter. Here I simply ask: Are there any reasons to believe that a polycentric legal system has better prospects than a monocentric system for advancing justice in a community? The preceding arguments suggest many such reasons, from various angles. Here I suggest one additional reason. I suggest it tentatively because I recognize, with the Noahic covenant (Gen 8:21), that sin pervades all human activities, and hence development of law by any means will fall far short of the ideals of justice discussed in chapter 9. Many horrific customs have existed, and some noble pieces of legislation have tried to rectify them.

Nevertheless, everyone (sinful as we are) would prefer to gain his own special advantage through the law, even at the expense of what is just. In monocentric legal systems, in which the vote of even a slight legislative majority can define the law, laws can easily be made to benefit one special interest over another. But where law is truly based upon widespread popular consent, as in a customary legal order, people are unlikely to embrace practices that work to someone else's advantage over their own. Therefore, what is just—that is, what is to no one's special advantage or disadvantage—seems most likely to gain the needed consent. The custom of forming lines so as to observe the principle of first-come-first-served may provide a simple but pertinent example.

Someone might note that most horrific customs do not enjoy the genuine consent of all parties involved, and thus do not fit the idea of "customary legal order" as I defined it. That is true, and will be relevant when we address authority and resistance in the following chapter.

---

103. On the danger of the politicization of society and law creation, and the benefits of customary law in restraining it, see, e.g., Stoner, *Common-Law Liberty*, 16; Jouvenal, *On Power*, 341; Anthony de Jasay, *Before Resorting to Politics*, The Shaftesbury Papers, 5 (Cheltenham: Edward Elgar, 1996), 54–55; and Benson, *The Enterprise of Law*, 77, 88.

CONCLUSION

While the Noahic covenant obviously provides no detailed vision for the substance of a legal code, I have argued that it provides good reasons to support a polycentric rather than a monocentric conception of law.[104] No system of making, interpreting, and enforcing law guarantees the achievement of the natural justice considered in chapter 9. But in light of Noahic concerns about human sinfulness, humans' identity as creative and dignified image-bearers of God, and the communal and cumulative way of attaining wisdom, a polycentric legal system that identifies the law with the customary legal order seems better poised to order society in just directions.

I have noted several times in previous chapters how the concerns of the Noahic covenant suggest that civil government ought to be limited and modest in its ambitions. The analysis of legal polycentrism in the present chapter buttresses this conclusion. Acknowledging the *jurisgenerative* activity of many activities and institutions in human society puts inherent constraints on government power and provides an important means of restraining state officials within the bounds of justice and the rule of law. Having undertaken these studies of justice and the law, we now turn to consider the nature and limits of government authority specifically.

---

104. Cf. Christopher J. Insole, *The Politics of Human Frailty: A Theological Defense of Political Liberalism* (Notre Dame: University of Notre Dame Press, 2005), 167, on how traditional English thinking about the common law rested upon a *modest* but not *ambitious* theological vision.

CHAPTER 11

AUTHORITY AND RESISTANCE

Many writers claim that authority is one of the central issues, if not *the* central issue, of political philosophy. Readers may thus wonder why I postponed this topic for the penultimate chapter. To be sure, I could have arranged part 2 in a coherent way that promoted discussion of authority to the front of the line. But my overall strategy—to consider perennially weighty topics in political and legal theory through an organic unfolding of the implications of the Noahic covenant—suggests that authority belongs near the end of the study, not the beginning. My conclusions about authority depend heavily upon the analysis in preceding chapters.

At the outset of both chapters 9 and 10, I noted the interconnection among justice, law, and government. Justice is foundational to law and government, since we wish our law and our political officials to be just. Law, in its own right, is foundational to government, since most of us wish our civil officials to act lawfully: we desire the "rule of law, not of men." There is also movement in the other direction. The action of government officials shapes what the law is, and the law in turn defines concretely what is just in a particular society. But the basic order is clear and important: the law ought to be just, and civil officials ought to act lawfully. Therefore, it makes most sense to consider government authority now, after extensive treatment of justice and law. As we ponder legitimate authority, however, our minds also move to the abuse and usurpation of authority. It thus seems fitting to confront difficult questions about civil resistance in this chapter as well.

To fulfill these goals, I begin by setting out a *general* theology of authority, developed through reflection on the Noahic covenant and its natural law.

Building upon this, I explain why *government* authority is legitimate, despite all the difficult problems it presents. Next, I address three chief functions that most governments take up—what I call protectionist, perfectionist, and service-providing functions. I consider whether, and to what extent, legitimate government authority extends to each. Finally, I reflect on how far obligation to obey the government extends, and thus what the rights and responsibilities of resisting corrupt authority may be. As in previous chapters, the Noahic covenant provides no exhaustive solutions to these issues, but does offer a substantive framework for thinking well about them.

A THEOLOGY OF AUTHORITY

Earlier reflections on the Noahic covenant and its background in the biblical creation story establish important foundation for Christian thinking about authority. In creation, God exercised supreme authority over the world. Genesis 1 describes God as the true Lord who makes all things, orders its various parts, and gives to each its own function. At the end of this work, God created human beings in his own image, which entailed a grand commission to subdue the other creatures, fill the earth, and exercise benevolent rule (Gen 1:26–28). That is, God granted the human race a delegated authority over creation. They were to rule it under him and within the bounds of his ultimate authority.[1]

If human authority were simply about human rule over other kinds of creatures, it would be a considerably easier topic (if not uncontroversial). But discussion of authority usually focuses upon one human being's claim to authority over another human being. Here we immediately confront a theological challenge. Genesis 1 and the Noahic covenant ascribe the image of God to *all* human beings. This implies that everyone has a rightful share in God's delegated authority over the world. In fact, the universality of image-bearing and hence of ruling authority is one of the striking features of the creation story. But if so, how can one image-bearer rightfully exercise ruling authority over another image-bearer?

The analysis in chapter 3 suggests a way to resolve this initial challenge. The Noahic covenant republishes the moral commission God delivered at creation, but in refracted form suited for a fallen world. The Noahic

---

1. David T. Koyzis, *We Answer to Another: Authority, Office, and the Image of God* (Eugene: Pickwick, 2013) also develops an account of authority through a theology of the image.

commission is basic and short. It sets a broad course for the human race without providing details. Yet contemplating the Noahic covenant and our experience in the world indicates how the details might need to be worked out. We recognize that we are social creatures who have to collaborate with one another to fulfill our mandate. We also recognize that to collaborate effectively we must establish institutions that will order and harmonize our activities. These institutions, furthermore, require authority structures for successful operation. We thus come to something like the following: for the human race to fulfill its general mandate to exercise authoritative rule over creation, it needs to establish institutions that recognize the authority of some human beings over others.[2] The exercise of authority *within* the human community, therefore, does not entail that some people are worth more than others but is an implication and outworking of the general authority they all share equally.[3] To be legitimate, the former kind of authority should serve the latter. Considering the three basic kinds of Noahic institutions identified in chapter 3 can help us see what this might look like.[4]

First, the basic authority in familial institutions is parental. This derives from obvious necessities of human nature. Young children do not understand their world very well, are unable to provide for themselves, and thus need the guidance of a fairly comprehensive authority. The best candidates for such authority are a child's parents, as argued in chapter 8. But the realities of nature also require that the character of parental authority change over time. As children grow, they gain understanding of their world and become increasingly able to provide for themselves and to make their own decisions. Proper parental authority, therefore, is dynamic rather than static. It seeks to help children attain responsible adulthood and exercise parental authority themselves one day. It aims to make itself obsolete. Parents pervert their authority when they regard children as their permanent subjects.[5] Parental authority is therefore natural but also provisional. It entails no inherent superiority of one human being over another: in due time, the younger generation

---

2. Therefore, Victor Lee Austin seems correct to write, "The work of authority has to do not primarily with human inadequacies . . . but with human excellences." See *Up with Authority: Why We Need Authority to Flourish as Human Beings* (New York: T&T Clark, 2010), 18.

3. For a somewhat similar analysis, see Koyzis, *We Answer to Another*, 23, 163.

4. On authority in these three types of institutions, cf. Richard T. De George, *The Nature and Limits of Authority* (Lawrence: University Press of Kansas, 1985), 68.

5. See Yves Simon, *A General Theory of Authority* (Notre Dame: University of Notre Dame Press, 1962), 133–34. Cf. De George, *The Nature and Limits of Authority*, 75. Of course, there may be exceptions, as in the case of severely handicapped children becoming adults.

must exercise the same authoritative functions as the older generation, for they share the same image of God.

Second, enterprise associations demand a different analysis. While parent-child relationships and hence parental authority emerge naturally, enterprise associations under the Noahic covenant arise voluntarily. People establish businesses, clubs, and schools to pursue endeavors for which humans are naturally fit, but such associations may take a variety of forms. They only exist because individuals have decided to establish and sustain them. A person is not born naturally into a business venture the way one is born naturally into a family. But enterprise associations require authority structures too. Because they need to make decisions about rules, budgets, strategic plans, and the like, and because unanimity among members is often elusive, enterprise associations need certain people to assume leadership, with authority to act on behalf of the whole.[6] Unlike parental authority, enterprise authority does not reflect natural relationships. Enterprise authority structures are created and entered voluntarily.

But like parental authority, enterprise authority can also honor the equal dignity inherent to image-bearers. People participate willingly in the authority structures of voluntary associations. Those who submit to the authority of a company employer, club president, or university professor do so of their own choice. Operating under another person's authority in one venue does not prohibit someone from exercising authority over that same person in another venue. People in an authoritative relationship that proves unproductive or unsatisfying can terminate it, and if such a relationship proves abusive, the victim can seek legal remedy. Furthermore, such authority is inherently limited, for it extends only to purposes for which the association exists and not to a general control of someone's life. In voluntary enterprise associations, therefore, relationships of authority can and ought to advance the general authority of the human race as a whole and respect the equal worth of all.

A still different, and considerably more complicated, analysis applies to *judicial* institutions. Judicial institutions are necessary to secure justice, and thereby to support and protect familial and enterprise institutions. Chapter 9 argued that judicial institutions can be voluntary and thus nongovernmental. Private mediation and arbitration services are prime examples. Because they

---

6. What I suggest here is similar in many respects to Simon, *General Theory*, ch. 2, although the way I relate political authority to other forms of authority later in this chapter differs from the way Simon relates them. See also Yves R. Simon, *Philosophy of Democratic Government* (Chicago: University of Chicago Press, 1951), ch. 1.

are voluntary, private judicial institutions resemble enterprise institutions, and the nature of their authority can be described and defended in the same way.

The analysis becomes difficult when we come to civil government. Government is, at least, one type of judicial institution (we consider below whether it is also more than this). But government is not voluntary. It asserts jurisdiction over all people within its geographical bounds and exercises physical coercion against those who resist it. The authority of government, therefore, cannot be justified in the same way as enterprise authority. Or at least that is how it initially seems. Nevertheless, many political theorists have attempted to justify government authority through some notion of voluntariness. This is the case with classic "social contract" theories in their various Hobbesian, Lockean, and Rousseauian varieties,[7] as well as with states that claim to rest on "the consent of the governed."[8] The idea is noble: governments exercise authority over residents of a territory because those residents have willingly agreed to it. But in fact, few people have explicitly agreed to submit to their governments. Some thinkers, therefore, have defended government authority by appealing to the "tacit consent" of the governed. Yet such claims are complicated to defend and inevitably controversial.[9] Many recent writers have proposed other kinds of theories to justify government authority, often well aware of compelling complaints about contract and consent theories.[10] Still other writers proclaim the failure of all such attempts, and conclude that no one has yet offered a satisfactory general account of government authority and/or its corresponding obligations.[11]

---

7. See Thomas Hobbes, *Leviathan* (1651); John Locke; *Second Treatise of Civil Government* (1689); and Jean-Jacques Rousseau, *The Social Contract* (1762).

8. As expressed, e.g., in the United States Declaration of Independence: "Governments are instituted among Men, deriving their just powers from the consent of the governed."

9. For detailed consideration and critique of consent theories, see, e.g., A. John Simmons, *Moral Principles and Political Obligations* (Princeton: Princeton University Press, 1979), chs. 3–4; Leslie Green, *The Authority of the State* (Oxford: Clarendon, 1988), ch. 6; Joseph Raz, *The Morality of Freedom* (Oxford: Clarendon, 1986), 80–99; and George Klosko, *Political Obligations* (Oxford: Oxford University Press, 2005), ch. 6.

10. Among other examples, many have developed a Thomistic approach, including Simon, *General Theory*; John Finnis, *Natural Law and Natural Rights* (Oxford: Clarendon, 1980), chs. 9–12; and Jean Porter, *Ministers of the Law: A Natural Law Theory of Legal Authority* (Grand Rapids: Eerdmans, 2010). For neo-Calvinist approaches, see Koyzis, *We Answer to Another*; and Philip D. Shadd, *Understanding Legitimacy: Political Theory and Neo-Calvinist Social Thought* (Lanham: Lexington, 2017). Klosko builds a case from *fairness* and *reciprocity* in *Political Obligations*. James F. Childress presents an argument based on the notion of *fair play*; see *Civil Disobedience and Political Obligation: A Study in Christian Social Ethics* (New Haven: Yale University Press, 1971), ch. 3. And Margaret Gilbert invokes the idea of *joint commitment*; see *A Theory of Political Obligation: Membership, Commitment, and the Bonds of Society* (Oxford: Clarendon, 2006).

11. E.g., see Simmons, *Moral Principles*, 191–92; Green, *The Authority of the State*, vii, 220; and

GOVERNMENT AUTHORITY

The justification of government authority ought to be a serious one for Christians and other morally thoughtful people. Entrusting the power of the sword in a unique (and perhaps even exclusive) way to a small cadre of people is a bold and weighty move. All are sinners to begin, and power tends to corrupt. States and state-actors are the main perpetrators of injustice in the world today—not only millions of small injustices but also most of the large-scale wrongs.[12] Through all of history, state officials have often been knaves, thieves, and thugs. Yet we not only entrust civil officials with the power of the sword but also acknowledge their right to levy taxes, which are extracted under threat of punishment. Scripture, of course, states on a few occasions that God has ordained civil magistrates and that people should submit to them. But on many more occasions, Scripture exposes their pride and corruption and brings them under divine judgment.[13] It is easy to understand why people submit to the state to stay out of trouble, but explaining why people recognize the state as having legitimate authority is another matter.

To stress the seriousness of the issue, I wish to clarify two assumptions. I am assuming, first, that the use or threat of physical coercion against fellow human beings is illegitimate unless justified. Image-bearing human beings may presume to have a right not to be coerced by another human being unless the other person can justify her authority to coerce. I do not deny that coercive authority exists, but the burden of proof lies with the coercer, not with the coerced. I also assume, second, that all actions of government are either overtly coercive or operate at some level under threat of coercion.[14] Putting these two assumptions together means that everything government

---

Raz, *The Morality of Freedom*, 99–105. The preceding page numbers refer to summaries of these authors' broader case. Such writers typically claim, however, that *some* people may have political obligations and that many people have good reasons to support their governments and to obey laws.

12. Abram de Swaan summarizes, regarding mass extermination in the past century, "Unlike common criminals who work outside the mainstream of society, in secret, on their own or with a few accomplices, mass murderers almost always worked in large teams, with full knowledge of the authorities and on their orders. Without exception, they operated within a supportive social context, most often firmly embedded in the institutions of the ruling regime." See *The Killing Compartments: The Mentality of Mass Murder* (New Haven: Yale University Press, 2015), 1–2.

13. For discussion of some of this manifold evidence, see Jacques Ellul, *Anarchy and Christianity*, trans. Geoffrey W. Bromiley (Grand Rapids: Eerdmans, 1991), ch. 2. Perhaps needless to say, I have many reservations about Ellul's exegesis and do not concur with his anarchic position.

14. The only exceptions I can think of are state-run services that no one is required to utilize and that operate entirely by user fees—a public museum, perhaps. How many such services truly exist I do not know, but I suspect the number is small, and in any case, they constitute a minute fraction of the things governments undertake.

does needs to be justified. The burden of proof for state activity should lie with the government, not with the governed.

The governments of the world claim authority to execute many functions. In light of my two assumptions, there is no reason to presume they have legitimate authority to do all of them. In fact, if the Noahic covenant implies that governments ought to be *limited*, as noted repeatedly in part 2, then it stands to reason that government's legitimate authority is considerably more constrained than the authority most real-life governments assert for themselves. My treatment of the subject in the following pages reflects these initial considerations.

Scripture and the State

Several biblical texts, summarized in chapter 1, teach Christians that legitimate government authority actually exists. Were that the only question on the table, the inquiry could end here. But as Christian political thinkers have long recognized, even the most detailed of these texts, Romans 13:1–7, fails to answer many pressing questions about government authority and our obligation to it. What exactly is the scope of legitimate government authority, for example, and how comprehensive does Paul intend our duty of obedience to be?

Thus we must do more than just assert and believe Romans 13:1–7 but also to try to *explain* it. It is not immediately evident *how* God ordains civil magistrates, as Paul says he does. God does not send down a word from heaven every time a new state official takes office. In fact, I cannot think of a single biblical text in which God *establishes* civil government by an act of special revelation.[15] Previous chapters have suggested that government emerges organically and legitimately as image-bearing human beings pursue their divine commission under the Noahic covenant. We need to consider that more closely here, with special attention to the question of authority. This study will be a kind of natural-law inquiry within the framework of Scripture. Through this study, I believe we can explain why Paul could speak of God instituting government authority and begin to specify its scope and limits.[16]

---

15. Contra Meredith G. Kline, "Oracular Origin of the State," in *Biblical and Near Eastern Studies: Essays in Honor of William Sanford LaSor*, ed. Gary A. Tuttle (Grand Rapids: Eerdmans, 1978), 132–41. This is an interesting article that makes a number of challenging exegetical claims. But it seems to me that even if Kline is correct that God promises to Cain in Genesis 4:15 that the fallen world will have a judicial order and that human beings will not be left in lawless chaos, he still begs the main point that his essay allegedly establishes, namely, that this judicial function will be exercised by a *state*.

16. Readers might therefore see my approach as a Reformed, covenantal version of an organic,

Legal Authority

To explain the legitimacy of government authority, I begin by discussing legal authority, that is, the authority of the law. Legal authority and government authority may initially seem to be two ways of speaking about the same thing. It is important to understand why this is not the case.

Chapters 9 and 10 noted that all people in all cultural contexts are obligated to observe the standards of natural justice but also that natural justice is underdeterminative. It sets general boundaries for human conduct but does not specify the concrete rules we need for living together and collaborating productively. For this, we need law.[17] Law ought to reflect the standards of natural justice while also providing the necessary specificity to regulate real-life human conduct. By providing this, law determines the details of what is just in a particular political community. Legal order is thus *necessary* for life in political communities under the Noahic covenant. Members of a community can have disagreements and arguments about what their laws ought to be, but the need for law is indisputable.

Legitimate *legal* authority, as just described, refers not to the authority of judges or the like but to the authority of the *law itself*. A human being who lives under the authority of her community's law suffers no injury to her dignity as image-bearer. To be under the authority of law is to live as God designed: as a social creature pursuing the Noahic moral commission in organized collaboration with fellow humans.

Still, law can take shape in ways that wreak harm and thus hinder rather than promote the ends of the Noahic covenant. Thus we wonder how legal authority can arise in legitimate ways that genuinely protect the equal dignity and general authority of all image-bearers.

This brings us back to the argument in chapter 10 that the *customary legal order* is what the law really is. Law is not the dictates of the government or solely its creation, as legal positivism and other monocentric conceptions assert. Instead, law is polycentric, residing in the practices and expectations of the members of a political community in their complex interrelations.

---

bottom-up Thomistic approach. It has important similarities to, amid many differences from, the approaches of Roman Catholic Thomists such as Finnis and Porter. I am inclined to agree with Porter that government authority does not arise from "a specific act of divine authorization"; rather, "we are in a position to defend political authority in terms of its status as a reflection of God's wisdom rather than seeing it as primarily a manifestation of God's will." See *Ministers of the Law*, 179. Simmons's distinction between a backward-looking deontological approach to political obligation and a forward-looking teleological approach may also be a helpful way to understand what follows. My approach is clearly of the latter type rather than former. See Simmons, *Moral Principles*, 45.

17. Cf. Porter, *Ministers of the Law*, 131–35.

For monocentrists, legal authority is simply one means of exercising government authority. Since law is conceived as the creation and instrument of government, whatever authority the law or legal officials exercise is governmental in nature. Monocentrists thus make the state more fundamental than the law. The notion of legal authority can provide no help for them in explaining the legitimate authority of government.

On a polycentric conception, in contrast, law emerges through a variety of sources, particularly through the establishment of voluntary enterprise associations, which form their own internal norms and develop ways of interacting with one another. State action can influence the shape of the customary legal order but never wholly determine it—even when it tries. The previous chapter explained why a polycentric conception best captures and protects the idea that all human beings bear God's image and have a rightful share in the commission to exercise authoritative rule in the world. Law emerging spontaneously through the customary order is the joint exercise of the many, not the imposition of the few. It is the product of widespread collaborative agreement rather than coercive direction from the top. It protects the reasonable expectations of ordinary people. Such considerations indicate not only that legal authority is legitimate (since the human community needs law in order to coordinate its activity in pursuit of the Noahic commission) but also that legal authority properly arises through a polycentric process. In other words, the law, as customary legal order, bears authority in the political community in which it develops.

Government Authority

What do these conclusions about legal authority imply about the authority of government? Some polycentrists are anarchists, believing that the legal authority inherent in the customary order is sufficient for coordinating activity in a just society and that no legitimate authority extends beyond this. But most polycentrists acknowledge that the state has a role, and perhaps even a very important role, in the development and enforcement of law and other governing functions. I now argue that legitimate government authority may arise out of legitimate legal authority. This claim, I believe, is simply an implication of the *rule of law*. In making this argument, I seek to follow a long stream of the Western political tradition holding that the authority of political rulers derives from the law and that these rulers must answer to it.[18] It is not the only

---

18. See Jean Bethke Elshtain, *Sovereignty: God, State, and Self* (New York: Basic, 2008), 23.

stream of the Western political tradition, and not well appreciated today, but the implications of the Noahic covenant suggest it is worth recapturing.

The basic argument is not complicated. If legal authority emerging through the customary order is legitimate, then other forms of authority it authorizes are also *prima facie* legitimate. And among other forms of authority the law may authorize, and which it seems likely to authorize, is civil government. That is to say, where the customary legal order recognizes certain bodies and offices of government, approves of certain means of staffing those offices, and defers to certain kinds of government action for enacting and defending just rules for the good of the community, these various provisions are legitimate. This perspective seems consistent with Paul's remarks in Romans 13:1 that God has ordained the existing government powers and that people ought to submit to them. Those who actually do the work of governing, Paul indicates, are the ones properly recognized as authorities. In terms of my argument here, the customary legal order has obviously not authorized people and institutions who *claim* government authority but whose words and actions are widely ignored. On the other hand, the people and institutions which members of a political community *actually* acknowledge and obey are evidently authorized by the customary legal order.[19]

In short, the law, as legitimate legal authority, may recognize and thereby authorize legislative, executive, and judicial functions of civil government. But as argued in chapter 10 and revisited below, the law is more fundamental than government and therefore government institutions and officials are ministers of the law rather than lords of the law. This suggests that there remains an important place for the customary legal order to repeal and replace the enactments of government. From this perspective, there is a problem with the contemporary notions that the state properly holds a monopoly on coercive power and that its authority preempts all others.[20] Government officers may properly exercise influential leadership roles in a community, and the customary legal order may incorporate the substance of state legislation and judicial decisions. But in the chain of authority, the law, rather than the

---

19. For related discussion, cf. Oliver O'Donovan, *The Ways of Judgment* (Grand Rapids: Eerdmans, 2005), 147; and Finnis, *Natural Law and Natural Right*, 246–50.

20. The common notion is sometimes attributed to Max Weber, although its inspiration may lie especially with Thomas Hobbes. Klosko puts it in this way: the state is that which "successfully claims a monopoly of legitimate force in a given territory." See *Political Obligations*, 21. Steven B. Smith comments, "The modern concept of the state as the possessor of the means of force within a given territory is the essence of the modern politics and is unthinkable without Hobbes." See *Modernity and Its Discontents: Making and Unmaking the Bourgeois from Machiavelli to Bellow* (New Haven: Yale University Press, 2016), 68.

government, rightly has the final word in governing the community's life. Where this is true, government authority is not mere power, in which the stronger few impose their will upon the weaker many. Rather, government authority is a legitimate exercise of human rule in fulfillment of the Noahic commission, an exercise that respects the dignity and calling of all human beings as divine image-bearers.

According to this argument, therefore, when texts such as Romans 13 say that God has ordained civil magistrates, these texts are not *establishing* government authority by special revelation. Instead, such texts *confirm* that the human community has acted in a legitimate way under the Noahic covenant by acknowledging, through its law, the authority of a government.

A couple of points of clarification are in order. First, I do not claim that this argument is the only possible way to explain the legitimacy of the state. But I believe this argument best corresponds to our consideration of authority through the lens of the Noahic covenant. Second, I also do not claim that existing government institutions whose lineage cannot be clearly traced through a fluid, organic, and collaborative process, as envisioned in the preceding argument, are necessarily illegitimate for that reason. My argument has attempted to provide a general, theoretical explanation of the legitimate authority of *government* as an implication of the Noahic covenant, not a description of how *particular governments* must have originated. The argument implies that if someone wonders what to do in the face of a brutal government, she cannot refuse to obey it because it is a government. No, government is legitimate. But there may be other grounds for refusing to obey her particular government; we will consider issues of civil resistance below.

The sad reality of government corruption raises important questions that must concern us for the rest of the chapter. I have argued that the law may recognize government bodies and offices, but what sort of government functions does it *rightfully* recognize, and hence legitimately authorize, from Noahic-covenantal perspective? What is the proper response when a government or even the law itself misfires? We take up the former question first.

THE RIGHTFUL EXTENT
OF GOVERNMENT AUTHORITY

The preceding section defended government authority in general terms: through the concept of law, we can understand how the institutions and offices of government can be part of the organic tapestry of life under the

Noahic covenant and thus why government officials can bear legitimate authority. The preceding section also made a narrower claim about government authority. Government institutions are not natural in the sense that familial institutions are, and they are not voluntary in the sense that enterprise associations are. Governments claim jurisdiction over every person within their territories, do not allow these people to opt out, and back up their policies and taxation codes with threat of physical coercion. Thus every action of government needs to be authorized in a specific sense. Since everything government does entails coercion or threat thereof against an image-bearer of God who holds authority in his own right, the burden of proof for justifying government action should lie with the government that bears the sword rather than with the person or institution at whom the sword points. Therefore, we now inquire what specific kinds of things the law rightfully authorizes government to do.

There are three broad functions that most governments pursue with some plausible claim of legitimacy.[21] (Of course, there are plenty of other things governments do that have no such plausible claim—such as genocide.) First are *protectionist* functions. Governments typically claim to protect and vindicate people from wrongs that other people do to them, that is, violations of their (negative) natural rights. Second, governments often pursue *perfectionist* functions. That is, they seek to make the members of their community better people. Third and finally, governments commonly *provide services*. They build infrastructure, dispose of garbage, run schools, offer health care, and the like—the specifics vary from state to state. These categories are far from airtight. It is not immediately clear, for instance, whether prosecuting the use of cocaine is perfectionist or protectionist: does it aim to keep people on good life paths or to curtail the harm addicts do to their communities? Or are public libraries service-providing or perfectionist? That is, do they aim to make desirable products available in a convenient and affordable way or to make people wise? Nevertheless, these seem to be reasonably clear distinctions that get our discussion going. I consider each of these three functions in turn.

Protectionism

Of the three, protectionist functions present the easiest case. As chapter 9 argued, whatever other responsibilities government may have, its core

---

21. We might categorize the functions most governments assume in different ways. While I have grouped them into just three, Klosko, for example, makes it seven. See *Political Obligations*, 24–40.

responsibility is to enforce rectifying justice. And if enforcing rectifying justice against a wrong is legitimate, stepping in to prevent the wrong from happening is also legitimate.[22] To exercise protectionist functions is thus to do precisely what Genesis 9:6 prescribes: "Whoever sheds the blood of man, by man shall his blood be shed."

For Christians, this kind of government authority is easy to justify theologically because this is what Romans 13 says God has appointed civil magistrates to do: the magistrate is God's servant, bearing the sword as an avenger against the one who does wrong (13:4). According to the New Testament, therefore, government officials are proper executors of the general human commission of Genesis 9:6.

This kind of government authority is also easy to justify from another angle. As discussed above, claims of government authority present special challenges because states do not operate simply by free and consensual collaboration with other people and institutions but through coercion or threat thereof. Ordinarily, no image-bearer ought to exercise or threaten violence against another image-bearer. But there are situations in which coercion is clearly justified: when inflicting just retribution and/or securing just compensation in response to violation of a person's natural rights, and when trying to prevent such a violation from happening in the first place. To use or threaten coercion on such occasions is not only permissible but just. Thus, when government performs these protectionist functions, it acts justly. In these circumstances, government should have no problem meeting its burden of proof in justifying the use of coercion. If the law authorizes government institutions to perform protectionist functions, therefore, the government has legitimate authority to do so.

And it is not difficult to imagine why the law (the customary legal order) would authorize government institutions to perform protectionist functions. Voluntary enterprise associations can protect and vindicate natural rights, and they often do. Theoretically, all violations of natural rights could be rectified through such private associations.[23] But many troublesome scenarios

---

22. This may be obvious and need no defense. But I would reason in this way: As wrongs such as murder, battery, rape, and theft are unjust and demand response, so also *threats* of such wrongs are unjust wrongs that demand response. This explains the almost universal recognition of the legitimacy of self-defense. And if judicial institutions are required to help people who suffer murder, battery, rape, theft, and the like (as argued earlier), they are required by the same reasoning to help people who are threatened by such acts.

23. E.g., see Randy E. Barnett, *The Structure of Liberty: Justice and the Rule of Law*, 2nd ed. (Oxford: Oxford University Press, 2014), chs. 13–14.

come to mind. What if poor people are unable to afford the services of a private judicial association and need help prosecuting a claim or defending themselves against one? What if two parties contractually agree to submit their disputes to the decision of a private mediator, but then one party refuses to abide by the mediator's decision? What if two parties with no contractual relationship have a dispute, and they can find no mutually agreeable judge to resolve their case? What if two disputing parties with no contractual relationship subscribe to different private security companies, and the stronger of the companies begins to bully the other rather than make a good-faith effort to resolve the dispute fairly? One could imagine many other examples.

In light of this, we can understand why communities acknowledge the authority of government police and courts to protect natural rights. This could well be the only solution able to garner widespread consent and hence able to take root in the customary legal order. When protecting natural rights, the police and courts function as a neutral referee among all members of society. They can stand behind the lawful actions and verdicts of private judicial institutions, and they themselves can provide protection and judicial remedies when these cannot be attained privately. Government-run national defense is even easier to explain (provided it is truly for *defense*). Faced with credible threats from abroad, communities understandably doubt the ability of purely private, voluntary action to raise and maintain a viable military. *Perhaps* a purely private military might be sufficient to stave off foreign attack. But there is no need to wonder why people are unwilling to risk such an experiment, and thus why authorization for government-run national defense can gain a strong foothold in the law.

Perhaps implicit in the notion of government authority to protect natural rights, but worth saying explicitly, is that governments should be especially vigilant about defending the rights of vulnerable people, whether the poor, ethnic minorities, or the unborn. Such people are usually the least able to defend themselves or to get the government's attention, and they have surely endured many more affronts to their natural rights than have the prosperous through the course of history.

Perfectionism

Perfectionism refers to a government's quest to make the members of its community better people. This raises the question whether legitimate government authority extends beyond the protectionist function described in Genesis 9:6 and Romans 13. Are governments properly authorized to use its coercive power not only to rectify violations of natural rights but also to try to improve people's moral character?[24]

The sort of analysis being pursued in part 2 cannot provide a dogmatic answer, but I argue that if legitimate government authority arises out of the Noahic covenant, then perfectionist functions are an uncomfortable fit. Nevertheless, insofar as governments effectively administer their *protectionist* functions, they will shape people's behavior in good directions and be able to address various social problems stemming from destructive conduct. This means we can account for many of the most attractive reasons for perfectionism on protectionist grounds. I will suggest that this is probably the way we *should* account for them. But the initial discussion that follows focuses upon perfectionism per se, that is, government attempts to shape people's moral character for its own sake.

The arguments earlier in the chapter suggest that we should address the question of perfectionism by considering whether government perfectionist functions are rightly authorized by the law. But before getting there, I note that many of the most common kinds of perfectionist rules should probably not be recognized as *law* at all. I say this because such rules are regularly ignored and inconsistently enforced. Despite the prevalence of rules against prostitution, gambling, narcotics, and the like, large numbers of people continue to dabble in them. And law enforcement often turns a blind eye to such behavior, at least when practiced in certain ways and places.[25] Where this is true, we have evidence that the government's perfectionist rules have not been absorbed into the customary legal order. In such cases, arguably, these rules are not really the law. Nevertheless, from this point forward, I give perfectionism the benefit of the doubt and assume that perfectionist rules can attain legal authorization. We focus on whether the law *rightly* authorizes perfectionist state action.

Is there evidence internal to the Noahic covenant that provides an answer? I conclude that three considerations, especially when taken cumulatively, make perfectionism an uncomfortable fit with the nature and purposes of the Noahic covenant.

First, the Noahic covenant takes a sober view of human sin: "the intention of man's heart is evil from his youth" (Gen 8:21). Any person holding

24. Among fairly recent, although different, perfectionist theories, see Raz, *The Morality of Freedom*; Robert P. George, *Making Men Moral: Civil Liberties and Public Morality* (Oxford: Clarendon, 1993); and Cathleen Kaveny, *Law's Virtues: Fostering Autonomy and Solidarity in American Society* (Washington, DC: Georgetown University Press, 2012).

25. Cf. Lon L. Fuller, *The Principles of Social Order: Selected Essays of Lon L Fuller*, ed. Kenneth I. Winston, rev. ed. (1981; Oxford: Hart, 2001), 252–53.

government office suffers from exactly the same sinful corruption as everybody else, and history and experience show that having power often has a harmful effect on moral character. Power tends to corrupt. Thus, when the Noahic covenant acknowledges a legitimate use of coercion (Gen 9:6), it makes sense to interpret this as *limiting* coercion to the kind of case it mentions (that is, to protecting against violence). Second, the purposes of the Noahic covenant are important but narrow. God promises merely to preserve the world and human society, not to redeem them or bring them to eschatological glory. Accordingly, the Noahic covenant, while not morally neutral, prescribes only modest social obligations: be fruitful and multiply (9:1, 7), eat plants and animals responsibly (9:3–4), and administer justice (9:5–6).[26] Thus government attempts to shape people's moral character arguably depend upon a richer moral vision and more grand goals than the Noahic covenant provides. And third, the Noahic covenant authorizes political communities that do not exclude or marginalize people for holding minority views about religion or the deepest issues of life, as argued in chapter 7. Yet matters of moral character are intimately connected with religion and other deeply held convictions. This provides reason to doubt that the Noahic covenant authorizes government *both* to protect a society's pluralistic character *and* to promote directly the personal moral improvement of its members.[27]

These three considerations suggest a lack of fit between the Noahic covenant and a perfectionist government, although they are not conclusive evidence. We might well wonder whether the broader biblical context strengthens or weakens the case for this conclusion. We first consider the immediate canonical context: the larger story of Genesis 6–9.

Prior to the post-flood Noahic covenant, Genesis recounts the story of the great flood itself (6:14–8:20). Genesis 6:1–13 describes the wickedness of the world and how God decided to destroy the earth because of it. These verses state God's rationale twice. The second time, God sees that the earth is "corrupt" and "filled with violence" (6:11–12), and thus he says to Noah, "I have determined to make an end of all flesh, for the earth is filled with violence through them" (6:13).

---

26. Some writers treat antiperfectionism as if it rests largely on a commitment to government's moral neutrality on the good life; e.g., see Raz, *The Morality of Freedom*, 110. For reasons explained in chapter 1, I do not believe governments are morally neutral.

27. See Nicholas Wolterstorff, *The Mighty and the Almighty: An Essay in Political Theology* (Cambridge: Cambridge University Press, 2012), 123, for observations that helpfully reinforce this point. As discussed below, Raz tries to develop a perfectionist theory compatible with moral pluralism; see his summary in *The Morality of Freedom*, 161.

The preceding verses explain what led to this verdict (6:1–7). The text states, "The sons of God saw that the daughters of man were attractive. And they took as their wives any they chose" (6:2). Shortly thereafter it adds, "The Nephilim were on the earth in those days, and also afterward, when the sons of God came in to the daughters of man and they bore children to them. These were the mighty men who were of old, the men of renown" (6:4). Biblical interpreters have often taken these mysterious statements to refer to angelic beings copulating with human women and producing prodigious offspring. But while the phrase "sons of God" does refer to angels in some biblical texts, it is unlikely here. Calling attention to angelic sin serves little point in a text meant to establish why God would judge the *human* race, and Scripture nowhere else mentions the strange idea of angel-human procreation.[28] More likely is that the "sons of God" are kings who promiscuously took wives from the human community, perhaps to amass harems. Others have defended this view effectively. It reflects both the ancient Near Eastern idea that kings are divine sons and the common biblical association of divine sonship with the exercise of royal authority.[29] Crucial for present purposes is that the violence and corruption God saw on earth, which provoked the great flood, was, in an important part, *governmental* in nature. Kings abused their positions of power by taking whichever women they wanted. David Novak describes it bluntly: it was "politically sanctioned rape."[30]

The statement about the "Nephilim" may confirm this. Genesis 6:4 does not say that these enigmatic Nephilim were the offspring of the sons of God and daughters of man but that they were on the earth in those days and later as well (cf. Num 13:33).[31] That is, kings were illicitly taking whichever women they wanted for wives at the same time as the Nephilim were roaming the earth. By describing the Nephilim as "mighty men" and as (literally) "men of name," the text suggests that they were arrogant military warriors.[32]

---

28. Rita F. Cefalu summarizes objections to this view in "Royal Priestly Heirs to the Restoration Promise of Genesis 3:15: A Biblical Theological Perspective on the Sons of God in Genesis 6," *Westminster Theological Journal* 76 (2014): 354–56. For a recent defense of the angelic view, see Jeffrey J. Niehaus, *Biblical Theology*, vol. 1, *The Common Grace Covenants* (Wooster, OH: Weaver, 2014), 164–73. A large study of this issue was published just as I was finishing editing this book: Jaap Doedens, *The Sons of God in Genesis 6:1–4: Analysis and History of Exegesis* (Leiden: Brill, 2019).

29. For further argument see Cefalu, "Royal Priestly Heirs," 356–67; David Novak, *Natural Law in Judaism* (Cambridge: Cambridge University Press, 1997), 36–37; and Meredith G. Kline, "Divine Kingship and Genesis 6:1–4," *Westminster Theological Journal* 24 (1962): 187–204.

30. Novak, *Natural Law in Judaism*, 36.

31. As argued in Cefalu, "Royal Priestly Heirs," 359–60.

32. Elsewhere in the Old Testament, the Hebrew term here translated "mighty men" often indicates strength and heroism in battle. Being "men of name" suggests *arrogance* especially in light of

Thus, again, the violence upon earth was, in an important part, governmental—or *state-sponsored*, to speak anachronistically.

In light of this context, we ask which is more likely: that Genesis 9:5–6 intends to set a boundary upon the lawful exercise of coercion (that is, limiting it to protectionist functions) or to give one example among many possible lawful exercises of coercion (perhaps including perfectionist functions)? The former is considerably more likely. Violence provoked the great flood, and the Noahic covenant addressed that problem of violence (Gen 9:5–6). But kings and military warriors were the chief perpetrators of violence before the flood. For the Noahic covenant to constrain human violence effectively, *limiting government power* had to be a primary concern. Therefore, it makes good sense for Genesis 9:6 to put boundaries on use of the sword. This implies that government officials should use physical coercion only for protectionist purposes. In contrast, it would be counterproductive for Genesis 9:6 to give one example among many legitimate occasions for coercive force.

Evidence from the rest of Scripture fortifies the preceding reasons to doubt the legitimacy of perfectionist government.[33] One relevant set of Old Testament texts are those addressed to (or about) the gentile nations surrounding Israel. As discussed in chapters 1 and 3, many prophets spoke of the rulers of these nations as servants of God who possessed legitimate authority. The prophets often condemned these nations and their rulers for hubris and unjust violence.[34] Yet no prophet judged them for failure to perform perfectionist functions. Thus the Old Testament prophets, if anything, confirm rather than rebut the picture presented in the Noahic covenant.

New Testament evidence points to a similar conclusion. A number of texts ascribe lawful authority to civil magistrates as servants of God and instruct Christians to honor and submit to them (e.g., Matt 22:15–22; Rom 13:1–7; 1 Tim 2:1–2; Tit 3:1; 1 Pet 2:13–17). But the New Testament never teaches that these magistrates ought to pursue a perfectionist project.

It may help to revisit Romans 13:1–7, since it presents the New Testament's most positive picture of government authority. If the New Testament has

---

the subsequent description of the tower-builders in Babel as those proudly wishing to "make a name" for themselves (Gen 11:4). Genesis 10:8–12 identifies Nimrod as a "mighty man" and the founder of many cities, including Babel in the land of Shinar. Scripture describes Babylon, the great city later to rise in Shinar, as brimming with arrogance (e.g., Isa 13:19; 14:12–17; Dan 4:28–30). All of this confirms the link I posit between arrogance and government-military might.

33. The Mosaic law obviously had perfectionist provisions, but chapter 3 explained why the Mosaic law does not define the proper functions for governments of common political communities.

34. See David VanDrunen, *Divine Covenants and Moral Order: A Biblical Theology of Natural Law* (Grand Rapids: Eerdmans, 2014), ch. 4.

a perfectionist streak, this is the most likely place to find it. Romans 13 speaks clearly of government's protectionist responsibilities. I see one possible argument that it also refers to perfectionist responsibilities: its statement that magistrates praise those who do "good" and punish those who do "wrong" (13:3–4). Does this envision magistrates with the authority to shape moral character?

It is unlikely. The reference to government praising those who do "good" is somewhat enigmatic, but evidence suggests that Paul was referring to Roman officials who honored wealthy public benefactors,[35] not to the promotion of community virtue. Likewise, Paul's statement about magistrates punishing the one who does "wrong" does not refer to the suppression of vice. Paul's precise claim is that the magistrate is an *"avenger* unto *wrath* for the one who does *evil"* (my translation).[36] With this terminology, as argued in chapter 9, Paul alludes back to the immediately preceding verses, Romans 12:17–21. He indicates that what Christians (at least in their private capacity) ought not to do, government officials should do: exercise the principle of *lex talionis*. And the *lex talionis* is precisely what Genesis 9:6 prescribes as just response to intrahuman violence. Thus the "wrong" ("evil") of 13:4 probably refers only to wrongs done to other people in violation of their natural rights.

Rather than add something to the protectionist responsibilities described in the Noahic covenant, therefore, Romans 13:1–7 simply echoes them. To bolster this conclusion, we might step back for a moment and ask: Would Paul, given all his knowledge and experience with Roman government, *really* have envisioned them as nurses of virtue, even of *Christians'* virtue? I find it difficult to disagree with Nicholas Wolterstorff's conclusion: "Not a chance."[37] Thus I conclude that New Testament teaching about civil government, like that of the Old Testament prophets, is consistent with the nonperfectionist tenor of the Noahic covenant.

Yet one might still wonder whether any broader moral-theological considerations tip the scales in the other direction. To test this possibility, I consider a few points that Cathleen Kaveny raises in her moral-theological defense of a modest perfectionism.[38] In general, I concur with the moral con-

---

35. See Bruce W. Winter, "The Public Honouring of Christian Benefactors: Romans 13.3–4 and 1 Peter 2.14–15," *Journal for the Study of the New Testament* 34 (1988): 87–103.

36. To clarify, the same Greek word is used in 12:17 and 13:4, although the English translation I am using has "evil" in 12:17 and "wrong" in 13:4.

37. Wolterstorff, *The Mighty and the Almighty*, 118.

38. In this work, *Law's Virtues*, Kaveny uses the terms *law as moral teacher* and *law as police officer* to represent, respectively, perfectionist and protectionist approaches.

cerns underlying her critiques of a strict protectionism, but I do not think they weigh against the arguments above.

One of Kaveny's objections against protectionism is that its view of freedom is individualistic.[39] This charge is *possibly* true against the position of Joel Feinberg (Kaveny's chief protectionist interlocutor) but it is not *necessarily* true of every protectionist theory.[40] The Noahic covenant does not deal with human beings merely as individuals. God established the covenant with the human race corporately, and the covenant's first and last requirement is to be fruitful and multiply. Genesis 9:6 surely calls for protection not only of individuals but also of families and other human associations. If a protectionist government defends such associations, charges of individualism cannot really stick.

Kaveny also critiques protectionism for resting upon a subjectivist view of value.[41] This may well be a fair critique of Feinberg, but it is clearly not true of the arguments above. The Noahic covenant authorizes protection of human beings made in the image of God, and God has commissioned image-bearers to serve him and their fellow creatures. Protection from unjust coercion thus protects image-bearers from those who hinder them from using their skills and resources to fulfill that calling. Of course, such protection often means protecting people in their poor pursuit of this calling. But it is not fair to assume that the law endorses the evil conduct it permits.[42] Broadly speaking, the Noahic covenant indicates that government should have a high view of human life, a high view of family and child-rearing, and a respect for animals and the broader creation order. This is not a subjectivist view of value.

A third concern of Kaveny is that human law inevitably communicates a moral vision. It "communicates something to its subjects about the ways in which they should and should not go about living their lives." Perfectionism

---

39. Kaveny, *Law's Virtues*, 22. Cf. Raz, *The Morality of Freedom*, 18.

40. Kaveny speaks of Joel Feinberg's individualism in *Law's Virtues*, 27. Yet Feinberg goes out of his way to deny individualism. He says that "the most significant truth about ourselves" is "that we are social animals"; see *The Moral Limits of the Criminal Law*, 4 vols. (New York: Oxford University Press, 1984–88), 3:46. Later he speaks of "the central and indispensable importance of community in human lives" (4:81; cf. 4:84). And see all of ch. 29A.

41. Kaveny, *Law's Virtues*, 19.

42. Kaveny draws often upon Thomas Aquinas's claim in *Summa Theologiae* 1a2ae 95.3, following Isidore of Seville, that law should be "virtuous, just, possible to nature, according to the custom of the country, suitable to place and time, necessary, useful," and so on. This translation is from *Summa Theologica*, 5 vols., trans. Fathers of the English Dominican Province (Allen, TX: Christian Classics, 1981). Thomas thus thought that law should not punish many things that are sinful. But he clearly did not think that permission entailed endorsement. See also his discussion of why human law does not repress all vices, in *Summa Theologiae* 1a2ae 96.2.

"recognizes, emphasizes and takes responsibility" for this fact.[43] But she says protectionism fails to take this seriously, since it wants law to function only negatively and does not inculcate a positive vision.[44] Kaveny is surely correct to say that law and governments inevitably communicate something about how people ought to live. But it is not true that protectionism fails to point to any positive social vision. Insofar as a protectionist government administers justice in cases of intrahuman wrongs, it communicates that members of a community ought to uphold justice in their mutual relations and thus that they should live together and collaborate peacefully, as far as possible, whatever their religion, ethnicity, or geographical origin.[45] That is a positive—albeit modest—moral vision that can hardly be taken for granted in most of the world today.

Looking beyond the field of Christian moral theology, we might also consider the perfectionist proposal of political philosopher Joseph Raz, especially since he presents it as consistent with a pluralistic society. Raz argues that each person's autonomy is morally valuable and, to be exercised, requires legitimate life choices among *good* options. The government, Raz claims, ought to ensure access to these opportunities where they are lacking.[46] By doing so, the government "promotes morality," even though it should not try to force people to make good decisions.[47] From a Christian perspective, Raz's emphasis upon "autonomy" has a troubling feel: human beings should never seek to be a law to themselves but are always under the law of God—under the natural law, if nothing else. But if we repackage Raz's proposal by envisioning *image-bearing* human beings instead of *autonomous* human beings, it becomes more plausible. As image-bearers, all people are responsible before God and have a rightful share in the general human rule of this world. The more good life choices people have, to use Raz's terms, the more meaningful and responsible their contribution to fulfilling the Noahic commission can be. With this modification, is a Raz-like perfectionist proposal compelling?

I am not persuaded. For one thing, Raz's argument depends upon his belief that the perfectionist measures he advocates involve no resort to

---

43. Kaveny, *Law's Virtues*, 28; cf. 17, 77.

44. Kaveny, *Law's Virtues*, 19, 77.

45. Cf. Feinberg, *The Moral Limits of the Criminal Law*, 4:100.

46. See Raz, *The Morality of Law*, 204–5, 265, and part 5. Richard H. Thaler's and Cass R. Sunstein's perfectionist vision seems similar to the spirit of Raz's, although in less heavy theoretical garb; see *Nudge: Improving Decisions about Health, Wealth, and Happiness*, rev. ed. (New York: Penguin, 2009). Like Raz, Thaler and Sunstein exalt each individual's free choice but think *good* choice is important and part of government's concern.

47. Raz, *The Morality of Law*, 415.

coercion.[48] But this is not really the case. True, Raz does not wish government to coerce the individual into making particular decisions but simply to ensure a slate of good options. But even ensuring good options requires decisive government action. This at least requires tax revenue, garnered from workers and investors under threat of coercion. Perhaps such coercion can be justified, but to claim that a government can achieve Raz's perfectionist policies without coercion is misleading.

A second concern relates to Raz's assumptions about the availability of options for good life choices. Do we need government to ensure such options? A market economy encourages and coordinates the innovative creativity of image-bearers under the rule of law. This should generate plenty of good opportunities for members of the human community to test their various aptitudes, develop their skills, and strike out on entrepreneurial paths. The idea that government would imagine and create excellent opportunities that no one in a vibrant market economy would have thought of seems unlikely. (And when government tries to do so, it drains resources from private actors better suited for the task). What is plausible, however, is that certain members of society may need financial or other kind of help in order to avail themselves of the ample opportunities an entrepreneurial economy will afford. With respect to both of these points, therefore, the real question is whether governments have legitimate authority to provide some sort of relief to the needy. But that issue belongs to the discussion below on *service-provision* functions and is not really a question about perfectionism.

I offer no theoretically conclusive argument against perfectionism. But in light of these various considerations, I conclude that a perfectionist vision of government is an uncomfortable fit with an understanding of political community grounded in the Noahic covenant. I now close this section with two final comments.

First, the discussion above need not imply that state action has no effect on people's character (an unlikely proposition) or that the state should have no concern about it at all. A protectionist government, which effectively defends people's natural rights, provides a sort of training that steers community members toward respecting other people's life, property, and reputation. And a just government presumably *desires* this, since no government is able to preserve order and justice when community members do not respect others'

---

48. Raz thus thinks it is consistent with the so-called "harm principle," a common feature of liberal theories like his own; see *The Morality of Freedom*, 420.

rights most of the time. Furthermore, government protection of natural rights helps to secure the conditions in which community members can voluntarily form institutions and pursue activities well-suited to achieving a more richly substantive virtuous life—that is, the kind of life the Noahic covenant suggests we should not entrust to government supervision.[49]

Second, while it may be relatively easy to dismiss government attempts to turn people into saints, its attempts to keep people from the most self-destructive kinds of behavior are considerably more attractive. The disturbing opioid crisis currently gripping segments of the United States provides a poignant example. Undoubtedly, many nonperfectionists are uncomfortable with the state sitting by indifferently while heroin addicts destroy themselves and damage their families and communities. The increasingly familiar stories about small children abandoned in cars and houses next to their overdosed parents starkly illustrate how seemingly private vices can cause grave harm to others. Even if government does not have rightful authority to shape the character of the drug user per se, it does have responsibility to protect people from others' harmful conduct. This arguably gives government a kind of preemptive jurisdiction over access to substances by which people regularly devastate the lives of others. Of course, the American experiment with Prohibition and its more recent war on drugs have had manifold failures. Such failures provide a sobering reminder that government attempts to control what people ingest often create unforeseen problems that make communities worse off than otherwise. Private, voluntary initiatives to help addicts can explore innovative solutions and probe underlying spiritual issues in ways governments cannot and should not. They are surely preferable where possible.

The Noahic covenant cannot answer these questions precisely, but provides a framework for thinking about them in theologically sound ways. The Noahic covenant does not dictate whether and to what extent government should regulate narcotics, for example, but it does suggest that we should evaluate the options on protectionist rather than perfectionist grounds.

Service-Provision

We now come to the last of the three categories of government action: the provision of services. I assume again that any legitimate government action must have legal authorization. The question before us is whether service-providing functions are the sort of thing that the law *properly*

---

49. Cf. Porter, *Ministers of the Law*, 140–41.

authorizes government to do. Does the Noahic covenant provide any guide for reflection?

I begin with two preliminary points. First, since governments can potentially provide such a great number of services, it may be helpful to make some distinctions. One distinction is between "nonexcludable" public goods (such as a lighthouse) and goods that private individuals and institutions can easily provide (such as garbage removal).[50] Another distinction is between services that entail controversial decisions about deep moral issues (such as education and health care) and those that may not (such as a public swimming pool). There is no bright line demarcating the categories in each case, especially since *anything* is potentially controversial. But this offers a rough way to identify some important differences in potential government activity. These distinctions will facilitate the analysis below.

The second preliminary point revisits my (controversial) claim in chapter 9 that natural rights exist but take only negative form, that is, as rights not to be harmed by others. Natural rights do not take positive form: no one has a natural right to have others provide her with particular goods and services, such as garbage removal, a university education, or well-paved roads.[51] Thus I will not try to answer the question before us by appeal to natural rights. But chapter 9 also noted that this does not mean governments should *not* provide goods and services. There may be other legitimate grounds for this.[52]

With these preliminary matters in hand, we may now consider government service provision through the lens of the Noahic covenant. Genesis 8:21–9:17 obviously provides no direct authorization for anyone to provide services for the community with the backing of coercive force. Thus, as with our study of perfectionism, we have to widen our scope of analysis and inquire whether any features of the Noahic covenant provide indirect insights. Let us reconsider a few of its features.

---

50. By nonexcludable public goods, I refer to goods that are widely desired and which, once available, are accessible to all people in the community. Because it is difficult or impossible to exclude anyone from using such goods, it is uncertain how a private party would provide them when there is no way to ensure that those who benefit from them will contribute to their cost.

51. As noted in chapter 9, the case of children with respect to their parents is likely an important exception.

52. This way of thinking about things differs from Wolterstorff's in *The Mighty and the Almighty*, 90–91. There he moves quickly, with little analysis, from the idea of government as a rights-protecting and injustice-curbing institution (with which I agree) to the idea that governments ought to provide welfare benefits to the poor as a matter of protecting their rights and correcting injustice. Helping the poor is a great good, of course. But because I do not believe that the idea of positive welfare rights is compelling or even coherent, I cannot come to such an easy answer about whether government is properly authorized to pursue this good.

First, all human beings are sinners, including government officials, who face special temptations that accompany power. For many government-provided services, this creates no special problem. For example, the reality of universal human depravity hardly determines whether a government agency or private company should pick up the garbage. But the fact that all are sinners should make us wary of concentrating a great deal of coercion-backed power in any small group of hands. Thus keeping service-provision dispersed among many private hands seems generally preferable to entrusting many services to government hands.[53]

The Noahic covenant also prescribes that political communities should welcome all peaceful people and not exclude anyone on the basis of religious profession or philosophy of life. State programs, therefore, should operate accordingly. The pluralistic character of a community creates no special problem in the case of government services that can operate largely without exposing people's differences in the deepest and most meaningful areas of life. But it becomes a problem when government services expose these differences. Developing health care policies and educational curricula, for example, requires choices on weighty religious and philosophical issues about which people adamantly disagree. Insofar as government offers such services and has to make such choices, it privileges some members of the community on religious-philosophical grounds and alienates others to the detriment of the pluralism it ought to protect.[54]

A final feature of the Noahic covenant relevant here is its implicit

---

53. A related issue is whether, on similar theological grounds, it might be well-advised for government to take control over some services to prevent too much economic and social power from accumulating in too few private hands. In other words, perhaps the government needs to take up a sufficient number of responsibilities to counterbalance the power of nonstate elites. This has a theoretical plausibility, although it seems unlikely that, in a free-market, enterprise economy in which the law protects natural rights (along the lines chapters 8–9 suggest), a small group of people without recourse to special government favors will be able to accumulate a significant percentage of economic power in a sizable political community, at least over time. In addition, it seems naïve to trust state officials to provide a just and non-self-interested counterbalance to private elites. What seems more likely is that state elites will collude with nonstate elites to create genuinely dangerous and unjust concentrations of economic and political power—that is, various versions of the crony capitalism that flourish around the globe. On this latter point, cf. Gary Chartier, *Anarchy and Social Order: Law and Politics for a Stateless Society* (Cambridge: Cambridge University Press, 2013), 227–28.

54. In part 1, I suggested that a political theology grounded in the Noahic covenant provides support for a notion of the "common good," but only a modest one. The present discussion reinforces the importance of that point. When discussing government service provision, a number of writers appeal to the "common good" in ways that, in my judgment, overestimate the ability of government officials to identify it and/or fail to reckon with how controversial identifying it can be within a political community. E.g., see Simon, *General Theory*, 145–47; Simon, *Philosophy of Democratic Government*, 5; and Klosko, *Political Obligations*, 111–15.

requirement that image-bearers pursue economic and technological development, to enable them to multiply and fill the earth. This may suggest that at
least some kinds of government services are authorized. The complex commission to fill the earth can advance largely spontaneously, that is, through
the free interaction of individuals and institutions. But some problems may
resist spontaneous resolution and thus require coordination from a central
authority. The distinction between "nonexcludable" public goods and goods
easily provided through private means is relevant here. Goods that are necessary for a community to carry out its Noahic commission and that are truly
nonexcludable seem to leave us no choice: if the state alone can provide goods
the community needs to fulfill God's calling, it must be proper for the law to
authorize the state to do so.

That said, how many genuinely nonexcludable public goods are there?[55]
Many breezy references to nonexcludable public goods seem to underestimate the generosity of wealthy benefactors and the ability of resourceful
entrepreneurs to discover ways to turn a profit by providing such goods. And
as technology advances, this ability will likely increase. Roads are a classic
nonexcludable public good and provide a fine example. The development of
electronic toll payment makes it increasingly easy to charge drivers for their
use of roads with minimal expenses for the payee and minimal inconvenience
for the payer. This makes private administration of roads more feasible and
viable (and arguably more just, in that those who do not use the roads are not
forced to pay for them).

To sum up the discussion thus far: The Noahic covenant does not directly
authorize the state to provide services, and several pieces of evidence suggest
that providing certain sorts of services runs at cross-purposes to the covenant.
But other kinds of services do not face the same objections, specifically, those
providing nonexcludable public goods that do not ordinarily expose differences on deep and controversial moral issues.

What insight does other biblical evidence add? The earlier consideration
of perfectionism observed that state-sponsored violence was a key reason why

55. This is an important question in light of some theories of political authority and obligation.
Among recent writers, Klosko's defense of political obligations relies especially on the indispensability
of many public goods whose provision depends on the government; see *Political Obligations*, ch. 2.
Unfortunately, his argument turns into a runaway train that places little constraint on government action
other than vague standards such as the "public interest," "fairness," what is "reasonable," democratic
decision-making, and cost-benefit concerns; see *Political Obligations*, 111–15. Some writers engage such
claims critically, noting both the highly subjective character of determining what is indispensable and
the unlikelihood that private actors will be unable to find ways to provide what is truly indispensable.
E.g., see Chartier, *Anarchy and Social Order*, ch. 3.

God judged the world through the great flood. This suggests that Genesis 9:6 should be read as a limitation on the authorized use of force. If anything, this adds another reason to be generally wary about ambitious, service-providing government programs.

Discussion of government officials and actions elsewhere in Scripture provides no reason to modify this general perspective. The Old Testament speaks of rulers who provided services of a sort, but none of them seems to be exemplary. The most attractive example is perhaps the Pharaoh who oversaw a massive welfare program to preserve Egypt through seven years of famine. But this can hardly be a model, since the program depended on God's special revelation of future events to Joseph, knowledge unavailable to government officials today. Also, the Egyptian people sold their livestock, land, and themselves to Pharaoh through the program (Gen 47:13–26)—a form of slavery hardly ideal for those bearing God's image. Nebuchadnezzar claimed to have built much of Babylon, but God condemned him for his hubris (Dan 4:30–33). Ahasuerus gave great parties for his people (Esth 1:3–8), but this ended in a drunken debacle of injustice (Esth 1:10–22). Such texts provide no models for contemporary governments, although they may offer warning about abuse of welfare and public-works projects.

The New Testament adds little to this. The most detailed text concerning government, Romans 13:1–7, states that God has authorized its protectionist efforts but is silent on service-provision. Again, this silence does not prove that governments should only pursue protectionist functions. I simply observe once again that although the Roman government did many things, Paul only speaks of one of them as divinely authorized.[56]

Do any broader moral-theological considerations provide insight? I suggest two. First, most services that governments commonly provide relate in some way to the Noahic-covenantal responsibility for the human community to provide for its material needs, to develop technology, and to fill the earth. Chapter 8 concluded that a market economy promotes these purposes. Such an economy is obviously compatible with some provision of government services.

---

56. Wolterstorff's reasoning in *The Mighty and the Almighty*, 98–99 is curious to me. He writes that although Paul is silent about states doing things that are not strictly required in justice, such as building roads, nothing Paul says implies that such activity is wrong, and he suspects Paul would have no problem with it. Yet Wolterstorff finds Paul's silence about state perfectionist responsibilities highly significant. Why exactly is Paul's silence so significant for perfectionism but basically irrelevant for service provision? I suspect other political-theological reasons drive Wolterstorff's conclusions here. Other considerations *are* necessary to fill in the silences of Romans 13, but I doubt that different conclusions should be drawn about perfectionism and service provision from the silence itself.

But I observed that free, noncoerced human interaction in the marketplace is especially effective in promoting industriousness, resourcefulness, and innovation for the general benefit of the human race and broader created order. If that is true, it indicates that providing important goods and services is best left to private means where possible. In real life, government agencies are notorious for their inefficiencies and failures. Americans are rarely impressed by the customer service at the Department of Motor Vehicles. Customer service at private companies is not always stellar, but when people in a market economy are displeased with their experience at a grocery store or restaurant, they can find another one. Removed from the discipline of the competitive market and the knowledge it provides about customer preferences, government-run services naturally sag in quality. Governments even struggle to win trust and satisfaction for performing the *protectionist* tasks it is most clearly authorized to carry out. For example, there is no more quintessential government work than running a police department. Yet in the contemporary United States, accusations of unfairness and racial bias against the police proliferate in poor minority neighborhoods, while many middle- and upper-class people move into gated communities, buy guns, and install home-security systems.[57] When possible, people often prefer to pay a bit out of the pocket for security services of their choice than to rely completely on what the government provides through tax revenue. Even those who have relative confidence in the state-run police like to have a backup plan.

This confirms the initial conclusion that there are good reasons to be wary of ambitious government programs to provide services, and that the most defensible programs are those that provide genuinely nonexcludable public goods without compromising the pluralism that ought to be honored in political communities.

A second relevant moral-theological consideration concerns the old slogan: the rule of law, not of men. This means making political institutions, offices, and activities perpetually accountable to the law (the customary legal order). Another way to say it is that communities ought to keep "politics" as limited as reasonably possible. To the extent that everything is "politicized" we lose the rule of law. Whatever is politicized is made subject to the coercive power of the majority, or even a clever and powerful minority. Where everything is politicized, people have motivation to try to improve their lot

---

57. Cf. Sean McFate, *The Modern Mercenary: Private Armies and What They Mean for World Order* (New York: Oxford University Press, 2014), 45–46, on why private military companies are better than state militaries in many respects.

by coercion rather than cooperation. They form factions and lobbies to secure the state services they want, funded by other people's taxes—if not from their own bad motives, at least to protect themselves against other people's. The rule of law demands keeping important activities away from the clutches of politics and the social divisiveness it fosters.[58] This also gives reason to be wary about expansive state service-provision programs.

An important, lingering moral issue is what all of this has to do with the poor. As noted in chapter 8, the maturing and expansion of market economies over the past few hundred years has raised billions of human beings from horrible poverty to previously unimaginable material wealth. Introducing a vibrant market economy under the rule of law to societies that still lack one would soon enrich most of those who remain destitute. This should surely be a high priority of global efforts to reduce and then end true poverty. Nevertheless, there are still relatively (if not absolutely) poor people in market economies. And thus there remains reason to be concerned about the plight of those who lack the resources to avail themselves of the services and opportunities that such an economy produces.

Under these conditions, might the law properly authorize the state to run a welfare system of some sort? The political framework of the Noahic covenant provides no final answer. We have considered how this covenant extends to all people universally, acknowledges all people as the image of God and thus as inherently dignified, and commends benevolence and kindness from all toward their neighbors, particularly the poor.[59] It is clear that governments authorized under the Noahic covenant ought to protect the poor zealously from those who violate their natural rights through rape, battery, theft, and the like, as most governments historically have failed to do. This would help the poor immeasurably. But in light of discussion above, there seems good reason to keep charity toward the poor in private hands as much as possible. Given the industriousness and creativity fostered by free interaction in a market economy, private endeavors to help the poor are likely to be more robust, efficient, and innovative than programs run through a government bureaucracy. And the best help for the poor—that is, help which aims to get

---

58. For related reflections similar to mine, see Anthony de Jasay, *Before Resorting to Politics*, The Shaftesbury Papers, 5 (Cheltenham: Edward Elgar, 1996), 54–55; and Michael van Notten, *The Law of the Somalis: A Stable Foundation for Economic Development in the Horn of Africa*, ed. Spencer Heath MacCallum (Trenton, NJ: Red Sea, 2005), 6. For a very different perspective, see Porter, *Ministers of the Law*, 300–301. Porter lauds the "social service state" and associates it with *communities* in which people "deliberate together on matters of public concern as free individuals."

59. See also VanDrunen, *Divine Covenants*, 409.

them out of need and into a self-supporting existence, when possible—often requires dealing with deep moral and spiritual issues, which government programs are poorly equipped to handle.

Even so, given the universal reach and concern of the Noahic covenant, it is plausible that a community's law could rightly authorize government to extend relief to the needy who stand outside the reach of other assistance. Yet the larger argument of the chapter suggests that this stands on the outskirts of legitimate state authority. Unfortunately, state welfare programs tend to create disincentives for private charity, give societies more of what they subsidize, and be difficult to curtail once instituted. Thus there is danger that such programs will tend to drift away from the outskirts and consume increasing government attention.[60]

CIVIL RESISTANCE

To this point in the chapter, I have defended the general legitimacy of government authority as grounded in legal authority and have explored how far that legitimate authority might extend in particular areas. These discussions provoke weighty questions I have postponed until now. Governments have legitimate authority but often abuse it. Laws and governments can wreak injustice rather than promote justice. Under what circumstances should justice-loving people disobey their state authorities or offer other resistance to their rule?

Civil resistance has been a contested issue in the history of the Christian church. Opinion was divided in the early years of my own Reformed tradition. One of its prominent figures, John Calvin, held a famously strict view of people's obligation to submit to government authorities.[61] Calvin recognized only two narrow exceptions: a person should disobey if a magistrate commands her to disobey God's law and a lesser magistrate should resist a tyrannical higher magistrate if his constitutional responsibility requires him to do so.[62] In contrast, several of Calvin's fellow French Reformed leaders promoted a much broader conception of legitimate resistance to tyrants. They appealed to ancient constitutional rights, covenants between ruler and ruled, and the like.[63]

---

60. Illustrated in detail in John F. Cogan, *The High Cost of Good Intentions: A History of U.S. Federal Entitlement Programs* (Stanford: Stanford University Press, 2017). "The book's central theme is that the creation of entitlements brings forth relentless forces that cause them to inexorably expand" (4).

61. John Calvin argued that although magistrates should rule justly, people ought to submit even to tyrants who do horrible things; see *Institutes of the Christian Religion*, 4.20.24–29.

62. Calvin, *Institutes*, 4.20.31–32.

63. For translations of the most important of these works, see Theodore Beza, *Concerning the Rights*

My own sentiments run much closer to the views of the latter. But despite the differences, a common thread unites the thought of these sixteenth-century Reformed writers: they all appealed to some law that was more fundamental than the command of the magistrate and believed that this law could justify resistance to government authority. I share this view, and think it is crucial to a theologically sound approach to civil resistance. Accordingly, the account of resistance developed below builds on the understanding of law defended in chapter 10. And this entails reflecting on resistance through the familiar lens of the Noahic covenant.

Romans 13, the Noahic Covenant, and the Rule of Law

Romans 13:1–7 obviously raises acute questions about the obligation to submit to civil authorities and the right and/or responsibility to resist them. At first read, the obligation to obey sounds absolute. Paul says that everyone should be subject to the governing authorities, that whoever resists them resists God, that obedience should flow both from fear of their sword and for sake of conscience, and that magistrates are servants and ministers of God. Paul mentions no exceptions. But it is impossible not to wonder about this. According to Paul, magistrates are a terror to evildoers, approve of those who do good, and bring God's wrath on the wicked. Yet Paul knew that many government officials act in just the opposite way. Did he intend to say that people should be subject even to magistrates who do not fit his description of them?

Some scholars answer no, pointing to evidence internal to Romans 13:1–7. Stanley Porter, for example, argues that Paul only requires obedience to just magistrates. A key part of his argument is that Paul refers to magistrates not as "higher" or "governing" authorities (13:1), as often translated in English, but as those who are *better*, that is, morally superior.[64] But Porter's translation of the Greek term, though theoretically possible, is contextually unlikely. If, in the first clause of Romans 13:1, Paul meant to tell the Roman Christians to submit only to morally superior magistrates, it is strange that he says, in the

---

of Rulers over Their Subjects and the Duty of Subjects towards Their Rulers, trans. Henri-Louis Gonin, ed. A. H. Murray (Cape Town: H.A.U.M., 1956); Stephanus Junius Brutus, *Vindiciae, contra Tyrannos: or, Concerning the Legitimate Power of a Prince over the People, and of the People over a Prince*, trans. and ed. George Garnett (Cambridge: Cambridge University Press, 1994); and François Hotman, *Francogallia*, ed. Ralph E. Giesey and J. H. M. Salmon, trans. J. H. M. Salmon (Cambridge: Cambridge University Press, 1972).

64. Stanley E. Porter, "Romans 13:1–7 as Pauline Political Rhetoric," *Filologia Neotestamentaria* 3, no. 6 (1990): 123–25.

very next clause, that they should do so because God has ordained *all* magistrates: "For there is no authority except from God, and those that exist have been instituted by God" (13:1). Furthermore, 1 Peter 2:13–14, when giving instructions similar to Romans 13:1–7, uses the same Greek word at issue to describe the emperor, but in a way indicating status rather than moral excellence (which is understandable, since it was likely referring to Nero).[65]

Wolterstorff arrives at a conclusion similar to Porter's but by different means. He argues that interpreters of Romans have too often taken 13:1 on its own and treated it as the controlling statement for the larger text. Instead, the key is 13:4–5, which amplifies what Paul writes in earlier verses. Paul does not mean to say that whichever magistrates are in power have their position because God has placed them there. Rather, Paul says that God appoints magistrates to do justice—whichever magistrates are in power, however they got there. Hence, officials who promote injustice act outside of their divine authorization and people have no obligation to submit under these circumstances.[66] Wolterstorff's case is stronger than Porter's, I believe. Romans 13:4–5 does emphasize that God has commissioned magistrates for a purpose: to enforce justice. Officials that commit injustice indeed act outside of their divine authorization. Nevertheless, Wolterstorff somewhat overstates his case. The text does not say that God has appointed magistrates (who happen to exist) to do justice, but that God has *both* appointed magistrates *and* commissioned them to do justice. According to Paul, all existing magistrates are divinely appointed. The text indicates that it is a travesty when civil officials perpetrate injustice, but it says nothing to indicate that disobedience, resistance, or revolution is justified in such circumstances. If Romans 13 leaves a place for resistance, it is not because the text itself says so.

In short, Paul simply does not address whether there are exceptions to his general teaching in Romans 13:1–7. What he writes is just that: general. It is entirely plausible that there are exceptions. Many biblical texts give broad exhortations about a particular issue without mentioning exceptions, while other biblical texts provide exceptions for the very same issue.[67] Romans 13:1–7 could very well be the kind of text that gives a broad exhortation with-

---

65. This text describes the emperor as "supreme," in distinction from governors who are sent for the punishment of evildoers and praise of those doing good.

66. Wolterstorff, *The Mighty and the Almighty*, 92–95, 117.

67. For example, some texts simply prohibit killing, divorce, and work on the Sabbath; others provide nuance demonstrating that these prohibitions are not absolute. On killing, compare Exod 20:13 with Exod 21:15–17; on divorce, compare Mark 10:11–12 with Matt 19:9; and on the Sabbath, compare Exod 20:8–11 with Matt 12:9–13.

out mentioning exceptions that do exist. Thus we need to inquire whether other biblical texts provide helpful perspective.

If the authority of civil government is indeed rooted in the Noahic covenant, this provides a clue about the scope of Paul's exhortation in Romans 13. Chapter 4 noted many similarities between Romans 13:1–7 and Genesis 9:5–6 in its covenantal context. But one difference between these texts points to the limits of our obligation to government authority.

The difference is that in the Noahic covenant God delegates authority to the human race in general, while Romans 13:1–7 speaks of God delegating authority to civil magistrates in particular. The authority residing in the human race generally comes to vest in special ways in particular people who hold government office. That is, God originally delegated authority to the human community, and this community has rightly delegated some of that authority to civil magistrates. As argued previously, this delegation to magistrates does not supersede the original delegation from God to humanity. Romans 13 does not supersede the Noahic covenant. Just as God's delegation of authority to the human community does not eliminate God's ultimate authority, so a community's delegation of authority to government officials does not eliminate the community's higher authority. Thus the general human commission to enforce justice must continue to stand somewhere behind magistrates' specific commission to enforce justice. And this general human commission implies that *anyone* who sheds human blood ought to be held accountable, including government officials. Therefore, the human community as a whole must retain a right—even an obligation—to correct, resist, or remove magistrates who fail to promote justice according to their divine commission.

What does this mean in practice? The Noahic covenant hardly provides a detailed resolution. Determining whether and how to resist unjust government is not an exact science. But I offer some reflections on how my conclusions thus far might work out with respect to civil resistance.

In all other spheres of life, legitimate authority exists, but always within bounds. When those who hold positions of authority act outside those bounds, the obligation to obey them ceases. An employer has authority over employees with respect to their performance on the job but not over what they eat for dinner; an employee has no obligation to obey his boss's culinary orders. A teacher has authority over students with respect to classroom conduct and course requirements, but not over their choice of friends; a student has no obligation to obey a teacher's commands about her social life. There is no compelling reason to think that this dynamic is any different with respect to government authority. If the mayor of my town calls me this morning and orders me to pick up lunch and deliver it to his office at noon, I would have a good laugh and get back to work. He has legitimate authority over me, but not to do that sort of thing. I have no obligation to follow such orders.

I should pause to emphasize that I refer to *obligation* to obey authorities who act outside their jurisdictions. While there is no such obligation per se, there may be prudential reasons for obeying in some situations. I can laugh at my mayor if he commands me to deliver lunch to him because no one would enforce his command. But if I know the police would beat me if I refused, my decision would not be so simple. Since delivering lunch to someone is not inherently evil, I might obey to stay out of trouble. Christians, furthermore, have a distinctive calling to endure unjust treatment in circumstances in which there is no way out (e.g., 1 Pet 2:19–25; cf. 1 Cor 7:21).

To return to the main point and put things in terms of my argument above: Government agencies and officials have legitimate authority only within the bounds granted by the law (that is, the customary legal order), and the law has authority only within the bounds of the natural law (which is the law of God). Therefore, people may have to disobey or resist government action for the sake of honoring a higher authority, the law, and may have to disobey or resist the law for the sake of honoring a still higher authority, God's natural law.

I have just claimed that submission to the law is more basic than submission to government. This implies that in situations involving genuine conflict between the law and a mandate from the state, we owe our allegiance to the law, at least as a general rule. (I consider exceptions below.) This may seem to be a bold claim, so I suggest considering two test cases.

The first takes us back to the ranching community in Shasta County, California, mentioned in chapter 10. According to Robert Ellickson, the ranchers developed a rather elaborate set of unwritten rules that governed how they interacted with each other and resolved disputes about boundary fences, property damage, lost cattle, and the like. These rules were in many ways different from state statutes that ostensibly governed these matters but about which the ranchers (and often their attorneys!) were largely misinformed. What actually governed were their unwritten, spontaneously developed norms.[68] Thus a conscientious rancher moving into the area would face quite a pressing decision: should she obey these unwritten norms or the official state statutes?

---

68. See Robert C. Ellickson, *Order without Law: How Neighbors Settle Disputes* (Cambridge, MA: Harvard University Press, 1991), part 1.

My argument that legal authority is more fundamental than governmental authority indicates that this rancher ought to follow the unwritten norms. The unwritten norms are part of the customary legal order, and thus the norms, rather than the state statutes, are truly the law. I recognize that additional facts might create need for further analysis, but I am willing to follow the logic of this conclusion. That this conclusion is morally sound is reinforced by the fact that the new rancher's neighbors expect her to follow their unwritten norms. They have organized their lives and planned their futures around the expectation that these norms will govern the community. For her to follow the state statutes instead would be disruptive and unneighborly. By honoring legal authority over government authority, she will better promote the social collaboration necessary for fulfilling the Noahic commission.

A second test involves a more common matter: driving a car. Most drivers encounter circumstances in which the speed limit actually being observed on the road is considerably different from the posted limit. On a foggy night, for example, the pace of traffic may be well under what is posted, while on a clear day on an open road the pace is well above it. Should a conscientious driver persist in driving as though the state-posted speed limit is binding at all times? My earlier argument suggests not. The actual pace of traffic represents the customary legal order and hence is the law. This too is a morally sound conclusion, in my judgment. Under most road conditions with at least a moderate amount of traffic, the vast majority of cars spontaneously move within a relatively narrow range of speeds. Drivers expect other drivers to be moving within this range and gauge their actions—passing, braking, switching lanes—accordingly. Those who drive outside this range endanger the safety of their fellow drivers. Doing so is disruptive and unneighborly. Again, honoring the authority of the law over that of government decree better promotes social collaboration under the Noahic covenant.

Clarifying Legal Supremacy

The preceding discussion considered the general principle that people are obligated to obey the law rather than government when the two conflict. Below I will address situations in which the law is fundamentally unjust. Before doing so, I discuss two kinds of situations that clarify my claim about the supremacy of law.

The first situation is when a legally authorized legislature decides that it would be better for the law to be different from what it is and votes to change it accordingly. What then is the law? To what is a person obligated? The logic of my larger argument suggests that the legislative statute deserves deference. If the legislature itself is legally authorized, presumably it is authorized to do what it did. The legislature acted against a particular law but did so with the authority of law more broadly. Law needs to be able to change in some way, and legally authorizing a legislature is one way a community can try to accomplish this. Nevertheless, my larger argument also suggests that the broader community could veto such a statute by failing to incorporate it into its customary legal order over time, or it could effectively annul such a statute by desuetude as the customary legal order further evolves.

The second kind of situation is when an aspect of the law (as customary legal order) has developed without the genuinely free participation and consent of the whole community. For example, one part of the community may have intimidated another part into submitting to certain practices. The latter group thus gives the appearance of consent to these practices but in fact follows them out of fear. What if the legislature tries to overturn these practices, while the customary legal order remains resistant to change? I suggest that even if these practices are not substantively unjust, there is reason to think that the legislative act ought to trump the customary legal order. Chapter 10 argued that the customary legal order is the law, but essential to that argument was that the customary legal order coordinates a community's life by free, mutual, and consensual interaction.[69] The scenario I have just envisioned lacks this freedom, mutuality, and consent.[70] In such circumstances, we might conclude that we do not have *law* at all but a forcible imposition of will. A legally authorized legislature rightly seeks to remedy it.

When the Law Is Unjust

One type of situation still deserves attention: what about when the law is fundamentally unjust? In other terms, what about when the customary legal order runs counter to the natural law? What are the options and responsibilities for people in these circumstances?

---

69. Cf. Alexander M. Bickel, *The Morality of Consent* (New Haven: Yale University Press, 1975), 106–11.

70. I recognize that this point may invite a kind of endless deconstruction of one customary practice after another on the ground that social interaction always occurs among unequals and is an occasion for one to assert power over another. Logically, then, no custom really develops through true consent. But I am not looking for a practically unattainable and philosophically/theologically suspect ideal of completely autonomous individuals interacting and negotiating apart from any social context. As I have described it, people interact in the political community as members of a variety of institutions in which each individual bears a variety of relationships with others. We need to be able to distinguish these normal and legitimate circumstances from occasions of clear coercion and threat thereof, such as the segregation laws of the American South.

If the situation is such that the law requires an individual to do something in direct violation of the natural law (or of a requirement of Scripture), it is clear that she must disobey the law. The biblical precedent is unambiguous (e.g., Dan 3:16–18; 6:20; Acts 4:19–20; 5:29). To conclude otherwise is to honor human-made law over the divinely revealed natural law and ultimately to honor fellow human beings over God.

Even if a law does not require direct violation of natural law or Scripture, if it is fundamentally unjust it is surely good to seek to overturn it through lawful means. (I stop short of saying it is a moral *requirement* of all individuals, since time and opportunities are always limited, and no one person can pursue all goods.) It is difficult to say in theory what forms such lawful means should take. Legislators might seek to change it through the power the law authorizes them to exercise. Ordinary people can, if nothing else, exercise their powers of persuasion toward their children, their neighbors, or their coworkers in hope of shifting community opinion and thereby pushing the customary legal order in more just directions.

Matters get more complicated when attempts to overturn a fundamentally unjust law by legal means repeatedly fail. Does a point come at which people may or ought to resist it through unlawful means? Scholars and activists have developed technical terms and distinctions to describe different forms of opposition to unjust laws.[71] In what follows, I remain at a fairly general level of analysis without descending into some of the more technical details.

To begin, it is helpful to revisit the notion that legitimate authority does not extend beyond its proper jurisdiction, and obligation does not extend beyond the bounds of legitimate authority. In the case of the law, authority cannot extend to promoting what is unjust. Law properly emerges from the collaborative interaction of members of the human community pursuing the Noahic moral commission. Law coordinates their activities and specifies how to administer retributive and compensatory justice against those who wrong others. Unjust law hinders the tasks that law ought to promote, and thus the human community has no authorization to develop unjust laws. A person confronted with such a law has no obligation to obey it per se.[72]

---

71. For example, in much of the literature, "civil disobedience" has come to mean technically a nonviolent and public violation of the law as an act of protest, which accepts the punishment legally specified. E.g., see Martin Luther King Jr., "Letter from Birmingham City Jail," in *A Testament of Hope: The Essential Writings and Speeches of Martin Luther King Jr.*, ed. James M. Washington (New York: HarperCollins, 1986), 294; Childress, *Civil Disobedience*, 3; and Austin, *Up with Authority*, 140–41.

72. Cf. Thomas Aquinas, *Summa Theologiae* 1a2ae 96.4; and Finnis, *Natural Law and Natural Right*, 359–60.

But this cannot conclude the analysis. A law might be unjust because one aspect of it is unjust, yet it forms a part of a larger complex of just provisions that accomplish good things. No body of human law will be perfect. Thus it may well be the better part of wisdom and neighborly love to bear with some injustice for the sake of a greater good (without giving up on lawful means to remedy the injustice). Therefore, although an unjust law does not obligate per se, taking into account all relevant moral considerations may indicate that tolerating it is the best course of action.[73] At what point does an injustice become so harmful that unlawful resistance is justified or required? The political framework of the Noahic covenant cannot specify.

Is there a point at which a government becomes so corrupt, and redressing its injustices through lawful means so futile, that *revolution* is permissible or even required? Given the arguments thus far, I do not see why not. But those who find themselves tragically approaching this point should be alert to strong countervailing considerations that may counsel toleration of even very wicked regimes. Revolutions often bring no improvement. Overthrowing Batista may give you Castro. Overthrowing the Shah may give you Khomeini. A revolution itself can produce massive suffering that outweighs the injustice it was meant to remedy.[74] While the Noahic covenant provides no precise directions, it does indicate that the residual responsibility to overturn a government is a responsibility resting in the human *community*, not in an *individual*—a reminder to any solitary would-be revolutionary.

CONCLUSION

As the Noahic covenant has provided a framework for understanding natural justice (chapter 9) and the law (chapter 10), so here it provides a framework for thinking about government, especially its legitimate authority and the rights and responsibilities of a community to resist its injustices. Although the Noahic covenant has not provided a comprehensive public policy or political theory, exploring its implications has confirmed that natural justice ought to ground the law, and that the law ought to ground government authority. Yet in turn, government action appropriately shapes the law, and the law specifies concretely what is just in a particular community.

---

73. Cf. Wolterstorff, *The Mighty and the Almighty*, 117.
74. Cf. Thomas Aquinas, *Summa Theologiae* 2a2ae 42.2 ad. 3; and Aquinas's discussion in book 1, chapter 6 of *De Regimine Principum*. For English translation, see *Aquinas: Political Writings*, ed. and trans. R. W. Dyson (Cambridge: Cambridge University Press, 2004).

CHAPTER 12

REFLECTIONS ON THE LIBERAL AND CONSERVATIVE TRADITIONS

Part 2 has considered several perennial questions of political and legal theory through the lens of the Noahic covenant. These studies have explored practical dimensions of the political theology in part 1. It seems fitting in this final chapter to reflect on two longstanding political traditions—*liberalism* and *conservatism*—that continue to shape my own context and many others. Exploring these controversial traditions provides the opportunity to synthesize many themes of previous chapters, in conversation with some of the great debates of Western political thought.

Closing on this note carries some risks. It risks abandoning my goal of staying several steps removed from the political drama and crises of the present day and helping readers think through important questions with a perspective broader than the latest headlines. It also risks contradicting my claim that the Noahic covenant offers a framework for thinking about perennial legal and political issues without providing a detailed public policy or promoting a specific party agenda. I acknowledge the risks but think they can be managed.

With respect to getting sucked into the intrigues of the moment, I will simply resist the temptation to opine on all the salient material contemporary politics provides. The liberal and conservative traditions existed long before today's scandal and will surely outlast it too. As we have considered topics such as religious freedom, justice, and authority in a mostly general and principial way, we ought to be able to do the same with liberalism and conservatism. In fact, pondering these traditions in broad perspective could provide welcome resources for engaging concrete policy proposals and party agendas as occasion demands.

The risk of advocating a particular party line is not insuperable either. The Noahic framework developed in preceding chapters does not correspond neatly to either the liberal or conservative tradition. On the contrary, a Noahic perspective has reason to appreciate elements of both traditions, and it points toward a vision in which the strengths of each can ameliorate the other's weaknesses and in which the emphases of one can balance those of the other. Furthermore, I understand "liberalism" and "conservatism" here in older, classical ways that do not correspond to conventional use of these terms today, at least in the United States. By "liberalism" and "conservatism," I do not refer to the respective agendas of the Democratic and Republican parties. In fact, it is helpful to distinguish liberalism and conservatism from other popular ways of thought, which I will call "progressivism" and "nationalism." These latter two, more than liberalism and conservatism, have gained increasing influence among the Democratic and Republican parties, respectively. And since I appraise both progressivism and nationalism negatively in light of the Noahic covenant, I believe the Democratic and the Republican parties would be better—and give Americans more attractive options—if they really were liberal and/or conservative. But this is all I will say about any political party. This chapter has no interest in party propaganda.

In this chapter, I reflect on the liberal and conservative traditions in light of the Noahic covenant and suggest that the conclusions in previous chapters point toward what I will call *conservative liberalism*. I begin by trying to identify what I mean by *liberalism* and *conservatism*. I then examine both traditions under Noahic light and suggest what might be appreciated, appropriated, and avoided in each. In so doing, I chart the basic contours of a conservative liberalism and explain its differences with both progressivism and nationalism.

LIBERALISM AND CONSERVATISM

There is no universally shared understanding of what it means to be "liberal" or "conservative." Before evaluating these two traditions, therefore, I need to clarify how I understand them.

Liberalism

Two common understandings of "liberalism" differ from liberalism as I evaluate it here. The first, prevalent on a popular level in the United States, thinks of liberalism as the policy agenda of the political left. This agenda advocates aggressive regulation of the market economy, extensive welfare programs, and recognition of morally progressive civil rights such as rights to abortion and homosexual marriage. This is not what I mean by liberalism.

A second understanding of liberalism different from mine is typical in many scholarly circles. It takes liberalism as a kind of philosophy, ideology, or worldview. This philosophical liberalism, to borrow terms from Patrick Deneen, believes in "radically autonomous human beings," "individualism," "non-judgmentalism," a "radical rejection of the past as a source of wisdom," and utility maximization. It is "the world's first ideology" and constitutes "a system of ideas that proposes a seamless political architecture, outside of which existing political arrangements are deemed to be illegitimate and require immediate remaking."[1] Or as John Safranek characterizes it, liberalism is centered in the ideal of personal freedom and is justified in terms of liberty, rights, autonomy, equality, or dignity. Yet none of these justifications work, for they are "performatively self-contradictory." For Safranek, liberalism is a myth.[2] Other writers characterize liberalism similarly.[3]

Such a liberalism sounds like a not-so-veiled repudiation of Christianity. Yet Deneen and Safranek are Roman Catholic critics of liberalism, so we might wonder whether they have unfairly described their opponent for rhetorical purposes. The fact is, however, many self-identified liberals provide such critics plenty of material to support their case.[4] John Rawls, for example, asserts that the "fair terms of cooperation" that constitute his famous "justice as fairness" are not determined by "God's law" or "natural law" but simply

---

1. Patrick J. Deneen, *Conserving America? Essays on Present Discontents* (South Bend: St. Augustine's Press, 2016), 2, 3, 8, 10, 118, 121, 197.

2. John F. Safranek, *The Myth of Liberalism* (Washington, DC: The Catholic University of America Press, 2015).

3. For example, Yoram Hazony, whose work I consider below, says liberalism is based on the principle of individual freedom. It is imperialistic and a "universal ideology" comparable to Christianity, Islam, and Marxism. See *The Virtue of Nationalism* (New York: Basic, 2018), 30, 43, 74, 228–29.

4. Cf. Helena Rosenblatt, *The Lost History of Liberalism: From Ancient Rome to the Twenty-First Century* (Princeton: Princeton University Press, 2018). She presents a "*word history* of liberalism" meant to illuminate what self-described liberals have meant by "liberalism" (2–3). From this perspective, she strongly identifies liberalism with liberal Christianity and portrays liberalism as in frequent tension with Roman Catholicism especially.

by *agreement* among "free and equal citizens."[5] Similarly, Bruce Ackerman states that *neutrality* toward different visions of the good is a hallmark of the liberal state. No assertion of right can rest upon a claim that one's "conception of the good is better than that asserted by any of his fellow citizens," for everyone has a right "to express his ideals *in the words that make most sense to him*."[6] Or we might consider Robert Audi's conviction that protecting individuals' autonomy is paramount, and that to do so a political community should make decisions on the basis of "secular" argumentation and avoid "religious" argumentation.[7] These versions of "liberalism" have serious problems and are obviously out of accord with the political theology developed in this volume. I will discuss some of these problems below.

In this chapter, I understand liberalism as a kind of polity or practical political arrangement. Classical and medieval thought typically conceived of the ideal political community as unified on a moral-metaphysical-religious foundation. Through this foundation, citizens could together attain their perfection or highest earthly ends. Christendom was one expression of this vision. In contrast, liberalism relinquished it. Liberalism accepted the fact of diversity in moral-metaphysical-religious conviction among members of the political community and sought ways to maintain a peaceful social order within which individuals, families, and voluntary associations could pursue their own particular ends.[8] Along with this important shift in thought, classical liberalism supported a number of other political ideas that were not necessarily unique to it but which it did emphasize.[9] Among these were broad freedoms of speech and religion, state authority resting on consent of the people, justice as the protection of rights, the rule of law, and a market economy.[10]

---

5. John Rawls, *Political Liberalism* (New York: Columbia University Press, 1993), 22–23; see 406 for Rawls's clarifying remarks on his liberal theory and natural law.

6. Bruce A. Ackerman, *Social Justice in the Liberal State* (New Haven: Yale University Press, 1980), 10–11, 54.

7. Robert Audi, "The Place of Religious Argument in a Free and Democratic Society," *San Diego Law Review* 30 (1993): 677–702.

8. For a helpful description of this from a critic of liberalism, see, e.g., Alasdair MacIntyre, *Whose Justice? Which Rationality?* (Notre Dame: University of Notre Dame Press, 1988), 210. From an advocate of liberalism (as a polity or practical arrangement), see, e.g., Christopher J. Insole, *The Politics of Human Frailty: A Theological Defense of Political Liberalism* (Notre Dame: University of Notre Dame Press, 2005), 5.

9. I am using the term *classical liberalism* in a way different from Rosenblatt; see especially *The Lost History*, ch. 7. She presents "classical" liberalism as a later invention of proponents of *laissez-faire* economics, who wished to deny the "liberal" designation to those promoting heavy state interference in the market.

10. For a similar though not identical list from a proponent of liberalism (as a polity or practical arrangement), see, e.g., Christopher Wolfe, *Natural Law Liberalism* (Cambridge: Cambridge University Press, 2006), 144–45.

This sort of liberalism is thus different from a philosophical or world-view liberalism because it does not presume to rest upon individualism, autonomous rationality, or a voluntaristic account of justice. As a practical political arrangement, this liberalism is open to people of any religious or philosophical conviction who are willing to seek peaceful coexistence among diverse people along the lines just described. The United States may be the quintessential liberal polity. Although many other countries came to embrace liberalism to one degree or another, the United States was the first and perhaps only country to be founded explicitly on liberal principles. And yet the United States has always been a very religious country, and a variety of Christians have embraced (or at least come to peace with) its liberal polity. Obviously, people of certain theological convictions cannot accept liberalism of this (or any) sort. Theocratic forms of Christianity and radical Islam, for example, must oppose it in principle. Nevertheless, many recent writers from various Christian circles have embraced liberalism as a polity or political arrangement—to use my terms, not necessarily theirs.[11]

Conservatism

The term "conservatism" also needs clarification. As many Americans associate liberalism with the political left, so they associate conservatism with the political right. The characteristics of this sort of conservatism include enthusiasm for lightly regulated global markets, a strong and assertive military, and support for "family values," among which are opposition to abortion and defense of traditional marriage. In this chapter, however, I take "conservatism" as an older tradition different in important respects from this more recent American version. I now identify five of its crucial features. I draw on a number of writers widely regarded as traditional conservatives and attempt to identify points of broad agreement if not unanimous opinion.

First, and perhaps most important, conservatism expresses respect for the wisdom of the ages accumulated over many generations. According to

---

11. Among Protestants, see, e.g., Insole, *The Politics of Human Frailty*; Michael W. McConnell, "Old Liberalism, New Liberalism, and People of Faith," in *Christian Perspectives on Legal Thought*, eds. Michael W. McConnell, Robert F. Cochran Jr., and Angela C. Carmella (New Haven: Yale University Press, 2001), 5–24; and Nicholas Wolterstorff in both *The Mighty and the Almighty: An Essay in Political Theology* (Cambridge: Cambridge University Press, 2012) and *Understanding Liberal Democracy: Essays in Political Philosophy*, ed. Terrence Cuneo (Oxford: Oxford University Press, 2012). Among Roman Catholics, see, e.g., Wolfe, *Natural Law Liberalism*; and Daniel J. Mahoney, *The Conservative Foundations of the Liberal Order: Defending Democracy against Its Modern Enemies and Immoderate Friends* (Wilmington: ISI, 2010). Among the Eastern Orthodox, see, e.g., Aristotle Papnikolaou, *The Mystical as Political: Democracy and Non-Radical Orthodoxy* (Notre Dame: University of Notre Dame Press, 2012).

its proponents, people acquire this wisdom more through inheritance and intuition than through rational investigation. This gives an important role to tradition, prescription, and "prejudice" (in its etymological sense of the foundational things a person knows prior to making deliberate judgments).[12] This perspective does not oppose all social change but desires change to come gradually and organically.[13] Of course, conservatives think social change usually happens far too abruptly, and their cultural analysis tends to be pessimistic.[14]

Second, conservatism acknowledges the existence of a moral order that stands behind all human communities and provides knowledge of a transcendent justice.[15] Because of this, many conservatives also advance a perfectionist view of law and government.[16] Conservatism's belief in a moral order may also explain its respect for religious belief and support of religious institutions for the good of society,[17] although many prominent conservatives are not all that religious themselves, at least in orthodox ways.[18] Some conservatives lament the loss of Christendom and express nostalgia for things

---

12. E.g., see Edmund Burke and Thomas Paine, *Reflections on the Revolution in France and the Rights of Man* (New York: Anchor, 1973), 100–101; Russell Kirk, *The Conservative Mind: From Burke to Eliot*, 4th rev. ed. (New York: Avon, 1968), 17, 18, 45–46, 49, 72; Russell Kirk, *A Program for Conservatives*, rev. ed. (Chicago: Henry Regnery, 1962), 4, 43, 302; and Roger Scruton, *The Meaning of Conservatism*, rev. 3rd ed. (South Bend: St. Augustine's Press, 2002), 13–14, 30–36, 71–72. Cf. Robert Nisbet, *Conservatism: Dream and Reality* (Minneapolis: University of Minnesota Press, 1986), 28–32; and Clinton Rossiter, *Conservatism in America*, 2nd ed. (Cambridge, MA: Harvard University Press, 1962), 27, 51.

13. E.g., see Burke, *Reflections*, 43, 45; Kirk, *The Conservative Mind*, 53; and Kirk, *A Program for Conservatives*, 301.

14. An excellent example, in my judgment, is Richard M. Weaver's *Ideas Have Consequences* (Chicago: University of Chicago Press, 1948), which criticizes just about everything about the modern world, including jazz, impressionism, and the radio. See also Kirk, *The Conservative Mind*, 338–48; Nisbet, *Conservatism*, 17–18; and Christopher Dawson, *The Judgment of the Nations* (New York: Sheed & Ward, 1942), 8.

15. E.g., see generally Leo Strauss, *Natural Right and History* (Chicago: University of Chicago Press, 1953). See also Harry V. Jaffa, "The False Prophets of American Conservatism," in *A Moral Enterprise: Politics, Reason, and the Human Good: Essays in Honor of Francis Canavan*, ed. Kenneth L. Grasso and Robert P. Hunt (Wilmington: ISI, 2002), 256–57, 262; Kirk, *The Conservative Mind*, 18; Kirk, *A Program for Conservatives*, 166; and Deneen, *Conserving America*, 140. Cf. Rossiter, *Conservatism in America*, 45.

16. E.g., see generally Walter Berns, *Freedom, Virtue and the First Amendment* (Baton Rouge: LSU Press, 1957). See also T. S. Eliot, *The Idea of a Christian Society* (New York: Harcourt, Brace and Company, 1940), 33; Weaver, *Ideas Have Consequences*, 101; Scruton, *The Meaning of Conservatism*, 68–75; Strauss, *Natural Right*, 129–35; and George H. Nash, *The Conservative Intellectual Movement in America: Since 1945* (New York: Basic, 1976), 176, 225–26.

17. E.g., see Burke, *Reflections*, 104–13; Kirk, *The Conservative Mind*, 17, 43, 99–100, 139, 143, 312; Dawson, *The Judgment of the Nations*, 12, 21–24, 94, 133, 148–50, 153–57, 220–22; Scruton, *The Meaning of Conservatism*, 158–59, 162–63; and R. R. Reno, *Resurrecting the Idea of a Christian Society* (Washington, DC: Regnery Faith, 2016), 130–38. Cf. Rossiter, *Conservatism in America*, 42.

18. E.g., although Kirk was a middle-aged convert to Roman Catholicism, he was apparently less than devout; see Bradley J. Birzer, *Russell Kirk: American Conservative* (Lexington: University Press of Kentucky, 2015), 369. On Kirk's quasi-paganism, see Birzer, *Russell Kirk*, 94, 361–63, 376, 387.

medieval.[19] Not surprisingly, a number find Roman Catholicism attractive and Protestantism distasteful.[20]

Third, conservatism perceives human nature and human experience as complex[21] and intractably flawed.[22] Accordingly, it tends to shun grand and abstract programs designed to solve social problems, however well-intentioned. Its proponents emphasize instead the importance of circumstances, the need for prudence, and the value of experience as they confront the challenges of life.[23]

Fourth, conservatism prefers things on a small scale and remains wary of the large. This attitude applies on several fronts. For example, conservatives often praise the rural and agrarian while critiquing the urban and industrial.[24] They also embrace private property and enterprise but not grand accumulation of wealth.[25] Conservatives thus warn against consumerism and materialism[26] and lament the disruptions of modern capitalism.[27] Conservatism also has high regard for mediating institutions, that is, small voluntary associations that stand between individuals and the state.[28] Its advocates often

---

19. E.g., see Eliot, *The Idea of a Christian Society*, 33, 40–41, 46–56; T. S. Eliot, *Notes towards the Definition of Culture* (New York: Harcourt, Brace and Company, 1949), 27–32, 67–68; Weaver, *Ideas Have Consequences*, 175, 187; Robert A. Nisbet, *The Quest for Community: A Study in the Ethics of Order and Freedom* (New York: Oxford University Press, 1953), 79–86; Bradley J. Birzer, *Sanctifying the World: The Augustinian Life and Mind of Christopher Dawson* (Front Royal, VA: Christendom, 2007), xi, 137, 139, 151; Brad S. Gregory, *The Unintended Reformation: How a Religious Revolution Secularized Society* (Cambridge, MA: Belknap, 2012), 2, 11, 294; and Deneen, *Conserving America*, ch. 8.

20. E.g., see Birzer, *Russell Kirk*, 2, 94, 365; and Nash, *The Conservative Intellectual Movement*, 60, 80.

21. E.g., see Burke, *Reflections*, 73–74; Kirk, *The Conservative Mind*, 107, 128; and Scruton, *The Meaning of Conservatism*, 1. Cf. Rossiter, *Conservatism in America*, 21.

22. E.g., see Kirk, *The Conservative Mind*, 92, 94, 231, 241; Kirk, *A Program for Conservatives*, 4, 41, 80; and Eliot, *The Idea of a Christian Society*, 16, 57–60. Cf. Rossiter, *Conservatism in America*, 20.

23. E.g., see Burke, *Reflections*, 19; Kirk, *The Conservative Mind*, 17, 31, 450–51; Kirk, *A Program for Conservatives*, 4, 5; Scruton, *The Meaning of Conservatism*, 2, 26–27; and Birzer, *Russell Kirk*, 36, 100–101. Cf. Rossiter, *Conservatism in America*, 21.

24. E.g., see Kirk, *The Conservative Mind*, 371; Kirk, *A Program for Conservatives*, 105, 303; Eliot, *The Idea of a Christian Society*, 19, 32, 62–63, 65; Weaver, *Ideas Have Consequences*, 30–31, 115; and Birzer, *Sanctifying the World*, 20, 127.

25. E.g., see Burke, *Reflections*, 63–64; Kirk, *The Conservative Mind*, 18; Kirk, *A Program for Conservatives*, 40, 42, 150–54; Weaver, *Ideas Have Consequences*, 131; and Birzer, *Russell Kirk*, 160–61. Cf. Nisbet, *Conservatism*, 14–15, 56; and Rossiter, *Conservatism in America*, 52.

26. E.g., see Kirk, *A Program for Conservatives*, 194–95; and Gregory, *The Unintended Reformation*, 257–61.

27. E.g., see Kirk, *The Conservative Mind*, 142, 217, 423; Kirk, *A Program for Conservatives*, 40, 143–50; Dawson, *The Judgment of the Nations*, 190–201; Weaver, *Ideas Have Consequences*, 32, 37, 132–33; Nisbet, *Conservatism*, 64–68; Scruton, *The Meaning of Conservatism*, vii, 4, ch. 5; Gregory, *The Unintended Reformation*, 16–18, ch. 5; Reno, *Resurrecting*, 109–10; and Birzer, *Sanctifying the World*, 46–47. For a larger study of this issue, see also Peter Kolozi, *Conservatives against Capitalism: From the Industrial Revolution to Globalization* (New York: Columbia University Press, 2017).

28. E.g., see Nisbet, *The Quest for Community*, 32–37, 49, 54, 85, 99–100, 121, 144, 156, 192–93, 202, 265, 270; Nisbet, *Conservatism*, 22, 49, 103–4; and Reno, *Resurrecting*, ch. 5.

delight in the spontaneous differences evident from person to person and locale to locale while despising uniformity and mass culture.[29]

Fifth and finally, conservatism has an interest in politics, but it resists the common urge to make politics ultimate. Instead, conservatives emphasize the cultural attitudes and practices that underlie a political community.[30]

LIBERALISM, CONSERVATISM, AND THE NOAHIC COVENANT

If we take "liberalism" and "conservatism" in the way just portrayed, how should we evaluate these traditions in light of a Christian political theology grounded in the Noahic covenant? In this section, I develop an argument for a *conservative liberalism*. This term may sound initially oxymoronic, but I hope to show that it follows the trajectory of previous chapters. In short, the political theology of this volume suggests reasons to appreciate many aspects of both liberalism and conservatism without endorsing either in any comprehensive way.

Liberal and Conservative Themes in Previous Chapters

The claims of this volume have reflected various conservative and liberal themes. In fact, part 2 has unfolded in a way that largely alternates liberal and conservative emphases—although I did not do this intentionally.

Part 2 began by defending the pluralistic character of political communities under the Noahic covenant and a broad measure of religious liberty. These are familiar features of a liberal polity. Then I turned to the three core elements of the Noahic moral commission. The first—to be fruitful, multiply, and fill the earth—suggests the importance of marriage, procreation, and diligent child-rearing: conservative emphases, to be sure. The second, calling the human community to provide for its material needs, entails the good of enterprise, technology, and a market economy—common emphases of liberalism. The third delegates judicial authority to the human race. My discussion of this topic began with a defense of retributive justice, likely to resonate with conservatives more than liberals. But my discussion went on to

---

29. E.g., see Kirk, *The Conservative Mind*, 18, 65–66, 200, 209; Kirk, *A Program for Conservatives*, 42, 177; Eliot, *Notes*, 17–18, 112; ch. 3; Nisbet, *The Quest for Community*, 265; Dawson, *The Judgment of the Nations*, 64, 116–17, ch. 7; Weaver, *Ideas Have Consequences*, 33, 35; Nash, *The Conservative Intellectual Movement*, 46; and Birzer, *Russell Kirk*, 82.

30. E.g., see Eliot, *The Idea of a Christian Society*, 7–8, 15; Eliot, *Notes*, 11; Birzer, *Russell Kirk*, 5, 37, 82, 183; and Birzer, *Sanctifying the World*, 59.

defend natural human rights, likely to impress liberals more than conservatives. The inquiry next turned to law. A conception of law as polycentric has liberal and conservative strains, an important point I revisit below. Finally, I considered authority and resistance. The legitimacy of authority is a theme more comfortable in conservative hearts, while the possibility of resistance is dearer to liberal souls. Has my case in part 2 been liberal or conservative, therefore? From a wide-angle perspective, it seems to be both partially but neither purely.

Noahic Liberalism: One Big Idea

Among the many themes traditionally associated with liberalism as a political polity, is there one that really gets to the core of what makes it distinctive? In my judgment, liberalism's one big idea is maintaining a social order marked by pluralism and tolerance. Liberalism abandoned the predominant classical and medieval ideal of a theologically, metaphysically, and/or morally unified political community. For a liberal polity, instead, a political community aims at the peaceful coexistence of individuals and institutions that hold different conceptions of ultimate truth and seek their own distinctive ends, achieved through voluntary cooperation and the protection of basic rights.

If this indeed gets to the heart of liberalism, then the political theology developed in this volume supports liberalism generally, if not every specific version of it. A few additional comments clarify what sort of liberalism may be harmonious with the Noahic covenant.

First and foremost, Noahic liberalism is liberalism as a polity, not a philosophical, ideological, or worldview liberalism. In other words, a Noahic liberalism will not answer the deepest questions about life but provide a basic framework for human interaction in political community. Several themes explored in chapter 7 are crucial to this framework. For one, a Noahic liberalism will recognize that there must be *some* substantive unity to hold a political community together. Even the relatively low bar of peaceful coexistence requires a certain level of moral commonality. Noahic liberalism requires moral bonds and a common good but insists that they are modest. Chapter 7 also indicates that Noahic liberalism will refuse to impose legal liabilities on people based on designation of "race" (a spurious construct) and will grant full rights of participation in public life to all law-abiding people of whatever ethnic background. Furthermore, Noahic liberalism will refuse to grant established status to any particular religious body or attach legal liabilities to a particular religious profession, doctrine, or worship. It will acknowledge a broad measure of religious liberty and avoid constraining it except when attempts to assert religious liberty violate others' natural rights. Along related lines explored in chapter 11, a Noahic liberalism will be wary of political perfectionism.

A Noahic liberalism, however, will not succumb to the myth trafficked among many self-identified liberals that certain areas of social-political life are morally neutral. As chapter 1 emphasized, Christian political theology should recognize that all people have many objective things in *common*, insofar as they share the same human nature as God's image-bearers and stand together under God's covenant with Noah. But political communities are morally *accountable*. Convictions and practices in political community can never be neutral. They are never independent of all moral commitment. As covenant participants, each person and association is accountable to God for all aspects of life in political community, and no one can be neutral toward God and his claims.

This implies, for one thing, that a person's view of justice can never be a matter of pure rationality detached from underlying theological and philosophical convictions. A Noahic liberalism will therefore not embrace Rawls's famous conception of "justice as fairness," since he views it as "reasonable," "freestanding," and "impartial" among "comprehensive views." Some aspects of Rawls's later work do get closer to a Noahic liberalism. He advocates a "political" liberalism different from a "comprehensive" liberalism.[31] This political liberalism represents an overlapping consensus among people of various comprehensive views. Thus Rawls thinks people will defend political liberalism differently from within their own comprehensive views, which are mutually incompatible. Thus far, it may be consistent with my own proposal. Nevertheless, Rawls believes that political liberalism's conception of "justice as fairness" is independent of any of these comprehensive views and hence is "freestanding." Although Rawls thinks that a multitude of comprehensive views inevitably emerges when people exercise reason within free institutions, he deems only some of these views as "reasonable"—precisely those that embrace the liberal project.[32] Therefore, Rawls constructs a liberal theory that is decidedly not "impartial" among competing comprehensive views. Justice is perennially controversial. No conception of it can be freestanding and independent of a comprehensive view. And no judgment about the reasonability

---

31. E.g., see Rawls, *Political Liberalism*, xxvii.
32. See Rawls, *Political Liberalism*, xix, xxvii–xxviii, 9–10, 39, 49–50, 60.

of a comprehensive view can proceed apart from the criteria some other comprehensive view provides. True, a liberal polity will not succeed unless diverse groups of people can agree to recognize some basic notions of justice, but it obscures matters to assert that there are realms of reasonable discourse about justice that can stand free of people's ultimate commitments.

Noahic liberalism's skepticism about "neutrality" should surely also extend to some popular notions of "public reason" and "secular" argumentation. These notions arise from an admittedly difficult problem: how can people in a liberal society, who have different comprehensive views, engage in intelligible political discourse? Rawls's theory of "public reason" purports to describe the proper way to discuss constitutional essentials and questions of basic justice in the public forum. He envisions citizens affirming the ideal of public reason "from within their own reasonable doctrines" (i.e., comprehensive views). Yet he also thinks public reason should appeal "only to presently accepted general beliefs and forms of reasoning found in common sense, and the methods and conclusions of science when these are not controversial." Such discussions are "based on values that the others can reasonably be expected to endorse."[33] Along similar lines, Audi distinguishes between "secular" and "religious" argumentation, the former of which should be the chief basis for political decision-making. Audi believes protecting individuals' autonomy is paramount, and therefore coercing people must be justified by arguments that the coerced people themselves would find persuasive, provided they had sufficient information and were thinking rationally. Secular but not religious reasoning meets this requirement.[34]

The problem is that "public" and "secular" reason inevitably ends up importing assumptions into its argumentation that are dependent upon comprehensive views or religious doctrines.[35] Many religious people, even those sympathetic to a liberal polity, are unable to meet Rawls's and Audi's requirements for public reason without giving up central convictions of their faith. I myself could never make a nonreligious argument according to Audi's "epistemic criterion,"[36] since I believe all knowledge is derived from divine revelation of some sort.

---

33. Rawls, *Political Liberalism*, 213–15; 218, 224, 226.

34. See Audi, "The Place of Religious Argument," 677–702.

35. For a defense of this claim, see, e.g., Wolterstorff, *Understanding Liberal Democracy*, ch. 1. For other critical engagement of Rawls on public reason, see Michael J. Perry, *Religion in Politics: Constitutional and Moral Perspectives* (New York: Oxford University Press, 1997), 54–59; and Kent Greenawalt, *Private Consciences and Public Reasons* (New York: Oxford University Press, 1995), ch. 10.

36. See Audi, "The Place of Religious Argument," 680–81.

This reference to revelation points to a better way to think about discourse in the public square. The conception of natural law defended in chapter 5 presumes a distinction between natural and special revelation. Along typical Reformed lines, I affirm that all true knowledge, and hence any valid argument, must derive from one or both of these sources.[37] God has given natural revelation (including natural law) to all people as created human beings and has ordinarily delivered special revelation only to Israel and the church as communities in redeemed covenant relationship with him. Thus natural revelation seems to be the more appropriate basis for political discourse in a liberal polity grounded in the universal Noahic covenant. Although arguments from natural law are never secular, impartial, or neutral in the sense intended by many liberal theorists, they are *appropriate* for political society insofar as God holds all people accountable through natural revelation (see Rom 1:19–20).

A Noahic liberalism will contest not only some conceptions of liberalism emerging from so-called secular sources but also some conceptions emerging in the name of Christianity. To mention a recent example, Noahic liberalism has fundamental differences with Timothy Jackson's "prophetic liberalism." Prophetic liberalism makes Christian love (rather than justice) its foundational norm and polemicizes against distinctions between church and world or between Christians and non-Christians that somehow privilege Christians and the church.[38] A Noahic liberalism will obviously share Jackson's concern about distinctions that posit "a clean cut between 'the church' and 'the world,' such that Christians, truth, and goodness are on one side and non-Christians, falsity, and evil are on the other."[39] But I suspect Jackson would not be pleased with grounding a liberal polity in the Noahic covenant (in distinction from the covenant of grace), although this distinction works with no "clean cut" of the kind he defines. Jackson believes that "secular forms of liberalism" focus on "duties of justice," while "prophetic liberalism" focuses on "duties of love [*agape*]."[40] In contrast, I have argued on theological (rather than "secular") grounds that natural justice and *not* Christian love is the proper organizing principle for law and government under the covenant with Noah.

---

37. For a detailed Reformed exposition of natural and special revelation, see, e.g., Herman Bavinck, *Reformed Dogmatics*, vol. 1, *Prolegomena*, ed. John Bolt, trans. John Vriend (Grand Rapids: Baker Academic, 2003), 283–385.

38. Timothy P. Jackson, *Political* Agape: *Christian Love and Liberal Democracy* (Grand Rapids: Eerdmans, 2015).

39. Jackson, *Political* Agape, 11.

40. Jackson, *Political* Agape, 42.

There is a distinctive Christian *agape* rooted in Christ's atonement that is not part of the Noahic covenant's moral fabric, and Christian *agape* is thus an improper foundation for a political community grounded in this covenant. Jackson's Christian defense of liberalism, I fear, saps *agape* of a good deal of its redemptive power and vitality in an attempt to make it universally applicable. Noahic liberalism is not Rawlsian liberalism, but neither is it Jackson's prophetic liberalism.

Noahic Conservatism: One Big Idea

I have just described how the political-theological vision unpacked in this book might plausibly be described as liberal. I now try to identify how it might plausibly be described as conservative. When discussing conservatism above, I suggested that its most important feature may be its emphasis on long-acquired and hard-won wisdom. This emphasis is rooted in a couple of key convictions. First, conservatives ordinarily believe in an objective moral order that underlies human justice. Second, they tend to think of human beings as flawed creatures whose experience in this world is complicated. In my judgment, this core of the conservative mind explains many of its other characteristic features, including its love for continuity, the small, and the local.

If respect for a long-acquired and hard-won wisdom indeed gets to the heart of conservative thought, then the political theology of this book represents a kind of conservatism. Chapter 5 argued that theological reflection on public life and political community must consider the natural law, the divinely established moral order that underlies earthly institutions. As a moral order, natural law cannot be reduced to a collection of discrete rules (although rules may helpfully describe and summarize it). This means that people learn the natural law not through memorization but through gaining a perception and understanding of how the world works and how to make one's way effectively and fruitfully within it. Such perception is *wisdom*—a natural or proximate wisdom, as I described it. In short, coming to know the natural law is the same thing as maturing in wisdom. Wisdom is the subjective human faculty suited to perceive the objective moral order. Natural wisdom is perception of the natural law.

I argued further that growing in wisdom and hence learning the natural law in its practical concreteness cannot be a solitary endeavor. It requires immersion in communities that for generations have been figuring out ways to live in accord with the order and constraints of this world. Each of these communities develops its own customs and practices. Some customs are better and some worse, but no community can claim to have found the only right way to live by the natural law. Although all people ought to exercise critical discernment as they participate in their inevitably imperfect communities, the way to wisdom runs through the instruction of parents, the counsel of elders, considering many opinions, and learning the new through comparison with the old.

This thread of argument seems to capture the core of the conservative tradition as described above. This implies that a Christian political theology grounded in the Noahic covenant is indeed conservative in an important, if not every, respect.

The Contours of a Conservative Liberalism

In light of the one big idea of liberalism and the one big idea of conservatism, this book's political theology plausibly points toward a conservative liberalism. Why not a "liberal conservatism" instead? I have no dogmatic preference and assume no sharp distinction between the two.[41] Yet I prefer to speak of "conservative liberalism." The heart of liberalism involves a substantive commitment to a particular kind of polity (that is, a polity that tolerates pluralism), while the heart of conservatism is a commitment to a way of understanding how to live in light of human nature and the nature of the world (that is, the way of wisdom). It seems best to make the substantive commitment the noun and the way of understanding the adjective. The political theology of these pages points toward a liberal polity but one attained and maintained conservatively.

To call oneself a conservative liberal can feel a little lonely at times, but such a perspective is not oxymoronic or eccentric. A number of impressive thinkers in recent centuries arguably fit this description, including Edmund

---

41. Daniel Mahoney, however, mentions such a distinction in the work of French scholars; see *Conservative Foundations*, 2. I am not utilizing these categories but mention them for interested readers: "French analysts of the liberal intellectual tradition distinguish between 'conservative liberalism' and 'liberal conservatism.' Conservative liberals have no objection to the fundamental presuppositions of the liberal order (i.e., the rights of man, constitutional liberalism, and the moral and civic equality of human beings) while recognizing the crucial dependence of liberal society upon extraliberal and extrademocratic habits, traditions, virtues, and 'inheritances.' Liberal conservatives, on the other hand, defend liberty against every form of despotism but are more openly critical of the Enlightenment categories that are used to justify the regime of modern liberty. They more forthrightly reject the illusions of modernity—including the affirmation of the individual and collective 'autonomy' or 'sovereignty' of human beings, the drift toward indiscriminate relativism, and the 'blind worship of progress.'"

Burke in the eighteenth century,[42] Alexis de Tocqueville in the nineteenth,[43] and Wilhelm Röpke,[44] Isaiah Berlin,[45] Michael Oakeshott,[46] and Bertrand de Jouvenal in the twentieth.[47] The American Founding might also be described as conservatively liberal. It established a liberal polity with a tolerant pluralism unusual for its day (although still tragically inconsistent), while maintaining a profound continuity with the insights and achievements of its ancient English heritage, particularly as embodied in the common law.[48] Insofar as the United States has maintained a liberal polity in continuity with its founding, liberalism is arguably America's conservative tradition.[49]

In what follows, I reflect on a number of points of comparison and contrast between the liberal and conservative traditions. I suggest, from Noahic perspective, how the traditions might complement, correct, and strengthen each other. I speak only in terms of general tendencies, without constantly hedging my statements with nuance and qualification. Following brief discussion of eight salient issues, I will explain why the conclusions about legal polycentrism in chapter 10 may point to the most important convergence between the traditions.

First, liberalism and conservatism agree that political community ought to be grounded in an objective morality. Liberals understand this morality

---

42. Burke is widely regarded as a giant of the conservative tradition. But Burke was also a liberal: he was a Whig (not a Tory), supported a relatively broad religious freedom, sympathized with the American colonists, and liked Adam Smith's economics. See, e.g., Insole, *The Politics of Human Frailty*, 15–40; and Kirk, *The Conservative Mind*, 22–23 (although Kirk does not emphasize this aspect of Burke's thought).

43. This is a fair reading, it seems to me, of Tocqueville's famous *Democracy in America*, trans. Harvey C. Mansfield and Delba Winthrop (1835–1840; Chicago: University of Chicago Press, 2002). For relevant discussion, see, e.g., Stephen B. Smith, *Modernity and Its Discontents: Making and Unmaking the Bourgeois from Machiavelli to Bellow* (New Haven: Yale University Press, 2016), ch. 10; and Mahoney, *Conservative Foundations*, ch. 1.

44. E.g., see Wilhelm Röpke, *A Humane Economy: The Social Framework of the Free Market* (Chicago: Regnery, 1960).

45. E.g., see Isaiah Berlin, "Two Concepts of Liberty," in *Four Essays on Liberalism* (Oxford: Oxford University Press, 1969). Cf. Smith, *Modernity and Its Discontents*, ch. 13.

46. E.g., see Michael Oakeshott, *On Human Conduct* (Oxford: Clarendon, 1975), ch. 2. Cf. Smith, *Modernity and Its Discontents*, 349.

47. E.g., see Bertrand de Jouvenal, *On Power: The Natural History of Its Growth*, trans. J. F. Huntington (1948; Indianapolis: Liberty Fund, 1993). And see Daniel J. Mahoney, *Bertrand de Jouvenal: The Conservative Liberal and the Illusions of Modernity* (Wilmington: ISI, 2005). Mahoney's own *Conservative Foundations* provides a twenty-first century example.

48. For similar comments, see Mahoney, *Conservative Foundations*, 6. From an antiliberal conservative perspective, Deneen basically agrees with the point but laments America's liberal founding and calls for America to be founded anew; see *Conserving America*, 8–10, 158–59.

49. Other writers have suggested this too. E.g., see Friedrich A. Hayek, *The Constitution of Liberty* (Chicago: University of Chicago Press, 1960), 397; and Alexander M. Bickel, *The Morality of Consent* (New Haven: Yale University Press, 1975), 118.

along relatively modest lines and describe it in terms of rights—the right over the good. Conservatives understand it in richer terms and describe it in terms of responsibilities—the good over the right. Accordingly, many conservatives support perfectionist policies, while liberals often do not. It seems to me that a conservative liberalism under the Noahic covenant should appreciate the liberal case for a modest, rights-based justice as what properly unites a political community and should also appreciate liberal wariness about perfectionism. Yet conservatives helpfully insist that individuals and institutions need to find a deeper purpose for life than a modest, rights-based justice can provide. People require richer strands of culture, training in virtue, and religious commitment, even if the state is not the one that provides them. A modest, rights-based justice may be the appropriate foundation for political coexistence, but it is a poor philosophy of life.

Second, liberalism desires the new and better and conservatism respects the old and proven. Several related convictions flow from these tendencies. Liberals take a more positive view of the "creative destruction" that an open and dynamic society instigates, while conservatives look warily upon the disruption it brings.[50] Along similar lines, conservatives have nostalgic thoughts toward things medieval, but liberals are glad to have escaped them. And while liberals have an optimistic bent, conservatives trend pessimistic.

Previous chapters indicate that each tradition could profitably chasten the other. Conservative wisdom should remember that there is still much to be learned, and liberal progress should remember that new achievements profoundly depend on achievements of the past. Conservatives can remind liberals of the lack of centralized state power during the Middle Ages (thus tempering liberal disdain for the medieval), while liberals can remind conservatives of the medieval era's religious persecution and poor living conditions (thus tempering conservatism's nostalgia for it). And both sides, with humility, might admit how difficult it really is to evaluate our own times. Is our age one of horrific violence or of steadily more peaceful coexistence?[51] Do we live in a blossoming cultural emporium or are we sliding into a new Dark Ages?[52] From Noahic perspective, we should be grateful for profound

---

50. I borrow this term from Joseph A. Schumpeter, *Capitalism, Socialism and Democracy*, 3rd ed. (1950; New York: Harper, 2008), 81–86.

51. Or, who understands the times better, Pankaj Mishra or Steven Pinker? See Pankaj Mishra, *Age of Anger: A History of the Present* (New York: Farrar, Straus and Giroux, 2017); and Steven Pinker, *The Better Angels of Our Nature: Why Violence Has Declined* (New York: Viking, 2011).

52. Or, do we party with McCloskey or take cover with MacIntyre? See Deirdre Nansen McCloskey, *Bourgeois Equality: How Ideas, Not Capital or Institutions, Enriched the World* (Chicago: University of

human accomplishments over the past few centuries, and yet the specter of sin haunts every political community under Noah's rainbow (Gen 8:21). With wonderful new accomplishments come dreadful new occasions for evil.

Third, liberalism strongly supports a market economy and conservatism lauds the importance of private property on a small scale while being wary of globalization and big business. Chapter 8 defends the good of a dynamic enterprise economy that reaches across the world and thus suggests sympathy with liberal support of globalization. But its sympathies also extend to conservative concerns, particularly about the moral dimension of economic activity and the special dangers of materialism and consumerism in a wealthy society. The Noahic covenant's emphasis upon family means we should be concerned about the disruptive effects of economic innovation, and this covenant's emphasis upon justice condemns the crony capitalism that powerful business interests often encourage. Conservative liberalism, then, supports an expanding enterprise economy but should be alert to its challenges, temptations, and abuses.

Fourth, liberalism embraces the cosmopolitan while conservatism is patriotic and loves what is local. In my judgment, the Noahic covenant encourages a cosmopolitan spirit insofar as it treats the human race as a unified body, recognizes natural human rights, and entails a worldwide commission in which all people have a share. At the same time, the Noahic covenant implicitly demands formation of families and voluntary institutions of many sorts, recognizing that human beings need more than membership in an abstract universal community. They cannot mature or fulfill their callings without particular, personal, and local attachments that provide resources for navigating a fallen and complex world. Conservative liberalism, it seems to me, rejects a narrow localism while resisting a cosmopolitanism that swallows the particular.

Fifth, conservatives love the mediating institutions that stand between the individual and the state. It seems that liberals should love them too, since such institutions are products of voluntary human interaction and help to keep government power in check. Many liberals do indeed praise mediating institutions.[53] But conservative critics often charge that liberalism's excessive individualism and creative destruction tend to weaken these institutions and

---

Chicago Press, 2016); and Alasdair MacIntyre, *After Virtue: A Study in Moral Theory*, 2nd ed. (Notre Dame: University of Notre Dame Press, 1984).

53. E.g., see how Friedrich A. Hayek ends one of his later books: *Law, Legislation and Liberty*, vol. 2, *The Mirage of Social Justice* (Chicago: University of Chicago Press, 1976), 150–52.

thus leave little else but individual and state—and the state, so the charge goes, inevitably fills up the vacuum created when mediating institutions dissolve.[54] This is largely a factual dispute: Will individuals who enjoy a broad measure of liberty tend to multiply voluntary associations or destroy them? Does love for mediating institutions therefore demand expanding or restricting such liberty?[55] The Noahic covenant indicates that people are both social creatures and sinful creatures, and thus, given sufficient liberty, they are likely both to create and to destroy useful institutions. Conservative liberalism embraces mediating institutions, I conclude, and does well to heed the concerns of both traditions.

Sixth, liberalism and conservatism both support a robust social diversity but in their own ways. Conservatives delight in a multiplicity of little associations and locales, each with its distinctive flavor, quirks, and idiosyncrasies, while liberals think in terms of cosmopolitan variety. Conservatives envision diversity expressed in the uniqueness of every country hamlet, while liberals envision a metropolis offering many kinds of cuisine, music, and art. A number of previous arguments suggest that the political communities under the Noahic covenant should welcome and encourage diversity. The size and complexity of the Noahic moral commission means that the world needs people with a variety of aptitudes and ambitions. And the relative indeterminacy of the natural law opens many possible avenues for ordering community life in productive ways. Both liberals and conservatives identify legitimate forms of diversity. From the perspective of conservative liberalism, liberal concerns might helpfully temper the stifling local parochialism that may creep into the conservative vision of diversity, and conservative concerns might helpfully temper the rootless globalized conformity that may tend to make urban centers indistinguishable from one another.

Seventh, both liberalism and conservatism believe in the legitimacy of government authority. Both also desire limits on state authority and are wary of ambitious government projects. Liberals seek to constrain state power especially through enforcing rights, while conservatives trust mediating institutions to keep the state in check. Liberals thus focus on protecting individuals from the state and conservatives focus on protecting smaller communities. I have argued throughout part 2 that the Noahic covenant implies limited though legitimate government. Since the Noahic covenant recognizes both

---

54. E.g., see Deneen, *Conserving America*, 4, 178, 201.

55. From liberal perspective, see Hayek, *The Mirage of Social Justice*, 151; from conservative perspective, see Reno, *Resurrecting*, 118.

the dignity of each individual and the importance of familial and enterprise institutions, conservative liberalism welcomes restraints on state power arising from rights and mediating institutions alike.

Eighth, liberalism emphasizes the use of critical reason while conservatism appreciates the insight of sentiment and custom. Again, both have valid concerns. As argued in chapter 5, individuals and communities gain wisdom through a long, multigenerational process. Conservatives thus properly seek insight from hard-earned knowledge inherited from previous generations and dismiss the abstract rationality of the lone individual. Yet long-standing customs err. Each generation is responsible for refining its inheritance through critical reflection and passing along an improved version. Conservative liberalism thus cannot do without reason but knows that rationalism is not the path to wisdom.

Conservative Liberalism and Legal Polycentrism

Earlier in the chapter, I identified the heart of liberalism and the heart of conservatism. Is there a heart of conservative liberalism? I do not wish to be reductionistic, but I think there may be one, and it lies in the conception of human law defended in chapter 10. Law is polycentric. It cannot be reduced to decrees of the state—whether statutory codes, administrative regulations, or court decisions—though all of these provide important evidence of what the law is. Instead, law is the customary legal order. In the extended argument of chapters 9–11, it was law as customary legal order that kept natural justice and civil government linked. My defense of law as customary legal order also corresponds to the discussion of pluralism and human institutions in chapters 7–8. And as this conception of law enjoyed a crucial place in these previous chapters, so it also offers a promising way to integrate key liberal and conservative insights—though not to create a perfectly consistent intellectual scheme.

To clear some ground first, I recognize that not all conservatives and not all liberals will be enthusiastic about interpreting law as customary legal order. Each side, from its own perspective, has understandable reasons for doubt, but I fear that they betray their best insights by holding out. Let me explain why for each in turn.

Legal positivism holds that the law is what political authorities command. In chapter 10, I discussed legal positivism as prime example of a monocentric perspective on law. Although I focused there on John Austin and Hans Kelsen, some recent conservative theorists have also expressed

strong positivist views. For example, former United States Supreme Court
Justice Antonin Scalia writes as though judges have only two options: they
either make law or follow a strict statutory textualism. He dismisses the idea
that law might exist independently of legislative or judicial decree and thus
need to be *discovered* by judges. For Scalia, law derives from one government
body or another. In a democracy, it ought to be the legislature.[56]

To be sure, in the context of American jurisprudential controversies of
the past half century, it is understandable why conservatives such as Scalia
have resorted to positivism to check the power of left-leaning judges. "Judicial
activism" and the idea of a "living constitution" have regularly aligned
courts against conservative causes. But this may be a short-sighted strategy.
Enthusiasm for robust legislative supremacy seems to lie in tension with
traditional conservative respect for the deep-seated wisdom of many generations. Treating law only as the product of deliberate government design and
insisting that discrete legislative acts ought to trump everything else cuts off
law from insights of experience, prescription, and custom that conservatives
allegedly treasure. I agree that some of the judicial cases most objectionable
to conservatives have been little more than assertions of power rather than
acts of lawful authority. But positivism is likely to be a false friend to the
conservative cause in the long run.[57]

The liberal perspective on law as customary legal order is also unsettled.
A prominent strain of the (broader) liberal tradition exudes confidence in the
power of critical reason to reform the law. It has distained customary legal
sources and sought to enact new measures unconstrained by the deadweight
of the past. Jeremy Bentham's utilitarianism may be the best example,[58] but
arguably it finds precedent in the philosophies of René Descartes, Thomas
Hobbes, Jean-Jacques Rousseau, and Voltaire. Another strain of the liberal
tradition, however, has been skeptical about reason's ability to rebuild the law

56. See Antonin Scalia, "Common-Law Courts in a Civil-Law System: The Role of United States
Federal Courts in Interpreting the Constitution and Laws," in *A Matter of Interpretation: Federal Courts
and the Law*, ed. Amy Gutmann (Princeton: Princeton University Press, 1997), 3–47.

57. The long-running debate between conservative scholars Walter Berns and Harry Jaffa probed
many issues related to conservatism and positivism. For recent analysis of these debates, see Steven F.
Hayward, *Patriotism Is Not Enough: Harry Jaffa, Walter Berns, and the Arguments That Redefined American
Conservatism* (New York: Encounter, 2017).

58. See Jeremy Bentham, *An Introduction to the Principles of Morals and Legislation* (1789; New
York: Hafner, 1948). In this work, Bentham portrays areas of the law governed by the common law as
"uncertain and incomplete"; see *Principles of Morals and Legislation*, 335. As Shirley Robin Letwin puts
it, Bentham represents "the urge to remake the world according to a rational pattern"; see *The Pursuit
of Certainty* (Cambridge: Cambridge University Press, 1965), 5.

effectively by legislative decree. Its proponents—including Edmund Burke, Adam Smith, Adam Ferguson, and David Hume—believe that modern societies are more the product of spontaneous order than deliberate planning. These liberal thinkers thus respect the common law and other customary legal sources not orchestrated by a political sovereign.[59] Which stream of the liberal tradition is most genuinely liberal can be debated. But on my working idea that the core of classical liberalism is embracing a tolerant and pluralist social order, then the latter stream has the stronger case. A spontaneously developing, polycentric law incorporates and reflects the diversity of a society in a way that law rationally decreed by a group of legislators cannot.

These are complicated debates internal to the liberal and conservative traditions, but I conclude that both traditions are faithful to their own best insights when they recognize law as customary legal order. For conservatives, it is fidelity to their quest for wisdom, while for liberals, it is fidelity to tolerating pluralism. Liberalism and conservatism also have other respective reasons to embrace legal polycentrism, some of them similar and others different. The polycentric strains of both traditions are modest about the powers of abstract human rationality, and hence the ability to create an effective law solely by legislative means. But we would expect each tradition to defend its modesty differently: conservatives are especially cognizant of human moral corruption, liberals of human ignorance. But from Noahic perspective, both are true, which suggests another way to see these traditions as complementary.

As it draws upon the strengths of liberalism and conservatism, emphasis upon law as customary legal order might also restrain some worrisome tendencies of both traditions. By curtailing abrupt and drastic legal change, law as customary legal order checks the liberal tendency to exalt the new and innovative. It defers to conservatism's respect for the hard-won wisdom of the ages. But by providing an open-ended way to change and refine the law incrementally, law as customary legal order checks the conservative tendency to romanticize the past. It accounts for humanity's ongoing responsibility to pursue the Noahic moral commission through the resourcefulness, creativity, and innovation that liberalism appreciates.

Finally, understanding law as customary legal order may helpfully integrate the liberal and conservative perspectives on why government should be limited. Law as customary legal order envisions society as ordered primarily

---

59. In making this distinction between two kinds of liberalism, I am especially indebted to the analysis in Friedrich A. Hayek, *Law, Legislation and Liberty*, vol. 1, *Rules and Order* (Chicago: University of Chicago Press, 1973), ch. 1.

from the bottom up, rather than the top down. Liberalism's emphasis on the individual's dignity and conservatism's passion for mediating institutions share a fundamental allegiance to the bottom-up vision. Polycentric law is the enemy of all rationalistic, detailed, comprehensive programs to make or remake the human community. Both liberals and conservatives should appreciate that and in doing so appreciate each other.

Progressivism and Nationalism

The Noahic covenant provides reasons to appreciate both the liberal and conservative traditions. Are there other prominent political traditions or movements that should *not* receive such appreciation? Before concluding this chapter and book, I wish to mention two prominent ones that deserve more negative assessment, in my judgment: *progressivism* and *nationalism*. As with liberalism and conservatism, there is no universally accepted way of defining these ideas. But at least as I understand them here, they stand in much greater tension with a political theology grounded in the Noahic covenant than do the liberal and conservative traditions.

Despite the large differences between progressivism and nationalism in certain respects, they both depend and thrive upon an adversarial mindset that pits one group against others in the life of political community. Another way to say it, in popular lingo, is that both promote versions of *identity politics*.[60] It is obviously true that humans are much more than individuals. As previous chapters have explored, we are the kind of creatures who form families and associations of various sort, and we enjoy a sense of meaning and belonging as we participate in them. Yet identifying with social groups can have dangerous as well as benevolent results. The political theology of this volume suggests that a prime goal of political community (and hence a prime responsibility of politics) is to find ways for people to flourish within their families and voluntary associations without setting their own groups in conflict with others. The Noahic covenant points to the goal of a peaceful coexistence through the bonds of a substantively modest common good. Conservative liberalism heads in this direction. I fear that progressivism and nationalism do not.

From an American perspective, *progressivism* has been associated historically with economics. Some proponents believe it should retain this focus, and theoretically it probably could. Even in this form, however, progressivism

---

60. The identity politics of progressivism and nationalism I have in mind here is very similar to the identity politics of the American left and right identified by Amy Chua in *Political Tribes: Group Instinct and the Fate of Nations* (New York: Penguin, 2018), 166.

has drawn its primal energy from a narrative of conflict, pitting the interests of workers over against the interests of owners. Be that as it may, in recent decades progressivist circles have spawned the multiplication of smaller and smaller identity groups—defined not only by economic class but also by race, sexual preference, gender identity, and many others. What differentiates people increasingly crowds out what they have in common.[61]

This becomes politically problematic especially when each identity group understands itself as an aggrieved minority. Oppression and conflict become the prime political narratives. Each group claims the right to be recognized and even celebrated by all others.[62] People who express moral reservations about the way some group identifies itself, or who simply decline to celebrate what it stands for, open themselves to charges of hatred and phobias. Arguably, this is the fruit of a conception of positive natural rights critiqued in chapter 9. Were it just a matter of people claiming (negative) rights to be unmolested in their person and property as they peacefully live in ways that express their self-identity, such claims could be largely consistent with everyone else's (negative) rights to live peacefully and without molestation. But the demand that all others provide positive support and encouragement for anyone's identity *du jour* inevitably entails that one person's rights-claim will conflict with others' rights-claims. People who assert an array of contrasting identities may be able to avoid killing each other, but there is no way they can all affirm and celebrate each other.[63]

Perhaps the obvious alternative to the dead end of (at least this sort of) progressivism is to try to recapture a sense of corporate unity in the political body.[64] In a sense, this is precisely what *nationalism* purports to provide. Yet nationalism also has troubling features from the perspective of a political theology rooted in the Noahic covenant. Just how troubling depends upon the form nationalism takes. We may briefly consider three distinct versions.

First, some forms of nationalism take a racial form. For any nationalism to gain traction, it must assert some sort of bond that unites the nation. In recent American forms of "white" nationalism, proponents promote a

61. Mark Lilla puts it in terms of "narrow and exclusionary self-definition," such that "the focus of American liberalism . . . shifted from commonality to difference." See *The Once and Future Liberal: After Identity Politics* (New York: Harper, 2017), 9–10, 78. Chua speaks of how identity politics "inevitably subdivides, giving rise to ever-proliferating identities demanding recognition." See *Political Tribes*, 183.

62. Cf. related comments in Lilla, *The Once and Future Liberal*, 67; and Chua, *Political Tribes*, 181.

63. Or as Carol M. Swain puts it, identity politics often divides people "by separating them into numerous tribal groups *with competing interests*" (emphasis mine). See *The New White Nationalism in America: Its Challenge to Integration* (Cambridge: Cambridge University Press, 2002), 312.

64. As in Chua, *Political Tribes*, 203, 208–9; and Lilla, *The Once and Future Liberal*, 119–30.

unity based upon a shared European culture among those of pure European descent, even if that can only be attained in a truncated geographical version of the current United States.[65] I argued in chapter 7 that the very concept of race is illegitimate and not a valid basis for marginalizing or excluding people from a political community. Given that discussion, I add nothing here about the complete inconsistency of a race-based nationalism with a vision shaped by the Noahic covenant.

Another sort of nationalism is economic in nature. Patrick Buchanan, an American journalist, former White House staffer, and several-time presidential candidate provides an interesting example, especially given the unmistakable echoes of his "economic nationalism" in the rhetoric and agenda of Donald Trump.[66] In *The Great Betrayal* (1998), Buchanan focuses his polemic against international free trade, which he portrays as sacrificing good American jobs for the benefit of consumerism, multinational corporations, and foreign countries. Our interest here is not on the details of trade policy but on Buchanan's nationalistic defense of his position. As with other nationalisms, an adversarial posture is palpable throughout this work. Although Buchanan seeks to avoid pitting some members of the American nation over against other members (unlike the white nationalists),[67] he places American workers in conflict with workers in other countries—naming Mexicans, Hondurans, Chileans, and Japanese in his opening pages.[68] For Buchanan, "nations are rivals, antagonists, and adversaries, in endless struggle through time to enhance relative power and position."[69] He uses military metaphors ("war," "invading and capturing") to describe free trade's assault on American markets, which has ended America's "economic hegemony."[70] International trade does not bring mutual benefit but produces winners and losers. If one nation benefits, another nation must have been harmed. Foreign "rivals" "loot us blind" and "pick our pockets." "Asian prosperity" comes at America's "expense."[71]

---

65. For a thorough study of recent American white nationalism, see Swain, *The New White Nationalism.* As she summarizes, "Contemporary white nationalists draw upon the potent rhetoric of national self-determination and national self-assertion in an attempt to protect what they believe is their God-given natural right to their distinct cultural, political, and genetic identity as white Europeans" (16).

66. *Economic nationalism* is his own term. E.g., see Patrick J. Buchanan, *The Great Betrayal: How American Sovereignty and Social Justice Are Being Sacrificed to the Gods of the Global Economy* (Boston: Little, Brown and Company, 1998), 21.

67. E.g., see Buchanan, *The Great Betrayal*, 286.

68. Buchanan, *The Great Betrayal*, 5–8.

69. Buchanan, *The Great Betrayal*, 66.

70. Buchanan, *The Great Betrayal*, 34, 37, 49.

71. Buchanan, *The Great Betrayal*, 8, 37, 91.

One could perhaps argue that as long as this economic nationalism retains a united and inclusive front within the national political community, a protectionist trade policy is consistent with a Noahic covenantal framework. But does Buchanan's nationalism meet this condition? The way he defines "a nation" raises serious doubts. A nation is "a people, separate and apart, with its own destiny and history, language and faith, institutions and culture."[72] A single faith? A single culture? "The people of a nation are a moral community who must share higher than economic interests."[73] Perhaps, but how morally substantive do the interests of this community have to be? It seems likely that even an economic-focused nationalism will need to recognize only *some* of the members of a nation as the *real* members. *They* will get to define the nation's faith, culture, and rich moral vision and thus also the national interests worth protecting. This fits uncomfortably with the political theology defended in this volume.

Finally, Yoram Hazony has recently made a robust case for nationalism of a third sort. At the outset of *The Virtue of Nationalism*, Hazony defines nationalism as the conviction that maintaining independent nation-states is the best form of world political order in distinction from various forms of *imperialism*, the only viable alternative.[74] If this truly is all that nationalism is, it is rather persuasive to me. At least, it raises no objection from the standpoint of a political theology grounded in the Noahic covenant. This is especially true if nations committed to nationalism are just as insistent about other nations' sovereign independence as they are about their own, as Hazony would wish.[75]

But there is more to Hazony's nationalist vision than the defense of independent nation-states. His vision has its own undertones that raise problems similar to those of Buchanan's nationalism. For Hazony, members of a nation have "mutual loyalty" "derived from genuine commonalities."[76] It is true that a political community must have some shared goods, but how substantively rich does Hazony envision them being, and is this vision compatible with the pluralism of the Noahic covenant? He makes a number of statements indicating that a common religious faith is among the things that must characterize a nation. For example, a nation's inheritance includes "a way of life,

---

72. Buchanan, *The Great Betrayal*, 51; cf. 286.
73. Buchanan, *The Great Betrayal*, 287.
74. See Hazony, *The Virtue of Nationalism*, 3.
75. E.g., see Hazony, *The Virtue of Nationalism*, 111–20.
76. Hazony, *The Virtue of Nationalism*, 140.

a religion and a language, skills and habits, and ideals and ways of under-
standing that are unique."[77] He associates the nation with what is *sacred*.[78]
Protestantism is crucial for understanding the United States as a nation, as is
Judaism for Israel.[79]

It is important to note that Hazony sometimes speaks more loosely about
religion as a source of political commonality and that he advocates tolerance
for religious minorities. (In fact, he argues that nationalism is the best way
to promote tolerance.)[80] Nevertheless, he identifies Old Testament Israel as
the origin of the conception of independent nation-states and as exemplary
for contemporary nations.[81] That is a troubling model. He himself notes
that foreigners could be welcomed into ancient Israel only if they embraced
Israel's God,[82] and he completely ignores the fact that ancient Israel only
became a nation-state with its own geographical borders by forcibly expelling
many other nations, as described in the book of Joshua. Old Testament Israel
was united in very thick moral bonds of commonality and the Mosaic law
permitted only an extremely limited toleration of those who were different.
To a lesser but real degree, in Hazony's vision, many people within a nation
will have to submit to a forced cultural and religious conformity or face outsider status.

As I argued in chapter 3, the idea that contemporary political communities emerge out of the Noahic covenant, not the Mosaic covenant, is crucial
for a sound political theology. Hazony's nationalism has its attractive features, but I fear that it is inspired by the wrong biblical covenant. Political
communities are not the kind of community meant to be united by the sacred
or by religious faith. And Christianity is not the kind of religion meant to
unite a nation.

CONCLUSION

Part 2 has explored the theological framework the Noahic covenant provides for Christians reflecting on central issues of legal and political theory.
According to this framework, political communities are properly pluralistic

---

77. Hazony, *The Virtue of Nationalism*, 88.

78. Hazony, *The Virtue of Nationalism*, 158–59.

79. See Hazony, *The Virtue of Nationalism*, 160, 163–65.

80. E.g., Hazony speaks of "religious traditions" (plural) and "commonalities of language *or* religion"
(emphasis mine); see *The Virtue of Nationalism*, 101, 140. On religious tolerance, see, e.g., 47–48, 164–65.

81. E.g., see Hazony, *The Virtue of Nationalism*, 19–20, 22–23, 80, 100, 111–12.

82. Hazony, *The Virtue of Nationalism*, 19.

in the present age, welcoming people of various backgrounds and granting a broad measure of religious freedom. Marriage, procreation, and child-rearing are foundational for the health of society, and a vibrant market economy effectively advances the enterprise responsibilities of divine image-bearers. This framework also affirms the objective reality of justice, which prescribes retribution and compensation in response to violations of natural human rights. The specific content of this justice must be defined through law, most helpfully understood as customary legal order. In turn, law properly recognizes but also limits the authority of government office.

These conclusions should make the liberal and conservative traditions attractive to Christians. Both traditions are bound by time and place, having emerged under particular cultural circumstances. Neither has a corner on the truth, expresses all that Christians should think about public life, or escapes the distortions of any fallible human construct. But insofar as they embrace pluralism and the hard-but-honorable road to wisdom, certain strains of liberalism and conservatism (respectively) provide Christians with traditions of political engagement worthy of their cordial attachment. These traditions do not point the way to utopia, but neither can any social philosophy in the present age. And when we consider the temptations of this and every age, the Noahic covenant should make us grateful for traditions that grasp much that is good.

SUBJECT INDEX

and Romans 13:1–7, 106–13
and technological innovation, 81, 82, 83
and tolerance, 185–86, 204
universality of, 63, 86, 110, 179, 181, 182–85,
  199–200, 213, 233, 234, 256, 320, 347
Noahide laws, the, 79, 104–6
nonviolent vision, the, 45–47, 53, 54
norms, 292, 293, 294, 304, 310, 327, 352, 353
Novak, David, 79, 335
Novak, Michael, 52, 55n51
Nussbaum, Martha, 142
Oakenshott, Michael, 142, 371
O'Donovan, Joan Lockwood, 255
O'Donovan, Oliver, 115, 116–17, 116n25, 255,
  257–58, 257n24
offspring, 66, 67, 68, 69, 70
oracles, prophetic, 96, 98
overlapping consensus, 164–65
overpopulation, 241, 242
Papanikolaou, Aristotle, 169n24
participation, 131, 132
pattern recognition, 140, 140–41 n33, 146
perfectionism, 109, 320, 332–41, 344, 362, 366, 372
personal knowledge, 142
Pikerty, Thomas, 254, 254n11
pluralism, 235, 257, 294, 343, 364
  and the church, 186–87
  and commonality, 159
  and the Noahic covenant, 181–89, 191, 193, 204,
    205, 207, 213, 235, 257, 364
  and perfectionism, 339
  and political communities, 181–88, 304, 205,
    228, 249, 364
  and polycentrism, 294
  racial, 189–93
  and Western society, 16
Polanyi, Michael, 142, 146n46, 164n19
polis, the, 17, 17n1, 85, 86, 100, 120
political communities
  and the Abrahamic covenant, 87–88, 90, 92, 93,
    94, 95, 99, 119
  accountability of, 17, 25, 32, 34–36, 93, 94, 95,
    97, 98, 121, 125, 156, 176, 366
  authority of, 100, 122–23
  Christians' place in, 150–51, 152, 154, 155, 156,
    157–59, 161–62, 173
  and the church, 102–3, 119
  claims of redemption of, 117–23
  as common, 17, 25, 32–36, 80, 80n2, 86, 92, 94,
    95–99, 156, 159, 176, 256
  and the common good, 187–88
  definition of, 17, 85, 86
  and the Genesis narratives, 93–95
  as holy, 80, 80n2, 87, 88, 89, 92, 94–95n20, 95, 97
  and immigration policy, 184–85

injustice in, 94, 95, 96, 97
and Jesus Christ, 112–23
legitimacy of, 17, 25–29, 93, 94, 95, 96, 97, 99, 122,
  156, 176
and limited government, 227, 346
and the Mosaic covenant, 87, 88–92, 93, 95, 99,
  100, 119
and the new covenant, 102, 103, 119
New Testament views on, 101, 103–13, 122–23,
  158
and the Noahic covenant, 79–86, 89, 92–93, 95,
  97, 99, 100, 101, 103–4, 113–23, 124, 130, 137,
  149, 188, 231, 256, 343, 366, 382
and objective morality, 371–72
Old Testament views on, 80, 92–99, 122–23
and justice, 205, 210, 249, 256
as penultimate, 92n17
and pluralism, 181–88, 228, 249, 364, 382
as preservative, 119
as provisional, 17, 25, 29–32, 117, 119, 120, 151,
  156, 157, 176
and radical Islam, 160–61, 160n6
and religious liberty, 198, 201–2, 205, 207, 212,
  227
and shared moral vision, 187–88
and treatment of strangers, 94, 94–95n20, 95,
  184–85
as universal, 227, 233
political theology, Christian
  basic tenets of, 25–37
  and conservative liberalism, 370
  context of, 36–53
  definition of, 17
  Noahic covenant as foundational to, 79, 80, 101,
    122, 123, 161, 179
polyandry, 224
polycentrism
  and conservative liberalism, 371
  definition of, 291, 294
  and the identity of the law, 300–4
  and the information problem, 311–13
  and justice, 317
  and law, 291, 294, 295–304, 295–96n14, 309–11,
    313, 315, 316, 318, 326, 327, 364, 375
  and natural law, 295–96
  and the Noahic covenant, 291, 294, 304–17, 318
  and pluralism, 294n3
  and prevention of concentration of power, 305–6,
    318, 327
  and the rule of law, 315, 318
polygamy, 222, 224
poor, the, 238–39, 347–48
Porter, Stanley, 349
positivism, 294–95, 296, 297n26, 300, 326, 375–76
Pound, Roscoe, 308, 316n98

SCRIPTURE INDEX